THE KING'S CUSTOMS

VOL. I

GEOFFREY CHAUCER.

Controller of the Custom and Subsidy of wool, fells, and hides, in the port of London, 1374 to 1386. (Area of control: London to Tilbury.) Controller of Petty or Aliens' Custom in the port of London, 1382 to 1386.

Frontispiece.

THE KING'S CUSTOMS

VOL. I

AN ACCOUNT OF MARITIME REVENUE &
CONTRABAND TRAFFIC IN ENGLAND,
SCOTLAND, AND IRELAND, FROM
THE EARLIEST TIMES
TO THE YEAR 1800

BY HENRY ATTON & HENRY HURST HOLLAND

WITH A PREFACE BY F. S. PARRY, C.B.
DEPUTY-CHAIRMAN OF THE BOARD OF CUSTOMS

REPRINTS OF ECONOMIC CLASSICS

AUGUSTUS M. KELLEY · PUBLISHERS
NEW YORK · 1967

First Edition 1908

(London: John Murray, *Albemarle Street W*, 1908)

Reprinted 1967 by
AUGUSTUS M. KELLEY · PUBLISHERS

LIBRARY OF CONGRESS CATALOGUE CARD NUMBER
67 - 21884

PRINTED IN THE UNITED STATES OF AMERICA
by SENTRY PRESS, NEW YORK, N. Y. 10019

PREFACE

'GREAT is the glory, for the strife is hard,' should justly
be the verdict earned by this very welcome attempt
to investigate the dark backward and abysm of a most
interesting branch of Revenue history. The task of
retrospective research, always difficult, is rendered doubly
so in the case in question through the scarcity of ancient
departmental records, a scarcity attributable to the fact
that the central Customs Office, with untold documentary
treasures, perished in the Great Fire of London, and that
a similar catastrophe occurred early in the nineteenth
century. The registers and letter-books kept at the outport custom-houses have in most instances been abandoned to moth and mildew, and those that have survived
furnish pathetic testimony of the extent of the loss sustained. But at last, despite all difficulties, two members
of the staff have merited the gratitude of all tariff students
by producing that long-desired work, a popular history
of the Customs. It is in no sense an ordinary departmental record, prepared during office hours and at the
public expense, like Chisholm's great Blue Book of 1869
on the Public Income and Expenditure, or the more recent
official 'History of the National Debt.' The work is
purely a private venture; the credit and the responsibility alike rest with the authors, as in the case of any
ordinary history. They have not attempted to compile
a masterpiece of antiquarian lore, but to do that which,
perhaps, is just as difficult—viz., to assort the results of
research in correct sequence, and then relate them with

due conciseness, moderation, and simplicity. In short, their object has been the production of a direct narrative of Customs legislation and procedure, from the earliest periods of our history to the present day.

Few will deny the need for a popular history. The general ignorance on matters concerning the department is amazing. Quite recently a well-known periodical, edited by an equally well-known public man, produced an article entitled ' Baffling H.M. Customs,' in which the modern British customs officer was represented as detecting and seizing ' badly fitted bodices that contain hundreds of yards of Point de Venise and Honiton, waistcoats that bulge in the wrong place so as to hide bags of unset gems, even top-boots specially made for smuggling jewellery and gloves,' besides watches, silks, etc. Not a single article mentioned is liable to duty in this country !

Any true history of the Customs is essentially an obituary notice of Prerogative. It must show the Civil List, at first the provision for all the national expenditure (Navy, Army, and Civil Service), dwindling slowly into little more than the Privy Purse—the King's ' customary ' privileges shrinking and vanishing under the assaults of Parliament—the King's ' customers ' gradually becoming the servants of the nation—and the popular attitude towards the revenue official undergoing corresponding modifications. Once the bugbear of the public, in the end he becomes its trusted guardian and provider, collecting the national dues with as little trouble to the payers as possible, and in many instances rendering valuable assistance to merchants and shipowners.

To a member of the Board of Customs contemplation of these changes suggests consideration of one most attractive among the many interesting points of a narrative such as this—the ancient *internal* history of the department. The mediæval customs officer was exempt from practical *Customs* control. The great officials (often sinecurists), who were appointed by royal patent, were responsible only to the King's treasurer and to the barons of the Exchequer. Parliament occasionally thought fit to intervene by the cumbrous method of legislation, but there is no great reason to suppose that the mediæval customs officers were more immoral than the average men of the period. The issue of various restraining statutes does not necessarily prove that they systematically abused their powers, but rather that Parliament took advantage of derelictions to assert itself in the only way then possible. The evidence for the prosecution has come down to us; we know but little of the evidence for the defence. It is hard to learn how far the barons of the Exchequer exerted themselves to enforce discipline, but there is no doubt that they exercised a rigid scrutiny of accounts at the periodical days of payment. Often the King's Treasurer, the Chancellor, and the barons of the Exchequer were bishops; the mediæval Civil Service was largely officered by incumbents of Crown livings, and mediæval churchmen were notorious for their tenacity in money matters. ' The Exchequer officers,' says Camden in his ' Remaines concerning Britaine,' ' were extorters in the time of King Henrie the 4th, otherwise Henrie Bell, Collectour of the Custome (as he stiled himself at that time) would never have written a riming long Satyr against them, which beginneth thus :

> O Scacci Camera, locus est mirabilis ille,
> Ut referam vera, tortores sunt ibi mille.
> Si contingat ibi temet quid habere patrandum,
> Certe dico tibi cœtum reperire nefandum ;

and concludeth in this manner :

> O sic vexate tortoribus et cruciate,
> Non dices vere propter tales Miserere.'

The system of administration was bad. Complaints against customs officers were treated as complaints against the Exchequer, or in later Tudor times, when the President overshadowed the whole of his colleagues, as

complaints against the Lord Treasurer, the final hearer
of appeals and framer of verdicts. An effort to establish
more direct responsibility was made by the Long
Parliament, but their system of temporary committees
can scarcely have been adequate, for blame could easily be
shifted to the shoulders of a previous committee. A
more satisfactory method was introduced after the
Restoration. A permanent Customs Board was instituted, and thenceforward for any sins of omission
or commission specific persons could be—and were—
pilloried, the primary requisite of good administration.

Another century had to elapse before Adam Smith
laid the foundation of the modern theory of taxation, and
Burke and Pitt purged the antiquated Exchequer, and
established the modern system of Treasury finance.
Almost another century passed before the slow Anglo-
Saxon mind realized the justice of Burke's pregnant
text : 'A teasing Custom House and a multiplicity
of perplexing regulations ever have and ever will
appear the masterpiece of finance to people of narrow
views.'*

The fascinating annals of the smugglers (the 'Sea-
Cocks,' after whom was named the country-seat of a
modern Chancellor of the Exchequer, at once their enemy
and prey) require no introduction. Yet another matter
is worth passing comment—the very close connexion
which has always been maintained between H.M. Customs
and H.M. Navy. From the first the welfare of the Fleet
has depended upon the efficiency of our Service. In days
of old the merchants' natural disinclination to meet the
demands of the King's Customers was mitigated by the
knowledge that the King in return would protect 'such
as pass on the seas upon their lawful occasions ' (as the
Prayer Book still puts it) from the violence of foreign foes
and of the pirates who used to swarm in the narrow seas.

* ' Observations on a Late State of the Nation.' (The slip is
Burke's.)

It was expressly for the needs of his Navy that the King first imposed tunnage and poundage. It was distinctly laid down that the proceeds 'soient entierement appliez *sur la salve garde de la meer* et nul part aillours' (5 Rich. II., stat. 2, cap. 3). The merchant who paid was vitally interested in ' the Navye of this Realme and the multitude of the shippes of the same, which to-fore this tyme hath been not onely a greate defence and suertie to this Realme of Englande in tyme of warre, but also a high commoditie to all the subjectes of the same *for transporting and conveyance of merchantdises in and from this Realme*' (23 Henry VIII., cap. 7); and again, ' the guarding and defending of the seas against all persons intending or that shall intend the disturbance of your said Commons *in the intercourse of trade* and the invading of this your Realm' (12 Chas. II., cap. 4). The practice of appropriating specific taxes to specific purposes has passed away, but Customs revenue still supports Naval expenditure, and when the latter increases, the former usually follows suit.

Like the great sister service under the White Ensign, ours of the Blue Ensign and Crown has gradually ' suffered a sea-change ' into something which would certainly appear strange to the Norman collectors. Posted, as we of the Customs are, at the gates of the Mistress of the Sea, to watch the ebb and flow of trade, every generation burdens us with fresh responsibilities. The receipt of custom, which was everything with the old riming collector, is but one, though still most important, among many other Customs duties. Mercantile Marine work, the registration of ships, the collection of Light dues, the administration of the Merchandise Marks and Quarantine laws, other duties connected with wreck, Alien Immigration and the public health, and the collection and record of innumerable statistics—labours of which several other departments of Government reap the benefit and credit—all these fall to us to execute, and over all the Treasury stands, Argus-eyed, where once stood the Norman Exchequer. But, however much the conditions of Customs service have altered, its essentials remain. We can look back with some pride upon centuries of public service ; we may hope loyally that in the future—

STET FORTUNA DOMUS CUSTUMARIÆ.

F. S. PARRY.

INTRODUCTION

In compiling this treatise we have followed a settled and perhaps peculiar plan. Aiming at the production of a sustained narrative, we have when practicable opened each chapter with a statement of the more important Customs statutes. In dealing with the eighteenth century, a period prolific of contraband, we have opened with accounts of the 'tariff Acts,' and followed with sketches of the laws intended to prevent smuggling. We have found it impossible, in this small volume, to specify every Customs statute, but we have done our best to display those which have appeared influential and interesting.

To avoid undue complication, we have put a brief statement of the older history of the Scottish Customs directly ahead of our account of the Union between England and Scotland. The older Irish revenue history has been treated in similar fashion ; the account appears at the end of the volume, and extends to the period immediately preceding the Union between England and Ireland.

Realizing that a mere enumeration of tariffs and restrictions would be exceedingly uninteresting, we have striven to clothe the skeleton with selections from the immense mass of Customs incidents available. For the more antique we have sampled the Rolls, the works of Hale and Rymer, and Mr. Hubert Hall's scholarly treatise on the older Customs. For the period subsequent to the accession of James I. we have used the collection of Treasury Papers (an almost exhaustless mine of reference on Customs matters) the State Papers, and the files containing the correspondence between the Admiralty and the important office of maritime revenue in Thames Street (not without amazement at the huge share taken by our venerable department in every sphere of ancient procedure). For information as to actual Customs 'practice' during the eighteenth century we have relied upon the outport Letter Books extant, and the ' Memoranda ' left by that industrious and learned Commissioner of Customs, Sir William Musgrave. The Letter Books and Memoranda contain much interesting matter—matter which we think few except practical customs officers are competent to interpret for the benefit of the reading public.

These last-mentioned documents the Honourable Commissioners have placed at our disposal, and we take this opportunity of thanking them most cordially for their kindness. As a matter of course, the whole of our work has been done either outside official hours or during the annual leave allotted us, and this has rendered the grant of convenient access to the quaint old ' documents of practice ' an inestimable favour.

We shall be grateful if readers can inform us whether there are any records extant—other than the ' Revenue documents '—that furnish evidence upon the following matters (*vide* pp. 449, 459, 462) :

1. The grant to Raleigh of ' over-length cloth customs,' and whether the same disproves to any extent the prevalent idea that he lavished his own means on the equipment of privateers.

2. The collection of Plantation customs by Washington's ancestor.

3. The endowment of Congreve with *two* Customs offices.

THE AUTHORS.

CONTENTS

LIST OF ILLUSTRATIONS

THE KING'S CUSTOMS

CHAPTER I

THE DOMAIN OF CONJECTURE—THE PERIOD OF PARTIAL
ILLUMINATION—EDWARD I.—EDWARD II.

To 1327

THE older English revenue historians and lawyers, while
admitting their inability to furnish exact information as
to the most ancient form of English ' Customs,' were
unanimously of opinion that impositions upon maritime
commerce had existed ' from time immemorial.' Even
the compilers of Revenue handbooks cautiously supported
this contention, and with good reason. Customs taxation
must have been coeval with the earliest oversea traffic,
for the maintenance of such traffic must have depended
upon royal protection, and it is certain that the protectors
would be rewarded by tribute.

It is matter of general knowledge that the Phœnicians
traded with Britain long before Cæsar's invasion, and
that there was frequent commercial intercourse between
the southern Britons and the Gauls ; but there is no record
of customs levied, either in kind or the rude coinage then
current. Yet the time-honoured conjecture recurs. Trade
could only have been carried on with the sanction of the
maritime chiefs, and sanction would not be given gratis.

Commerce increased and became regular under Roman
rule, the imports being munitions of war, and goods, such
as wine and spices, which could not be produced in

Britain ; the exports lead, tin, wool, hides, horses, and cloth. Inland taxation was comprehensive and severe, for the chief object of Roman aggression was revenue. It is unlikely, with such ingenious inquisitors in power, that maritime commerce escaped exaction, but the Roman rates of duty and methods of collection in Britain are quite beyond discovery.

The Saxon system of taxation was quaint and characteristic. The king had his occasional ' feorm ' or method of purveyance, under which goods were appropriated for the maintenance of the royal household. Purveyance was conducted by the reeves, each of whom controlled a district and held a monthly court. The thanes were subject to the martial and picturesque tax of ' heriots,' an exaction of arms and armour from each estate on its holder's decease. The king also profited by fines paid in condonation of deeds of violence. There were three immutable taxes—the ' bryg-bot,' for repairing roads and bridges ; the ' burg-bot,' for equipping fortresses ; and the ' fyrd,' for maintaining soldiers and mariners. The maritime districts were assessed in ' ship-geld ' for the repair and maintenance of war-vessels. The ' Dane-geld ' was at first a special ' ship-geld,' afterwards a standing tax to provide means of repelling invasion, later still a collection to furnish tribute.

The absence of any allusion to ' Customs ' in the records and legends of the Heptarchy may be due to the fact that during the earlier centuries there was little English commerce. The triumph of barbarism on the Continent paralyzed merchant navigation, and the Saxons seem to have taken kindly to a pastoral life, the rich soils and sheepwalks of the southern and midland districts supplying them plentifully with corn, wool, and flesh. The cities left by the Romans may have existed as centres of homely handicraft, but the southern ports retained little of their ancient trade. Fugitive traffic occasionally enlivened them, being no doubt made subject to slight port dues, or occasional levies in kind by the maritime reeves.

Commerce increased with the advent of the seventh century. There was a little trade with the Levant, principally conducted by Italians, and occasional traffic with the south-western cities of Europe, the route being across the Channel and then overland. A message from Charlemagne to one of the Saxon kings is quoted in the records, conveying assurance of protection to English pilgrims visiting Rome, and stipulating that such as were merchants should pay the usual custom upon their wares. It may be concluded that the Saxon monarch extorted a similar acknowledgment when the pilgrim-traders returned.

The depredations of the northern pirates discouraged traffic during the succeeding centuries, yet English traders were occasionally adventurous ; witness Athelstane's grant of thaneship to every native merchant who had made three voyages to the Levant. Queenhithe was the London mooring-place for ' aliens ' (foreign merchants). Some of the revenue historians quote certain dues levied in the port of London on corn, ale, and herrings, erroneously describing them as ' customs.' At the time mentioned it would be neither profitable nor necessary to import corn and ale, and the duties obtaining on those commodities must have been city tolls levied at exportation. The tax on herrings was undoubtedly a local levy on fish caught on the coast and brought to London. The same writers quote a local levy upon charcoal, brought by river from the forests of the Kentish Weald, as a customs tax upon ' coal,' and specify as ' customs ' the London impositions upon craft and water-borne timber. The error in regard to the last-quoted article appears strange when the immensity of the contiguous Kentish forests is taken into consideration, and the fact that two centuries later, according to Fitz-Stephen of Canterbury, the country to the north of London was for many miles densely wooded.

It is likely that the Saxon kings rarely or never exacted maritime dues in coin. But there is good reason to assume that they made levies in kind upon foreign cargoes, and that such levies were not systematic, but imposed in cases of royal need. The charters and rolls of the earlier Norman period contain allusions to Saxon levies upon sea-borne merchandise, notably upon wines—allusions which, though perhaps not absolutely corroborative, should not be overlooked. These will be quoted in their proper sequence.

William I. instituted startling changes in the system of taxation. His inland exactions were immense and grievous, and it is inconceivable that maritime commerce escaped. The Norman coinage seems to have resembled the Saxon, but evidence is in favour of the assumption that until the establishment of the Court of Exchequer during Henry I.'s reign the amount of silver available was so small, and the exactions were so vast, that most of the taxes were collected in kind, the amounts of goods taken being merely *computed* in coin figures. Therefore it is likely that the early Norman ' customs ' took the form of purveyance or ' prisage.' It may also be assumed that when the Conqueror and his successor ' prised ' merchandise they prised extensively, and made the more valuable cargoes special subjects of operation.

During the period extending from the accession of Henry I. to the promulgation of Magna Carta most of the royal impositions were answered in coin. The maritime exactions may be specified as Prisage, the Maltolte, and Ancient custom. By customs Prisage must be understood the appropriation of a portion of merchandise at or before landing or shipment. This was extensively practised, the goods being usually taken by the Chamberlain of the City of London, ostensibly for the use of the king's household. At intervals prises were made of foodstuffs, and, as England was an agricultural country, it may be concluded that these prises were in most cases of goods intended for exportation. Wine, of which there seems to have been a steady and abundant supply, was *systematically* prised at import. The Chamberlain had power to taste all wines, to select the most suitable, and to use wine from the unprised casks to fill those taken. There were two kinds of Prisage. The regularized appropriation was a tun from every ten when the cargo prised amounted to ten and was less than twenty tuns. If the cargo amounted to twenty tuns or more one tun was taken before and one behind the mast. Cargoes of less than ten tuns were exempt.* (A sum, stated as 20s., was paid to the merchant as ' freight ' upon each tun taken.) This method was called ' rightful Prisage,' and appears to have been cheerfully submitted to. The other kind, known as ' evil Prisage,' was simply ' pre-emption.' The Chamberlain or his deputies enforced it under sanction of the king's special writ, empowering them to arrest all incoming wines at a certain port for a period, to ' buy ' as much as the king needed at ' the king's price ' (usually much below the market rate), and then release the rest upon payment of a ' fine.' This form of imposition was extremely distasteful to merchants. The kings frequently took much more than they really needed, and then made presents of wine to their favourite churchmen and courtiers, sometimes even to servants of the household. Occasionally, too, they became traders, and sold wines, both of rightful and evil Prisage, in the open market. Most of the records of prises and pre-emptions refer to ' Gascon wine.' For a long period all French wine went under that appellation. ' Gascon ' was plentiful and cheap, despite the royal impositions.

The ' Maltolte ' was an occasional heavy tax in coin upon merchandise, and was enforced at the larger ports by ' customers ' or collectors. (It is likely that the collectors at this period were not permanent officials.) At remoter ports the levy was usually made by the sheriffs or port-reeves. The Maltolte, though not a systematic duty, was in most cases accounted for at the Exchequer, but now and then its proceeds were intercepted by the king.

---

* Exempt by popular interpretation of the unwritten law, but, as will be subsequently shown, the Exchequer barons of a later period insisted that under certain conditions cargoes of nine tuns might be prised.

There was one systematic tax in coin, the 'Ancient Custom' upon exported wool, wool-fells, and leather.* Some commentators quote 1275 as the earliest date of this levy, because its conditions were then fully expressed in an Act of Edward I., but it is probable that the Act in question merely *ratified* a long-standing tax. The exact rates prior to 1275 are unknown, but they may have been reaffirmed by the rates mentioned in Edward's Act, which were as below :

	£	s.	d.	
On every sack of wool exported (28† stone of 14 pounds)	0	6	8	(half a mark).
On every 300 fells (skins with the wool on)	0	6	8	,, ,,
On every last of leather (240 hides) ..	0	13	4	(a mark).

Certain taxes upon exported lead and tin, and upon imported cloth and wax, are also quoted as 'Ancient Custom,' but it is not clear that these were regularly levied, and it is safer to apply the term solely to the taxes on wool, fells, and leather. It is evident that Ancient Custom existed long prior to the date of the historic conference at Runnymede, for Magna Carta expressly provided that only 'the old and rightful customs' should be taken of foreign merchants. 'The old and rightful customs' could not have signified

---

* English wool had for many years been supreme in quality, and was eagerly sought after, especially in the Flemish markets. Most of the carrying trade was in 'foreign bottoms'; indeed, the 'aliens' appear to have dominated the export wool trade down to the end of the fourteenth century. Each race of foreign traders had its guild or mercantile society, and the societies were extremely powerful and enterprising. The principal alien traders were the Hanse merchants, who appear to have been popular in England, both with kings and people, for they were allowed easy rates upon their merchandise, their interests were protected by charter, and their transactions were rarely resented by the barons and burgesses. Next in importance were the various Italian guilds, known afterwards as the Friscobaldi of Florence, the Ricci of Lucca, etc. The Italians were disliked, on account of their skill in 'forestalling' (cornering), and the sinister powers which they often acquired by lending money to royal personages. The Venetian merchants were especially unpopular, being renowned as incorrigible usurers, arrant cheats, and subtle foes of English commerce.

† In Edward III.'s reign made 26 stone.

Prisage, or the unpopular and erratic Maltolte. The words could only have applied to an ancient and easily borne tax collected in coin—in short, to the 'Ancient Custom.'

It would seem that, though the kings made frequent levies upon merchants' goods and purses, there was no comprehensive arrangement of ports and places of collection. Some of the ports were ' farmed ' by the principal burgesses, who paid a certain sum yearly to the Crown, and collected their ' customs ' and port dues together. Occasionally the greater part of the collection was farmed by one or more of the foreign trading guilds ; indeed it has been stated on excellent authority that during the middle of the thirteenth century the Hanse merchants farmed the entire customs of England.

The Act of 1275,* reciting the rates upon wool, fells, and leather, applied to England, Wales, and Ireland ;

* ' *De Nova Custuma Lanarum, Pellium, et Coriorum, in Originali Anno 3. Regis F. R. H.*

' A la novele custume, ke est graunte par tous les graunz del realme, par la priere des comunes des marchaunts de tout Engletere, est purveu, ke en chescun conte, ou la grem'ore vile ou port est, soient eslut deaus de plus leaus e plus pussaunz, ke averont une pece de un seil en garde, en un, ke sera assigne par le roi, avera un autre pece, e seront jurez, ke leaument resceveront et responderont des deniers le roi, c'est asavoir de chescun sak de laine demi mark, e de chescun treis cent peauls ke funt un sak demi mark, e de chescun last de quyre un mark, ke isceront hors del realm, ausi bien en Hyrlaund en Wales come en Engletere, de denz fraunchise e de hors. Estre ceo en chescun port, ou nefs pount issir, seront deus prodes hommes jurez, k'il ne sufferount a issir laynes peaus ne quyrs sanz leattre overte a la seel, ke sera au chef port en le counte. Et s'il est mil ke autrement sen isse hors del realme, ausi bien il perdra tous les chateus k'il a, e sun cors sera a la volunte le roi. Et pur ceo ke ceste chose ne pouv tost estre per furing, est purveu, ke le roi enveie ses lettres a chescun vesconte per tout le realme, e fait crier et defendre par touz les contes, ke nul, sor forfeture de son cors e de touz ses chateus, ne face mener hors de la terre laynes peaus ne quyres avaunt la feste de la Trinite en cest an, et adunkes par lettres overtes od le seaus si com est andudroe encime autrement sir les avantdites forfetures. Et le roi ad graunte de sa grace, ke touz les seigniorages, par quy porz laynes ou quyres isteront, averont les forfetures quant eles deviendront, chescun en sun port, sauve a roi demi mark de chescun sak de layne e des peaus, e un mark de chescun last de quyres.'

but it is probable that so far as Wales was concerned this was a mere assumptive declaration of authority. Sir Matthew Hale, from whose illuminative treatise on the older English Customs the specimen of the Act given below is quoted, states that many ' merchant strangers ' were fined for infringing its provisions. It will be observed that the imposition was called ' Nova Custuma,' but this may only imply that the duties were levied at a new rate intended to be permanent, and may even be held proof that there *was* an earlier custom on wool. Later it will be shown that when higher rates were levied, and described as ' Subsidy,' this ' new Custom ' of 1275 came to be called ' Ancient Custom,' and retained that title during many years. Indeed Hale, and several other ancient writers, were inclined to believe that there was a customs duty on wool, hides, and fells long prior to 1275. No doubt they were correct, for what other regular duties could the Hanse merchants have farmed ? And it is plainly shown in the Patent Rolls that the Lucca guild farmed the customs from the beginning of the reign, which proves there were standing customs prior to 1275, and affords good reason for concluding that they existed prior to 1272.

The collection of the ' new Custom ' on wool, etc., was entrusted to the Lucca merchants. The Rolls display several ' writs *de intendendo*,' empowering them to collect it, and to search for goods concealed, both in England and Ireland. In 1279 their accounts were checked by the Chancellor, who was assisted by the Archdeacons of Dorset and Durham. The period brought under audit extended from Easter, 1272, to Michaelmas, 1279.

It has been generally held that Edward's Charter of 1278, announcing that the barons (burgesses) of the Cinque Ports were free of Prisage on their wines, was the first grant of such exemption, but there is good reason for believing that the Cinque Ports had been exempted from Prisage by previous kings. A brief examination of Edward's Charter may be of service. It commenced with the usual formula : ' Edwardus, Dei gratia, Rex Angliæ,

Dominus Hiberniæ, et Dux Acquitaniæ, Archiepiscopis, Episcopis, Abbatibus, Prioribus, Comitibus, Baronibus, Justiciariis, Vicecomitibus, Præpositis, Ministris, et omnibus Ballivis et Fidelibus suis, salutem,' and proceeded to state confirmation to the barons of the Cinque Ports of all their liberties and freedoms, ' as they and their ancestors have had in the times of Edward ' (the Confessor), ' William I., William II., Richard I., John, and Henry III., *which we have seen.'** ' We forbid lest any unjustly disturb them or their merchandise.' ' We have also granted them of our special grace that they have " utfangtheff " ' (power of trying felons for offences committed within the ports, even if the felons were captured elsewhere). The barons were also freed from service on assize or ' recognition ' outside the ports, even though they owned lands in the districts in which such proceedings were held. Then came the exemption from Prisage. ' Et quod de propriis vinis suis de quibus negotiantur, quieti sint de recta prisa nostra : videlicet, de uno dolio vini ante malum, et alio post malum ' (' And that of their own wines for which they trade they be quit of our rightful Prise : that is to say, of one cask of wine before the mast, and another after the mast '). Then came exemption from wardships, with an explicit avowal that Edward's ancestors had granted similar exemption. ' Our *aforesaid confirmation* of the liberties and freedoms aforesaid, and other our *grants following*, we now have made to them of our special grace.'

Although the direct statement that there had been prior exemption may to some readers of the Charter appear to apply specially to wardships, others will agree that it included all ' the liberties and freedoms ' previously enumerated, or, to put matters more clearly, all the exemptions.

---

* In 1678 Jeake, the annotator, stated that in the records of Rye there was a document announcing that the Cinque Ports were enfranchised by Edward the Confessor, and that Edward I. granted a *Charter of Confirmation* in 1278. ' Whatever became of these old charters,' said Jeake, ' I cannot say, but it seems they were extant at the time Edward I. granted his Charter. It is likely length and tract of time hath worn them out.'

For this statement follows : ' That the barons and their heirs for ever may have all the liberties and freedoms aforesaid, as the charters aforesaid do reasonably testify.'

But there is convincing testimony elsewhere. In the Close Roll, I Edw. I., Membrane 5, appears a royal mandate to the mayor and bailiffs of Southampton, directing them to forbear prisage on certain wines belonging to Cudel and de Sere, barons of the Cinque Ports, till the king shall arrive in England, as the said barons claim that they and their fellows of the Cinque Ports have been quit of Prisage ' time out of mind.' Edward's Charter was dated at Westminster, June 17, 1278. It may be assumed, therefore, that the Cinque Ports burgesses were exempted under the previous charters, and the extreme antiquity of Prisage becomes almost a matter of certainty.

The audit of 1279 did not in any way loosen the hold obtained by the Lucca guild upon the customs, but it may have tended to convince the Exchequer barons that some systematic check upon collection was necessary. In 1282 a royal mandate was sent to the maritime sheriffs, enjoining them to appoint in each port ' two of the better and more faithful men ' to collect the ' new Custom.' It is not apparent whether these new officials actually collected the duties and handed them over to the Lucca merchants, or whether the merchants collected under supervision by the officials. It is probable that the latter course was adopted, for Edward continued to borrow extensively from the Italians, and they in return were granted many privileges. They did not always go free with their booty. There is record of a commission of oyer and terminer in 1282, touching certain persons in Kent who had been charged with harbouring an outlaw named Bushe, with a large sum of the ' king's Custom ' which the said Bushe had stolen from the merchants of Lucca.

The Prisage of Wine was taken out of the hands of the City Chamberlain, and put under the control of the king's

Butler or Wardrobe Chamberlain.*   The supply of wine
was large, and ' Gascon ' was cheap.   At one period the
king fixed the maximum retail price of Gascon wine in
London at 4d. a gallon (say about 4s. in modern money).
The vintage had been deficient, and 4d. was considered
a high price.   Later one Peter de Denhull acknowledged owing the king's Pantler six tuns of wine (about
1,500 gallons), value £13 10s.—barely 2¼d. a gallon.
Again the king, after debate with the Gascon merchants,
fixed the maximum retail price of French wine in London
at 3d. a gallon ; in Oxford at 3½d.   Rhenish was dearer,
the price being usually about 5d. a gallon.   It should be
borne in mind that the gallon was about one-seventh less
than the modern measure.

Although Edward I. made assignments of the custom
to people and societies from whom he had borrowed
money or received supplies, it does not appear that he

* A few extracts from the Wardrobe Account may be interesting :

'From Adam de Rokesle, the king's Butler,
    for 135½ tuns of wine, the same being wine
    purchased, prisage wine, and wine remaining
    after the withdrawal of Matthew de Colum-
    bar (a previous Chamberlain), sold by the
    said Adam at various prices, etc.   -   - £293 13 9'

(This sum was profit upon wine bought at the king's price and
afterwards sold, wine prised with an allowance of 20s. a tun as
freight and afterwards sold, and wine on hand in the royal
cellars—also sold.)

' From the same, for monies from fines of sundry
    merchants coming with wines to various
    ports, in order that there should not be
    taken from them two tuns of wine of prisage in
    accordance with the custom of the realm, etc.   £23 16 0'

(This sum was made up of money paid to escape ordinary
prisage.)

' From the same, for ten tuns presented to the
    king by the burgesses of Yarmouth, and sold
    to the same burgesses at the price of 40s. a
    tun -   -   -   -   -   -   - £20 0 0'

(It is likely that the burgesses had taken the wine as prisage
for the king, and, the king's cellars being overstocked, the Butler
left the goods with the burgesses and accepted £20 instead.)

spent much on his private pleasures. His household expenses were anything but extravagant ; but he was a born warrior, and it may have been necessary for the maintenance of government that warlike employment should be provided for the barons. Sudden and effective war meant expeditious borrowing, expeditious borrowing meant unbusinesslike methods of discharge. Edward became heavily responsible to the inhabitants of certain towns in Aquitaine, for goods supplied to his troops. The mayors of the towns in question were put upon the English custom at intervals, but neither in this reign nor the next did they obtain full recovery. Edward also became a debtor of John, duke of Brabant, and his attempts at payment may have made the duke's subjects wish that the debt had been forgiven. For the king invited Brabant merchants to trade to England for wool, promising them safe-conduct and various privileges, and when they became involved in business he laid the Maltolte upon their purchases. Then he put the duke upon the wool custom, and also allowed him to buy and export a large quantity of wool *duty-free*.

A short review of the position provides further enlightenment. The carrying trade was to a large extent in the hands of Italians, the most unscrupulous usurers of the period. Most of the wine consumed in England, and therefore made liable to Prisage and occasional impositions in coin, came from France, yet frequently at each of the larger ports the actual owner of the custom was a merchant of Lucca, Pisa, Florence, or a provost of Aquitaine. Extortion and smuggling must have been rife, especially as the assignees' proceedings were 'checked' by officials who received but nominal salaries, and who were either aliens or Norman-English.

In 1303 Edward issued his famous ' Carta Mercatoria,' reiterating the provisions of Magna Carta with regard to the privileges of merchant strangers, but prohibiting the ' aliens ' from selling anything by retail except ' mercery.' Their wines were freed from Prisage, and their merchandise from purveyance except at trade price. In recognition of exemption from Prisage they were called upon to pay a tax called 'Butlerage' of 2s. per cask (afterwards levied at 2s. per tun) upon all wines they imported. This tax was to be paid in 'pence' (cash) within forty days after the wines were landed. It is probable that the aliens at once took to importing their wine in tuns, the tun being the largest convenient package, and that consequently the butlerage came to be collected on every 252 gallons, irrespective of size of cask.

Carta Mercatoria also prescribed a tax of 2s. upon every 'scarlet' and every cloth 'dyed in grain'; 1s. 6d. upon every cloth mixed with grain; 1s. upon every cloth without grain; and 1s. upon every quintal of wax, imported by aliens. This was likely to please the English cloth manufacturers, who appear to have been unable to compete with the Flemings in making the more valuable and showy kinds of cloth. The aliens had also to pay an *ad valorem* duty of 3d. in the £1 upon all other imported merchandise, and specially high rates upon wool exported. Thus amended, the wool duties stood as below :

Denizens.	£	s.	d.	*Aliens.*	£	s.	d.
Upon every sack of wool	0	6	8	The same sum and an additional quarter-mark ..	0	10	0
Upon every 300 fells	0	6	8	The same sum and an additional quarter-mark ..	0	10	0
Upon every last of leather ..	0	13	4	The same sum and an additional half-mark ..	1	0	0

The 'King's Weight,' or standard scale, was directed to be placed in every market town and fair, to secure the proper weighing of articles in which the aliens dealt. Goods bought in the realm by aliens and exported paid 3d. in the £1 value. Wine which had been imported by aliens might not be exported without royal licence, but other aliens' merchandise which had paid poundage on importation might be exported duty-free. It was maintained that in paying these special duties the aliens made due acknowledgment of the privileges granted them by Magna Carta, of the protection promised by the king, and of his guarantee, by establishing an accessible standard scale, that English goods bought by foreigners would be correct as to weight. The third part of this contention was justifiable, but the first and second may be dismissed as mere sophistry. Magna Carta had provided that aliens should pay ' only the ancient Custom.' This Edward considered, and rightly, a great boon, but he destroyed the privilege whilst claiming reward for maintaining it. As for the ' protection,' one has but to scan the Rolls to find what royal protection meant.

To return to Carta Mercatoria. Denizens' wines were still liable to Prisage, except those imported by the chief burgesses of the Cinque Ports. Merchandise imported by denizens was duty-free ; the only legal impositions upon their foreign trade were Prisage, Pre-emption, and the ancient Custom outward. Soon after the promulgation of Carta Mercatoria Edward summoned a colloqium at York, and attempted to cajole his subjects into accepting the same duties as the aliens, but without avail.

The extra Carta Mercatoria duties on aliens' goods became known as ' the new Custom,' and were made a separate branch of receipt. At the larger ports special collectors were appointed to manage them, and one may often fall across references in the records to an official who was ' collector of Ancient Custom,' sometimes called ' the great Custom,' and to another at the same port who collected ' the new Custom,' sometimes called ' Aliens' Custom,' and at other times ' Petty Custom.' This means that the first collector accounted for the custom on denizens' wool, etc., outwards, and for that portion of the wool custom, paid by aliens, which was the rate prior to Carta Mercatoria, while the other collector accounted for Butlerage, the aliens' special duties on cloth and wax, the aliens' poundage on imports and exports, the quarter-mark extra on wool and fells, and the half-mark extra on leather.

On the accession of Edward II. the Customs revenue was saddled with the expense of a gigantic outburst of conviviality. The Seneschal of Gascony and the Constable of Bordeaux were directed by royal mandate to provide 1,000 casks of French wine for the coronation festivities. It is probable that the casks were all tuns, but an equal proportion of tuns, pipes, and hogsheads would give a total of about 150,000 gallons, from which we may conclude the courtiers, and perhaps many of the London citizens, drank his Majesty's health deep and often. The sagacious Friscobaldi of Florence paid for the goods, and took an exhaustive pull at the Customs revenue in return.

In 1308 the king's Butler was directed to provide, out of the new custom on wine,* 600 tuns (over 150,000

* Certain new instructions were issued to the king's Butler. Below is a summary from the Wardrobe Account.

The Butler was directed, when carrying out mandates of pre-emption, to buy the wines 'honourably,' giving no cause of slander, and disturbing the merchants as little as possible. He was to bring all wines taken, whether of *recta prisa* or *mala prisa*, to the place appointed by the Wardrobe Treasurer, and then de-liver them into the custody of the chief Butler of the Household. He was to furnish an account in triplicate, specifying the number and description of the casks, the merchants from whom the goods had been taken or bought, and the charges of conveyance, etc. One of these accounts was to go to the chief Butler of the House-hold, one to the Clerk of the king's Cellar, and the king's Butler was to retain the other. The Clerk of the Cellar had to account to the king's Butler for the price and charges, and to the Butler of the Household for the way in which the wine was put to use. After the wine had been set up, and allowed time to 'settle,' it was to be viewed by the Knight-Marshal of the Hall, who was to inspect each cask and taste the wine therein. If the wine were found good, the prise charges were to be entered in the Butlery Roll, and allowed for as the goods were consumed. If the wine in any cask were found 'corrupt,' the head of the cask was to be knocked in and the wine spilt. The king's Butler had to bear the loss.

gallons) of Gascon for the army in the north. (By 'new custom' was meant 'Butlerage'). Some of the casks were sent to Berwick, the rest to Carlisle.

The king seems to have contracted debts in the blithest spirit, to have reposed great confidence in the resources of maritime collection, and to have been a mere tool in the hands of the Genoese and Florentine financiers. In 1308 the Italian guilds controlled the entire custom, and in the following year the king allowed them to assess their own export transactions at the ancient Custom rates. While enjoying the benefit of 'denizens' duties,' the Italians charged with aliens' duty 'such natives as were willing to pay.' The barons and commons detested the foreign assignees, and attempted to checkmate them by lowering or repealing duties. Thus king and legislators pulled different ways.

In 1310, while the Italians held the customs, the king considered the long-standing claims of the Aquitaine mayors, which were still undischarged, though the Frenchmen had been quartered on the customs at intervals. He allowed them to levy a special tax on imported wines. Then he still further complicated the collection of revenue by assigning 'the aliens' Custom of England' to certain Gascon merchants to whom he owed £3,254, for wines

---

(Prised and pre-empted wines were frequently deposited at various provincial towns whenever the king travelled, so that if he stayed a few days at any place he and his courtiers might be well supplied. When he left, the king's Butler took possession of any wine that was unconsumed, and removed it to some other place advised, usually to Westminster. Sometimes, by the king's order, it was given to the townsmen as largesse. The king's Butler's charges for such transactions were directed to be allowed.)

The purveyors and the king's Butler's deputies at the outports, etc., were enjoined to send all their wines to the appointed places of deposit as soon as possible after they collected them. Sometimes, if it were not convenient to send them, they were empowered to sell, answering to the king for the moneys received. (Chaucer's grandfather was assistant to the king's Butler, and collector of aliens' custom on wine. In 1308 he was charged with misbehaviour to some of the Gascon merchants. He appears to have succeeded in clearing himself, but it is possible the instructions quoted were issued in consequence of the charge.)

which his Butler had pre-empted.   As the Butler certainly bought at less than the market price, the sum represented about 1,500 tuns ! The Court and its purlieus must occasionally have been flooded with wine.

In 1311 a statute was issued abolishing all new imposts, including the Carta Mercatoria duties, which were decried as having been levied without the barons' consent, and against the spirit of Magna Carta.   The ancient Custom and Prisage were retained, and aliens' and denizens' duties thus made similar.   It was also enacted that the customs should be ' kept and received by denizens, not by aliens '; that the collectors of the ancient Custom should pay regularly at Easter and Michaelmas, answering for every ship, the quantities of wool carried, the ports of charge, and the owners of goods ; and that the issues of all customs should come direct into the Exchequer.   Merchant aliens who had held the customs were to be detained with all their goods, till they rendered full account to the Treasurer and barons of the Exchequer.   But the Italian experts were soon released by royal writ, the king announcing that they were prepared to render the account required. Soon after they were again arrested on account of pressure brought to bear by the barons, and their goods impounded. Yet the king continued to apportion sums out of the customs to his court favourites, to intercept moneys for his private expenses, to grant his servants small bites at the wool duty, and to send his providers of knick-knacks to the Customs for their money.   The queen bought trinkets from a Genoese, and the seller went on the Boston custom for pay.   A soldier asked for his wages ; the king sent him to the Customs.   Frequently a paltry debt to a tradesman was discharged in the same way. The queen was put on the Southampton custom for £4,000, part of a large debt.   Harassed as the Southampton custom was just then, the queen must have had but a poor chance of recovering.   In the end the king revived all the imposts, and arranged for the Ballardi of Lucca to farm the customs.   It is likely that he accepted secret loans and bribes from all the Italian syndicates in turn, and repaid with close writs that enabled them to batten upon Commerce.

An extraordinary riot over revenue matters took place during this reign. The citizens of Bristol, who had previously been allowed to collect their own customs and answer for them through the port-reeve, resented the appointment of a governor, empowered to act as collector. Despite the king's writ, they continued the ancient system. It is recorded. that they shut the governor up in his keep, and afterwards seized two of the king's justices who had been sent down to investigate matters, and threw them into prison. An army was dispatched to invest the town, but the valorous rebels appear to have treated the attack with contempt, and easily maintained their position. In the end the Bristol citizens were outlawed, and not till then did they make submission, agreeing to render an account of the moneys illegally collected, and to pay a heavy fine.

In Edward II.'s time London was the most considerable port. Southampton ranked next, then Boston, then Sandwich. The principal ports for shipment of wool were London, Boston, and Southampton. Southampton and Sandwich imported much French and Levant wine. English shipbuilding was on the mend, but most of the wine and wool traffic was still conducted in foreign bottoms. The method of computing a vessel's capacity was to estimate her stowage in ' tuns of wine.' Most of the English vessels were of the Cinque Ports, and used in both commerce and war. The fleet of the Cinque Ports consisted of ships, galleys, barges, cutters, and ' cogs.' The vessels of Yarmouth were mostly cogs, those of Dartmouth, Poole, and Fowey barges and ' balingers.' And it must be stated that these last were often used in intercepting and plundering the vessels of the aliens. In Edward's day, and for centuries after, the English of the West Country were eminent as wreckers and pirates. If a foreign ship happened to lie becalmed off the coast of

Dorset, Devon, or Cornwall, lucky were her company if in the night a galley did not come alongside, and a dozen desperadoes leap aboard and carry off the choicest of her cargo. If a foreign ship went ashore on one of those picturesque strands, down came a gang of whooping country-folk, who stole everything they could lay hands on, and stripped such unfortunates as escaped the sea. The character bestowed in Kingsley's novel upon the rugged fellow who brought tidings of the Armada would have fitted many a mediæval mariner of ' Dertemouthe ' or ' Fowy.' ' If he has not left his manners behind, look out for your pockets, gentlemen all! He's manners enough, and very bad ones they be, when he com'th across a quiet Flushinger.'

LIST OF AUTHORITIES.

Saxon taxation : Anglo-Saxon Chronicle.

Ancient system of collection : Hubert Hall's ' History of the Custom-Revenue.'

Act relating to ' Nova Custuma ' : Hale, quoted in Hargrave's ' Law Tracts.'

Assignments, pre-emptions of wine, etc. : Patent Rolls, 8 Edw. I., m. 28 ; 14 Edw. I., m. 19 ; 16 Edw. I., m. 13 ; 10 Edw. I., m. 17d. ; 1 Edw. II., p. 1, m. 18 ; 1 Edw. II., p. 2, m. 3 ; 11 Edw. II., p. 2, m. 27 ; and Close Rolls, 10 Edw. I., m. 5 ; 17 Edw. I., m. 6d. ; 22 Edw. I., m. 2 ; 1 Edw. II., m. 2 ; 5 Edw. II., m. 21 ; 5 Edw. II., m. 30 ; 5 Edw. II., m. 3.

Carta Mercatoria : Hale, quoted in Hargrave's ' Law Tracts ' as Carta, 31 Edw. I., No. 44.

Prisage routine, etc. : Tate's Transcript, quoted by Professor Furnivall.

Bristol riot : Hubert Hall's ' History of the Custom-Revenue.'

Legislation : Ordinances, Edw. II., c. 4, 5, 8, 10, 11

CHAPTER II

THE ' SUBSIDY ' OF WOOL, AND OF TUNNAGE
AND POUNDAGE

1327–1422

In the early part of Edward III.'s reign the barons dealt sternly with the alien merchants and the unsatisfied assignees. The mailed guardians of the young king temporarily prohibited the exportation of wool, in order to benefit the English cloth industry. By a charter granted in the first year of the reign, the citizens of London were made free from Prisage.

Many of the Italian merchants having gone home, and taken their riches with them, there was a scarcity of coin throughout the realm, and this the barons attempted to remedy. The customs searchers were instructed to rummage for money sterling carried on board foreign-going ships. Persons going abroad were forbidden to take more coin than would cover their reasonable expenses, and the statute even directed that the innkeepers at the various ports should be sworn to search their guests.

As soon as the king shook himself free of restraint, it became apparent that a foolish spendthrift had been succeeded by an audacious man of business. In spite of the repeated protests of Parliament and the native merchants, he proceeded to extort, in addition to the wool custom sanctioned by Carta Mercatoria, a special impost of 40s. on each sack of wool, 300 wool fells, and last of leather, urging as pretext the needs of his ' great business.' This kind of ' Maltolte ' had been occasionally used by previous kings, notably by Edward I. in 1297 ; but never had it been applied with such savage persistency as in this reign of the third Edward. The king repeatedly promised that when the period specified for continuance of the impost should expire he would take no more than the time-honoured customs—at any rate, of denizens. But in no case did he keep his word.

This imposition upon the richest product of English agriculture continued to the end of Edward's reign. Sometimes it was taken at the 40s. rate, sometimes at a rate even higher. Sometimes the rates were the same upon wool, fells, and leather ; sometimes the leather rate immensely exceeded that on wool and fells. The impost was accompanied after a period by a duty upon exported cloth,* a tax totally against the old export revenue doctrine, for it had always been held a justification of the wool tax that it benefited the native cloth industry by making English wool dear in the Continental markets. Yet, when the cloth tax was petitioned against, the king merely made answer that cloth was justly liable to taxation, it being a product of wool. Not only did Edward increase rates, he actually, at one period of his reign, instituted a gigantic system of pre-emption or evil prisage of wool, arresting exportation of the article, buying to the amount of 20,000 sacks at his own price, selling at contract price to merchants, and at once compelling the merchants to pay the Maltolte on their purchases. Worse even than the Maltolte were the extortions of the king's buyers, who charged the wool-producers heavy fees, and the tricks of the farmers of customs at various ports, who exacted for their own benefit extra duties as ' loans to the king.' Through the whole of this reign the commons and wool-producers protested and petitioned against the unjust officials, and the arbitrary imposts enforced by them.

* The impost was 14d. per ' short cloth ' upon woollens exported by denizens, 21d. on woollens exported by aliens. The various cloths ' dyed in grain ' were rated proportionately Though a mere arbitrary levy, the cloth tax became ' perpetual.'

It would be tedious to specify the fluctuations of the Maltolte, or ' Subsidy,' as it was called towards the end of the reign. The rates quoted below may be taken as something near averages :

	Denizens' Duties.			Aliens' Duties.	
	Sack of Wool, or 300 Fells.	Last of Leather.		Sack of Wool, or 300 Fells.	Last of Leather.
	£ s. d.	£ s. d.		£ s. d.	£ s. d.
Maltolte	2 0 0	4 0 0	Maltolte	2 0 0	4 0 0
Ancient Custom	0 6 8	0 13 4	C. Merc. Duties	0 10 0	1 0 0
Total	2 6 8	4 13 4	Total	2 10 0	5 0 0

(It must be taken into account that towards the end of the reign the tax was levied on 240 fells instead of 300, and that for a long period denizens were forbidden to export wool.)

Occasionally Edward's senators tried to ease the burdens of the nation by juggling with the incidents of the wool industry. They set themselves to organize a national ' Staple ' of wool, fells, and leather.*   Newcastle, Bristol, Chichester, Exeter, Carmarthen, Dublin, Waterford, Cork, and Drogheda were named as ports where goods might be weighed, inspected, and sealed, for exportation or for coastwise transport. Several inland towns were also made places of staple, and each was linked with an adjacent port, to which all its stapled

* Previously the great centres of staple seem to have been Bruges and Middelburg, places where various kinds of imported goods were inspected, and then passed as reliable articles of trade. The antiquity of staples is proved by a document in the Record Office, included in State Papers, Elizabeth, 1561.   It states that the Company of English Merchant Staplers was a corporation before Calais was English, the Staple being kept at ' various places beyond the sea, till by King Edward removed to Calais.'   It is apparent, too, that stapling towns for certain products had existed in England long prior to Edward's reign.

goods had to be sent. York was linked with Hull, Lincoln with Boston, Norwich with Yarmouth, Westminster with the port of London, Canterbury with Sandwich, and Winchester with Southampton. At the 'staple ports' wool for exportation was weighed, inspected, and sealed, in presence of the customs officers and the Mayor of the Staple. At the 'staple towns' it was weighed, inspected, and sealed, by the Mayor of the Staple, and the outward custom paid. Then the goods were advised to the linked ports, and on arrival they were examined and reweighed by the customs officers as a check. It is not exactly apparent how long the English Staple endured. Later in the reign the Staple went to Calais, then back to England, then to Calais again.

Edward's 'needs' continued to increase, and his sinister knack of 'business' soon provided him with a new source of revenue, the levy of 'Tunnage and Poundage,' at the rate of 2s. a tun upon all imported wine, and 6d. in the £, value upon *all* merchandise except wine, fresh fish, and 'bestial' inward, and exported wool, fells, and leather. The new duties were practically thrust upon Parliament, with a demand that they should be sanctioned for a brief period. The Commons repeatedly reaffirmed them. They were destined to become 'perpetual,' and to play, centuries later, a tragic part in English history.

The minor customs incidents of the reign are not without interest. The Archbishop of York claimed restoration of his ancient right of prisage in the Humber waters. The Exchequer barons granted the request, but later the grant was revoked, and the king renewed prisage in Hull.*

The long-standing debt to the Aquitaine mayors was discharged, the Mayor of London and another com-

---

* The Archbishop claimed that his predecessors had held power of prisage under a charter granted by the Saxon king Athelstane, and affirmed by Henry III. Edward I.'s Chamberlain, Matthew de Columbar, dispossessed the Archbishop of 1283 (Close Roll, 1 Edw. III., p. 1, m. 11).

póunding with the creditors for about half the sum claimed as due, and then going on the Southampton custom. Afterwards the new assignees complained that they had been unable to realize the amount of their advance, and were put upon the Staple at Winchester.

Towards the end of the reign several farmers of customs and their deputies were dismissed for fraud, and two of them imprisoned.* The statutes testify that there was much extortion. One statute declared that the king's Butler and his deputies had misbehaved in prisage, taking more wine than the king needed, keeping the best for themselves and giving the worst to the king, extorting gifts from merchants, and occasionally conniving at escape from prise. Another statute regularized the fees of the alnagers or cloth-measurers, who had oppressed merchants. It also recited the regulations as to gauging of wine at importation,† and expressed profound suspicion of the good faith of the gaugers. Another statute stipulated that no vessel might be held forfeitable ' for a little thing uncustomed.' Evidently some of the officers had strained the law to their own profit, and seized vessels for trifling irregularities which were probably the result of oversight.

Richard II. was granted his predecessor's customs— viz., the subsidy of wool, fells, and leather—over and above the Carta Mercatoria duties on aliens' wool, wine,

* The case most notable was that of Richard Lyons, who was a farmer of customs, and ' one of the king's council.' He was arraigned before Parliament during 51 Edw. III., and committed to prison. His estate was also seized. Richard II. pardoned him. After Lyons' death Richard reaffirmed the pardon, so that the dead man's estate, which was considerable, might be disposed of. (See Patent Rolls, 5 Rich. II., p. 2, m. 13.)

† It appears that wines had been gauged on importation even prior to the imposition of ' Butlerage ' in Edward I.'s reign. It may be interesting to experts to know that the gauging was mere ' dipping ' to find the ' wet,' with an occasional measurement as check upon the standards of tuns, butts, pipes, etc. The gauge fee was a penny a cask, and Mr. Hall points out that this was not a gauger's perquisite, but was paid into the Exchequer.

and merchandise, and the new subsidy of ' tunnage and
poundage.'* (Prisage and the Ancient Custom were of
course immutable perquisites.) The provision which
attached to Edward's tunnage and poundage was reaffirmed—viz., that the duties should be applied solely to
' keeping the sea.' (Sir Matthew Hale, in his treatise on
Customs, has called the tunnage and poundage a convoy
duty. At one period during this reign the collectors of
customs were instructed to deliver their takings direct
to the admirals of the fleet.) The rates of tunnage and
poundage, after several fluctuations, became fixed at 3s.
a tun on wine, and 12d. in the £, value upon merchandise. The method of estimating the value of goods
for poundage was peculiar, and no doubt conduced in
many cases to fraud. The collectors fixed the rate by
conferring with the merchants who owned the goods,
the merchants, if required, furnishing invoices from their
factors.

Both officers and traders received occasional warning
by statute. It was enacted that alnagers sealing faulty
cloth should be imprisoned during the king's pleasure,
that customs officers should not own or be concerned in
shipping, and that their patents (writs of appointment)
should endure during the king's pleasure only. The
Clerk of the Market of the King's House (purveyor) was
warned not to stay longer in one place than the legal
contingencies of purveyance rendered necessary, and not
to ride with more than six horses.† Merchant strangers
were forbidden to buy from other aliens to sell again
within the realm. Another act defined the lawful refuse
of wool (Cot, Gare, and Villein), and provided that the
' cocket ' or clearance for wool outward should be in the
owner's name. It was also enacted that all West-Country

* 5 Richard II., s. 2, c. 2, refers to a grant of the wool
duties by a previous Parliament. No doubt the tunnage and
poundage were collected from the beginning of the reign, but
Hale is of opinion they were not ratified by Parliament till the
issue of 10 Richard II., c. 18 (an Act that has not survived).

† The purveyors, while travelling on their unpopular duty,
were allowed to impress horses for carriage and transport.

cloth should be exposed for sale open, as merchants who had bought it by the bale and taken it abroad had been in danger of their lives from the incensement of buyers who had found the bales deceptive.

The wool trade provided cause for many writs, assignments, special licences, and royal interventions. The Staple was temporarily removed to Calais, but at the end of the reign came back to England. There appears to have been no little intrigue used, both in England and across the Channel, to gain possession of the stapling privileges.* Frequently the king granted licences to merchants of Newcastle to buy the rough wool of the counties north of the Humber, and ship it unstapled to Flanders and other places. There was a twofold excuse for such transactions. In the first place, the northern wool was of inferior quality, and thus rarely up to staple standard ; in the second, it was held that the privilege encouraged exportation from the northern shires, and thus prevented the smuggling of wool across the Scottish border. Whenever such exemption was allowed, the king demanded, in addition to the custom, the sum of 19d. per sack, which was the amount of the stapling fees imposed upon other wool.

One or two instances of exemptive licence will illustrate this. A Bristol merchant was allowed to ship northern wool from Carlisle to Bristol. He had to attend personally at the Exchequer, so that he might give bond to pay the outward custom on the arrival of the goods at Bristol, and to export the consignment within a specified period. In 1393 an unusual transaction was licensed ; a large quantity of Welsh wool was brought overland to Southampton, the outward custom paid there, and the goods shipped free of staple to Genoa.

* Occasionally, when the Staple was at Calais, the customs revenues accruing were applied to the maintenance of the English garrison, the duties being secured by bond, entered into with the English collectors of customs at the time of shipment. The moneys were collected when the goods arrived at Calais, and disbursed by the Mayor and Masters of the Calais Staple. The Mayor and Masters were English wool merchants, mostly of Lincolnshire.

The king equalled Edward II. in irresponsible extravagance, and incurred debts with great recklessness, flinging many of his semi-private liabilities upon the overburdened customs. He owed one Janyn, a Lombard, a sum amounting to over 10,000 marks, and, being also heavily in debt to the Mayor and Commonalty of London, divided the cocket or clearance seal of the port of London betwixt Janyn and the City Fathers, with the stipulation that if Janyn failed to collect the 10,000 odd marks within a reasonable time he might dispose of certain jewels, pledged with him by the king. Later other jewels were pledged with the Bardi of Florence, the Treasurer of the Exchequer formally handing them over. Later still ' a royal crown ' was pledged with the Mayor and Commonalty of London. The Treasurer and chamberlains were directed to deliver it, enclosed in a sealed coffer, and the mandate provided that if the debt for which it was security were not discharged before the following Easter the City officials might deal with crown and coffer as they pleased.

Yet the king, or perhaps some astute official acting as prompter, could execute a sharp business transaction when opportunity arose. In 1393 the royal sergeant-at-arms was sent into the counties north of the Humber, on the specious pretext that certain merchants had covenanted to lower the price of wool by stopping purchases. The emissary was directed to ' buy for ready money ' all the outstanding stock of wool, to ship it in certain vessels which had been forfeited to the Crown, and to press mariners. This was a notable commercial feat. The wool, which was free of the Staple, was really bought ' at the king's price,' the ships were prize, the provisions for them were pre-empted, the sailors were pressed.

The gradual enlightenment of the king's advisers on the matter of contraband traffic is worth notice. In 1387 the mayor of Bristol was directed to investigate as to English smugglers entering the Severn, and running goods

into Wales.   Inquiry was also made as to smuggling from
the eastern ports to Middelburg.   In 1390 it was discovered that extensive smuggling was practised off the
Wight, and from the unguarded coasts of the north-west
of England.   A controller of customs was thereupon
appointed for Cumberland.   Investigation was extended
to Yorkshire, Devon, and Cornwall, and in the end the
whole realm was by implication indicted.   Both aliens
and denizens took part in the illicit trade.   During part
of the reign the exportation of wool was vested in aliens
only, and then such denizens as smuggled wool outward
were liable under two counts—defrauding the revenue
and infringing the exportation laws.   The whole kingdom
was racked by lawlessness ;   indeed the contempt of
maritime law prevailing was as nothing compared with
the turbulence of the ' foresters ' in the woodland shires
of York, Nottingham, and Leicester, where there was a
continual succession of raids upon parks, warrens, and
manor-houses.

This reign is remarkable for the number of pardons
granted for acts of riot, violence, wrecking, piracy, and
smuggling.   In some cases the writs of oblivion appear
to have been granted at intercession of wealthy nobles
or influential churchmen, in others the reasons of grant
are undiscernible.   Recital of a few instances will afford
readers an opportunity of judging.

The mayor of Southampton, assisted by a body of
citizens and *the collector of customs*, illegally imposed
port dues upon vessels lying at Fareham, a place exempt
' from time immemorial.'   The dues being disputed, he
seized and carried off a quantity of merchandise, which he
sold in Southampton for his own profit.   He also heavily
forestalled provisions and other goods.   The Crown
pardoned him and his associates.

A Lincolnshire merchant was indicted for carrying corn
into Scotland, contrary to the statute that prescribed the
minimum price at which corn might be exported.   Pardoned.

A Hampshire smuggler who had carried uncustomed wool to 'the king's enemies' (the French) was pardoned.

Over two hundred defendants, mostly wool-merchants of Lincolnshire and the Midlands, who had been convicted of frauds in the weighing of wool, were pardoned in a batch.

One Geoffrey Blake, Irish merchant, impeached at the Exchequer for having, with the assistance of certain of his countrymen, defrauded the revenue at Bristol, was pardoned at intercession of his kinsman, a church dignitary.

One instance of scrupulous dealing may be quoted. A German trader approached the king, pleading that the Hanse merchants had expelled him from their guild because he had paid the king of England *more custom than was necessary*. The king admitted this incomprehensible Teuton to the privileges of a denizen, and the Mayor of London made him a freeman of the City.

Aliens had a parlous time, especially when cruising on the Cornish coast. When wrecked they were stripped, beaten, and their goods appropriated. Often their vessels were seized whilst cruising, on the pretext that they were owned and manned by 'the king's enemies.' When they petitioned the king for restitution he ordered a commission of inquiry. Usually the goods could not be traced. Occasionally the sheriff secured them, and the king restored them to their owners, charging double custom or a heavy fee for his trouble.

During this reign the 'scheme' of revenue ports was frequently exemplified in the various patents of office. The coast, from Berwick to Chepstow, was divided into customs districts, each district having as centre a 'great port.' (The record during the early part of the reign made no mention of Wales and the north-western maritime shires, and it is evident that such traffic as occasionally took place in the creeks and rivers from Land's End

to Carlisle enjoyed immunity from customs supervision.)
The districts were set out as below :

Great Ports.	Extent of Districts.
Newcastle.	Berwick to Scarborough.
Hull.	Scarborough to Grimsby.
Boston.	Grimsby to Wisbech.
Lynn.	Wisbech to Blakeney.
Yarmouth.	Blakeney to Ipswich.
Ipswich.	Ipswich to Tilbury.
London.	London to Gravesend.
Sandwich.	Gravesend to Dover.
Dover.	Dover to Winchelsea.
Chichester.	Winchelsea to Portsmouth.
Southampton	Portsmouth to Melcombe, including the Wight.
Exeter.	Melcombe to Bridgwater.
Bristol.	Bridgwater to Chepstow.

At each great port was stationed a ' customer ' or
collector, with a ' controller ' as check. (The larger
ports had two collectors and a controller.) The patents
appointing collectors stipulated that they should reside
at their places of employment. The controllers kept
duplicate accounts. There were also officers called
' searchers,' who supervised the actual landing and shipment of goods, and ' tronours,' who performed the weighing of wools, etc.

The salaries of the collectors were small. Their patents
empowered them to pay the controllers' salaries out of
the takings, but the sums thus paid were merely nominal,
and it is evident that both collectors and controllers were
allowed to levy fees. The searchers appear to have had
no pay except fees, and grants out of forfeitures and
seizures.

Occasionally a port was ' farmed,' the king granting a
lease of the takings for a specified period, and the farmers
paying a lump sum in anticipation. But it seems that
the collector and controller remained in office even while
the farm was in force, to check the proceedings of the
farmers' deputies. The following is a fair rendering of
an agreement between king and farmers :

' Between the King and A——, B——, C——, and

D——. The King leases to A—— and his fellows all the custom of wool, wool-fells, and hides that may be shipped in the port of E—— from Easter next unto Easter following, they paying to the King — marks, and grants to the said A—— and his fellows that the customers, weighers, and controllers in the said port shall be appointed with their free assent : And that all issues of the said custom in the port of E—— shall be delivered unto F—— and G—— as the attorneys of A—— and his fellows, and that the customers shall account with the said attorneys for the receipt of custom from Easter next unto Easter following, and shall be discharged by the said attorneys of their account towards the King : And the King wills that the passage of wool, wool-fells, and hides shall be open in the said port from Easter next unto Easter following, and if the said passage be by the King restrained abatement shall be made in rent of farm in order with such time as restraint shall continue.'

The subsidy of wool and the tunnage and poundage varied occasionally as to rate during Henry IV.'s reign, but for the greater part of the time they were as follows : Tunnage, 3s. ; poundage, 12d. ; wool exported by denizens, 50s. ; by aliens, 60s. ; leather—denizens, £5 per last ; aliens, £5 6s. 8d. A penny in Henry's time was worth about a shilling in modern money. Thus, the tax may, in our coinage, be stated as about 20d. a pound on denizens' wool, 24d. a pound on aliens', and, roughly, as 5s. on every hide of leather. The restrictions involved bore heavily upon the producers, and if, as the older economists claimed, they fostered the English cloth industry, the fostering was a costly and not altogether advantageous process.

In an early year of Henry's reign it was enacted that alien merchants should furnish security to the customs collectors that all money received for foreign goods should be expended in the purchase of English commodities. It was also provided that all goods should be shipped or unshipped at the great ports, not at creeks. To prevent forestalling, it was enjoined that aliens should sell their wares within three months of landing. This last statute was soon repealed, provision being made that all aliens' merchandise should be sold, not carried out of the realm. Petition was tendered that aliens should be debarred from acting as collectors of customs. The king agreed, stipulating that the customs officers should be courteous to Italian merchants.

The revenue officials were enjoined to live at their towns of employment, and later the injunction was reaffirmed, with the significant addition that customs searchers might not employ deputies, and that all customs officers should answer upon oath for their remittances. The searchers were forbidden to take money of shipmasters by way of ' welcome ' or ' farewell,' or to entertain merchants and mariners. Later still it was enacted that no common innkeeper should be a controller or searcher.

The king's stipulation that the Italian merchants should be courteously treated was perhaps made with a view towards his own accommodation, for he afterwards gave the Genoese merchants permission to export wool duty-free for a period, in discharge of loans which they had advanced him. Henry did not borrow so extensively and recklessly as his predecessor. His wars with Scotland were probably expensive, for in 1401 he directed the collectors of Hull, Boston, and Lynn to send money direct to the Earl of Northumberland and Harry Percy, in aid of the keeping of the Scottish marches.*

There were many complaints from merchants as to the improper taking of duties. The grant of 50s. and 60s. on denizens' and aliens' wool respectively had been intended to include the ' Ancient Custom ' of 6s. 8d., but at some of the ports the collectors took the 50s. and 60s. rates as

---

* This grant to the Wardens of the Marches appears in the Rolls more than once.

subsidy rates only, and afterwards collected the ancient
and the aliens' Custom.   Several petitions were tendered,
complaining of unfair practices used by alien merchants,
and the king consoled the petitioners by imposing for one
year double poundage upon aliens' goods.

It is evident that in spite of the enormous rating of
wool, etc., the out-turn of the customs was unsatisfactory.   For instance, at one period of the reign certain
merchants of the Cinque Ports were allowed the proceeds
of the tunnage and poundage, and a fourth of the wool
subsidy, on condition that they furnished a defensive
fleet.   A certain sum was to be advanced at once, but
the amount was not forthcoming, so the whole arrangement lapsed.   The deficiency in the revenue was popu-
larly attributed to extensive smuggling by aliens, whom
the native merchants charged with systematic evasion of
both wool and cloth duties.   It appears that the aliens
evaded the cloth tax by ' making up ' woollens, and
exporting them in the form of garments, paying only the
outward poundage.   The native merchants, in calling
attention to the falling off in the revenue receipts, quoted
the return during the latter part of the previous reign,
stating that then the proceeds of the custom and subsidy
of wool were £160,000 a year net.   This was a gross
exaggeration, and the petitioners may reasonably be suspected of a desire to harry their foreign competitors, and
thus secure for themselves a larger share of the outward
carrying and trading.   But the statement must have had
effect, for it was enacted that garments made of wool
should be liable to custom as well as poundage.

The Genoese and Venetian traders were unpopular
during this reign.   The Venetians appear to have been
enterprising folk, and they were ably assisted by their
skilful and far-seeing senators, whom the Venetian ambassador in England kept posted on matters of trade, on
the impositions' made by kings and customers, and on
the doings of the Venetian ' Factory.'

The Guild of St. Thomas à Becket, which afterwards

became famous as ' The Merchant Adventurers of London,' received a charter in 1404.   To the efforts of this powerful and enterprising syndicate may be ascribed much of the English agitation against foreign traders, which many years later culminated in the Navigation Acts and the mercantile dominance of England.   But there were other irritating influences, for which the aliens were clearly responsible.   For instance, towards the end of Henry's reign certain London ships in the Morocco trade were captured by Genoese pirates, and Henry granted the aggrieved shipowners permission to make reprisals on Genoese commerce.   He also extended favourable consideration to a petition that ' proper persons ' should be employed as customs collectors, not such as were ' hosts to aliens.'

The subsidy was taken by Henry V. at the following rates : 43s. 4d. denizens' wool and fells, 60s. aliens' ; 100s. denizens' leather, 106s. 8d. aliens' ; tunnage 3s. ; poundage 12d.   (According to Hale, the grant was made during 1 Henry V., and for life during 3 Henry V.)

In 1414 the Venetian Senate limited the loading-time of its fleet in England to fifty days.   All goods were to be shipped by the forty-sixth day, and it appears that the captains were held responsible if there were any delay through the outward duties not being paid.   There was a Venetian ' Council of Twelve ' in London, for regulating affairs of trade.   The English customers were exceedingly strict with the Venetians, and if any duties were unpaid as the sailing-time approached they removed the sails and rudders, thus effectually preventing the vessel's departure.

Henry renewed Carta Mercatoria, and the privileges granted by Edward I. to the traders of the Hanse.

The salaries of the customs collectors and controllers throughout England during one year of this reign are stated as amounting to £547 only, and the total Customs revenue, including customs, subsidy of wool, and tunnage and poundage, to just over £40,000. Thus it is evident that the officers were allowed to charge many fees. It must be borne in mind that during the continuance of the fee system no official statement of net revenue could convey even approximate information as to the actual amount extorted from the public.

It should be stated, too, that the returns furnished by various ancient writers, even of the net payments into the Exchequer, will rarely stand the test of comparison. The sums occasionally quoted by interested people who approached the throne with petitions were often flagrantly unreliable. The safest conclusion is that at the large ports, especially at London, collection was in a way systematic, and that at the small and remote ports the collectors did much as they pleased. It is practically certain that the Customs net revenue up to the end of Elizabeth's reign rarely approached £100,000 per annum. Of course the comparatively great value of money in mediæval times must be taken into account.*

LIST OF AUTHORITIES.
Legislation.

Wool : 11 Edw. III., c. 1 ; 14 Edw. III., s. 1, c. 21 ; 27 Edw. III., s. 2, c. 1 ; 13 Rich. II., s. 1, c. 9.

Coin : 9 Edw. III., s. 2, c. 9, 10, 11.

Cloth : Hale, ' Pars Tertia,' Hargrave's ' Law Tracts '; 13 Rich. II., s. 1, c. 11 ; 11 Hen. IV., c. 7.

---

* Mr. Hall furnishes many illuminative statements of the returns of certain duties, usually London returns. These must be accepted as quite authentic, but it is noticeable that he rarely attempts to estimate the *total* yield. No doubt after profound consideration, he makes the guarded statement that during Edward III.'s reign it may have been about £60,000 per annum. Sir William Petty, writing during Charles II.'s reign, avowed that he had come to the conclusion that the old returns of revenue were frequently, sometimes wilfully, misstated, to the great prejudice of speculators who relied upon them, and farmed the customs at rates founded on the Exchequer figures. If this remarkable statement be correct, it would seem that Mr. Hall's reticence should be applauded. It is to be wished that at least one other writer had been equally cautious.

Officers: 25 Edw. III., s. 5, c. 21 ; 3 Rich. II., c. 2 ; 14 Rich. II., c. 10 ; 13 Rich. II., s. 1, c. 4 ; 1 Hen. IV., c. 13 ; 4 Hen. IV., c. 20 ; 4 Hen. IV., c. 21 ; 11 Hen. IV., c. 2.
Wine : 27 Edw. III., s. 1, c. 4 and 8.
Ships : 38 Edw. III., s. 1, c 8.
Merchants : 5 Hen. IV., c. 9 ; 6 Hen. IV., c. 4.
Ports, etc. : 4 Hen. IV., c. 20.

Incidents.

Assignments : Patent Rolls, 6 Edw. III., p. 2, m. 1 and 5 ; 7 Edw. III., p. 1, m. 4 ; 5 Rich. II., p. 2, m. 25 ; 6 Rich. II., p. 1, m. 36 ; 2 Hen. IV., p. 2, m. 7.
Special licences : Patent Rolls, 16 Rich. II., p. 1, m. 7 ; 16 Rich. II., p. 3, m. 23*d.* ; 9 Rich. II., p. 2, m. 39.
Prisage and pre-emptions : Close Rolls, 1 Edw. III., p. 1, m. 11 ; Patent Rolls, 16 Rich. II., p. 3, m. 23*d.*
Frauds : Patent Rolls, 10 Rich. II., p. 2, m. 23*d.* ; 14 Rich. II., p. 2, m. 44*d.* ; 15 Rich. II., p. 1, m. 20*d.* ; 5 Rich. II., p. 1, m. 13 ; Hubert Hall's 'History of the Custom-Revenue.'
Pardons : Patent Rolls, 1 Rich II., p. 2, m. 6 ; 1 Rich. II., p. 4, m. 31 ; 19 Rich. II., p. 1, m. 30 ; 19 Rich. II., p. 1, m. 14 and 15 ; 19 Rich. II., p. 1, m. 34.
Reprisals : Fœdera (' De Reprisalia ').
Venetian trade : Calendar Venetian State Papers, 1414 and 1419.
Mercantile privileges : Fœdera (' De Confirmatione pro Mercatoribus ').
Revenue : Fœdera (' Declaratio Prosicuorum Regni et Onerum Supportandorum ').

CHAPTER III

HENRY VI. received the wool subsidy and custom as
below :

> Denizens : 33s. 4d. wool and fells, 100s. leather.
> Aliens : 53s. 4d. wool and fells, 106s. 8d. leather.

(Hale states that the wool duties were granted by a
statute of 1 Henry VI., but in the Patent Roll of 1423
there is allusion to an ordinance ' by advice of Council,'
specifying the rates on aliens' wool.)

Considering the length of Henry's reign, the revenue
statutes quotable are few. One Act defined the measures
of wine in cask according to the ancient standard—a tun,
252 gallons ; a pipe or butt, 126 ; a tertian, 84 ; a hogshead, 63—stating that of late the casks had been imported at smaller sizes ' through device and subtilty.'

It appears that the Danes had a staple for fish. In
the eighth year of Henry's reign English merchants were
enjoined not to trade in the Danish king's dominions,
which included Denmark, Norway, Sweden, and Iceland,
except at the fish Staple of Bergen.

It was announced that uncustomed goods were frequently smuggled through Wales and into England.

Patents empowering the holders to receive sums out of
the revenue, or to levy impositions, were directed to continue during the king's pleasure, not ' for life.' Certain

37

holders were exempted, mostly royal or titled personages, and the commonalties of privileged cities such as London and Winchester. The tunnage rate on ' sweet wines ' (Madeiras, Muscadels, etc.) brought by aliens was doubled, and so was the poundage upon tin exported by aliens. The Act of 1454, granting the subsidy for life, appears to have contained the first constitutional grant of the outward cloth duties, which duties, through the growth of the English cloth manufactures, were fast becoming important items of revenue.

The customs officials were directed to give warrants, instead of the usual ' tallies,' in respect of duties taken. In default merchants were empowered to sue, and the penalty in case of conviction was fixed at £10, half to go to the plaintiff. The statute stated that by withholding receipts many officers had embezzled duties and escaped Exchequer proceedings, the merchants concerned having no vouchers to show. The statute prohibiting customs officers from owning ships or acting as merchants, factors, or wharfingers was reaffirmed, and made applicable to officers' deputies. A special Act was issued condemning extortions practised by certain ' water-bailiffs, controllers of the search, and searchers,' particularly by those employed at the notorious ports of Fowey, Plymouth, Dartmouth, and Poole. These enterprising officials had ' by distress and arrests ' made heavy impositions upon merchants, both native and foreign. (It is to be presumed that the foreigners suffered most.) A general writ of trespass was issued, empowering the injured merchants to sue for £40 each, and to take the whole as damages if successful. If they failed to sue, any ' liege person ' might take action on their behalf, receiving half the penalty if he won his case, the other half to go to the Crown. The full details of the roguery practised are not exactly clear to him who merely reads the Act, but it almost seems that the officers, after fleecing the merchants most unmercifully, levied certain taxes of their own devising upon the ship's fittings.

The Staple* was at Calais during this reign. The usual exemptions by licence were granted to merchants of the north of England, for wool of Northumberland, Westmoreland, and Cumberland only. The Italian merchants were often licensed to ship wool unstapled to their own countries, it being provided that the goods should go by the Straits of Morocco (Gibraltar), *and not overland.* This seems to imply that there was still trade by the Channel and then overland to the Mediterranean.

It is apparent that the custom taken at the Staple fell off during Henry's reign. It is likely that this was due to the increased English manufactures, which provided a new market for the raw material. It was better for the producer to take a low price in England than to subject his goods to the burdensome outward expenses, and to risk of storm and piracy. The king's advisers seem to have attributed the falling-off to other causes, for they enacted that all wool or fells placed in remote places near the coast, except under indenture for legal exportation, should be forfeitable.† The desire of the English to dominate the trade had previously been made manifest in a petition that the export of live sheep to Flanders might be prohibited, as it improved the breed of Flemish sheep to the loss of English trade. The request had been acknowledged by prohibition of export, except under royal licence or to the Staple. Occasionally privilege was

* It is possible that the maintenance of the Staple at Calais instead of in England may have assisted in the prevention of smuggling, for no wool would be received at the Calais Staple unless ' cocketed ' in England, and secured by bond as to duty. Thus smuggled wool could not well be run directly across Channel into the parts of France subject to England, for the Masters of the Calais Staple, during such time as they held exclusive stapling privileges, kept a sharp watch upon all vessels arriving on the adjacent coast. Whether the Staple were in England or Calais, the smugglers could scarcely have cleared the whole amount of the custom, for they would have to sell their wool unsealed. Its quality would therefore be unattested, and the buyers would offer a low price, and refuse to believe that the goods were of the English counties south of the Humber.

† In 1427 a Commission had inquired into the unlading and lading of uncustomed goods on the coast of Sussex, and as to non-residence of officials.

granted to certain Welsh wool-producers to have their goods stapled at Carmarthen, the duty collected there, and the goods shipped via Bristol without further charge.

The yearly expenses of the king's household were stated as 10,000 marks—quite a moderate sum. 2,000 marks were appropriated towards this end from tunnage and poundage, 5,000 from the wool subsidy, and the rest from the Welsh revenues, the revenues of the Mint, and Wardships. But the king contrived to burden himself with debts, and his creditors, among whom the Bishop of Winchester and the Florentine and Venetian guildsmen were conspicuous, were frequently allowed to dabble in the customs receipts. Other curious assignments appear in the records. For instance, the Justices of the King's Bench were quartered on the Hanaper and the Customs for 180 marks each yearly, besides £5 6s. 11¼d. ' and the sixth part of a halfpenny ' for a furred robe every Christmas, and £3 6s. 6d. for a lined robe every Whitsuntide.

In 1450 Dutch and Flemish wares were prohibited for a period, the Netherlanders having prohibited English cloth.

There was much bartering and adjusting of commercial privileges between England and foreign states. A treaty betwixt Henry, the Master-General of the Teutonic Knights of Prussia, and the Consuls of the Hanse towns, renewed all commercial privileges granted between England and the Almains concerned during the previous hundred years, and provided that the duties and customs formerly prescribed should remain on the ancient footing.* The treaty does not appear to have been rigorously observed on either side. The Venetians' trade with England must have been on the diminishing scale, for the Senate enjoined that its London factory should not be called upon to expend more than £20 per ship in corrupting

---

* About this time the Hanse merchants began to lose their trade, which gradually passed into the hands of the English and Dutch.

the English collectors.* An amicable understanding seems to have existed between Henry and the king of Portugal. The latter was frequently granted licences to ship large quantities of English goods.

English merchant enterprise was manifested by the sudden emerging into importance of a company that in after years gained a firm grip of the export cloth trade, and commanded powerful legislative support. The Society of St. Thomas à Becket, extending its operations with immense vigour, entered into formidable competition with the Hanse traders. A 'great ship' belonging to one Taverner, of Hull, entered the Thames, and the king seems to have taken special interest in her. He granted a licence, empowering her to carry outwards 'all kinds of merchandise, either aliens' or denizens',' bringing back 'such goods as were most needed in England,' and named her *The Grace-Dieu*.

The southern English maintained their reputation as wreckers and pirates, and Spanish commerce in particular suffered terribly from their depredations. The Rolls furnish numerous records of their lawless doings. It appears they did not confine their excursions to the English side of the Channel. Below is quoted a complaint in Chancery presented by certain Breton merchants :

' *To the rev*en*d Father in God, Bysshop of Bath &*
Chauncellor of England.

' Besechith mekely John Bonodyn and Aleyn le Bihous, proctours and attornez of Gyan de Garne, Piers Bourdyn, John le Peyntor, Guyllam Maner, Piers Guyllam, Piers Tourell, Piers Duryan, and Richd. Kerbouter, merchauntes of Vennes† in Britaigne, that where the seide

* Bribing them to put a low value on goods for poundage. The 'loading period' was made ninety days instead of fifty, with an extra fifteen days for clearing through the Custom House. It would seem that the London customs men held, with their whilom controller Chaucer, that it was impossible to work ' bothe wel and hastilie.'

† Vannes in Brittany.

merchauntes, late beyng possessours and owners of a schipp called *Seint Gillian*, de Vennes in Britaigne, with divers marchaundisez, godes, and moneys beyng in the seide schipp, to the value of vjM crounes, the which yn a sedule to this bill annexed specially appearith, beyng on the costes of Britaigne yn the moneth of Octobr the XIX yere of the reigne of Kynge Herry the Sixte, saylinge toward the coste of Burdeux, having at that tyme the safe-conducte of the Erle of Huntyngdon, then beyng lieutenant of Guienne, and under the Kynges pees of Englond made and p'claymed betwene the Kynge of Englond and the Duke of Britaigne, yn way of marchaundise toward the port of Burdeux, fast by the entrynge into the ryver of the seide port, unto such tyme that the seide schipp and godes within the seide moneth of Octob'r there were taken by IIJ balyngers of were of the counte of Cornewayll : That is to sey, on balynger cleped the *Cristofre* of Trerewe,* and thereof Wolfe maister and Sr Ramfray Arundell and Sr John Trerys, Knyghtes, owners and vitallers : Another balynger cleped *Ihu* of Peryn in Falmouth, and thereof John Jetard maister and the seide Sr Ramfray Arundell, Knyghte, owner and vitaller : And the thrydde balynger cleped the *Flour de la Mare*, and th'of John Treehowe maister and the forseide Sr Ramfray Arundell owner and vitaller : And by another balynger yn their copeney as yet unknown : The seide safe-conducte and trewes natwithstondyng : And afterwardes the maisters and mariners of the seide balyngers ladde the seide schipp and godes into the ryver of Jerand,† and there dispoiled the seide godes and sold the seide schipp with grete pt of the seide godes to maister John Tregoran, clerke, Robt Maundeson of Hull, Edmond Mathewe, and Peter Gyles : The which, knowyng the seide schipp and godes soe to be dispoiled and robbet upon the see, bought the seide schipp and godes, and ladde the seide schipp and godes to the porte of Hulle within the roialme of Englond, and kepith the seide godes

---

* Truro. † Gironde.

agenst gode feith and concience : The which mat's youre
seide besechers bien redi to p've by resonable p'ves, lyke
as it plese youre g'cious Lordschipp that they schall doe :
Wherefor hit plese youre g'cious Lordschipp tenderly to
consider this p'misses, and to graunte severall writtes of
suppena directe to the seide mysdoers to appere afor you
at a certain day to aunswere to the p'misses, and th'upon
to restore youre seide besechers to the seide schipp and
godes, as gode feith and concience askith and requirith,
for the love of God and yn wey of charyte.'

One of the records may appear almost incredible. It
should be stated that in Richard II.'s time, when the
outlaws of the north Midlands made themselves busy in
plundering the estates and abodes of the rural land-
owners, they were sometimes headed by desperadoes who
in the subsequent writs of inquiry were described as
' priests ' or ' abbots.' Yet the account of such doings
in Richard's time, up in the ' lawless shires,' scarcely
prepares readers for the statement that in Henry VI.'s
reign the abbot of St. Augustine's, Canterbury, aided by
' other evildoers,' boarded a French vessel off the Isle of
Thanet, and appropriated ship and cargo.

Edward IV. received the subsidy on wool, etc., at the
following rates : Denizens' wool and fells, 33s. 4d. ; aliens',
66s. 8d. ; denizens' leather, 66s. 8d. ; aliens', 73s. 4d.*
He also received tunnage at 3s., with an extra 3s. on
sweet wines imported by aliens, and poundage at 12d.
in the £1, with an extra 12d. on aliens' tin outward. All
the above for life. Thus the total rates levied would be—

	Denizens.			Aliens.		
	£	s.	d.	£	s.	d.
On every sack of wool and every 240 fells outward	1	13	4	3	6	8
On every last of leather outward ..	3	6	8	3	13	4

* Hale states tunnage and poundage granted by an Act of
3 Edw. IV., but he is unable to give the date of the wool grant.

(The ancient Custom, and the Carta Mercatoria duties on aliens' wool, should be computed with the subsidy, and the whole of the wool and leather duties outward will thus come into the rate.)

	Denizens.			Aliens.		
	£	s.	d.	£	s.	d.
On every tun of wine imported, except sweet wines imported by aliens	0	3	0	0	3	0 (tunnage)
		—		0	2	0 (butlerage)
				0	5	0
On every tun of sweet wines imported by aliens ..		—		0	3	0 (tunnage)
				0	3	0 (impost)
				0	2	0 (butlerage)
				0	8	0
On every £1 value of merchandise imported or exported by denizens or aliens, except wool, fells, and leather exported by denizens or aliens, cloth exported by denizens, tin exported by aliens, wine imported by denizens or aliens, and imported fresh fish or bestial	0	1	0	0	1	0
		—		0	0	3 (C. Merc. duties)
				0	1	3

(Double poundage on tin exported by aliens. The cloth duties were maintained.)

Edward's parliaments appear to have busied themselves in defending native handicraft against foreign competition. They prohibited many articles of foreign manufacture, and granted extensive powers of search, to the end that the goods might be confiscated if found within the realm. 'The Liberties of Great St. Martin's' were exempted from the operations of this statute.

It was enacted that cloth unfulled in England should not be exported.

English archery having decayed through the scarcity of bowstaves, it was enacted that aliens should bring four bowstaves with every ton of merchandise. (The best foreign bowstaves came in the ships of Venice, but of course they were not Venetian produce.) It was provided that he who defrauded the king of tunnage and poundage should answer with body and goods.

It was also enjoined that no Scottish merchandise should enter England except by way of Berwick or Carlisle, and that no English goods should be sold into Scotland except at those places.

Edward seems to have made a less rigid estimate of official responsibilities than some of his predecessors, for he repeatedly relaxed by writ the provisions of the statute forbidding customs officers from acting as merchants, keeping taverns, and being interested in shipping. At the same time he or his advisers must have thought that a show of supervision was desirable, for ' Controllers of the Scrutiny '—*i.e.*, surveyors of the searchers—were appointed at various ports. A special surveyor was appointed at Poole, his district including Exeter, Bridgwater, and the irreclaimable ports of Fowey and Dartmouth. Special surveyors were appointed at London, with power to supervise all the revenue officials of the port, to examine books and memoranda, to rummage merchandise, and to arrest and imprison offenders. Previously a Commission had sat to inquire into extensive frauds at Bristol and Southampton, and the conduct of the officers there, and another Commission had investigated frauds in Devon and Cornwall, and accusations against the officers of taking bribes, being interested in merchandise, keeping taverns, and neglecting their duty.

The Staple was at Calais, and a portion of the wool custom and subsidy there collected was granted to the mayor and burgesses as usual for the maintenance of the garrison. At one period of the reign they expended a great sum in repairing the fortifications of the town, and were allowed to ship wool duty-free from England, giving security that a portion of the proceeds should return in the form of coin or plate, and thus be expended in the mother-country. There were many grants of duty-free shipment to creditors of the king, and to commonalties of towns that had incurred expense in repairing fortifications.

The increasing importance of English merchants rendered them useful as lenders, and they frequently made advances to the Crown. The Genoese and Florentines figured occasionally as royal creditors, but by no means to the same extent as of old. In 1471 the former were given exceptional privileges in discharge of a royal debt. The Florentines were quartered for a time on the London, Southampton, and Sandwich customs. Yet it is apparent that maritime commerce and the profitable business of financing the king were being gradually wrested from their original holders. A few of the royal obligations to English merchants and corporate bodies may be advantageously noted.

The king whilst at Calais borrowed £40 from one Sapcote, and allowed him to deduct half a mark from the duty on every sack of his own wool, shipped at Ipswich, up to the amount of the debt. (The deduction was of course made at Calais, where the duties were paid.) A quantity of woollen cloth was allowed shipment duty-free, in satisfaction of a royal debt due to English creditors. In 1478 the king acknowledged a debt of over £12,000 to the City of London.

In spite of the havoc wrought by the wars of the Roses, the extinguishment of many noble and wealthy families, and the reduced importance of others, the importation of wine was extensive, and it was found necessary to appoint one of the royal yeomen as deputy purveyor, ' the Chief Butler being fully occupied.' That English commerce in general was increasing is proved by the mention of Plymouth and Chester as rising ports, and the increase in the staff of London controllers. The port of Sandwich appears to have been prosperous. A petition sent to the king many years later by the burgesses of this ancient town alluded to the condition of Sandwich during Edward IV.'s time, stating that the port then had ninety-five ships, and yielded about £17,000 yearly in customs. The statement was no doubt an exaggeration, yet probably the petitioners were right in naming this as the summertide of Sandwich's prosperity.

The price of wine in England had slightly increased, Gascon occasionally selling at £4 a tun. The following goods were plentiful in the London markets : anise, cummin, worm-seed, wax, alum, grains of paradise, ginger, cloves, mace, cinnamon, rhubarb, scammony, spikenard, senna, turpentine, dyers' grains, zedoary, almonds, rice, dates, euphorbium, stavesacre, cassia, nutmeg, pepper, mastic, frankincense, litmus, and woad. In the early part of the reign the Commons petitioned Edward to investigate the manufacture of cloth, stating that ' through fraud and deceit ' in the making English cloth had ceased to be asked for in foreign markets, and much foreign cloth was imported into England ; but undoubtedly the Commons were either scheming or misled, and the movement was really inspired by some of the English manufacturers, who desired that their foreign rivals might be hampered by restrictions. There is every reason to believe that the English cloth industry was swiftly gaining ground. The returns of export revenue show it, for they indicate a steady decrease in the return from wool, and a corresponding increase in that from cloth. Much more reliable than the revenue returns are the records of wrecked and plundered ships, from which it may be seen that foreign woad was a large item of almost every import cargo.

It is likely that the fostering of manufactures, which had been conducted for many years with a ruthless disregard of the interests of agriculture, had made sad inroads upon the rich old English rural spheres of existence. Not only had the strain of the wars of the Roses been borne by the rural population, but the burden of this commercial conflict, victory in which meant the enrichment of hundreds of smug burgesses, and the transformation of thousands of sturdy peasants and shepherds into dejected weavers.

Besides the merchants bred, many of the country nobles were possessed by the frenzy of trade. One instance of knightly traffic is worth observation. William, Lord Herbert, fitted out a vessel called *The Gabriel*, and sent her abroad for merchandise. On her return she was cast away on the coast of Ireland, and the king by writ relinquished claim upon the wrecked goods. These matters, and the hints in the statutes as to the decay of English archery, indicate a growing change in English life, a change no doubt prophetic of wealth, yet to a certain extent destructive of national manhood. It must be admitted that the change *was* slow, and that the old rural industries died hard, for foreign potentates and noblemen, even in Edward's day, made large purchases of sheep and oxen in England under special licence from the king, and there is record of a Dorset gentleman who owned 14,000 sheep.

There was one peculiar industry that showed no sign of decay—piracy. It is highly necessary to devote a few paragraphs to the doings of the west-country adventurers, and Edward's reign is most suitable to the purpose, for no other period furnishes so many instances, and its revenue and piratical records intermingle in peculiar fashion. In many cases the king put the aggrieved parties upon the custom of the ports most convenient, and thus piracy became more disastrous to the revenue than direct smuggling, for the merchandise stolen was run to prevent identification, and its value afterwards taken from the outward custom.

For one case of piracy or wrecking on the eastern coast there were a score on the south-western. This was in a small part due to the circumstance that the vessels traversing the English Channel carried cargoes specially attractive, and principally to the peculiar instincts of the Devon and Cornish coast-dwellers. In most cases the malefactors were of Dartmouth and Fowey, the latter port being simply a nest of pirates. The sheriff of Cornwall seems to have had a busy time, for writs were continually issued, empowering him to make inquiries and arrest offenders. Inquiries may have been made, but for record of arrests one searches in vain. Perhaps 'Henry Bodrugan, knight,' and his partners, did not exert themselves much even in investigation, for year after year

Fowey continued to send forth companies of industrious buccaneers to intercept the alien merchant, laugh at the safe-conduct the king had granted him, ' grievously mal-treat ' his agents and mariners, and appropriate his goods. In some cases the ship was taken as well, and the crew and passengers put ashore, their bones sore with trouncing and their pockets empty. The unfortunate foreigners then made their way to London, and unfolded their burn-ing grievances to the king's advisers—gentlemen, it may be conceived, not particularly interested in the sufferings of their fellow-countrymen, much less those of a crowd of ' beggarly, forestalling aliens.' Lack of space forbids quotation of more than a few cases, yet these may cause readers to marvel that foreign merchants ever ventured into English waters.

John Heavey and Denis Lane, Irish merchants, having been legally customed and cocketed in Ireland, were ' sailing towards England,' and off Winchelsea they met one William Mather in his balinger, who promptly seized both ship and cargo.

Two Gascon merchants loaded a ship with wine, and set sail for England. They held a safe-conduct from the king, and the wine was intended to provide ransom of certain prisoners. Hardy mariners of Fowey encountered them, villainously maltreated them, appropriated the letters of safe-conduct, took ship and cargo, and *sold* the wine at Fowey.

In 1462 belated inquiry was made into the case of *The Katherine* of Bayonne. It appeared that while she lay at anchor off St. Ives *on Christmas Eve* a gang of Cornish pirates carried off her cargo.

Certain mariners of Sandwich boarded *The Pink* of Middelburgh, jocosely stating that they acted under authority of the earl of Warwick, and despoiled her of cargo and rigging.

In 1463 a Spanish vessel was wrecked on the Wight. Her crew came safely to land, and her cargo as safely into the hands of the islanders.

In 1467 the balingers of John Rawleigh or Raleigh, Walter Cock, and Ralph Mercer, Devon worthies, made up to six Flemish merchant ships which were ' sailing upon the sea,' and took from them wine to the value of 4,330 crowns of gold.   The king, as in the previously quoted cases, directed that restitution should be made. Probably by the time the sufferers reached London and made plaint, and the writ travelled down to the west country, most of the wine had disappeared, for no restitution was made except the usual grant of customs.   The king then issued orders to arrest the delinquents, but it does not appear that anyone was arrested, and it is likely that in bonny Devon the whole affair was regarded as an exquisite joke.   Perhaps the king, in his secret soul, was not overmuch offended.   Later an order was issued to arrest certain Cornishmen, who had helped themselves to the goods of Breton merchants.   The thieves could not be found.   It should be mentioned that one of them was the vicar of St. Keverne, and his share of the spoil had been three tuns of wine.

Yet the harvest of the Channel was but imperfectly gathered till John Wilcock, skipper of *The Barbara* of Fowey, went forth.   From February in 1468 to the Tuesday following Whitsun in the same year he plundered sixteen foreign vessels, mostly laden with the produce of the Gascon vats, and conveyed the spoil to Fowey.

Fowey continued her aggressions, and in 1474, Commissions being found useless, a royal writ was issued to arrest all masters, mariners, possessors, and victuallers of ships, *and all pirates*, that did inhabit there.   ' They have committed great depredations upon merchandise ' —thus ran the royal fulmination—' and do not heed the king's mandates, but daily do worse.'   The specification of ' masters, mariners, possessors, and victuallers ' appears superfluous.   ' Pirates,' one might think, would have included all the folk of Fowey, not excepting the revenue officers of the district, for it is impossible to conceive that these latter would be ignorant of what was going on, or able to collect much custom *for the king* in the turbulent little port they supervised. In 1476 the Fowey blades were again busy, as though mandates were things of nought.

These west-country feats provoked occasional retaliation, but, as is usual in such cases, the real culprits did not suffer ; indeed it may be assumed that few aliens would venture to attempt reprisal upon the shipping of Fowey. Worthy and innocent English traders suffered. About the time when the English Exchequer paid a large sum* to the merchants of Castile as part compensation for damage done them by west-country pirates, and put them on the English custom for further reimbursement, one Payne, a merchant of Bristol, went with a ship to Spain. He and his partner, with the ship and cargo, were captured by Castilian privateers. The two merchants succeeded in escaping to England, and appealed to Edward, who gave them letters to the Spanish king. Twice they visited Castile with no advantage, each time on their return appealing to Edward. They made a third essay, and, being unable to obtain audience, they nailed a written protest to the Castilian monarch's chamber door. For this act of justifiable effrontery Payne's partner was put to death. Payne escaped, and once more laid his case before Edward. The dilatory monarch, who had good reasons for avoiding a quarrel with the Castilian king, put the Bristolian upon the custom of Sandwich, Southampton, and Bristol for 3,600 golden crowns, of which 2,000 were to be reckoned compensation for loss, and 1,600 expenses of travel. It is doubtful whether Payne ever realized the sums.

In 1482 ' convoyers or wafters ' were stationed off the English coasts, to protect commerce and the fishing industry.†

---

* The sum paid down appears to have been for piracies committed during the time of Henry VI., and the further sum assigned from the customs was to cover transactions during Edward's reign.

† The fishermen had to contribute towards the expense (Patent Rolls, 22 Edw. IV., p. 1, m. 2).

Edward made many grants of prised wine to the Church, occasionally stipulating for the benefit of prayer. At the beginning of his reign he saddled the customs of London, Hull, Ipswich, and Boston with his deceased father's debts, directing the account to be specialized in the Exchequer memoranda, ' that the soul of the departed may soar to Paradise.'

Richard III.'s accession was signalized by vindictive edicts against aliens and their manufactures. The wording of these statutes illustrates vividly the antipathy of the older English to races (such as the Italians and Jews) who followed none but the inevitably crooked occupations of traffic and usury. It was stated that many merchant strangers, especially of Italy, had warehouses at the larger ports, in which they stowed their goods until prices were intolerably augmented ; that though allowed to buy English goods and sell them within the realm at pleasure they did not employ their ultimate profits within the kingdom, but conveyed them oversea ; that they acted in colonies and made secret bargains, and that they came to London in numbers as artificers and usurped the manufacture of native goods, instead of taking to laborious occupations such as those of ploughing and carting.* It was accordingly enacted that the Italians should sell by gross only, not by retail ; that all aliens should sell within eight months of importation, or remove their goods oversea ; and that alien artificers should not practise their callings in England. The almost incredible statement followed that bowstaves had risen in price to £8 per 100, and it was enjoined that aliens should bring ten bowstaves with each butt of malmsey. (This was levelled against the Venetians, who through their control of the

* Before readers blame the old English overmuch, let them bring to mind the doings of the Italian guildsmen in the days of the Edwards, and attempt to imagine what would have happened in Venice, if a body of London merchants had contrived to collect the Venetian customs.

Levant trade had opportunity of obtaining good bow-staves, and who were especially obnoxious.) It was further stated that malmsey had gradually risen from 50s. a butt of 126 gallons to more than twice that rate, and that the butts had come to hold 108 gallons only. Therefore it was prescribed that all casks of wine should be carefully gauged on importation, and the old standards maintained.

Another statute provided that no merchant stranger should bring into the realm girdles, wrought harness, points, leather laces, purses, pouches, gloves, knives, pins, shears, hangers, andirons, scissors, tongs, cupboards, grid-irons, fireforks, locks, keys, hinges, spurs, garnets, painted glass, painted paper, painted cloth, beaten gold, beaten silver, saddles, saddletrees, stirrups, boots, buckles, wire, hawks' bells, etc., the whole produce of the crafts of many classes of artificers being specified.

The first of these statutes was not destined to endure, and need only be regarded as an expression of national impatience. The great trading cities of the blue inland seas had tried similar expedients and failed, and down to the present day it has not been made evident that such edicts are likely to succeed.

There is not much more to be said with regard to Richard's short reign, except that he seems to have been able to trust Italian merchants to a greater extent abroad than in his own kingdom. He appointed Strozzi, a Florentine, English consul at Pisa, allowing him for his trouble ' one-fourth of one per cent.' out of the value on all English goods carried thither.

In 1484 the king's mother was allowed to ship a quantity of wool duty-free, to provide her with a specified sum, and it is worth notice that the duty thus remitted was computed at the aliens' rate. In the same year Richard presented the prior and canons of Carlisle Cathedral with two tuns of Gascon wine from the prisage of Hull, desiring them to pray for the king and queen during life, and for their souls after death.

Duties were as in the preceding reign.

Henry VII. received the usual subsidies ' for life.'   The Act of the previous reign against Italians and other aliens was revoked in deference to a request made by the Italian merchants, and it appears that the king granted the Italians temporary remission of a portion of the extra wool duties outward.   It was enacted that wine of Gascony and Guienne might only be imported in ships manned by English, Welsh, or Irishmen.   This Act also extended to woad from Toulouse.   The pretexts furnished were the encouragement of the English shipping industry, and the due maintenance of the navy.

It was enjoined that aliens who had been made denizens should still pay aliens' customs, and that all foreign goods carried coastwise from port to port in England should be advised to the collectors stationed at the ports of discharge, and their unlading certified.

The old Act providing that aliens should employ their takings in purchasing English goods, and the Act of Edward IV. prohibiting exportation of unfulled cloth, were reaffirmed.   Provision was also made that no woollen cloth might be exported unless barbed, rowed, and shorn. It was also enacted that no ' common officer ' of a town should act as collector of customs.

The Venetians, who had previously engrossed the Levant trade, found that English merchants were interfering extensively in that branch of commerce, and heavy duties were imposed upon English shipments from Candia. In retaliation the English Parliament laid a duty of 18s. per butt on malmsey brought to England in alien shipping, and at the same time fixed the selling price of malmsey at a rate which the Venetian ambassador, in a statement to the Senate, declared ruinous to Venetian trade.

There seems to have been a desire on the part of both king and legislators to foster English commerce, and to open up new channels of traffic.   The Merchant Adventurers of London, whom success had made more arbitrary and enterprising than ever, fomented hostility to foreign traders by every means within their power, and there can be no doubt that at this time the famous merchants known in London as Men of the Steelyard had lost much of the outward wool and cloth trade.

The arrangement made by Henry with the Cabots evinced astuteness and enterprise. In return for his substantial encouragement of their great venture, which brought about the discovery of Newfoundland, the king stipulated for one-fifth of the proceeds of the voyage, but at the same time he allowed them freedom from all customs duties on such goods as they brought back.

An Act was passed prohibiting the exportation of horses, except by royal licence, and the exportation of mares of a value exceeding 6s. 8d. It was provided that all entries of foreign goods should be in the name of the real owner.

Meantime many members of the public found as much reason to complain of the growing importance of the newly strengthened trade syndicates, and the villainies of certain native manufacturers, as of foreign competition. Two statutes of the reign, though not applying directly to revenue matters, illustrate this in striking fashion. It may be as well to furnish a summary of their provisions, to show that fraud inhabits the very arteries of trade, and that often when a nation is spurring itself into bitterness against a rival's methods it may have good reason to mend its own.

One was the Act rendered necessary by the practice of that arrogant company previously mentioned, which had come to be widely known as 'The Fellowship of Mercers and Merchant Adventurers of London.' They had originally levied an entrance fee of half a noble on each novice who joined their society. But this had been increased, 'contrary to every Englishman's liberty, of their own incharitable and inordinate covetise,' to £20. The Act abolished the fee.

The other statute revealed the existence of an ingenuity almost modern, and brought into relief the artifices of 'certain denizens,' who occupied themselves in preparing fustians which had been imported unshorn. Instead of operating 'with the broad shear,' they for purposes of expedition used an instrument that 'broke the ground' of the fustian, and to conceal the effect they 'sleeked' and singed the article, and then dyed it. Said the statute, 'The poor serving-men find that their fustians endure four months instead of two years.' Thus it will be seen that not only was expedition aimed at, but an enduring increase in the demand for fustians.

During the latter part of the reign the collection of custom and subsidy of wool was assigned to the Calais Staple for sixteen years, £10,000 odd of the receipts to go to the Calais Treasurer for the garrison and defences, and the rest to be accounted for at the Exchequer, subject to a small grant to the London 'customers' or collectors (probably as a formal acknowledgment) and the payment of certain fees.

Henry VIII. was granted the perquisites of his predecessor for life. (The impost on sweet wines imported by aliens was later made 6s. 8d. per butt by order in Council. The king seems to have obtained almost arbitrary powers in the regulation of trade, especially the trade in foreign wines, and his method of altering and increasing wine imposts was copied by more than one of his successors.)

Henry VII.'s statute as to entering of foreign goods was repealed, and it was provided that 'one Englishman might enter for another Englishman, and one alien for another alien.' Edward IV.'s Act, by which all who defrauded the revenue of tunnage and poundage were made answerable with body and goods, was reaffirmed, and made to endure during the king's life.

The penalties applying to customs officers who delayed the sealing of valuable imported cloths were increased, and the officers made liable to a fine of £20 if they extorted fees for such service.

The exportation of Norfolk wool was prohibited, in

order to secure a plentiful and ready supply to the Norwich cloth manufacturers. This was but one of many instances in English history, of the yeoman being hampered for the weaver's benefit. 'The Act of Apparel' was another concession to cloth, providing that no man not ennobled should wear woollen cloth, unless it were of the make of England, Wales, or Berwick.

In the tenth year of his reign Henry by charter exempted the burgesses of Southampton from Prisage, except to the extent of five tuns yearly, which had previously been allotted from the port prisage to various abbeys in the locality. Later the charter was affirmed by statute. (It is evident that the five tuns were taken even after the Reformation, for the final remission was not formally announced till 1608. It is likely that they were appropriated by the usurpers of the abbey lands.)

Many Englishmen had established themselves in Flanders and other countries and there sworn fealty, yet they continued to trade with England as denizens, thus gaining the advantage of preferential customs duties. It was enacted that they should be made to pay aliens' customs on all goods landed by them in England. The Merchant Adventurers of London and the English ambassadors were instructed to make inquiry as to all such English residents abroad. It is likely that the first-named had part in inciting the issue of the Act, and that, as many of their own agents lived abroad, they exercised their powers of inquiry with great circumspection.

A grant previously made to the citizens of York, that they might ship northern wool under the ancient privileges secured to the merchants of Newcastle, was annulled, it having led to the enrichment of a few of the citizens only, instead of to the advantage of all.

The privilege of exporting wool seems to have been the subject of many mercantile intrigues. The quantity of fells exported was still considerable, in spite of the persistent attempts to foster the cloth industry.

The Acts of Richard II., intended to confine the shipment of merchandise as far as practicable to English vessels, and the Act of Henry VII., restricting the importation of Gascon wine and Toulouse woad to English bottoms, were recited, with the significant statement that in spite of their provisions the navy had decayed, and it was apparent there would soon be few expert English mariners. Therefore it was enacted that the statutes quoted should be sternly observed. The retail price of French wine in England was limited to 8d. a gallon, and that of sweet wine to 1s. The enactment was to endure till the end of the next Parliament.* The next Parliament provided that the king might by proclamation or letters patent repeal or make void the restrictions upon French wine. (This appears to have been construed into a grant of power to the king to alter or levy imposts upon wines, and both he and his successors seem to have taken full advantage of the mysterious extension of prerogative.)

It was found that much leather was being exported uncustomed, especially from the south-western counties. Sworn ' tellers ' and packers were stationed at the principal ports, and their fees stated. Leather conveyed from inland towns to the coast for shipment was to be advised to the officers.

An Act was passed regulating freights, which contained the interesting stipulation that owners of ships outward-bound from London should advertise the dates of sailing by affixing written statements ' to some post in Lombarde strete, there to remain for the space of seven days.'

The terms of some of the licences granted to English merchants to import French goods during time of war with France are rather instructive. One was granted late in the reign to George Lazenby, London grocer,† the

* Towards the end of the reign the provisions were relaxed, import prices having risen (34-35 Hen. VIII., c. 7).

† In olden times ' grocery ' as a tariff and trade term had a wide significance, comprehending an immense number of articles, and the appellation ' grocer,' now usually bestowed upon a petty tradesman, often signified a wealthy and distinguished merchant.

cargo being wine, woad, canvas, and prunes. He had to import the goods in an English ship, or a ship of a friendly nation, to pay the ordinary custom and 13s. 4d. a ton besides, and to leave a copy of his licence at the Custom House when making entry. Another licence to a London merchant to import French wine stipulated that the king should have part of the cargo at a figure lower than the London market price. A licence granted to a Dutchman to import a mixed Dutch and French cargo described the goods as 10 tons plaster, 35 cases Normandy glass, 2 vats prunes, 28 dozen skins, 200 ells canvas, 1 empty vat with curious drinking-glasses, and 9 iron pots.

In 1546 a licence was granted to export certain packages of spikenard free of outward duty. They had formed part of the cargo of ' a great Venetian ship,' which had been seized for use by the English during the war.

In 1547 two Paris merchants brought a quantity of jewels to London, in order that the king might make selection and buy. But the king was sick unto death when they arrived, and the arrangement fell through. The merchants made a few sales in other quarters, and were directed to pay custom on the wares sold. The rest they were allowed to export duty-free.

Edward VI. received his predecessor's subsidies, the tunnage rates being 3s. (6s. on sweet wines imported by aliens, including Hanse merchants) and 12d. per aum on Rhenish. The poundage was 12d. on all merchandise imported or exported by aliens or denizens, and 12d. extra on wrought tin or pewter exported by aliens. Wool and fells by denizens paid £1 13s. 4d., hides £3 6s. 8d. ; wool and fells by aliens (including aliens who had been made denizens by letters patent) £3 6s. 8d. ; hides £3 13s. 4d. Goods shipped by denizens in caracks or galleys paid aliens' duty. The Hanse merchants' ancient rights of freedom from inland toll were affirmed. Besides these there were the Carta Mercatoria poundage on aliens' merchandise, the butlerage on aliens' wines, and the special impost on sweet wines brought by aliens (6s. 8d. per butt, levied by order in Council of Henry VIII.'s reign).

It was enacted that there should be no purveyance of victuals and provender for the king's household, except at market price and by owner's consent.

Certain Admiralty officers having made grievous exactions in money and kind from English vessels coming with fish from Ireland, Iceland, and Newfoundland, such exactions were forbidden under a penalty of treble the value of the amount extorted.

The exportation of ' white ashes ' was forbidden, they being useful in the making of soap and saltpetre, and the scouring of wool.

Wool was plentiful in England, but forestallers and engrossers* kept the price up. It was enacted that none should buy wool except for private use, or directly for use in the weaving of cloth for sale, except members of the Calais Guild, who might buy for shipment to the Staple. Aliens might not buy any of a season's wool prior to the Feast of Purification (February 2) in each year. Owners of wool were to sell within twelve months of shearing. Merchants of Newcastle dealing in northern wool were exempt.

The customs grants were the same as usual when Mary ascended the throne, the tunnage and poundage being specified as applicable to the defence of the realm and the keeping of the sea. A ' Book of Rates,' furnishing the values of merchandise for poundage, was issued. It was expressed in this document, according to a decree of the Lords of Council, that the existing rates on woollen cloths outward were too little. It appears that four ' short cloths ' could be made out of a sack of wool. (A

* ' Forestalling ' : buying goods on their way to market, or contracting to buy before the goods were ready for delivery.

' Engrossing ' : buying corn in the field, fruit on the tree, etc.

' Regrating ' : buying at public sale and re-selling in same market, or within a specified distance—in short, buying with no purpose save to ' turn over.'

short cloth was 28 yards in length, and weighed 64 pounds).
It was decreed that each short cloth exported by denizens
should pay 6s. 8d. (double if by aliens).*

Henry VIII.'s Act, fixing the sale price of foreign hats,
caps, and bonnets of woollen, was recited, and amended
to the effect that customs collectors were to apprise the
mayors of towns as to such importations, and on an
appointed day each collector in presence of the mayor
concerned was to sell the goods publicly at no more than
the price specified, and hand the proceeds to the importer.
Not more than a dozen articles were to be sold to any one
person.

Corn, victuals, and wood being at a great price, were
for a period forbidden exportation except by licence.

It was enacted that commissions for purveyance should
be expressed in English, and endure for six months only.
Purveyors were to give a ' docket ' to the High Constable
for all goods taken, and he was to submit it to the sessions
justices, who were afterwards to send it to the king's
steward.

In 1554 the burgesses of Southampton were by letters
patent given a notable concession. They had represented
that the trade of the port had fallen off, the merchant
strangers no longer bringing their Levant goods and sweet
wines to Southampton as of old, but landing them at
creeks and remote places in Sussex and Kent. It was
accordingly enjoined that all sweet wines brought by
aliens should be landed at Southampton, so as to revive
the customs receipts of that port, and enable the burgesses
to fortify the town and repair the sea bank as they had
formerly done. The grant brought little benefit to the
city, although made perpetual in 1571, for it appears that
it became the practice to issue licences to enable the aliens
to discharge at other ports. At first the issue of a licence

* The cloth duties remained at this rate till about the middle
of James's reign. It seems that the denizens' cloth duty was by
Mary's Rate-book made exactly equal to the denizens' wool duty,
minus the ancient custom. Thus, 4 cloths at 6s. 8d. = £1 6s. 8d.
The wool duty was £1 13s. 4d., made up of subsidy and ancient
custom. The ancient custom was 6s. 8d. *Hale* (doubtful.)

of this kind was made to appear a great favour, as, when the Venetian ambassador made suit upon one occasion to the Privy Council that one of his country's ships might be allowed to discharge her cargo of malmsey in the port of London, the transaction was allowed ' for this time only.' It appears that there was a special ' Southampton duty ' on sweet wines, for it was stipulated that the owners of this particular cargo should present the Southampton burgesses with four butts of malmsey, in recognition of the privilege granted of discharge in London. No doubt the expense and trouble of obtaining licences, with the alternative of confinement of discharge to one port, hampered the Venetians, and assisted the English merchants in gaining possession of the Levant trade.

In 1558 an impost was laid by order in Council upon all French wine imported. It was at the startling rate of 26s. 8d. a tun, and the collectors were ordered to take security for this duty, or to exact the duty, before the wines were landed. It was accompanied by an impost of extra poundage upon all French goods. It is evident that this tax caused consternation amongst importers, and that the officers had some difficulty in collecting it. On August 4, 1558, it was directed that the London officers responsible should be called upon for the impost on wines discharged in the port under their survey. One Fisher was the receiver, and he was summoned before the Council for being in arrear. My Lords gave him a fortnight's grace. At the end of the fortnight he appeared before the Council. His books were inspected, and found incomplete. He was ordered to put them right, to pay into the Exchequer a sum of £1,500 which he confessed he had retained, and to produce the receipt to the Council. Then he was called upon to find security in £5,000 for the speedy rendering of a full account.

A few days later the Council sent peremptory directions to Bristol that the officers should enforce payment of the impost, as ' we meane not to alter or change.'

During the following month the Council were apprised

that certain merchants refused to land their Spanish wines on account of the increased duties. (This seems to show that the Southampton duty on sweet wines was being imposed at all ports.) My Lords replied that the merchants might take their wines whither they pleased, but they should not be allowed to land them till they had given security for payment of the duties.

It will be perceived that the imperious Tudors took full advantage of the provisions of the Act of 26 Henry VIII., c. 10, empowering them to levy on wines by patent or order in Council. Indeed, during the period between the passing of that statute and the issue of James I.'s 'Book of Rates' in 1611, the variations of the wine duties are extremely puzzling, and the commentators, not excepting the careful and industrious Hale, seem to have regarded the duty actually collected on wine as mere matter of conjecture.

At the beginning of Elizabeth's reign the exportation of tallow, raw hides, and leather was forbidden for a period. When this Act determined, the price of boots, shoes, etc., increased, so the law was again put in force.

The hours during which cargo might be discharged and shipped were fixed by statute, and the limits of ports defined. It was enacted that the owner or master of every ship from foreign ports should furnish a full report of cargo, and that a declaration should be made of all goods shipped outward. In consequence of extensive smuggling, customs collectors were instructed to provide deputies at all creeks and remote places within their respective districts.

The provisions of Richard II. and Henry VII.'s Acts as to natives importing goods only in native ships were repealed, it having been found that foreign princes in defence made similar rules. But goods shipped in foreign ships by denizens were still liable to aliens' duty.

Elizabeth received the grants and customs that had been allowed at her sister's accession, and the proceeds of the impost on French wine and wares levied by Mary (this last not specified in the Act).

Coastwise traffic in English goods was restricted to ships owned by denizens, captained by Englishmen, and with at least three-fourths of the mariners English. Attempts were made to encourage English sea-fishing by freeing exported English fish from outward poundage, and prohibiting the importation of foreign fish. The latter provision had to be repealed, fish, especially herrings, reaching a great price. Denizens were then allowed to import herrings in English square-rigged ships, paying subsidy. (A trade appears to have sprung up in English-cured fish, principally with France, Portugal, and Italy.) Later the restrictions were relaxed, and aliens allowed to export English fish in English ships, and to import foreign fish at will, paying such customs as were charged on English fish abroad.

Foreign harness, etc., were prohibited, to encourage the decaying native industries.

The prohibition of the exportation of live sheep was revived, and embellished with terrific penalties. It was provided that he who offended should be imprisoned for ' one whole yere without bayle and maynepryse, and at the yere's ende in soome open Market Towne in the fulnesse of the Market on the Market Daye have his lefte hande cut off, and that to be nayled up in the openest place of suche Market.' This punishment was to be accompanied by forfeiture of goods.

The grant to the port of Southampton of the exclusive landing of Levant wines brought by aliens was made perpetual in 1571. (As before stated, the grant brought no great benefit to the town, for by the beginning of the next century the English Turkey Company had succeeded in dominating the Levant trade, especially the trade in sweet wines. Being an English company, it could carry wines into any English port.)

English vessels from foreign, on their arrival in English ports, were made to pay a tonnage tax, to be applied to the repair of Dover harbour. This was collected by the Customs, and paid into the Exchequer as a special account, the Exchequer handing over the moneys in instalments to the mayor of Dover.

The importation of logwood was prohibited, the article being held to produce a fraudulent dye. Later the provisions of the Act were strengthened, offenders being made liable to the pillory.

An Act was passed ordering that all casks imported for the use of brewers were to be gauged and marked by ' the masters and wardens of the Art and Mystery of Coopers,' as it had been found that beer had been sold in casks fraudulently marked as to content. The Act did not apply to casks imported by strangers and intended to be filled with beer for exportation, or to casks intended for shipment to Scotland.

In 1591 a new impost was levied on French goods, at the rate of 3s. a tun for wine and 3s. a ton for other merchandise. This was really a convoy duty, and the proceeds were devoted to ' waftage '—i.e., the maintenance of war vessels to defend the merchant fleets that periodically visited Bordeaux.

On February 20, 1593, the Council sent notices ' to the officers of all the Custom-houses,' commencing thus : ' Whereas her Maiestie of late time to her exceeding great chardge hath bin often occasioned to send over into Normandie divers troupes of souldiers to the aid of the French King : Forsomuch as by dailie experience yt falleth owt that manie of these souldiers do indirectly withdraw themselves '; and then instructing the officers to rummage all vessels arriving from France, and detain any deserters they might find.

On June 17, 1593, a letter was sent from Whitehall to the Lord Mayor of London, alluding to a practice, which appears to have existed for some time, of referring disputes on questions of mercantile assurance to a board of merchants chosen yearly by the City worthies, ' and by oathe enjoyned to attend and determyn these cawses according to equitie.' The Council directed the Mayor and aldermen to elect three merchant strangers to serve on the board. (Thus it would appear that the system of assuring ships and cargoes is of ancient origin.)

The importation of wool-cards was prohibited, in the interest of the cardmakers of London, Bristol, Norwich, Coventry, etc.

The Merchant Adventurers of London having repeatedly complained of their foreign trade being hampered by the Hanseatic League, and all attempts at adjustment having failed, the Privy Council abolished the privileges so long enjoyed by the Leaguers, so far as the German sections of the League were concerned, but intimated that the merchants of Polonia (Poland) might still trade in England. The German traders were ordered to depart, and the customs searchers of London and Gravesend were directed to satisfy themselves, before the Germans embarked, that all outstanding obligations had been discharged. In 1600 the Lord Mayor of London was directed to seize the famous ' Steel Yard ' (the London depot of the Hanse traders), which stood in the place now occupied by Cannon Street Station. The Steel Yard was made a naval store-house.

On September 16, 1600, it was conveyed to ' The Adventurers on the Voyage intended to the East Indies ' that the queen highly approved of their design. On October 26 they were encouraged by the Council to proceed with their fitting-out ' with all expedicion and possible speede.' ' Otherwise,' wrote the energetic councillors, ' you maie muche prejudice yourselves by your staggering and delaies.' It appears that some of the promoters were not quite as adventurous as their title implied, for on January 11, 1601, the Council threatened to commit them to prison unless they speedily made good their deposits.

This syndicate was the foundation of the celebrated

East India Company.   The first fleet left in 1601, and the
Council at once proceeded to urge the Adventurers to
bestir themselves in preparing a second.

It appears that the ancient system of adjudicating upon
assurance disputes was fast falling out of favour, despite
the interest taken in it by the Council in 1593.   An Act
was passed providing that the Lord Chancellor should in
future appoint Commissions to deal with such matters.
Each Commission was to consist of an Admiralty judge,
two doctors of law, two common lawyers, the Recorder of
London, and 'eight grave and discreet merchants.'
Litigants had power to appeal to the Court of Chancery.

Enterprising reformers, anxious to increase the customs
receipts, and at the same time secure valuable offices for
themselves, seem to have been plentiful in Elizabeth's
day.   'The humble petition' of three citizens of London,
dated 1568, is an example of the suggestions tendered :

'We crave your hyghnes to have our service in tryall
to bryng your highnes great gayne, whereas we know
your maiestie to be deceaved £3,000 or £4,000 by the
yere in coustome and subsidie inwarde onlie of the porte of
London, by merchant straungers dwelling alongst
divers the keys.'   The petitioners stated that they
would ask for no reward until they had increased the
revenue of the port.   They described themselves as men
who had been long accustomed to deal with merchandise,
and went on to state that whilst £100,000 worth of silks
and haberdashery were imported yearly only £30,000
worth paid duty ; that by reviewing the books at the
Exchequer they had found that scarcely any duty was
taken upon goldware and silverware, etc., yet such goods
were extensively imported ; that the landing-waiters had
each a fee of £4 a year only, yet could afford to pay large
sums to obtain their offices ; that many of the said waiters,
who before taking office had been poor and in debt, had
mysteriously become men of substance ; and that while,

according to the law, all costly and fine goods were to be examined at the Custom-house Quay, many aliens bribed the officers to allow them to take such wares to private quays, where they were entered as coarse goods and paid little poundage. Whether the statement was wholly credible cannot be ascertained. Possibly it was true ; undoubtedly it was not disinterested.

Two years later one Needham wrote a pamphlet on the same subject, and sent it to the Lord Treasurer. It commenced with a statement that the writer ' thought it his duty justly and truly to open to his Honour such notes and knowledge as by his service and travel he had gathered during ten or twelve years, devoted to searching how to reform such abuses, deceits, and disorders as were used all England through against the queen's Majesty, both by the officers of customs and by merchants and shippers, and how they might be redressed, and her Highness justly answered of her rights and duties.' He continued that the said officers, their clerks, and their ' clerks' clerks,' wronged many honourable merchants by imposing novel duties, delaying cockets, and not observing the proper hours of employment, and that ' by long sufferance ' the officers, with many merchants, and many of the watermen, were ' nestled and grown into a disordered liberty,' so extremely profitable that they could not be reformed except by severe measures.

Later one Thomas Ferrers threw down his soiled gauntlet in challenge of corruption, stating that if he could but be granted a certain lucrative post he would advance the customs receipts by several thousands a year, besides keeping all coin and bullion within the realm. If he failed in the attempt he would relinquish the office, and never be a suitor again.

A collector who was unable to meet his creditors' claims attributed his condition to ' having served without corruption, and dispatched the merchant without expectation of reward.' He pleaded that he had paid a vast sum for his collectorship, and that if he were deprived of his office his creditors would close upon him and take everything he had. In the proceedings on this case it was suggested that the defendant's dismissal should be kept as secret as possible, as public cognizance of such cases was undesirable, and it was urged as partial extenuation of the offence that an officer who had to give an unreasonable sum for his appointment could scarcely be expected to behave properly.

A pamphlet produced in 1601 by the secretary to ' The Merchant Adventurers of London ' contained a broad allusion to the privileges once enjoyed by the Hanse merchants, to their preferential customs, and the unfair advantage which they had till recently secured in trade. (Be it noted that the Merchant Adventurers had for over a century been busily undermining the Hanse men, and had captured most of their business.) It also complained of ' the great fraternitie, familiaritie, kindness, and inward friendship between the officers of her Majesty's Customs and strangers,' and hinted that there was a sinister reason for this good understanding. Apparently the same kindness had not been extended to the Adventurers, for the tone of the document hereabout soared into rhetoric. ' Let these customers, while they warn other men, be wise and warned themselves also, lest by too much leaning unto and favouring of such strangers they prove in the end bad customers to her Majesty, and consequently corrupt and unnatural members of the State.' It further complained that the aliens had tried to bring the trade of the Adventurers ' to confusion,' but hinted that the Adventurers expected to survive, ' even though these odd customers ' might assist the aliens to the fullest of their power. Then it pointed out the immense benefits conferred on the revenue by the Adventurers, calling attention to the fact that they paid their duties in lump sums yearly, instead of ' by driblets and small parcels.' It even tried to palliate the special impositions made by them upon cloth, both in England and abroad, and other incidental charges which they levied upon goods, urging that these surtaxes were systematically collected by skilled overseers, who were thus rendered able to furnish the English Customs with valuable information upon trade matters and upon customs due. It compared the dealings of the Society with those of other companies, greatly to the Adventurers' advantage, stating that they were not like other merchants, who shipped their goods at remote places, ' in covert manner, hugger mugger,' for the Adventurers shipped all their goods at London and the other great ports—ports at which, it was insinuated, the officers were well paid, and therefore not easily corrupted.

In the concluding statement of the Adventurers' recital there was undoubtedly a delicate hint to the ' well-paid ' officers at the great ports that it might be advantageous to extend a few special facilities to the Society.

The average amount collected annually as customs during Elizabeth's reign may be stated with something like confidence as about £80,000. One account for thirteen years renders an average of over £70,000, another for ten later years (perhaps more reliable) gives an average of nearly £94,000. The first appears in Stow's ' Survey,' the other in the State Papers of the reign of Elizabeth (1602).

LIST OF AUTHORITIES.

Legislation and Incidents.

Wine: 2 Hen. VI., c. 14 ; 1 Hen. VII., c. 8 ; 7 Hen. VII., c. 7 ; 26 Hen. VIII., c. 10 ; Acts of Privy Council, April 17, 1558 ; September 23, 1558 ; October 19, 1558.

Frauds: 20 Hen. VI., c. 7 ; 11 Hen. VI., c. 15 ; 28 Hen. VI., c. 5 ; 12 Edw. IV., c. 3 ; Patent Rolls, 6 Hen. VI., p. 1, m. 28d. ; 6 Edw. IV., p. 1, m. 4d. ; 13 Edw. IV., p. 2, m. 21d. ; Act 1 Rich. III., c. 13 ; 11 Hen. VII., c. 27 ; 27 Hen. VIII., c. 14 ; 2-3 Edw. VI., c. 6 ; 31 Eliz., c. 8.

Subsidies : Hale (quoted in Hargraves' 'Law Tracts '); 1 Hen. VIII., c. 20 ; 1 Edw. VI., c. 13 ; 1 Mary, s. 2, c. 18 ; 1 Eliz., c. 20.

Staples : 8 Hen. VI., c. 2.

Assignments : 31 Hen. VI., c. 5 ; Patent Rolls, 2 Hen. VI., p. 3, m. 13 ; 2 Hen. VI., p. 3, m. 6 ; Ordinance of 18 Hen. VI. ; Patent

Rolls, 2 Edw. IV., p. 2, m. 11 ; 1 Edw. IV., p. 4, m. 20 ; 11 Edw. IV., p. 1, m. 11 ; 2 Edw. IV., p. 1, m. 19 ; 18 Edw. IV., p. 1, m. 8 ; 1 Edw. IV., m. 23 ; 1 Rich. III., p. 4, m. 6 ; 1 Rich. III., p. 2, m. 20 ; Act 19 Hen. VII., c. 27 ; 21 Hen. VIII., c. 17 ; 23 Eliz., c. 6.

Special licences: Patent Rolls, 1 Hen. VI., p. 3, m. 13 ; 5 Hen. VI., p. 2, m. 19 ; Acts of Privy Council, October 17, 1545 ; June 21, 1545 ; January 18, 1546 ; March 3, 1547.

Cloth : 31 Hen. VI., c. 8 (Hale) ; 7 Edw. IV., c. 3 ; 4 Hen. VIII., c. 6 ; 6 Hen. VIII., c. 1 ; ' Book of Rates ' (Mary).

Wool and Sheep : 14 Hen. VI., c. 5 ; 3 Hen. VI., c. 2 ; 6 Hen. VIII., c. 12 ; 5-6 Edw. VI., c. 7 ; 8 Eliz., c. 3.

Protective measures and prohibitions : 28 Hen. VI., c. 1 ; 3 Edw. IV., c. 3 and 4 ; 12 Edw. IV., c. 2 ; 22 Edw. IV., c. 8 ; 1 Rich. III., c. 9 ; 1 Rich. III., c. 11 ; 1 Rich. III., c. 12 ; 3 Hen. VII., c. 9 ; 3 Hen. VII., c. 12 ; 14-15 Hen. VIII., c. 4 ; 22 Hen. VIII., c. 8 ; 23 Hen. VIII., c. 7 ; 2-3 Edward VI., c. 26 ; 1 Mary, s. 2, c. 11 ; 1-2 P. and Mary, c. 5 ; 1 Eliz., c. 10 ; 14 Eliz., c. 4 ; 18 Eliz., c. 9 ; 1 Eliz., c. 13 ; 5 Eliz., c. 5 ; 5 Eliz., c. 7 ; 23 Eliz., c. 9 ; 39 Eliz., c. 11 ; Acts of Privy Council, 1591-1592 ; Act 39 Eliz., c. 14.

Venetian trade : Calendar Venetian State Papers, 1444 and 1456.

Mercantile arrangements and privileges : Fœdera (' De Confirmatione Appunctuamentorum inter Regem et Magistrum Pruissiæ '; ' Pro Rege Portugaliæ '; ' Super quadam Navi, quæ ex Concessione Regis de Causa Magnitudinis, Nominetur Carraka ') ; Patent Rolls, 5 Edw. IV., p. 1, m. 21 ; 20 Edw. IV., p. 1, m. 1 ; 20 Edw. IV., p. 2, m. 9.

Piracy : Chancery Rolls ; Patent Rolls, 4 Hen. VI., p. 2, m. 19d. ; 1 Edw. IV., p. 1, m. 15d. and 5d. ; 2 Edw. IV., p. 1, m. 21d. and 20d. ; 7 Edw. IV., p. 2, m. 4d. ; 8 Edw. IV., p. 1, m. 8d. ; 9 Edw. IV., p. 2, m. 17d. ; 14 Edw. IV., p. 2, m. 15d. ; 21 Edw. IV., p. 2, m. 8 and 16.

Wrecking : Patent Rolls, 3 Edw. IV., p. 2, m. 11d.

Consular appointment : Fœdera (' Pro Laurentio Strozzi ').

Officers : Patent Rolls, 1 Edw. IV., p. 1, m. 7 ; 13 Edw. IV., p. 1, m. 13 ; 18 Edw. 4, p. 1, m. 10 ; 20 Edw. IV., p. 2, m. 20 ; Act 3 Hen. VII., c. 8 ; Acts of Privy Council, September 13, 1558 ; and of 1591 and 1592.

Preventive : 11 Hen. VII., c. 14 ; 3 Hen. VII., c. 8 ; 1 Hen. VIII., c. 5 ; 1 Eliz., c. 11.

Merchant Adventurers : 12 Hen. VII., c. 6.

Southampton Privileges : Davies' ' History of Southampton,' Act 22 Hen. VIII., c. 20 ; Acts of Privy Council, July 20, 1556.

Freights and assurance : 32 Hen. VIII., c. 14 ; Acts of Privy Council, 1593 ; Act 43 Eliz., c. 12.

Purveyance : 2-3 Edw. VI., c. 3 ; 2-3 P. and Mary, c. 6.

Schemes of reform : State Papers, Eliz., 1568 ; Stow's ' Survey '; State Papers, Eliz., 1575 ; Wheeler's ' Treatise of Commerce.'

CHAPTER IV

THE PERIOD OF PROCLAMATIONS AND ORDINANCES

1603–1660

FEW historians have had a good word to say for James I., and all agree that he was not popular with his English subjects. The latter circumstance deserves consideration, for the English have usually been inclined to make liberal allowance for kingly deficiencies. It is possible that the principal causes of his undoubted unpopularity were his industry in augmenting taxes, his disdain of constitutional methods of imposition, and the Stuart facility in getting rid of an immense amount of money without having anything to show for it.

As soon as he was familiar with the English throne he turned his attention to the Customs revenue. Consulting his personal antipathies, he laid an astounding impost upon tobacco, amounting to 6s. 8d. a pound ' over and above the custom of 2d. hitherto paid.' Then, dissatisfied with the return of the outward subsidy, the cloth duties, tunnage and poundage, the aliens' Custom, and the wine imposts, he with the assistance of Robert Cecil altered the values of most goods liable to poundage, making startling additions to Mary's rates. The new list was issued, James probably furnishing the preamble. ' We let you wit,' said he, ' reasonable and indifferent values and prices ought to be paied unto us.' The public, much to James's chagrin, stigmatized the new imposts as monstrous, and the high rating of currants led to the celebrated Bates case. Bates, a dealer in goods from the Levant

ANCIENT CUSTOMS SEALS (SILVER).

1. Fowey, in the port of Plymouth (Royal Arms ; date, prior to 1603).
2. Dartmouth, in the port of Exeter (Royal Arms ; date, Stuart period).
3. Lyme Regis, in the port of Poole (Fleur-de-Lys and letters 'C.R.,' probably Charles I.) : Controller's Seal.
4. Spalding, in the port of Boston (Portcullis and 'G.R.,' probably George I.).
5. Poulton, in the port of Chester (Rose and Crown and 'G.R.,' probably George I). : Comptroller's Seal.
6. Ramsey, Isle of Man (Arms of England—being three lions passant-guardant—and 'G. III. R. 1765) : Collector's Seal.

From 'Seals in the Board Room,' by H. V. READE, Assistant Secretary of Customs.

(then called a ' Turkey Merchant '), being assessed on a parcel of currants at the old poundage plus the new impost, refused payment of the latter. The case was tried at the Court of Exchequer in 1606, Bates pleading that the impost was illegal, it being levied without the sanction of Parliament. The judges decided in favour of the Crown, ruling that the king was entitled to levy imposts at will.

In 1609 appeared a fresh list of imposts, many of them doubling the rate, and logwood, long prohibited on account of its use in the manufacture of fraudulent dyes, was—' so much the better to suppresse and hinder both the bringing in and use thereof within the Realme '—admitted at a heavy value rating ; the king thus proposing to profit by the toleration of fraud. Numerous petitions were presented against the new schedule, in spite of the many assurances it contained that the public benefit was dearer to James than the prospect of gain. It is evident that he found it prudent to temporize.

In 1611 he brought out his final ' Book of Rates,' dedicated to Cecil, and fervently commended to all revenue officials.

In his preface to the new book James described the method by means of which the assessments of 1609 had been made. ' Certain of our counsell conferred with the principal merchants.' (He had in 1604 used the old plea to justify a special tax on exported cloth—viz., that he was entitled to profit by the shipment of manufactured as well as of raw wool.) He proceeded to explain that in his schedule of 1609 he had exempted the following goods from the new impost inwards :

Corn, fish, cheese—viz., merchandise of sustenance.

Naval requisites, arms, and ammunition—munitions of defence.

Wax, hides, and tallow—merchandise usually tran-shipped.

Cotton, silk, and hemp—raw material of handicraft.

Gold, silver, and jewels—articles of enrichment.

' Yet,' he went on, ' some of those whom reason cannot satisfie continue their complaints.' He affirmed :

1. That the law of Nature incited every man to prefer his own people.

2. That most foreign articles were vain and unprofitable, and should be kept out by impositions.

(This had to some extent been the opinion of more than one of his predecessors, but they had adopted the expedient of *prohibition*. Elizabeth had prohibited logwood ; James had allowed that ' vain and unprofitable ' article to be imported, and had profited by the grant. And it is unlikely that he contemplated closing a fruitful channel of revenue by shutting out a large portion of foreign merchandise.)

3. That the Crown had previously lost through the undervaluing of foreign goods, which was a matter against the national welfare.

(Be it noted that James had previously stated that foreign goods were vain and unprofitable, yet here he insisted that their values had often been understated.) He withdrew the obnoxious privilege he had so recently granted to logwood. ' Wee desire not to make profit by disgrace.' The list ended with an order to all concerned to observe the provisions of his ' Book of Rates.' ' On pain of our heavie indignation and displeasure, and as they will answer the same at their uttermost perill.'

Below are specified most of the articles ' raised ' in value by the new list :

Argal (crude tartar deposited by wine-lees, and used in dyeing), ashes of soap or wood, bombasin (a twilled fabric of silk and worsted), buckram (coarse linen stiffened with gum), caddas (tape or lint riband, used in dressing wounds), camlet (thin woollen stuff, sometimes mixed with silk), candle-wicks, carpets of certain kinds, cochineal, drugs of certain kinds, flax (wrought), fustian, galls, groceries, grograin (coarse fabric of silk and mohair), gum, hemp (dressed), hides (tanned), hops, indigo, latten (ornamental brass), linens of certain kinds, madder, oil (except train oil), onion seed, pans of certain kinds, plates of copper, plates of earthenware, printing paper, quicksilver, serge, silk (wrought), starch, steel, succades, sturgeon, tapestry, thread (except crossbow thread), vinegar, wainscots, wood of Brazil, woad* (the plant).

Beaver wool was raised in value immensely, the impost upon it being fivefold. Mary's value for pins had been 4s. per 12,000 ; James added 10s. ; total, 14s. The value of wrought flax was more than doubled, and that of leaf tobacco quadrupled.

	Subsidy Value.	Impost Value.	Total Value.
	£ s. d.	£ s. d.	£ s. d.
Tobacco, leaf, per pound ..	0 6 8	1 0 0	1 6 8

(Thus the poundage was raised from 4d. to 1s. 4d.)

	Subsidy Value.	Impost Value.	Total Value.
	£ s. d.	£ s. d.	£ s. d.
Tobacco, manufactured, per pound	0 10 0	1 0 0	1 10 0

(Thus the poundage on manufactured tobacco was trebled, being raised from 6d. to 1s. 6d.)

Even if the subsidy value be taken as the real value, and James's impost rate as an utter overcharge, it is evident that tobacco was dear.

French wool was admitted at the old rating ; Polonia wool was surtaxed. Flemish soap escaped the impost ; Venice soap was charged. Muscovy leather and Muscovy yarn were specially surtaxed.

The subsidy value given for oranges and lemons was 6s. 8d. per 1,000. Bowstaves were valued at £4 per 120, quails at 4s. per dozen, ' sucking-bottles ' at 5s. the gross. Dripping-pans and frying-pans were subjected to the impost, warming-pans escaped.

Sugar was classed as white, panellis, candy, and muscovado. There was no loaf sugar.

The only export goods raised in value were bays, lead, and tin. Woollen cloth paid a special tax as of old, instead of poundage. The impost on uncast lead outward was two and a half times the subsidy rate, and on

* ' Woad ' : a plant with four petals, yielding a permanent blue dye.

unwrought tin double. (Merchant strangers exporting unworked lead or tin of course paid twice as much as denizens.) Bays manufactured at Barnstaple escaped the impost ; other bays were charged. All exported goods, except those specified above and beer, remained at the old values for poundage.*

The tunnage rates, as settled by James's list, stood as below. The exact wine duties during the latter part of Elizabeth's and the early part of James's reign are difficult to specify. The statute that granted James his original subsidy is explicit enough, yet its rates do not agree with those quoted as ' subsidy rates ' in James's book. There appears to have been a ' composition tax ' levied in 1609 on all wines imported into London, and a smaller composition tax on certain wines imported into Southampton and Bristol. These extra taxes may have been surtaxes charged on account of the special facilities for unshipment, sale, etc., at the ports mentioned, or mere adaptations of the old wine imposts.

James's tunnage rates were as below :

Duties for Wines brought in by Englishmen.

Gascon and French wines, and all other wines of the growth of the French King's dominions.	Brought into the port of London, the tun.	Subsidy, 3s. Impost, 42s. Composition, 15s.	60s.
	Brought into any of the other ports, the tun.	Su sidy, 3s. Impost, 37s.	40s.
Rhenish wine.	Brought into any port, the aum (42 gallons).	Subsidy, 12d. Impost, 8s. 8d.	9s. 8d.

* By 1 Jas. I., c. 25, it had been enacted that corn might be shipped oversea when the price in England did not exceed a specified sum (26s. 8d. a quarter for wheat, 14s. for barley, 15s. for rye). The outward custom was 2s. a quarter on wheat, and 1s. 4d. on other grain. By 3 Jas I., c. 11, beer might be exported when the price of malt did not exceed 16s. a quarter. The reasons for allowing exportation of beer were quaintly expressed. It was stated that the merchant navy would thus be increased, because one shipload of barley might be brewed into four shiploads of beer ; also that the brewing trade would be made prosperous, and ' divers Port Townes greatly comforted and relieved.' The duty outward was 1s. 6d. a tun (custom) and 8s. 6d. (impost).

Muscadels, Malmseys, and all other wines of the growth of the Levant.	Brought into the ports of London, Bristol, or Southampton, the butt.	Subsidy, 1s. 6d. Impost, 20s. 4d. Composition, 2s. 6d.	24s. 4d.
	Brought into any of the other ports, the butt.	Subsidy, 1s. 6d. Impost, 20s. 4d.	21s. 10d.
Sacks, Canaries, Malagas, Madeiras, Romneys, and Hollocks.	Brought into the port of London, the butt or pipe.	Subsidy, 1s. 6d. Impost, old, 18s. 6d. ,, new, 7s. 6d. Composition, 2s. 6d.	30s.
	Brought into Bristol or Southampton, the butt or pipe.	Subsidy, 1s. 6d. Impost, 18s. 6d. Composition, 2s. 6d.	22s. 6d.
	Brought into any of the other ports, the butt or pipe.	Subsidy, 1s. 6d. Impost, 18s. 6d.	20s.
Bastards, Teints, and Alicants.	Brought into the port of London, the butt or pipe.	Subsidy, 1s. 6d. Impost, old, 17s. ,, new, 7s. 6d.	26s.
	Brought into any of the outports, the butt or pipe.	Subsidy, 1s. 6d. Impost, 17s.	18s. 6d.

Duties paid for Wines brought in by Strangers.

Gascon or French wines, and all other wines of the growth of the French King's dominions.	Brought into the port of London, the tun.	Subsidy, 6s. Impost, 42s. Composition, 15s. Butlerage, 2s.	65s.
	Brought into any of the other ports, the tun.	Subsidy, 6s. Impost, 37s. Butlerage, 2s.	45s.
Rhenish wines	Brought into any port, the aum.	Subsidy, 12d. Impost, 8s. 8d. Butlerage, 4d.	10s.
Muscadels, Malmseys, and all other wines of the growth of the Levant.	Brought into the ports of London, Bristol, or Southampton, the butt.	Subsidy, 3s. Custom, 6s. 8d. Southampton duty, 10s. Impost, 20s. 4d. Composition, 2s. 6d. Butlerage, 12d.	43s. 6d.
	Brought into any of the other ports, the butt.	Subsidy, 3s. Custom, 6s. 8d. Southampton duty, 10s. Impost, 20s. 4d. Butlerage, 12d.	41s.

Sacks, Canaries, Malagas, Madeiras, Romneys, and Hollocks.	Brought into the port of London, the butt or pipe.	Subsidy, 3s. / Impost, old, 18s. 6d. / ,, new, 7s. 6d. / Composition, 2s. 6d. / Butlerage, 12d.	32s. 6d.
	Brought into the ports of Southampton or Bristol, the butt or pipe.	Subsidy, 3s. / Impost, 18s. 6d. / Composition, 2s. 6d. / Butlerage, 12d.	25s.
	Brought into any of the other ports, the butt or pipe.	Subsidy, 3s. / Impost, 18s. 6d. / Butlerage, 12d.	22s. 6d.
Bastards, Teints, and Alicants.	Brought into the port of London, the butt or pipe.	Subsidy, 3s. / Impost, old, 17s. / ,, new, 7s. 6d. / Butlerage, 12d.	28s. 6d.
	Brought into any of the outports, the butt or pipe.	Subsidy, 3s. / Impost, 17s. 6d. / Butlerage, 12d.	21s. 6d.

Note that for such wines as shall be landed in any of the outports, and afterwards brought to London, there is to be paid	For every tun of Gascon or French wines	20s.
	For every butt or pipe of Sacks, Canaries, Malagas, Madeiras, Romney, Hollocks, Bastards, Teints, and Alicants	7s. 6d.

NOTE.—The Southampton duty on Levant wines imported by strangers was paid at all ports.

An arbitrary impost of 3s. 4d. per short cloth was levied on exported woollens. This tax became known as ' pretermitted customs.' (The explanation of the title may perhaps be found in Sir Matthew Hale's suggestion that the impost was recommended by certain officious collectors, who represented to the king that 3s. 4d. too little had been charged in the old subsidies, through misapprehension as to the ancient Custom on wool being included in the wool tax.)

The yield of the Customs in 1610–11 (during publication of the new list) is stated by Mr. Hall as £137,000. In 1613 it appears to have been £148,000.

Cecil died in 1612, and James, deprived of his great financial pilot, seems to have adopted a policy of taking all he could, both by customs and inland impositions. After Cecil's death, one Cranfield was appointed Surveyor-General of customs, and, if some of the statements of Customs revenue may be credited, the returns increased enormously.   But the accounts are dreadfully conflicting (one writer puts the return of 1623 at £323,000, an incredible sum, considering the misappropriation that prevailed).*

In 1616 it was proclaimed that the merchants of London had gone beyond their rights in disputing the officers' fees prescribed in the ' Book of Rates.'   They were enjoined, if they desired to benefit by an abatement of 5 per cent. on duties, promised to all who paid the duties promptly, to render unto Cranfield, ' our faithful and well-beloved servant . . . Surveyor-General of Customes great and small, Subsidies, Imposts, and Impositions throughout the Realm . . . such fees as have heretofore been allowed to the holder of the office.'   (The order when issued contained a table of fees, but this is now missing.)

In 1620 James, by means of one of the proclamations to which he was so hopelessly addicted, prohibited the planting of tobacco in England.   The proclamation stated that the king disliked the weed, and that its use was hurtful to both body and mind, but that he considered it wiser to allow importation of the evil article, ' with many other varieties and superfluities coming from beyond sea,' than to tolerate its growth within the realm.   All persons having tobacco to the amount of 10 lbs. or upwards in their possession were to bring the goods to the Hawk and Pheasant, Cornhill, to be sealed and marked.   Officers were empowered to search for and seize any tobacco withheld.   Certain historians have attributed the issue of the proclamation to a motive far different from that announced by James, and accused him of a desire to engross profits, he having assumed pre-emption of all Plantation tobacco, and made its importation subject to special licence.

In 1622 a Commission was appointed to inquire into the

* See also the paragraph as to a Commission in 1622.

cause of a sudden falling off in Customs receipts. The matters submitted for consideration were many and puzzling. The Commissioners were directed to inquire why the price of wool had fallen, how the cloth laws might best be systematized, and whether joint-stock companies were beneficial. The old craving for coin inspired the putting of a couple of time-honoured questions—viz., whether the exportation of English goods might be regulated so as to ensure an ample return of bullion, and if it would be wise to compel foreign merchants to expend their takings within the realm. Another question, as to how foreign ships might best be kept from carrying English goods, was no doubt vaguely expressed, the subject intended for consideration being the best means of securing English dominance in the carrying trade. (This matter was destined to be dealt with thirty years later, by men much wiser and more determined than either James or his counsellors.) Then came a brace of questions which have been debated upon many times since, and are even at the present day subjects fruitful of discussion.

1. ' Whether an excess of imports over exports may be held disadvantageous ?'

2. ' Whether such excess may be prevented ?'

It appears that the customs receipts in 1621 were less by £30,000 than in 1613.*

The method of compiling total values of imports and exports at this time was to multiply the customs poundage receipts inward and outward respectively, less the extra aliens' Custom under Carta Mercatoria, by twenty. Then an estimate was made of the values of such goods as were not subject to poundage—the tunnage, wool, and cloth Customs totals, with other incidentals, being used. Then an amount was added for ' goods run.'

In 1624 James by proclamation forbade the use of any tobacco not Plantation-grown. He had previously secured

* Yet, according to one statist, in 1623 the customs yield exceeded that of 1613 by £175,000 !   If this be correct, the labours of the Commission were crowned with success.

pre-emption of all Plantation tobacco.   But afterwards, when it suited him to do so, he granted licences at heavy rates for occasional importations of Spanish tobacco.

The celebrated Hanger Prisage case, by means of which the conditions governing exemption of London citizens from Prisage were clearly laid down, was decided during the early part of James's reign. ' Prisage,' said the judges, ' is a duty which the kings of England by themselves or their officers have taken from time immemorial.'   They decided that Prisage was not legal until after bulk was broken (unloading begun), and that they who imported wine for private use were ' naturally Prisage-free.'   ' The Prisage of Wines,' continued the judges, ' is a Flower of the Crown,' and they defined such qualities of citizenship as secured exemption.   A freeman not in residence was liable to Prisage.   A freeman resident, yet not a house-holder, was liable.   A resident and householder, yet not a freeman, was liable.   Those exempt were freemen hold-ing houses and residing within the City, and if even they imported wine for sale the goods were not free of Prisage unless they were the sole property of the importers, and intended for sale to none but citizens for the use of citizens. Sex of importer no bar.

Charles I. came before his Parliament with two decided disqualifications—a pile of debts left by his accomplished father, and a reputation for high-handedness.   War with Spain was contemplated, and the royal needs were urgent. The attitude of Parliament was discouraging, and highly incensed the king.   Then began that venomous struggle between the Crown and the people's representatives, in considering which most readers find their sympathies distracted with the varying aspects of the contest, now inclining to the king, now to the champions of those who contributed towards the support of the realm (at the same time enriching the farmers of taxes and their subordinates.) The Parliament of 1626 was also averse to granting money, and desirous of impeaching the king's favourite, Buckingham. Charles dissolved it.

It must be admitted that the conduct of the Parliaments was rather unreasonable, especially in avenging upon the king his father's debts and antics, but it has always been the English way to endure overlong and then resent in stubborn fashion. It is possible that many of the more thoughtful amongst the better classes, and nearly all the merchants, were tired of Stuart rule. The king was apt in furnishing pretexts for quarrel, and perhaps a large number of his most influential subjects were determined that quarrel should be. Indeed this is almost rendered clear by the action of the third Parliament.

It contained a host of implacable economists, and announced its true character by formulating the Petition of Right, and stating that no supplies would be granted until the claims of the petition were met. Charles by an ungracious acknowledgment obtained temporary supplies, but in 1629 he was again protesting. The Commons countered by charging him with infringing the Constitution. It appears that the king's officers had met with opposition in collecting his arbitrary levies of tunnage and poundage, and certain refractory merchants had been imprisoned. He declared that the recusants had been incited by the action of Parliament, and ordered the House to confirm the tunnage and poundage. ' I do not desire it out of greediness,' said he. ' I must be instant with you ; proceed with this business. . . . You must not think it much if I finding you slack shall give you further quickening.' But quickened the stubborn assembly would not be. Charles dissolved it, and for eleven years governed without a parliament.

It should be noted that the Commons, in reproaching the king, referred with unmistakable resentment to James's arbitrary increases of poundage. Undoubtedly the im-

posts rankled in the commercial mind, and the poor suffered by the inflation of prices.   This may explain the
rigid adherence of the mercantile class to the Parliamentary cause during the subsequent hostilities.

Charles's needs soon became urgent, and he revived in
full the system of farms and assignments.   The proceeds
of the old imposts were divided amongst royal favourites
and royal creditors, the names ' Hay,' ' Montgomery,' and
' Murray ' figuring side by side in the grants with ' Pindar,'
' Wolstenholme,' ' Dawes,' and ' Jacob.'   Pindar, Jacob,
and Dawes seem to have been in the thick of affairs.   At
one period they farmed the entire customs, and were
allowed to keep back from the rent a huge sum which
they had advanced or disbursed.   Pindar was a collector
of customs as well as a farmer.   Jacob was receiver of
tobacco duties.   Dawes was a distinguished pluralist, collector of customs, surveyor of customs, and clerk of the
Rolls.

In 1635 was published a new ' Book of Rates,' extending
the impost on poundage to many articles left untouched
by James, and here and there adding special imposts.
The new scheme had many other unfavourable points.
For instance, payment of duty was demanded *before entry*.
Prisage was instituted on imported groceries, with heavy
composition fees, and additional tunnage was levied on
wine at outports.   The poundage on Barbadoes tobacco
was reduced to 6d., on Virginian to 4d. ; on Spanish roll
tobacco it was raised to 2s.

While thus juggling with the Customs, the king raised
money by many other arbitrary expedients.   The obnoxious ship-money tax was in full swing.   Two years
later Hampden's case was tried in the Exchequer, and
a majority of the judges decided in favour of the Crown.
The soap, glass, and other manufactures were vested in
syndicates, that paid large sums to the king for their
privileges, and then made the public pay excessive prices.
(In 1630 Charles had renewed his father's prohibition of
tobacco-planting in England, prohibited all foreign tobacco

unless imported under royal licence,* and copied his father in pre-empting all Plantation tobacco.   In 1631 appeared the grotesque ' Licentia Thome Badger Militi et aliis pro exportatione Canum,' providing that Sir Thomas Badger and Thomas Potts, Masters of Harriers, and Sir Timothy Tyrrell, Master of Buckhounds, should enjoy sole privilege of exporting ' hounds, beagles, and hunting-dogs.' Indeed, it would seem that any company that tried the king with a purse might obtain almost any unfair privilege that could be asked for.   The Merchant Adventurers of England obtained the power of levying monstrous fees on all desirous of becoming members of their society, and threatened to increase the rates after a specified period had elapsed.)   In 1636 proclamation was made that the monopoly of retailing tobacco, which had been vested in a patentee, was being infringed by ' divers vagrant ped-lars,' who made it a practice to ' carrie tobacco upp and doune in packs, . . . and sell and retail the same to the damage of the pattentee.'   It was enjoined that such hawkers might be arrested, and dealt with as rogues and vagabonds.   Mayors, bailiffs, constables, etc., were ordered to ' bee ayding and assisting unto ye said pattentee ' in repression of the irregular traffic.

The celebrated Long Parliament met, voted tunnage and poundage and the wool duties for a brief period, and then impeached as ' delinquents ' a number of farmers and officials.   It is apparent that the rest did not pay much regard to the ominous proceedings, but continued when practicable to collect unwarranted dues for the king and intolerable fees for themselves, for later Parliament, while renewing tunnage and poundage for a limited period, enacted that if any officer continued the collection beyond the date specified, *or collected any illegal customs*, he should be liable to the provisions of the Statute of Præmunire. The act of grant stated that farmers had taken duties not

* See the Proclamation, ' That our Subjects may not un-thriftely vent the solid commodities of our owne kingdoms, and return the proceed thereof in smoak.'

sanctioned by any parliament, and that this had been proved on examination before the House and by confession of certain of the culprits. The tunnage granted was the ancient rate of 3s. only ; 6s. on sweet wines brought by aliens. Thus the wine imposts enduring from the times of Mary and Elizabeth were practically condemned as illegal. Plantation tobacco was freed of all duty except 2d. a pound.

The revenues sanctioned were continued again and again for brief spaces of time, as though purposely to exasperate the king. All grants of tunnage and poundage by letters patent (assignments, etc.) were annulled, and it was stipulated that no forfeiture for breach of the laws relating to tunnage and poundage should hold unless the act of grant had been proclaimed. Meanwhile the Customs revenues were being most improperly collected, the officials at certain ports scraping up what they could for the king, others conforming outwardly to the new regulations, yet collecting little. Others no doubt there were who did the best they could for themselves, yet went hourly in dread of the formidable Parliament and the Act of Præmunire.

The last rumble before the storm was a mutter at Westminster that the nation was drifting fast into debt for naval expenses. Then, while swords were being secretly sharpened for the inevitable conflict, Parliament made public certain of its recent dealings with the king in the matter of tunnage and poundage. The ordinance of disclosure accompanied a new ' Book of Rates,' and was a terse and ably-expressed document.

It stated that fifty-two ships of war were in commission, and that a debt of £200,000 had been incurred on behalf of the navy ; that a bill of tunnage and poundage and the annexed ' Book of Rates ' had been sent to the king ; that the king did not acknowledge them ; and that he gave no audience to a commission sent to move him in the matter.

It alluded to an Act passed for the relief of captives taken by Moorish pirates, under which Act all merchants importing or exporting goods were required to make entry of them promptly and correctly.   It reiterated the injunction, and enjoined the customs officers at all ports to vigilance in enforcement.

It admitted that, as the Bill for tunnage and poundage had not received the royal assent, none was bound to obey it, yet payment of the duties therein expressed was invited as a loan for national purposes at 15 per cent.   It continued that, though the king had the Bill in his possession, he was not competent to ratify it, except by his patent, declared in the Upper House in full presence of Lords and Commons.

The ordinance pledged both Houses to secure and confirm to all who paid duties in advance the 15 per cent. allowance before perfecting the subsidy in question or any future subsidy, and provided that all delinquents should be charged with full arrears.

It assured the officers of customs that they would be acting legally in obeying its instructions, and that ample provision would be made for their security.

(It alluded afresh to the Act for the relief of Moorish captives, under which all merchants were called upon for an advance of 1 per cent. on their contemplated revenue transactions to meet urgent necessities under the said Act, and stated that such as had not complied would be held liable, but the definition of the liabilities consequent was by no means clear.)

It empowered collectors to allow the 15 per cent. as a defalcation upon all duties paid under the provisions of the ordinance.   They were to make monthly return of all moneys received, and the returns were to be sent to William Toames, Surveyor-General of Customs, who in turn was to furnish an abstract to a committee of members, appointed by the full House. Copies of the Bill and ' Book of Rates ' were to be sent to every port.

It may be concluded that this ordinance was the guarded expression of a profound and subtle scheme.   The Bill was void, yet Parliament, by publishing its provisions, secured to the party of revolt the power of taxing most of the goods imported. London was with the Parliament men, and in case of hostilities would be the stronghold of their cause. As soon as war broke out Parliament would, for revenue purposes, be able to control the ports of Boston, Yarmouth, Lynn, Ipswich, London, Dover, Sandwich, and Southampton. The king would be restricted to the remoter and smaller ports, and be compelled to raise money by impositions upon the inland towns. The allowance upon duties paid appealed powerfully to the commercial mind. It is noteworthy, too, that for the first time in history Parliament took the revenue officers into its confidence, indirectly adjuring them, the London officers especially, to do their best to support constitutional liberty.

The Bill to which the ordinance alluded was also remarkable. It affirmed :

1. That no national charges on merchandise, inward or outward, could legally be made without the full consent of Parliament, except as provided (*vide* 4).

2. That grants made by Parliament were not immutable, but might be altered even by the parliament that made them.

3. That all such grants to the king were made solely that he might defend the seas.

4. That the ' old customs ' were the king's own. It recited them as the ' ancient Custome upon wool,' Prisage, Butlerage, the Carta Mercatoria duties, the ancient duties on the exportation of corn and grain, the duties of 3 James I. upon the exportation of beer, and Elizabeth's ' licence duties ' upon the exportation of leather, tallow, and hides. It then proceeded to give the rates and define the incidence of the ' old customs,' and certainly went astray, for it quoted Edward I.'s Carta Mercatoria duties on aliens' wool, etc., outwards as being ' the ancient wool Custom ' rates ; it stated Prisage as obtaining upon *every* vessel bringing ten or more tuns of wine ; and it described Butlerage as a ' fraight.'

The Bill prohibited the importation of currants.   (This was against the Venetians.)   It continued the officers' fees at the legal scale, hinting that they might soon be regulated by Parliament.   In the accompanying 'Book of Rates' appeared concise rules for the guidance of merchants and officers.   Below is a précis :

1. All masters of ships from foreign ports were directed to report, furnishing a full account of cargo.   If they proceeded to other English ports to complete discharge, the collectors at such ports were to be furnished with an account of all goods previously discharged.

2. The privileges previously extended to certain merchants by the late farmers were to be extended to all other merchants.

3. Casks of wine much reduced by genuine leakage were to be admitted duty-free.   Wine ' gone corrupt, fit only to distil into hot waters ' (spirits), ' or to make vinegar,' received the same privilege.   Twelve per cent. was to be allowed for ' leakage ' on all wines duly entered.

4. Aliens were to pay the same poundage inward as denizens, except on lead, tin, and woollens, and the Carta Mercatoria duties as well.   On lead, tin, and woollens they were to pay double poundage, and the Carta Mercatoria duties.   They were to pay double customs outward on native manufactures of wool, and on all other goods outward the usual poundage plus the Carta Mercatoria duties.

5. Wine imported and afterwards exported was to be available for drawback of the tunnage paid at import, less 20s. per tun withheld from denizens and 25s. from aliens.

6. Foreign wool imported and duty-paid was not available for drawback if afterwards exported, but might be shipped free of the outward custom, if the shipping and cocket fees were paid, and the goods exported in English bottoms.

7. Other goods duty-paid inward and exported were available for drawback of half the inward duty, if exported within a specified time.

The hours and places for unlading and shipping were defined. The landing and shipping officers were to give attendance between 6 a.m. and 6 p.m. in summer, and from sunrise to sunset in winter, *if actually required.* Officers neglecting to attend when duly notified were made liable to a fine of £5, part of the fine to go to the merchant aggrieved.

The indoor officers at outports were to attend from 9 to 12 in the morning, and from 2 to 4 in the afternoon. Those in London were to attend from 9 till 12, and in the afternoon were to help at the waterside, ' an able clerk ' remaining within ' to attend the book.' The merchants were to be dealt with in fair rotation. Officers who showed favour with a view to extort gratuities were to be punished.

Emphatic reference was made to the table of fees ratified by Parliament, and it was announced in plain terms that if an officer exceeded he was to be dismissed.

The searchers of outward-bound ships were warned not to detain any vessel beyond a specified time (three tides at Gravesend, one tide at the outports).

Certain privileges of slight defalcation in entry outward of cloth, long enjoyed by the merchants of York, Hull, Newcastle, and Exeter were confirmed.

The rates mentioned in the Book were not to entrench on any dues such as package, scavage, balliage, portage, or on any local custom dues levied by cities and ports upon aliens' merchandise for the upkeep of quays, harbours, etc.

It will be perceived that the Parliament extended consideration to the convenience of merchants, and was determined to see that the officers did their duty fairly and efficiently. Gentlemen appointed by royal patent, and accustomed to partnership with the employés of revenue-farmers, would probably scan the new regulations with disapproval.

Two years later, when the land resounded with conflict, Parliament issued another ordinance, continuing its

'Book of Rates.' It appears that a Committee of members supervised publication of the Book, with the ordinances and bill appertaining.

The ordinance of 1644 appointed Samuel Avery, Richard Bateman, Charles Lloyd, Christopher Pack, and Walter Boothby Commissioners of Customs, and referred to 'the late Commissioners' (the dispossessed farmers). It reaffirmed that the officers would be protected, and held accountable to Parliament only, and stated that in future schemes of tunnage and poundage provision would be made, not only for indemnifying merchants who might make advances, but for the security of collecting officers. It gave elaborate instructions as to dealing with seized goods. The account of all such goods was to be kept by a London officer, and the proceeds of the seizures were to be divided between the Treasury and the seizer. All proceedings against revenue defaulters were to be in the Court of Exchequer.

The allowance of 15 per cent. was withheld from payments upon imported tobacco. The prohibition of currants was repealed, and one-third of the proceeds of the currant duty appropriated to the maintenance of the garrison of Gloucester.

The Parliamentary Committee appointed to deal with naval business was notified of all customs after collection, and its order became the Commissioners' discharge. The customs officers were enjoined to be vigilant in the performance of their work, to conform closely to the 'Book of Rates,' and to obey Parliament and its committees. (The printer of the volume containing the 'Book of Rates,' Bill, and Ordinance was specified, and granted monopoly of publication. The price of the volume was fixed at 2s. 6d.)

Nearly all the values for poundage were increased, for the Parliament had no sustained source of revenue except the customs of the south-eastern ports. Spanish and Venetian goods were heavily surtaxed, as may be seen by the following comparison with the rates of 1635 and 1611 :

1635.			
Total tunnage in London:	£	s.	d.
Levant wines imported by Englishmen—Venetian Cargo (the butt),..	1	14	4

1642–4.			
Tunnage in London:	£	s.	d.
The butt	2	5	o

1611.			
Total value at which rated for poundage:	£	s.	d.
Spanish tobacco, leaf, per pound ..	1	6	8
Total poundage ..	o	1	4

1642–4.			
	£	s.	d.
Value for poundage	3	o	o
Poundage	o	3	o

(Tobacco from the English Plantations was rated extremely low—value, 3s. 4d. ; duty, 2d.)

The rating of several articles was doubled. For instance :

1611.			
Aqua vitæ (per hogshead)	£	s.	d.
	4	o	o
Poundage ..	o	4	o

1642–4.			
Aqua vitæ (per hogshead)	£	s.	d.
	8	o	o
Poundage ..	o	8	o

Outward Rates for Poundage.

1611.			
	£	s.	d.
Tallow (the cwt.) ..	1	o	o
Poundage ..	o	1	o

1642–4.			
	£	s.	d.
Tallow (the cwt.) ..	2	o	o
Poundage ..	o	2	o

The Parliament believed in rigid protection. During its control of the revenue there was no attempt at reducing the tariff, although strenuous and highly successful retrenchment of public expenditure was practised whenever opportunity arose. The martial Puritans had no love for foreigners ; their political motto appears to have been : ' England for the English, and England against the world.'* (Cromwell was much more disposed to toleration, both religious and racial, than the shrewd

* See preamble to the Commonwealth Act of 1656, c. 5 : ' Forasmuch as the prosperous estate of all islands is maintained by a just endeavour and care that the exportation of native commodities overbalances the importation of foreign commodities.' ' The balance of trade ' was a serious consideration with the old Puritans.

and fierce sectaries who followed, admired, and bitterly suspected him.)

The ' Book of Rates ' furnishes evidence that a sugar-refining industry had sprung up in England. In the 1611 Book there was no mention made of refined sugar. In the 1635 Book ' refined sugar in loaves ' was listed at an extremely high rate for poundage, but the item did not appear in the outward list. ' Refined sugar in loaves ' appeared amongst the imports in the 1642–4 Book, and was almost the only item standing at a lowered value.

Value for Poundage Inward.

	1635.			1642–4.		
	£	s.	d.	£	s.	d.
Refined sugar in loaves (per cwt.) ..	21	6	8	17	0	0

Apparently the refining of sugar in England had lowered the value of the foreign article. In the 1642–4 Book's *export* list appeared :

Value for Poundage Outward.

	£	s.	d.
Sugar (coarse), having paid custom inward, refined, and made into loaves and exported (the cwt.) ..	2	0	0

The Parliament's Ordinance and ' Book of Rates ' were to endure until a specified date in 1647. Meantime additional funds were raised by an Excise duty, levied on the ' first buyer ' of certain foreign commodities. Wine was included, and, to make sure that the tax should be diverted from the importer, the retail selling price was fixed at 14d. per quart for Spanish wine and 8d. for French, a higher price than had previously obtained. Excise duties were also placed upon beer, ale, and spirits, produced in England. The standards for wine-casks were recited thus : Tun, 252 gallons ; pipe or butt, 126 ; puncheon (anciently called ' tertian '), 84 ; hogshead, 63 ; tierce, 42 ; quarter-cask, 31½.

Messrs. Towle, Langham, Foot, Kendrick, Cullum, Evans, Lamot, and Claxton were appointed Excise Commissioners. Mr. Faulconbridge was made controller, and Mr. Bond auditor. The oath to be taken by each Commissioner ran as follows :

' You shall swear to be faithful and true in your place of Commissioner of the Excise during the time you shall be a Commissioner, according to the Ordinance of both Houses of Parliament in that behalf made. You shall according to your knowledge execute the same diligently and faithfully, having no private respect to yourself in prejudice of the Commonwealth. You shall make and deliver a true account of all your receipts and disbursements to such Auditor or Auditors as is or are or shall be from time to time appointed by the Houses of Parliament according to the said Ordinance : so help you God and the contents of this Book.'*

The operations of the ' New Impost,' as the Excise was called, were for a time restricted to London and the neighbouring districts, but as the Parliament gradually wrested control of the various counties from the king, they were extended to England, Wales, and Berwick. At first there was much evasion by ' roomaging and removing of goods,' and the New Impost was received in no friendly spirit by the nation, especially as extensive powers of search were granted to the officers. The professed reason for the tax was that the eastern ports, which were friendly to the Parliament, would by their contributions of tunnage, poundage, etc., have borne the bulk of the expense of the war, had not this new method been applied to the inland counties, many of which had at first taken the part of the king. The Ordinance instituting the tax described it as a ' New Impost, whereby Malignants and Neutrals may be compelled to pay proportionate parts of the charge for the preservation of the Kingdom.' Yet it does not appear that Parliament,

* Later the wording of the oath was altered, each Commissioner being required to vow allegiance to the Commonwealth.

though capturing county after county, called upon any of them for arrears.

The only foreign goods exempt from Excise duties on sale were bullion, corn, victuals, arms, ammunition, and ordnance. (Thus it seems that the revenue maxims of the Parliament were the same as those of James I., whom the leading men of the new school held a blundering tyrant.) Goods imported for private use were liable. Barter counted as sale. There was no escaping the tax. More remorseless exacters of dues never lived than the stern and incorruptible English Republicans. But they accounted honestly for the moneys they collected, and used them to the best advantage.*

The next Ordinance worth note was that of 1646, which freed export trade between England and the Plantation of New England and the West Indies of all duties.

In the same year the Act granting Tunnage and Poundage was renewed.

The exportation of wool was prohibited in 1647.

In 1651 the Rump passed its momentous Navigation Act, stipulating that no merchandise of Asia, Africa, or America should enter England except in ships built and owned by Englishmen, navigated by English captains, and manned by crews of which more than the half part were Englishmen. Such merchandise as came direct from Europe, and was in ships of the country of shipment, was excepted. Fish might not be imported into or exported from England unless it had been caught by English fishermen.

This, of course, was a deliberate attempt to provoke a quarrel with the Dutch, and gain an opportunity of

* In 1649 Parliament, in one of its Acts, described the New Impost as 'the most useful and indifferent' (fairly apportioned) 'levy that can be laid upon a people.' The tax brought in a deal of money, and at the time Parliament was in great need. The King had been beheaded, the Rump was in power, and executive government had been entrusted to the strongest body of men that ever ruled a nation—the famous Council of which Bradshaw was president and Milton foreign secretary.

making England supreme as a carrier of goods. Nothing in history is more remarkable than the resoluteness of this Parliament, unless it be the efficacy of its measures. It had dethroned the king, tried him as a common criminal, and beheaded him as a traitor. Through its wonderful general and peerless soldiers it had shattered the opposition of Scotland, and been able to strike enduring terror into the hearts of the Irishry. Withal it had an eye to the ports and the ocean beyond them, and had resolved to stake the existence of the Commonwealth upon a novel and tremendous venture.

It seems that the Dutch at once realized the danger at hand. They sent an embassy of remonstrance, but it was received coldly. The Commonwealth demanded—

1. A sum as damages for fishing carried on by the Dutch in English waters.
2. Cession of the Spice Islands.
3. Compensation for an outrage upon Englishmen at Amboyna.
4. Satisfaction for the murder of Dr. Dorislaus, Parliamentary Envoy at the Hague.
5. Reparation for damage caused to English shipping by the Dutch.

The third and fourth items of demand were reasonable ; the rest could be granted by no self-respecting nation. The sum claimed for damages to shipping was really an outrageous item, yet there is good reason to believe that, had it been instantly paid, fresh demands would have been made. Parliament had but one object—to shatter the power of the Dutch.

'A fair fight, and the winner has the world's trade,' was the watchword on both sides when Blake and Van Tromp began their tremendous struggle. But during that brief and glorious space in her history, that commenced with the rise of Cromwell and ended with the death of Blake, the best of England gave England counsel and fought her battles, and England could not lose. The destruction of the Dutch fleet, and the death of its heroic commander, fixed the rule of the seas beyond successful challenge. The damage sustained by Holland was irreparable. Within two years she lost almost all her ships of war, and several hundreds of her merchantmen. She was made to 'pray and pay.' The English East India Company received notable concessions, and the Stuart cause was left for the time destitute of both support and hope. The Channel Islands and the Colonies had been forced to renounce it ; Scotland and Ireland had been bludgeoned into submission, and now even the stubborn Dutchmen were compelled to condone the execution of 1649.

In 1652 tobacco-planting within the realm was prohibited.

In 1653 Barebone's Parliament issued an Ordinance continuing the Customs until 1658, and provided that there should be no drawback of subsidy on goods which had been taxed at sale or altered in quality and afterwards exported. It was also provided that the pay of the Commissioners of Customs should take the form of ' poundage upon receipts '—1d. on every 20s. of net customs money.

In 1654, Barebone's Parliament having vacated office, a unique Ordinance was issued. Perhaps the grave Commissioners had been scandalized by the ribald outcry of Billingsgate, Fresh Wharf, and the Wool Dock, or some of Cromwell's men may have visited the Custom-house at mid-day. Below is the Act :

' An Ordinance empowering the Commissioners of the Customs and others for the better suppression of Drunkenness and prophane Swearing in persons employed under them.

' Whereas several persons such as Carmen, Porters, Watermen, and others who are employed upon the Keys* as also upon the River of Thames in Ships, Boats, and Lighters, and in Thames Street and other Streets and Lanes adjacent within the City of London, for shipping

* Quays.

and unshipping, packing, carrying, craning, and removing
Goods and Merchandise, are very ordinarily drunk, and
do also Prophane and Blaspheme the holy name of God
by Cursing and Swearing, to the great dishonour of God,
the scandal of the Professors and Profession of the Gospel
among us, and of the present Government : For the preventing whereof, Bee it Enacted by His Highness the Lord
Protector, by and with the consent of his Council, that the
Commissioners of the Customs for the time being bee and
are hereby authorised and required to take care that the
Laws of this Nation against Drunkenness, Swearing, and
Cursing bee put in execution against all such persons as
shall bee guilty of the crimes aforesaid : And for that
purpose shall and hereby have the Power and Authority
of Justices of the Peace within the said places : And every
Officer and Officer's Deputy and Deputies of the Commissioners of the Customs, having a Commission whereby
they are deputed and authorised to bee Officers and
Deputies under the hand and seals of the said Commissioners, shall have and hereby have power and are authorised to apprehend and attach and in safe custody to bring
before the said Commissioners, or anyone of them sitting
at the Customhouse in London, every person or persons
whom they shall see to bee Drunk, or shall hear to Swear,
Curse, and Blaspheme the holy name of God as is aforesaid : And shall have power, and hereby have power to
execute, any power or powers, authority, or authorities
in this case which by Law any Constable may or ought to
exercise or use, although the said Officer or Officers have
no particular warrant of the Commissioners aforesaid for
apprehending any of the offenders for the offences aforesaid, as in the like cases are usually issued unto Sworn
Constables by Justices of the Peace upon the like occay-
sions : And all persons whom any of the said Officers shall
require to bee aiding and assisting unto them for the
apprehending and bringing before the said Commissioners
any such offenders are hereby required to bee aiding and
assisting unto them therein accordingly : And in case of

refusal such punishment and proceedings shall bee had and awarded against them as by Law may bee and ought to bee upon every person that shall refuse to bee aiding and assisting to any Sworn Constable or Constables when required thereunto.

'*Friday, June 30th*, 1654.

' Ordered by His Highness the Lord Protector and His Council, that this Ordinance bee forthwith Printed and Published.

'HENRY SCOBELL, *Clerk of the Council.*'

It will be observed that Cromwell's councillors did not ' imitate the honourable Romans in brevity '; their ordinances were elaborate as sermons. It is possible that the language in Thames Street then may have been as bad as that used there at the present day. If it were, the proclamation may almost be excused, though it is certain that if the customs men tried to carry out its provisions they had little time to collect and safeguard the revenue.*

In an Ordinance fixing the retail prices of wine, French wine was listed at 7d. a quart, Rhenish at 12d., Spanish at 18d. Tunnage and poundage were continued, applying to Scotland and Ireland as well as England. Certain Spanish goods were surtaxed, thus :

	Additional Tunnage.			
	£	s.	d.	
Spanish wine imported by subjects	1	10	0	per tun.
,, ,, ,, ,, aliens	2	0	0	,,

	Additional Duty.			
	£	s.	d.	
Spanish ' raisins of the sun,' by subjects	0	3	0	per cwt.
,, ,, ,, ,, strangers	0	3	9	,,
Other Spanish raisins, by subjects	0	1	6	,,
,, ,, ,, strangers	0	1	10½	,,

---

* A letter from the Commissioners to Thurloe shows that the officers performed other incidental duties. The water-guard men seem to have acted as political detectives, and to have detained passengers suspected of being ' malignants.'

' Now is come into our hands a letter of the officers at Gravesend, signifying that there are divers persons come in there out of a ship,' etc.

Certain capital revenue regulations were initiated during the periods of the Parliament and the Protectorate. It was directed that foreign goods carried by lighter from a ship lying in the stream were to be accompanied by a 'lighter-note,' made out by the officer boarded on the vessel. The lighter-note was to be the warrant for the landing of the goods. The landing-waiters were to check the entry and out-turn of the goods by it, and inquire into any discrepancy. An Act of the Protectorate instituted what is now known as 'The King's Warehouse,' but which in the preamble was called 'His Highness's Warehouse.' One such place was to be maintained at every port of consequence. All fine goods or small packages, on arrival in port, and all goods remaining undelivered from vessels within twenty-eight days of their breaking bulk, were to be removed to 'His Highness's Warehouse' for safety, at owners' charges. The keeper of each warehouse had to provide 'good bond,' and was held responsible to owners for the safety of the goods in his custody.

The penalty for making incorrect entry of goods was fixed at £10. Smuggling was made punishable with a fine of treble the value at issue, and forfeiture of the goods. No proceedings were to take place until the seized goods had been warehoused and registered. (It would be extremely difficult to improve upon any of these regulations.)

Steps were taken to farm the revenue. (According to Thurloe, Cromwell had always favoured the idea.) A committee was appointed to contract, it being provided that none of the committeemen should be concerned in the farm, or deal in the commodities taxable. The Customs Commissioners were directed to practise similar abstention. Thus the Great Revolt, which at its outset was marked by bitter persecution of revenue-farmers, may be said to have expired amid requests for tenders.

Two rather interesting cases were tried in the Exchequer during the period of the Protectorate. In 1656 the Attorney-General proceeded against one Shirt, for prisage on nine and a half tuns of wine. The court were of opinion that Shirt imported his goods is small parcels purposely, to elude prisage, and that when such intent appeared any quantity between nine and ten tuns was subject to prise.

In 1658 a bill was presented in the Exchequer against Samuel Mico, ' for discovery of the truth ' in connexion with a charge of his having bribed Hawes and Oldenham, ' officers of customs and excise,' to allow him to import 290 casks of currants into the port of London, in a ship called *The Christopher*, without paying the custom due. Mico demurred, pleading that if he answered the charge he might be made to accuse himself of smuggling. He was defended by Hardres, a celebrated Exchequer lawyer. Hardress commenced with an appeal to ' the Law of God,' and ingeniously twisted St. Paul's reply to Tertullus into a contention that the Apostle considered himself not bound to answer to his own peril. He also instanced Christ's silence when interrogated by Pilate. After these illustrations of what ' the Law of God and the God of Law ' allowed ' in cases of crime,' the indefatigable pleader appealed to the ' Law of Nature,' and then unwound a mighty chain of ordinary legal precedents. This case is well worth reading, as a specimen of the methods used by ancient pleaders.

LIST OF AUTHORITIES.

Legislation and Incidents.

Imposts : Fœdera ('Commisssio pro Tabacco '), 'Book of Rates,' 1611 ; Hale (' Hargrave's ' Law Tracts '); 'Book of Rates,' 1635 and 1644.

Protective measures and prohibitions : Fœdera (' Proclamatio super abusu Herbæ Nicotianæ '; ' A Proclamation concerning Tobacco '; ' A Proclamation for the Utter Prohibiting,' etc.) ; Commonwealth Acts, 1648, 1651 (Navigation Act) ; 2 of 1652.

Officers : Treasury Papers, 1615-1616.

Commissions of Inquiry : Fœdera (' De Concessione speciali directa Domino Presidenti et aliis concernente Negotium Lanæ ').

Prisage (Exchequer trials) : Bohun, Hardres.

Excise duty : Commonwealth Ordinance, July 22, 1643, and others.

Wine : Commonwealth Acts, October 9, 1643, 8 of 1656.

British tunnage and poundage : Commonwealth Act 9 of 1656.

Revenue-farming : Commonwealth Act 31 of 1656.

Preventive : Commonwealth Act 9 of 1656.

Long Parliament's grants to Charles I. : 16 Chas. I., c. 8, 12, 22, 25, 29, 31, 36.

Frauds (Exchequer trials) : Hardres.

CHAPTER V

A CLEVER revenue historian of the time of the Georges, after enumerating most of the taxes imposed from the accession of Charles to the death of Anne, confessed that he had omitted some, which, ' like noisome meteors, made their appearance for a year or more, and then vanished.' As a similar method will be applied in this treatise, it may be well to quote his excuse, which ran as follows : ' These we have forborne to mention, because we believe that the reader will be as heartily tired of reading, as we are of collecting and writing, such a disagreeable scroll as that we have now given. Let him consider what kind of people they must be who are to pay these taxes, and on account of these taxes are made liable to an infinite number of pains, penalties, and hardships.'

The thing most intolerable in connexion with Charles's revenue business was not the extent of the impositions— at least so far as the Customs revenue was concerned— for his Parliaments were not much more extortionate upon maritime commerce than those of the Commonwealth had been. It was the conspicuous failure of the levies to realize the sums intended. The financial officials were always in straits, even though the peerless army had been disbanded.

It appears that the duties remained in farm up to the latter end of 1671.* During July of that year an under-

---

* It is curious that about the last official act of the Farmers was the issue of a code of regulations (the ' Index Vectigalium ') for the guidance of officers.

SECTION OF M. 1d. PART 2, PATENT ROLL 23 CHARLES II., SHOWING PREAMBLE OF DOCUMENT INSTALLING SIR GEORGE DOWNING AND OTHERS AS COMMISSIONERS OF CUSTOMS IN 1671.

(During the same year instructions were given to the Remembrancer of the Exchequer to proceed against the lessees of a Customs farm which expired in 1667, the said lessees being in debt to the Crown for a large sum.)

The Commission begins 'at ' Charles the Second by the grace of God,' and contains nearly 5,000 words. The lines above ' p · bre · de Privato Sigillo,' (' by writ of Privy Seal') conclude M. 2d. on same Roll, a document furnishing instructions to Lord Ranelagh and others, who farmed the Irish Revenue.

To face p. 104.

taking was entered into by Lord St. John and others to farm the customs upon all goods exported and imported, except the temporary imposition upon wine and vinegar, the temporary duty of 5s. a ton upon French shipping, the customs upon bullion, smalt, saffers, salt, timber, glass, potashes, and logwood, the Coinage duty, and such duties as were 'usually exempt from farming.' The farmers advanced £140,000, and undertook to pay a rent of £480,000 per annum. They were to pay the rent in monthly instalments, and to meet all debentures on goods duty-paid and afterwards exported. They undertook 'not to clogg the markett towards the end of the tearme.' The farm was to endure five years, and to commence on September 29.

Later they made another advance, and obtained permission to farm the imposts on wine and vinegar as well as the permanent duties. By September, 1671, they had advanced in all £226,000, and a Privy Seal warrant of that month directed the Exchequer officials to pay the interest upon the loan out of the forthcoming customs receipts, and to arrange for paying off the principal by instalments. They were also bidden to hold themselves in readiness to pay to Lord St. John and his associates in the lease such other sums as 'the king by Sign Manuall may appoint as gratuities in respect of their surrendering their farm.'

Thus it appears that the farm had been cancelled. On September 27, 1671, just two days prior to the date on which the lease should have come into effect, Commissioners were appointed to manage the Customs revenue. The patent (23 Chas. II., p. 2, m. 1*d*.) is too long to be reproduced *in extenso*, but a brief account may be of interest.

The Commissioners named were Sir George Downing, Sir William Lowther, Sir William Thompson, William Garway, Francis Millington, and John Upton. Downing had originally been an Exchequer Teller. (Pepys was his clerk in 1659.) He was made a baronet in 1663, and thenceforward was occasionally employed in adjusting the disposal of the customs takings.* Sir William Thompson and Garway had been employed as Commissioners of Accounts.† The new Commissioners were granted salaries of £2,000 per annum. Robert Sherwin ‡ was made Secretary—salary £400 ; and Richard Prowse Solicitor—salary £300.

The Commissioners were empowered to collect the subsidy and imposts, to appoint inferior officers by nomination, etc., from the Treasury or Exchequer, to remove or displace them by similar warrant, and to take security for their good behaviour ; to authorize the Receiver-General and the outport collectors to expend customs money for ‘ incidents ’ ; to administer oaths on customs matters ; to board and search vessels by day or night, and to search warehouses, etc., by day. Admiralty officers, Justices, Sheriffs, etc., were directed to assist them. They might grant Portage Bills,§ administer the Acts in encouragement of shipping, and compound petty seizures. Certain farming privileges previously allowed

* ‘ Thence to the Treasury Chambers, and there all the morning, to my great grief, put to do Sir G. Downing's work of dividing the customs for a year between the Navy, the Ordnance, and Tangier,’ (Pepys, March 22, 1669). (Large loans had been taken on the customs in 1669, and Downing had spoken to Pepys in despair of being able to do no more out of the revenue than pay the interest. Thus it would seem that the seeds of national indebtedness were sown long before the time of James II. or William III.)

† Garway and Sir William Thompson overhauled Pepys' account in 1666. Says Samuel : ‘ Sir W. Coventry says Garway is a man not well used by the Court, though very stout to death, and hath suffered all that is possible for the king from the beginning.’ Sir William Thompson was elected for the City, March 19, 1661. Says Pepys in 1666: ‘Capt. Cocke tells of Garway and those people what they object as to the mal-administration of things as to money. But they mean well, and will do well.’ Pepys quotes a statement of revenue based on their calculations. There is an item of £2,390,000 collected and not accounted for. Says Pepys : ‘ So what has become of all this sum ?’ Garway is also quoted as speaking against the maintenance of a standing army.

‡ ‘ Mighty strange to find myself sit here in committee with my hat on, while Mr. Sherwin stood bare as a clerk ’ (Pepys, January 17, 1665).

§ Sums of money as rewards to shipmasters for reporting their cargoes correctly.

and not determined were to endure till end of lease, and the Commissioners were to supervise the importation of the goods appertaining. They were exempted from answering for any deficiencies in the duties of Customs, etc., except such as were results of ' voluntary and particular misfeazance.'

Later* a Receiver-General was appointed, at a salary of £1,000. He was to keep separate accounts of the standing customs and temporary imposts, to pay in the moneys every Monday, and to furnish the Treasury and Board every Tuesday with a statement of the cash in his possession. The Treasury might demand an account every six months, or more frequently if necessary.

Several other important offices were ' erected.' For instance, Giles Dunster, John Man, and George Blake were made ' Surveyors Generall in all Ports and Creeks throughout the Realme.'

The institution of responsible officials in the place of mere speculators had been first ventured upon by the Long Parliament (*vide* p. 90). That the step was not taken earlier in Charles II.'s reign than 1671 may have been due to a desire to satisfy the outstanding claims of men like Wolstenholme and Jacob. There can be no doubt that the change was highly judicious, yet it might have been made much more effective had it not been thought fit to duplicate some of the existing offices. It seems that new collectors were appointed at many of the ports, yet the old ' customers,' with their ' controllers ' and ' searchers,' were allowed to retain their offices as sinecures. When the ' patents ' lapsed, other favourites were appointed, and the extraordinary system of having one set of officers to do the actual work, and another set of officers who were merely pensioners upon maritime trade, continued for more than a century.

* During the eighteenth century the system of accounting for cash lapsed, and the accounts became extensively muddled. The offices of Surveyors-General were abolished before the end of the seventeenth century, and revived during the eighteenth.

The arrangement of ports, etc., was as below :

Head Ports.	*Members.*	*Creeks.*
Berwick-on-Tweed	Nil.	The East Marches, Holy Island, Blyth Nooks, Alnmouth, Seaton Delaval.
Newcastle-on-Tyne	Shields, Sunderland, Hartlepool, Stockton, Whitby	with Middlesborough.
Hull	Scarborough, Bridlington, Grimsby	,, Gainsborough.
Boston	Nil	Saltfleet, Theddlethorpe, Mumby Chapel, Wainfleet, Fosdyke, Spalding.
Lynn	Nil, Wells	Cross Keys and Heacham. with Burnham.
Yarmouth	Blakeney., Southwold, Aldeburgh, Woodbridge	,, Lowestoft and Walberswick. ,, Dunwich and Orford. Nil.
Ipswich	Colchester, Maldon	,, Harwich, Manningtree, Wivenhoe, and Brightlingsea. ,, East Mersea, West Mersea, Burnham, and Leigh.
London	Nil	Gravesend.
Sandwich	Rochester, Milton., Faversham., Dover	with Queenborough. ,, Whitstable, Margate, Ramsgate, and Deal.
Chichester	Hythe, Rye, Hastings, Lewes, Shoreham, Arundel	,, Folkestone. ,, Romney, Lydd, and Winchilsea. ,, Pevensey. ,, Seaford and Newhaven. ,, Brighton. ,, Selsey.

Head Ports.	Members.	Creeks.
Southampton ..	Portsmouth	with Emsworth.
	Cowes	{ ,, Newport and Yarmouth.
	Nil	{ Lymington and Christchurch.
Poole	Nil	Wareham and Swanage.
	Weymouth	{ with Lulworth and Portland.
	Lyme Regis	{ ,, Charmouth and Bridport.
Exeter	Nil	{ Axmouth, Exmouth, Lympton, Sidmouth, Powderham, Topsham, Seaton, Starcross, and Teignmouth.
	Dartmouth	{ with Totnes, Torbay, Brixham, and Salcombe.
	Barnstaple	{ ,, Bideford, Appledore, and Clovelly.
	Ilfracombe	Nil.
Plymouth	Nil	Stonehouse and Saltash.
	Loowe.	
	Fowey.	
	Falmouth	{ with Truro, St. Mawes, and Penryn.
	Helston.	
	Penzance.	
	St. Ives.	
	Padstow.	
Bridgwater ..	Minehead	Nil.
Bristol	Nil	Uphill and Pill.
Gloucester ..	Nil	{ Severn from Bridgnorth to King's Road.
Cardiff	Swansea	{ with Chepstow, Newport, Penarth, Aberdare, Newton, Neath, and South of the Burry.
Milford	Pembroke	{ ,, North of the Burry Llanelly, Carmarthen, Tenby, and Haverfordwest.
	Cardigan	,, Liskeard and Newport.
	Aberdovey	,, Aberystwith.

Head Ports.	Members.	Creeks.
Chester	Carnarvon	with Barmouth and Pwllheli.
	Beaumaris	,, Amlych and Holyhead.
	Conway	,, Mostyn, Bagillt, Birkenhead, Neston, and Hilbree.
	Liverpool	,, the south shore from the Red Stones, also Frodsham and Sankey Bridge.
	Poulton	,, Preston and the Wyre.
	Lancaster	,, Grange.
Carlisle	Whitehaven	,, Milnthorpe, Ravenglass, and Workington.
	Nil	West Marches.

The legal landing and shipping places in London were Brewer's Quay, Chester's Quay, Galley Quay, the Wool Dock, Custom-house Quay, Porter's Quay, Bear Quay, Sub's Dock, Wiggon's Quay, Young's Quay, Ralph's Quay, Dice Quay, Smart's Quay, Somers Quay, Lyon Quay, Botolph Wharf, Hammond's Quay, Gaunt's Quay, Cox's Quay, and Fresh Wharf. At these wharves all goods might be landed or shipped. Billingsgate was approved only for fish, salt, victuals, fuel, fruit, and the shipment of English building material. Bridge House, Southwark, was approved for corn for the provisioning of the City.

The goods allowed to be discharged 'in the stream'— i.e., from vessels moored in the river—were iron, deals, and timber. These could be unladen between Westminster and Limehouse Dock, and the duties on them had to be paid prior to unshipment. The goods that could be *loaded* in the stream were horses, coal, beer, stone, corn, grain, and fish taken by denizens. Custom outward to be paid and cocket issued prior to shipment.

The officers levied fees upon merchants, masters, etc., for all revenue transactions of accompt, receipt, indenture, and declaration. Below appear a few of the authorized fees :

	£	s.	d.
For taking report of an English ship from the East Indies or beyond the Straits	0	2	6
For taking report of an English ship from Spain, West Indies, and the Plantations	0	2	0
For taking report of an English ship from other countries, including Scotland and Ireland	0	1	0
(Foreign ships paid double.)			

Custom Inward.

	£	s.	d.
For issuing a warrant to a Freeman of London	0	1	4
For issuing a warrant to any other merchant	0	2	0
For issuing a Bill of Sight	0	2	0
For any special employment	0	2	6
For issuing a certificate for foreign goods proceeding coastwise	0	1	0
For issuing a bond of any kind	0	0	6
To the collector for an oath	0	0	2
When goods were short entered to the amount of over 5s., they were sent to the King's Warehouse, and the warehouse-keeper charged per package for checking them on receipt	0	0	2
For a transire or let-pass for coastwise goods	0	0	6

Custom Outward.

	£	s.	d.
For the outward entry of a ship going beyond the Straits	0	4	0
For the outward entry of a ship going to other foreign parts	0	1	4
For the outward entry of a ship going to an outport in England	0	0	5
For the clearance of a ship outward	0	2	6
For endorsing a warrant or licence	0	0	8
For a cocket issued to a Freeman of London	0	1	8
For a cocket issued to any other merchant	0	2	6
For a cocket for goods going duty-free (having been duty-paid inward)	0	1	8
For a cocket for a ship going foreign and calling at an English outport	0	3	0
For a certificate for goods shipped duty-free on Treasury warrant	0	3	6
For a debenture for repayment of any part of outward custom	0	2	0
For a licence for a foreign ship to take beer as stores	0	2	0

There were many other clerical fees. The landing, shipping, and searching officers also charged fees on almost all transactions supervised by them. The landing and shipping officers' fees were usually taken in gross upon a number of transactions, and afterwards divided among the officers concerned. The searchers took large fees for rummage and final clearance of vessels outward.

The systems of assessment and collection were slovenly and imperfect, and the preventive regulations were erratically administered. There were no docks in England for merchantmen ; vessels unloaded and took in cargo at the ' legal quays '; and when there was a glut of shipping, which often occurred, the ships had to lie off until berths were vacant. In special cases they were allowed, notwithstanding the regulations previously quoted, to discharge into lighters, when the document called a ' lighter-note,' instituted in the Commonwealth time, was found useful.

The gauging of wines, etc., was unreliable in the extreme. The gaugers used callipers to ascertain the lengths of casks, but the bung diameters were merely taken by perpendicular measurement. The contents were cast by the pen, and a set of tables first published by Henry Phillips in his ' Mathematical Manual,' and reprinted in the ' Index Vectigalium.' The method gave tolerably correct results as regarded computation, but there seems to .have been considerable confusion upon the important matter of allowance for irregularities in shape. Worst of all, if the gauger checked his work by actual measurement it was likely that the measure used was incorrect, for the standard vessels were unreliable.*

The old gaugers relied upon the ' gauging-rod,' or dip-rod, a cumbrous and uncertain tool. It had a line of

---

* This was conclusively proved in 1688. One Wybard asserted that the standard ' wine and spirit ' gallon measure in the London Guildhall was too small by seven cubic inches. On May 25, in the Guildhall, in presence of the Lord Mayor, the Commissioners of Excise, the King's Astronomer, and ' other ingenious gentlemen,' Mr. Shales of the Excise filled a brass vessel of 224 cubic inches ' with clear water,' and emptied it into the standard measure, which it exactly filled. Thus Wybard's assertion was proved correct, for the standard should have contained 231 cubic inches.

inches for showing the perpendicular diameter, a line for
'contenting' casks by diagonal measurement, and no
less than eight additional lines for finding ullages of
various kinds of casks 'by the dip.' These lines were
adapted to standard casks only, 'as made by the London
coopers,' and had been constructed by the primitive
method of measuring successive wine gallons into the
standard casks, inserting the rod, and 'marking off' the
spaces covered by the liquid. The rods were thus marked
for tuns, butts or pipes, puncheons, etc. There were
separate rods for gauging ale, etc., the ale gallon being
larger than the wine gallon (282 against 231). As the
foreign-made casks were of irregular shape, and often
wide of the standard contents, the results of such 'gauging' must have been perplexing to the retailer, especially when, as was often the case, the gaugers used an
incorrect gallon measure to regulate their 'contenting'
of casks, and a correct quart was used in measuring the
goods for sale.*

In 1660 a subsidy, destined to become *perpetual* as ' The
Old Subsidy,' was granted Charles for life, and the grant
was accompanied by the issue of a new ' Book of Rates.'
The tunnage duties therein expressed were almost similar
to those levied by the Commonwealth. The wine duty
for London was higher than for outports, and, as of old,
when wine duty-paid at an outport was removed to
London it was liable to the extra duty. The poundage
was 1s. in the £1 value upon all goods imported and exported, except as below :

---

* In 1683 Thomas Everard, an excise officer, by an adaptation
of the logarithmic scale, constructed a sliding-rule for computing
gauges. It was of boxwood, 1 foot long, 1·2 inches broad, and
0·75 inch thick, and was an ingeniously devised and useful instrument. It is likely that as time went on the gauging became more
accurate, for an excise handbook of the middle of the eighteenth
century states that many of the customs officers of the port of
London were extremely expert in cask-gauging.

English-taken fish, and fresh fish and bestial imported. The latter had always been duty-free.

Sheep's wool, imported. This was made duty-free in aid of the manufacture of cloth.

English fustians and garments, exported. These were made duty-free to encourage manufacture.

Woollen cloths, or ' old Draperies.' These were free of poundage, but paid a special tax of 3s. 4d. a cloth if exported by English ; 6s. 8d. if by aliens, and the aliens also paid Carta Mercatoria duties.

English beer, exported. This also paid a special tax. If exported by English, it paid 2s. a tun ; if by aliens, 6s.

The ancient regulation prohibiting the exportation of corn when above a specified price in England was maintained. So was the ancient Custom upon English wool, English lead, and English tin—exported by English—but aliens paid double duties on those articles, and the Carta Mercatoria duties as well. The aliens also paid double outward poundage on all goods exported by them which had been manufactured from English material, or produced in England.

The general tendency of the rates was decidedly against the foreigner. Below are a few items of illustration :

	Rate for Poundage.			Poundage.		
	£	s.	d.	£	s.	d.
Spanish tobacco, inward, per pound	0	10	0	0	0	6
Hops, inward, per cwt.	15	0	0	0	15	0
Woollen cloth, inward, per yard (made up)	8	10	0	0	8	6
Aqua vitæ, inward, per hogshead ..	4	0	0	0	4	0
Loaf sugar, inward, per cwt. ..	17	0	0	0	17	0
Plantation tobacco, per pound ..	0	1	8	0	0	1
Hops, outward, per cwt. ..	1	10	0	0	1	6
Woollen cloth, outward, by English, per yard	(Special tax)	(about)		0	0	1½
Aqua vitæ (English spirits), outward, per hogshead, by English	2	0	0	0	2	0
Loaf sugar, outward, per cwt., by English	0	10	0	0	0	6

It is interesting to note that goshawks were valued at £3 6s. 8d. each, and falcons at £4.

An ox outward was valued at £6 13s. 4d., poundage 6s. 8d. Among the skins specified in the outward list were those of the coney, kid, hare, fox, dog, cat, swan, squirrel, and badger. The list also had as separate items Sheffield knives and London knives.

Oranges and lemons inward were valued at 20s. per 1,000, poundage 1s. Ordinary apples were valued at 4d. per bushel, pippins at 1s. Eggs were 1s. 8d. per 120, poundage 1d.

With a few exceptions, the poundage was almost similar to that imposed during the time of the Commonwealth.

Besides the subsidies inward and outward, there was granted a tax which afterwards was known as ' The Additional Duty,' and which became perpetual in a later reign. It took the form of an added tunnage on wine, and an added poundage of 6d. in each £1 value upon all wrought silk other than that of the East Indies, and all linen except Irish linen and calico ; also an extra 1d. per pound duty on Plantation tobacco. The added tunnage was to be paid within nine months after importation, the added poundage within twelve, and these postponed duties were to be secured by bond, entered into when the goods were landed. Thus the extra duty was for a space forborne, as all the duties on bonded goods are forborne at present until clearance from warehouse.

In 1662 the One per Cent. Inward and Outward duties (also destined to endure) were granted. These were vague imitations of the Long Parliament's tax for the relief of Moorish captives. They were levied upon goods brought from or taken to the Mediterranean beyond Malaga in English ships with less than two decks, and carrying less than sixteen guns with two men to each gun, and were intended to stimulate the use of vessels capable of resisting the Moorish pirates. (This tax was included in the ' Act against Frauds,' quoted later.)

These, with one or two temporary imposts, were the only important customs granted during Charles's reign. The Coinage Duty, a special tunnage of 10s. on foreign wine, beer, and vinegar, and 20s. on foreign spirits, although collected by the Customs, may scarcely be considered a customs tax, for the proceeds went to the maintenance of the Mint. It is necessary at this point to abandon tariffs, and approach matters even more important.

The most momentous statutes of the reign were those dealing with navigation and the Plantation trade. Under the Act ' for the Encouragement and increasing of Shipping and Navigation,' passed in the year of Charles's accession, many classes of goods were made liable to aliens' Custom, even if imported by denizens, unless in English-built ships, with English masters, and three-fourths manned by English mariners, and brought direct from the places of growth or manufacture. By ' English-built ' was meant built and owned in England, Ireland, or the Plantations ; by ' English mariners,' the king's liege subjects from the same dominions. Several subsequent statutes amended and explained this Act, and the main provisions then stood as below :

Goods might not be taken from Asia, Africa, or America to England or Ireland except in ' English ships ' that were ' English manned,' and direct from the place of growth or manufacture. Sugar, tobacco, ginger, cotton, indigo, and woods used in dyeing, all which were entitled ' enumerated Plantation goods,' might not be put on board ship in the Plantations,* except for landing at other Plantations, or direct carriage to England. If intended for a foreign port they were to be brought to England, landed, and then reshipped for their destination. Ship-masters

---

* When the word ' Plantations ' is used without qualification such as ' Spanish,' French,' etc., it must be taken to mean ' English Plantations.'

proceeding from England or Ireland to the Plantations had to enter into bond before an English or Irish collector of customs to bring their Plantation goods to England direct, and if they entered a Plantation port from foreign to load cargo they had to give similar security there before shipment. European goods for the Plantations were to be first brought to England, landed there, and reshipped, except victual, horses, and *servants*, from Scotland or Ireland. Similar exemption was granted to wine of Madeira and the Azores laden at places of production, and goods laden at ports south and east of the Cape of Good Hope. These excepted goods might go to the Plantations direct, if the regulations as to English shipping and mariners were complied with. The Plantation governors were to take oath to provide to the best of their power for the due observance of the Navigation and Plantation laws. Foreign ships might only bring goods to England direct from the countries in which such ships were built. They were excluded from the Plantation trade. Coastwise traffic in England and Ireland was to be in " English " ships, with " English " mariners.

It is to be hoped the above account of these important regulations is understandable. The main points of their subsequent history will be duly indicated, but it must be clearly understood there will not be space in which to explain fully all their meanderings. Readers will perceive that they were inspired by the Commonwealth Act of Navigation, and that two ideals were steadfastly kept in view, one being permanent English dominance at sea, the other the establishment of England as 'a universal Staple.' It cannot be denied that these ideals were realized.

Yet even at the outset colonial merchants, especially those located in the American Plantations, were dubious, and later the American colonists came to regard the complicated restrictions as intolerable. Their goods were rendered dear in foreign markets, for some one had to assist in bearing the expense of the extra journey, and of the unnecessary unshipment and relading. Frequently vessels from the Plantations, which might have performed the direct voyage to Europe in safety, were cast away on the storm-swept English coast, while attempting to reach Cowes, Bristol, or London, in order to land their cargoes. This of course tended to a great extent to prevent the colonists from trading with Europe, and gave England almost a monopoly of Plantation traffic. The Acts bore hard upon Ireland, too, for all Plantation goods carried thither had first to be turned over in England. It remains substantial matter of debate whether the subsequent triumphs of England in naval war, which were hugely assisted by this method of making a large number of her sons familiar with the sea, and the vast increase in her carrying tonnage and oversea trade, were or were not discounted by the gradual impoverishment of Ireland, and that irremediable disaster, the severance of England from the thirteen mighty Provinces. There remains one thing to be said in favour of the old legislators. Whilst striving to ' corner ' trade and shipping, they did not altogether forget their duty towards national manhood.

Parliament continued to exert itself in attempts, not always wise or well-directed, to regulate industries. It bountied the woollen manufacture at the graziers' expense by prohibiting the exportation of wool. Ireland and the Channel Islands were included by the prohibiting Act, but it was provided that they and England might trade with each other. The provisions soon had to be strengthened. ' Owling,' or smuggling of wool outward, became a common practice, especially in Kent and Sussex.*

Foreign bone-lace, cutwork, embroidery, etc., were prohibited, and, still further to assist manufacturers, expor-

* It appears that the French Government secretly encouraged this illegal traffic, being desirous of destroying the English woollen industry.

tation was encouraged by repealing the aliens' double outward custom on English products, and making the rate the same as with denizens, except with respect to coals.

Meanwhile, as these measures impoverished the agriculturists, Acts had to be passed 'in Encouragement of Tillage.' The poundage outward on horses and cattle was reduced, and an impost levied on imported sheep and cattle. The duty on foreign corn was increased. It would seem that not only did the legislators believe that an Act of Parliament was as direct an instrument of enduring benefit as a fine harvest or a favourable tradewind, but that they conceived that two such instruments might be made to work in different directions without friction.

An Act was passed in the early part of the reign prohibiting the blending together of wines of various countries, and the adulteration of wine. The adulterants quoted were cider, perry, honey, sugar, molasses, raisin juice, herbs, and *flesh*. The people of England must have been sadly deficient in discrimination if their palates were not sufficient protection against such grotesque ingredients of fraud. The mixing of wine with isinglass, brimstone, and lime was forbidden. It is scarcely conceivable that merchants would use such articles as 'adulterants.' Isinglass has generally been deemed a valuable agent in 'fining'; brimstone and lime, one might reasonably conceive, could only have been used in the cleansing of foul casks.

The celebrated 'Act against Frauds,' issued soon after the Restoration, seems to have been drafted, so far as its preventive provisions obtained, after comprehensive study of the Long Parliament's ordinance of 1644, and certain other Commonwealth enactments. It allowed only three days for vessels in transit between Gravesend and London (to prevent smuggling in the middle reaches). At all outports vessels from foreign were to go direct to the place of unlading. Masters were to report their cargoes on oath.   Small parcels were to be placed in the King's Warehouse for security.   Wharfingers, carmen, porters, watermen, etc., dealing with uncustomed goods, were made liable to heavy penalties.   Aliens under twenty-one years of age were forbidden from entering goods as owners.   Sight and sufferance entries were to be promptly perfected.   Mail-boats were not to carry merchandise unless specially privileged.   Goods were not to be carried coastwise without sufferance and cocket, and a certificate of their being landed in the kingdom was to be furnished within six months.   Scotch goods were to be customed at Berwick or Carlisle.   The officers were enjoined not to show partiality to merchants.

C. 7, of 25 Car. II., forbade the Plantations dealing *with each other* without first bringing the goods to England, unless certain duties were paid at shipment, and accounted for to the English Commissioners of Customs. The Plantation officers might take these dues in kind if money were not forthcoming.

During this reign there were immense inland impositions, and the odious tax of ' Hearth Money '—a duty upon chimneys—was instituted.   The importation of fat cattle from Ireland was prohibited.   (This last Act was diligently evaded, and the importers frequently mixed a few English bullocks with the smuggled ' runts,' so that if the herd were seized they might be able to enter action for damages.   In 1680 it was enacted that in all such cases the English cattle should be forfeited as well as the Irish.)

Amongst the Treasury papers preserved in the Record Office there is a terse and lucid statement, dated 1680, which deals with the revenues collected during the latter part of Charles II.'s reign.   From this it appears that the net yield of the customs in the port of London, for the year ending Lady Day, 1680, was £554,964, and in the whole of the outports £136,941 ; total, £691,905. This was called the ' net ' because it represented the sum remaining after debentures, etc., had been paid.   But there was a charge of about £46,000 for 'management,' so the amount paid to the Exchequer may be taken as about £646,000. During a year and a half, ending Michaelmas, 1680, the Treasurer of the Navy received out of the customs about £476,000. But it appears that loans had been taken in anticipation of customs receipts, and out of the 'Loans on Customs' the naval Treasurer had received about £234,000 more. It appears that ordinarily the navy cost about £350,000 yearly. The year and a half quoted had been a time of stress. The military expenses were about £200,000 a year. The king's allowance for household expenses, as settled in 1667, was £90,000 a year. Perhaps, after all that has been said, Charles was not so very extravagant. £90,000 was not a great allowance for household expenses, but it appears that his servants' wages were often overdue.

In 1662 the Attorney-General proceeded in the Exchequer against a merchant, for the double custom on certain goods imported 'contrary to the new Act of Navigation.' The defendant demurred, pleading that the goods were forfeitable under the Act granting the subsidy of tunnage and poundage, and that if he paid the double custom demanded his goods might afterwards be seized. The Court overruled the demurrer, stating that after the Attorney-General had 'informed' upon a penal law no further proceedings could be taken.

During the same year a similar action was entered with regard to a quantity of Asiatic spices imported from Holland. Verdict for the Crown, but the defendant pleaded in arrest of judgment that it had not been particularly stated in the charge that the goods were 'not of the growth of Holland.' The quibble was successful.

In the same year it was reaffirmed that when an importer brought several parcels of wine in different ships, such parcels being each of nine and under ten tuns, his goods were liable to Prisage, unless proof were furnished that at time of lading there was not room on board for more.

In 1663 Sir William Waller, who farmed the Prisage and Butlerage of England, took action against Giles Travers, a London citizen, who had imported wines at several outports, and had raised the novel plea that as London citizens were exempt from Prisage such exemption obtained on their wine even if not imported into London. Hardres defended Travers, and displayed wonderful skill in twisting plain statements into puzzling conclusions, and furbishing up old records.

He quoted several singular charters of the City of London in support of his contention that wide discrimination should be made between the charter freeing London citizens of Prisage and that granting exemption to the 'barons' of the Cinque Ports. It appeared from his statement that there were charters allowing—

1. That in the City of London a man might be arrested for debt before the debt became due.

2. That a beadle, by mere virtue of his office, had power to search a house for suspicious persons.

3. That an executor might pay a debt on a simple contract prior to a debt secured under bond.

In discriminating between the charter exempting London citizens and that exempting the Cinque Ports barons, he insisted that the latter was granted because the Cinque Ports defended the realm, but the former for advancement of London trade. He claimed that the City of London was 'the Heart and Epitome of the whole kingdom, the King's Chamber, the Merchants whereof fill his Coffers by their customs paid,' and that the privilege of exemption from Prisage, being annexed to the *goods* of the citizen, obtained in every English port into which such goods might be brought for landing.

It was urged for the plaintiff that exemption had never before been granted to a London citizen except for wine imported into London. Hardres replied that complete exemption had been intended by the granter of the charter, and that 'non-user' could never destroy the validity of a grant. Therefore he claimed that London citizens were Prisage-free *per totam Angliam.*

The barons decided in favour of the plaintiff, Sir Matthew Hale, Chief Baron, making a special point of the fact that he had found, by consulting the Red Book of the Exchequer, that in the days of the Edwards exemption from Prisage throughout the realm had been occasionally granted for limited periods to certain guilds of merchants; that in all such cases it had been particularly stated that such exemption was *per totum Regnum;* and that had Edward III. intended to make the London citizens Prisage-free throughout the realm that provision would have been fully expressed in the charter.

It appears that during the Plague of 1665 the foreign trade of the port of London was terribly hampered. Defoe discoursed upon this, stating that all the 'extraordinary' (temporary) officers of customs were dismissed. This is borne out by Pepys' remark that in November, 1665, Sir G. Carteret was amazed to find the Upper Pool 'so empty of boats,' and the Custom-house quays deserted.

Defoe stated that the trade from London to the Levant was stopped for a time, as soon as tidings of the plague's ravages in London reached the Mediterranean ports. The statement may have been correct, for during the seventeenth century the Mediterranean coast-dwellers were frequently visited by the ghastly disorder, and they who are thus afflicted rarely miss a chance of imposing restrictions upon folk who suffer occasionally.

But much of Defoe's history of the Plague was mere opportunist journalism. For instance, he asserted that the eastern ports, profiting by the isolation of London, exported immense quantities of goods to Holland. Yet Holland and England were at war. He also stated that during the height of the disorder the ships lay in tiers from the Pool 'down the river as low as Gravesend.' Yet that extremely keen-eyed observer, Samuel Pepys, spent much of the autumn of 1665 upon the river, and failed to record anything of the kind.

It is apparent that the Excise revenue suffered severely. It was let to a host of speculators, and the records for this period contain many copies of requests for remission of rent. In the next great lease a clause appeared, providing that allowance should be made if the plague revived.

The account of this reign would be incomplete without a further reference to the immortal diarist. Pepys found time, amid all his gossiping and prying, to converse occasionally with Sir Philip Warwick, historian and economist. Warwick appears to have considered the assessments made by the Long Parliament and Commonwealth more effective than those made by Charles's advisers. In this he was of course correct, but his estimate of the amounts raised by the Parliament and Protector may be discounted. The country was cheaply governed during the interval between the death of one Charles and the accession of the other, no matter what Sir Philip might think—cheaply and effectively; its army and navy then, compared with the forces during Charles's reign, were luminous items of instructiveness.

Warwick even went so far as to coach Pepys upon the balance of trade. It is doubtful whether at this point Pepys did not become muddled—perhaps his own record of the argument was not correctly stated—but the old slyboots dismissed the matter with the pregnant remark, ' Though I do not remember the argument, yet methought there was a great deal in what he said.'

Sir Philip appears to have been a kind of amiable and self-elected oracle at the Treasury. He worried Pepys a deal with figures, yet to the end Samuel held him a good man; and no doubt he was, for he would not talk even statistics on a Sunday. Yet on the death of the Lord Treasurer in 1667 Pepys mournfully remarked that the slowness and remissness of the illustrious deceased had gone as far to undo the nation as anything else that had happened, which would indicate that Sir Philip's advice had either not been taken, or had been taken with disastrous results.

Pepys, as the world knows, though an industrious official, was not over-scrupulous. He not only pocketed bribes, but defrauded the revenue more than once.* While on important public business at Gravesend he bought a quantity of smuggled goods at ' a blind ale-house,' and afterwards philosophized over the smugglers, the evils of smuggling, and other incidental matters. His dealings with prize goods were extremely crooked. One of his little hauls was temporarily seized by the customs officers, and the constable left in charge, no doubt realizing that Pepys was wide-awake, made a subtle proposal, a proposal which Pepys was merely too shrewd to accept.

Several imposts on foreign merchandise were levied during the short reign of James II. One took the form of an increase of the tunnage rates on wines and vinegar, the proceeds of the extra duty being appropriated to ' weighty and important occasions ' and repairing naval ships. The Prisage, which for some years had been given to royal favourites, was by this Act shorn of much profit, the holders being made to pay an abated duty upon their prised goods.

The second impost was upon tobacco and sugar, Plantation tobaccos and sugars being preferentially treated. The new duties might be postponed if bond

* It is evident that such matters were thought little of in olden days, yet at certain periods corruption reached such a pitch that it was found necessary to issue special enactments. For instance, see 33 Hen. VI., c. 3—a statute aimed expressly against Exchequer officials.

were given for their payment within a specified time. The proceeds went to the supply of the king's 'weighty and important occasions,' and the discharge of debts due to the late king's servants and family.

The third was upon silks, linens, calicoes, and spirits, to endure for a period of five years. The collecting officers were enjoined to keep a special account of the proceeds, and pay them into the Exchequer weekly. Loans were invited up to £400,000, in anticipation of receipts, interest being guaranteed at 8 per cent. per annum, payable quarterly. Thus was established a seductive and deadly precedent, and from this period the 'funding' of taxes became fashionable. Whence of course England's National Debt, that seems likely to endure as long as England herself.*

Charles II.'s Act 'for the Encouragement of Tillage' was amended, it being provided that the price of corn, in accordance with which the inward duty on corn lapsed or fluctuated, and the exportation of corn was permitted or prohibited, should be stated by the justices in the counties at the quarter sessions, and by the City Fathers in London twice a year. The prices thus fixed were to be advised to the various collectors of customs.

It is noticeable that the preventive statutes up to this period frequently contained references to extensive smuggling. These became more frequent as the tariff grew more complicated, but the illicit traffic did not attain full development till the time of George II. The account must tarry till that picturesque period is approached, when there was a systematic and permanent traffic in contraband, sympathized with by the bulk of the population of the maritime counties.

'The Glorious Revolution' occurred in 1688. The first Parliament, which was to a large extent composed

* The impost appears to have produced only £93,000.

of self-elected members, did one good thing by abolishing the ' Hearth Money ' tax. Having thus commended themselves to the nation, the legislators proceeded to grant money without stint. All Charles and James's revenues, except Hearth Money, were temporarily continued for William's benefit. The proceeds of James's three imposts were appropriated thus : £60,000 to satisfy the outstanding claims of Charles II.'s unpaid servants, £600,000 from the residue to reward the United Provinces for having provided England with a king, and the rest towards the subjugation of Ireland and the war with France.

(In 1689 tunnage and poundage were formally granted, and a loan of £500,000 invited upon the proceeds.)

Special commissioners and officers were appointed to carry out the Act prohibiting the exportation of wool, and it was ordered that wool taken coastwise entered at the intended port of shipment before being brought within five miles of the coast. A central account of all wool carried coastwise was instituted at the London Custom-house. The exportation of wool from Ireland was limited to traffic between the principal Irish and the western English ports, so that there should be less opportunity of running Irish wool to the Continent.

French goods, and foreign spirits such as brandy and *aqua vitæ*, were prohibited during continuance of the war with France. The excise duties on tea, coffee, and chocolate, levied on the goods *after infusion*, were repealed, and a customs tax substituted, to be paid at time of landing. Foreign ' thrown ' silk was prohibited, except Italian silk, imported in accordance with the Navigation Act.

' The impost of 1690,' granted upon fifty-five articles of foreign merchandise, came into force on Boxing Day. The articles made liable were linen, silks, and calico, besides many classes of goods extensively used in manufactures—goods such as unwrought iron, raw silk, steel, and wool, together with such absolute aids towards comfortable existence as soap and candles. With most of the fifty-five articles the impost took the form of an addition to the poundage. The provisions as to the rating of various kinds of paper were remarkably complicated.

The Board of Customs informed the Treasury that the privateers brought in many French prizes, but that the customs officers, who were supposed to take an account of the goods, were often not allowed to go on board until the privateers' crews had helped themselves freely to the best of the captures, while the collectors, having to appoint extra tidesmen to look after the wounded and captives, had no time left in which to do their ordinary revenue work. The Treasury promised to appoint special commissioners and tidesmen to look after the privateers and their prisoners, but a long time elapsed ere the promise was fulfilled.

During the war in Ireland many Irish protestants fled to England, carrying their goods and effects with them. In most cases the Treasury allowed them to land and remove the goods and effects duty-free. The collectors on the western coast of England were often directed to furnish sums to the Commissioners of Transport, to be used in conveying Dutch and Danish mercenaries to Ireland.

The tobacco manufacturers of Bristol complained to the Board of the customs method of deducting 5 per cent. from the drawback payable on tobacco manufactured into roll and exported, the said deduction being intended to account for the addition of moisture during manufacture. They used the ancient plea that if the Customs continued the method the trade would leave the country. The Board, in forwarding the application to the Treasury, advised that full drawback should be taken on ' the bright fair kinds,' admitting that after importation the merchant had to cut away the stalk and abandon it, thus losing much of the weight he had paid duty on. But they insisted on continuing the deduction with regard to ' the

darker kind.' Later they relented, and advised that full
drawback should be allowed in all cases.

An English frigate, after a desperate engagement, in
which her captain and sailing-master were killed, had
captured two French men-of-war that were engaged in
convoying sixteen merchant ships, and brought the captains prisoners into Plymouth. The customs collector
took charge of them, and during the night they escaped
from his custody by filing through an iron bar, and appropriating a small boat which lay in the harbour. It
was stated in the report that the frigate would have captured the whole fleet of merchantmen if darkness had not
come on.

During 1689 the Board of Customs received hundreds
of applications for appointment to the office of landing-
waiter at London, although there were only thirty such
situations in the port. All the applicants were nominees
of influential persons, and had been referred to the Board
by the Treasury. Shortly afterwards a Treasury minute
conveyed to the Commissioners the king's expressed
opinion that many customs situations had been traded.
The Board replied that they were 'greatly sencible' of
the aspersion, and reminded the Treasury that by law
anyone who bartered an appointment was held incapable
of public office. They insisted that under their method
of appointing landing-waiters strict selection was practised, each Commissioner taking his turn in nominating
a candidate, and the appointment being discussed by a
full Board. The king then intimated that it would be
better if a majority of the Commissioners undertook to
nominate.

In 1690 certain Irish Jacobites who had escaped to
England made an attempt to take ship at Dover for
France, but were detected. It was found that the Dover
surveyor of customs had assisted in trying to secure their
escape, and he was thrown into prison with them.

Many detentions of cargoes under the Navigation Act
took place, but the Act was not tyrannically enforced.

Most of the detentions were of goods of one European nation brought in the ships of another, and in such cases the parties concerned petitioned the Treasury, and were usually let off with an injunction to compensate the detaining officers. Occasionally an English captain would arrive with Asiatic goods, and a crew consisting mainly of aliens. Then the goods he brought became liable to aliens' duties; but the captain might obtain remission if he proved that he left England with an English crew, that sickness and death had reduced their number, and that he had been compelled to engage foreigners.

A petition for a customs appointment in Dorset reached the Treasury, and they referred it to the Board. The Board recommended it to be 'sunk,' stating that since the prohibition of commerce with France there had been little genuine trade on the southern English coast. So little custom was taken at the Kentish ports that the officers' salaries had to be paid out of the London receipts.

The Archbishop of Dublin asked the Treasury to let him have an officer to inspect certain goods which he was about to send from London to Ireland, stating that if this were not done the officers at Chester would charge exorbitant duties, 'making every pair of shoes, not cobbled, new.'

The Receiver of the 4½ per cent. duties in the Leeward Islands informed the Board that he could not send his account and the proceeds* of collection to England for lack of convoy, and because the rate of exchange on bills from the West Indies was 15 to 20 per cent.

During this reign many heavy inland impositions were made, including a huge excise impost and a searching poll-tax. Most of the taxes had been 'funded,' and the national indebtedness swelled daily. Fiscal schemes, and devices towards borrowing, were the standing topics of parliamentary debate.

* Duties collected chiefly in kind.

The eleventh Act of 1690 expressed alarm. ' Whereas many great revenues, sums of money, and provisions, have been expended, granted, raised, and assigned, since the 5th November, 1688, on which day the king landed in England. . . .' Thus ran the preamble. A commission was appointed to take account of the revenues from lands, firstfruits, fines, forfeitures, subsidies, and imposts, and of the nation's ships, goods, and stores. The Act stated that large sums had been granted for the navy during James's reign, yet the ships had neither been repaired nor properly maintained. This may have been a suggestion that James or some of his officials had carried off the money, or it may have been designed to avert responsibility, for it is certain that great peculation was practised during William's time. The contracts were often made at 50 per cent., in some cases at 100 per cent., above the market price.

The prohibition of commerce with France having been evaded by the bringing in of French cargoes falsely described as prizes, and by the agency of gangs of armed smugglers, an Act was passed which among other preventive provisions contained clauses amplifying the powers of the magistracy, and authorizing sessions justices to deal summarily with smuggling cases. In 1691 the exportation of munitions of war to France, and the taking passage thither, were made acts of high treason. Exporters of merchandise to France were made liable to the Statute of Præmunire. In spite of these prohibitions an immense amount of wool was run, principally from Romney Marsh, and the revenue sloops on the Kentish coast were quite unable to cope with the desperate and well-armed smugglers.

A miller of Cheltenham planted a field with tobacco. The excise officers destroyed the crop, and the miller was fined £360. He approached the Treasury, pleading ignorance of the law, and the fine was remitted.

A spy who had been sent by the English Government to France returned, and accused Abraham Hough, a customs officer stationed at Margate, of having sent information to the French, by means of which the mission of espionage was frustrated. He denounced Hough and several other customs officers as Jacobites, and expressed a hope that there were ' none of that kidney on the Board of Customs.' The Treasury exculpated the officers.

The Bristol collector of customs, suspecting collusion between some of his officers and the Bristol merchants, employed a spy to watch proceedings, and discovered many flagrant irregularities. The officers concerned were fined £500, and compelled to exhibit themselves publicly in Bristol during Assize time, and to display a paper declaring the nature of their offences.

It appears that the officers exerted themselves to obtain custom upon wrecked goods, and thus frequently came into collision with the proprietors of ' droits.' The Lord Warden of the Cinque Ports complained that the collector at Deal had forcibly taken wreck from the custody of the Admiralty sergeant, and held it till the duties were paid. But both the Board and the Treasury upheld the collector.

In 1692 the Commissioners wrote the Treasury that much of the clandestine carrying out of coin and bullion, and the illegal importation of East India goods from Holland, was conducted by officers of the navy.

The officers of customs at Whitby sent news that five French privateers had chased an English vessel into Robin Hood's Bay, and had held the master captive till he sent to Scarborough for £200 as ransom. The privateers had been observed hovering for some time, and it was thought they were on the look out for an opportunity of carrying Jacobites to France.

News came from ' down West ' that a French privateer of twenty-eight guns had engaged an English ketch of ten guns, which was carrying a cargo of pressed men to the fleet. The ketch was captured, and the Frenchmen put ashore her cargo, consisting of 106 victims of the press. This privateer had captured five English merchantmen within sight of Padstow.

James, Lord Mordington, petitioned ' the King's Most Excellent Majesty ' as follows : ' A seizure of silks, muslins, and other things prohibited by law, was made lately in the cuntrey in a Coach-and-Six, and the same was carried into your Majestie's warehouse [in] London in the custody of Mr. Isaacson, booke-keeper of the said warehouse, and are to be condemned Thursday next, and One Hundred Pounds only to be returned into Your Majesty's Exchequer : wherfor your Petitioner humbly prays Your Majesty wd. be gratiously pleased to grant him an order for your Majestie's share in kind, by which your Majesty will preserve yr. Petitioner, his Lady, and childring, from sterving, at present not having bread,' etc. ' Granted—to send to the Commissioners of the Customes, to know at what value these things are appraised, and how much the king's part comes to.'

A sheaf of charges against the collector of Bristol reached the Treasury, with a letter signed ' Ambrose Williams.' The papers were referred to the Board. (The Commissioners then furnished a general statement on the matters involved, and referred to a recent special survey of the port of Bristol.)

There were nineteen charges, dealing with receipt of bribes and presents, composition of frauds, appropriation of officers' seizure awards, receipt of a sum of £100 from a merchant concerned in the cargo of a ship called *The Constant Love* (as acknowledgment of services rendered in obtaining removal of an embargo), neglect to destroy a crop of English-grown tobacco (in consideration of a present of fifteen guineas), illegal release of a vessel detained under the Navigation Act (recompense, a pair of silver candlesticks), *impolite behaviour towards the Patent Officers of the port*, etc.

The Board reported at great length upon the matter. 'Ambrose Williams,' they stated, 'is a person unknowne to us, and, tho' enquired after, not to be found.' As to the affair of *The Constant Love*, they had summoned the merchant named as briber, a 'Mr. Gardiner, of good reputation,' and he had furnished denial upon oath. As to the English-grown tobacco, they had found that the collector was absent from the port at the time quoted, and they had failed to obtain corroboration with regard to the bribe of fifteen guineas. In short, after spending much time in investigation, 'the said severall persons being heard face to face,' they had decided to 'support' the collector. They ended by referring to a mass of enclosed 'testimony, which,' said they, 'is quite opposed' (conflicting).*

The following is a copy of a statement sent by the Board to the Treasury, with reference to disputes as to interest due on duties in arrear:

'*The State of the Account between the Officers of the Customs and the East India Company.*

'The East India Company are Debtors to their Ma^ts. for the Interest for forbearance on severall Entrys, made up from ye times of their first Entring at Sight to the placing the Same to Acco^t. in ye King's officers books, The Summe of:

	£	s.	d.
'The said Comp^y pretend that by reason that they paid in severall considerable Summs of money in part for the duties on their Said goods, severall months & days before ye quite P'fecting their said Entrys (which indeed wee doe find they did) that they are overcharged in that Acco^t of Interest† ye Summe of	5,428 663	10 18	2 6
	4,764	11	8

* The collector had previously been instrumental in discovering extensive frauds, and securing the pecuniary punishment of certain officers concerned (*vide* p. 130).

† The Customs had charged the Company interest on duties

	£	s.	d.
	4,764	11	8

' And more that they say is due to them for the Interest on Severall Tallys, which was not allowed them, this Acco^t being depending, ye Summ of ..   ..

	1,492	10	4
	3,272	1	4

' There is likewise due from the Said Company for their Duties on the last 4 Shipps ye Summe of—Estimate—   ..   ..

which they have not fully p'fected, because they would have allowance for Damage on tea, as they pretend, because at ye Sale they had not for ye whole anything considerable more than what ye same was sold for.*

	45,000	0	0
	48,272	1	4

' And they make another pretence : That a certaine Commodity they formerly past as floretta Yarne, at 8 p.c. value, is upon a better information a Raw Silk : But this is but a bare pretence, because Raw Silk is charged but with 5 p. cent. for this new Duty of Impost, when as Floretta Yarne, being a manufacture, is Lyable to 20 P. Cent.

' Of which Summe of   ..   ..   ..

according to this own Acco^t they have paid and promise to speedily pay in ye remainder, or one ½ thereof as ye last week and ye other within one month after : Yet for all that promise of their Govern^{or} Sr. Thom^{as} Cook : They have in fact paid not one penny more '

	48,272	1	4
	20,000	0	0
	28,272	1	4

From the above it seems that the Company were either in straits, or conscious of the undoubted fact that the customs accounts were in a muddled condition.

Later the Board complained afresh, and furnished, in place of the previous 'Estimate' of duties due, what purported to be an exact account.

---

overdue. From this charge, and the total of the duties, the Company claimed a deduction on account of duties paid in advance, and of interest due on outstanding tallies.

* This means that the Company claimed to have made little profit by sale of the tea, the goods being damaged by salt water, and the Customs having failed to make allowance for the said damage.

' Custom House,
    ' 31st August, 1692.

' To the Right Honble the Lords Commrs. of their
                        Matys. Treasury.

' *The Commrs. for managing and causing to be Leavied and
collected their Maties. Customs, Subsidy, and other Dutys.*

' The said Commrs. (after many disappointments in the
daies wherein the Committee of the East India Company
have promised to satisfy their demands of such sums as
appeare to bee due to their Maties. from that Company,
as well from the Customs and Imposts on the Entryes of
their ffoure Last Ships, as upon Accompt of Interest for
the time wherein they failed of their former payments)
thinke it their duty to lay before their Lordpps. (in the
paper thereunto annexed) the present state of that
Account, as it was adjusted by the Patent Officers to the
17th Currant, and since sent to the Govern^or of the Company, without further satisfaccon than a promise of payment, which has hitherto proved ineffectuall : Humbly
submitting it to their Lordpps. that such speedy and
effectual Remedy may bee taken upon the Bonds they
have entred into upon this Occasion as to their Lordpps.
shall seeme meet.

                        ' C. Godolphin.
                          G. Boothe.
                          J. O. Werden.
                          Robert Southwell.
                          Robert Clayton.'

They annexed a statement as to separate amounts due
upon the cargoes of certain vessels belonging to the Company ' for sights* yet unperfected.' It appears that the
following sums were owed and overdue :

* ' Sights ' : the entries ' upon sight,' sometimes called ' entries
upon view.' These were documents permitting the Company's
officials to ' view ' the cargoes upon landing. An account of the
goods was then taken by both Company and Customs, and the
Company were expected to ' perfect ' each sight within a specified
period, and pay the duty.

	£	s.	d.
Upon the cargo of the *Princess Anne* (Captain Maurice)	15,200	15	8½
Upon the cargo of the *Josiah* (Captain Gayer)	13,334	19	10
Upon the cargo of the *Royal James and Mary* (Captain Buck)	9,106	4	0½
Upon the cargo of the *Defence* (Captain Heath)	10,384	6	8
	48,026	6	3
As interest at 6 per cent. on the respective sums from the dates on which they were payable: £802 3s. 11d., £686 2s. 0d., £467 0s. 8d., £532 11s. 8d.	2,487	18	3
Arrears of interest upon other cargoes, incurred before November 1, 1690 ..	5,175	5	7

	£	s.	d.
Paid in part of this account	23,272	1	4
Interest to be forborne on account of above payment	419	4	7
	23,691	5	11
Moneys due ..	31,998	4	2
	55,689	10	1

55,689 10 1

At the foot of this account the Commissioners added the significant statement :

' Besides ye Customes for Tea and all Dutys for their China Ware in the *Defence*, for which wee had noe value to compute ye same by.'

(This statement is difficult to understand,* but it would almost seem that the Company had succeeded in landing, viewing, and disposing of the greater part of the *Defence's* cargo without the cognizance of the customs officers. For it appears from a general study of the records that at

---

* It is by no means safe to draw confident deductions from statements such as the above. The Commissioners themselves were often misled as to the true condition of affairs with regard to sums due, many of the clerical officers being vastly in arrear with their work. The clumsy methods of expression adopted by certain members of the secretarial staff, and the grotesque fashion in which they stated matters of accompt, render the documents extremely puzzling to the direct thinker.

this time the duties were not levied as percentages on the gross prices at the sales.)

A petition reached the Treasury from Mary Jones, daughter-in-law to the late collector of Lyme Regis. She stated that when the duke of Monmouth landed in England he took by force £200 from the Lyme Regis customs receipts. Her husband, who had succeeded his father as collector, had been ordered to make good the loss, and, dying shortly afterwards, had left his estate burdened with the charge. The Board reported favourably upon her petition, and the Treasury granted it. There were other customs charges on the estate, and the Board seem to have thought that this remission would enable the widow to pay them.

Another huge impost was laid upon many foreign articles, some being surtaxed by rate, others by direct additions to duty. This tax, which became historic as 'The Impost of 1692,' was appropriated to 'the king's extraordinary occasions.' The odious increases in the salt poundage commenced with this Act. The tunnage on French wine was increased, and an additional 25 per cent. *ad valorem* laid on other French goods.

During the time of the Commonwealth an ordinance had been issued against the false packing of butter and cheese for exportation. Its provisions had been practically reaffirmed by a statute of Charles II., but afterwards the control of the export trade in butter and cheese had been dominated by the Cheesemongers' Society of London. This syndicate, under pretence of enforcing the Act, frequently sent its agents to the various ports, where they behaved in arbitrary fashion, 'to the great oppression of farmers.' William's parliament prohibited the unfair preferences and extortionate actions of the London agents, and directed shipmasters to forbear the practice,

previously common, of refusing shipment to goods un-
controlled by the meddlesome Society.   Factors were
enjoined to put their own seals upon all their packages of
butter and cheese, and were made responsible for the
quality of their goods.

Later there were several enactments of prohibition,
affecting foreign 'hair buttons' and the importation of
brandy in casks of less than 60 gallons.   This latter was
to prevent the bringing in of small casks for running.
The foreign silk stuffs known as 'alamodes and lustrings'
were subjected to close supervision on importation, the
motive announced being the protection of the English
silk manufacturers.

The Act of 1692, for the encouragement of privateering,
appears to have had a disastrous effect upon the French
mercantile marine, which at this time was harried unmercifully by scores of privateers, mostly hailing from the
southern English ports.

A tonnage duty was imposed upon shipping, two-thirds
payable by the importers of goods, one-third by the shipowners.   The proceeds of this tax, together with those
of certain existing customs and excise duties, were to be
kept apart, and used to guarantee a loan from the public.
In connexion with this loan a famous national institution
came into existence, the sum of £1,200,000 being subscribed by a corporation, to be called the 'Governors and
Company of the Bank of England.'

In 1694 additional poundage was levied upon spices
and pictures, and the duties on tea, coffee, etc., were
increased.   The first part of this grant afterwards
became one of the standing branches of revenue, under
the name of 'The Spice and Picture Duty.'   The
right of customs officers to 'overtime' for attendance
beyond the legal hours was recognized under this Act

the Commissioners of Customs in London and the collectors at outports being directed to fix the amounts that merchants should pay.

About this time many requests to be employed in lucrative offices reached the Treasury, and many seductive proposals of reform. In the latter one curious point of similarity obtained. The success of the schemes was made to appear a direct consequence of the employment of the schemers. It will be as well to quote two or three.

One William Culliford, ex-Commissioner of Irish Revenue, asked to be made a surveyor-general of customs, and on being reminded that the post had been abolished, requested a London surveyorship, with a yearly grant of £500 in excess of the ordinary salary, and a commissionership when one became vacant. It would seem that he based his claim upon the fact that one George Cruffe, a customs officer out of employment, had shot him ' with two bullets,' and that he still carried the bullets in his body.

An enthusiastic reformer submitted a scheme, arranged under six heads thus :

1. That any officer who succeeded in getting a superior convicted of fraud should be rewarded with the superior's office. (The Board of Customs replied that this was impossible, as an illiterate tidesman might thus become a surveyor.)

2. That the practice as to compounding seizures should be amended. (The Board answered that the proposer appeared to know little of Exchequer practice.)

3. That shipmasters should be prosecuted for falsely reporting cargoes. (The reply was that this was the practice.)

4. That a surveyor-general of outports should be appointed. (The Board replied that they did better by sending experienced men occasionally.)

5. That the number of officers should be reduced.

(The Board stated that they had recently increased the staff, on account of loose management by the previous Commissioners.)

6. That the offices of such customs patentees as employed deputies should be abolished, especially that of the head searcher at Gravesend. (It was answered that there was no head searcher at Gravesend, and that all patent officers whose salaries were paid out of the Exchequer were empowered to employ deputies.)

The author of this proposal seems to have retired discomfited.

An enterprising person, named William Carter, appears to have directed his energies partly to the suppression of owling, and partly to the conspicuous advertisement of his abilities. In a petition to ' My Lords of the Treasury ' he claimed to have brought about the capture of thirty owling shallops within a period of fourteen months. He also wrote a pamphlet upon the prevention of wool smuggling, embodying a scheme of exact account and supervision of all wool produced in England—a scheme which, if carried into effect, would certainly have brought about a rising of the English yeomanry. Both Board and Treasury soon displayed signs of being tired of Mr. Carter ; but he persisted, repeatedly asking for grants of money in order that he might effect captures, and painting lurid pictures of the doings of the Kentish owlers. He succeeded in obtaining advances amounting to several hundreds of pounds, but in the end the Treasury repulsed him.

Then came forward Lord Lanesboro and his coadjutor, Onesiphorus Albin. They started with a statement that the aliens' duties were not properly collected, and that the ancient statute, providing that aliens should expend a moiety of their takings within the realm, was not enforced. They raised the old cry that aliens were usurping English trade, and tagged it with a hint that this would continue until Lord Lanesboro and Onesiphorus Albin were provided with extensive powers of supervision.

Their proposals were referred to the Board, and the

Board countered effectively by stating that the system of compelling aliens to expend their takings in England had lapsed since Charles I.'s time, and that aliens had since taken little part in the carrying trade. They also made cheerful comparison between the existing state of English commerce and its condition in days of yore. 'Then,' said the Board, 'there was no East Indian or Plantation trade, and such trade as existed was mostly in Aliens' hands.' They opposed the employment of extra officials at high salaries, stating that such appointments could only be justified by the multiplication of restrictions, and that too many restrictions were unfavourable to commerce. 'The freer and more easy trade is in any place, the more it flourishes.' A remarkable statement, surely, for a Customs Board to make.

The brace of reformers returned to the charge with a proposal to farm the aliens' duties. This scheme was also referred to the Commissioners, who reported against it, asserting that since Charles II. abolished the customs farm in 1671 it had been the general opinion that farming should not again be resorted to. (The Commissioners appended and approved a report of the Board of 1679 on a similar application. This report suggested that the impositions upon aliens should not be enforced too strictly, and propounded as a query 'whether the king in point of his customs as well as the Trade of the Kingdome is not a greater gainer by the not too Troublesomely collecting the Dutys upon Aliens.')

Onesiphorus made a third attempt single-handed, going back on his previous proposals, and graciously admitting that it would be unadvisable to let any portion of the customs to farm. Still, he was desirous of having a finger in the pie, and offered to advance a substantial sum for the use of the Crown, to be repaid out of the aliens' customs. So far as can be gathered, nothing came of this, and it is probable that the applicant turned his energies into other channels.

Applications of the kind were not always directed

towards obtaining appointments in the Customs, for in 1691 a gentleman who had been surveyor of Greenwax approached My Lords, asking to be restored to his office. He said that since his discharge he had employed all his means in detecting ministerial and official corruption, and had thus got into debt. He wound up with the following plaintive appeal : ' If My Lords will do nothing, please let me know it, that I may hide from my creditors till Parliament meets.'

It was directed that all ' molten silver ' exported should be stamped.

In 1696 French goods were again heavily surtaxed, the tunnage on French wine and vinegar being increased, a heavy tunnage laid upon French brandy, and an additional 25 per cent. *ad valorem* on all other French goods. This last was to endure for twenty-one years, but it eventually became one of the permanent branches, under the title of ' The second 25 per cent. on French goods.' Parliament had succeeded in establishing many incitements towards smuggling, but none so stimulating as this.

The exportation of stocking-frames was prohibited, and their removal or sale within the kingdom made subject to registration by the Wardens of the London Framework-Knitters' Society.

An Act was passed to allow the importation of plate and ' battered money for coining purposes,' and, to defray the expenses of coining, an impost, at varying rates of 20 and 25 per cent. *ad valorem* in excess of all previous duties, was laid upon foreign paper, vellum, etc.

Cap. 28 of 1696-1697 prescribed the methods of receiving and accounting for moneys paid into the Exchequer. (This is not Customs history, but it is as well to furnish a précis of the Act.)

Moneys received, whether as loans or revenue, were to be counted and weighed by the Tellers. They were to record the amounts and particulars on slips of parchment, which were to be thrown down the Pipe into the Tally Court, whence the tallies of receipt were issued. The Tellers were to be charged with the sums, and to hold the cash till authorized by debenture from the Auditor of Receipt to make disbursement. The Auditor-General's authority for issuing debentures was to be the king's order under the Great Seal, or an order under the Privy Seal, or an Act of Parliament. (A statement of the condition of the loan Funds was to be displayed constantly in the Auditor-General's office.)

The money received in the room above was to be kept in chests under three locks, one key being held by the Tellers, one by the Clerk of Pells, and one by the senior Deputy-Chamberlain who struck the tallies of receipt. At the end of each day the key-holders were to assemble in the Court of Receipt, and the Tellers to produce the day's takings, made up in bags. The Chamberlain and the Clerk of Pells were to weigh the bags as an approximate check, ticket them, and put them into the chests. Then each key-holder was to lock the chests with his own key.

The debentures issued below by the Auditors of Receipt were not to be paid till the following day. Then the key-holders were to assemble in the Court of Receipt, unlock the chests, take out sufficient money to discharge the account, and lock the rest up again. The amount thus withdrawn was to be left with the Tellers.

The Auditor of Receipt was to make an exhaustive survey every twenty-eight days.

Additional duties were levied for a period upon Scotch coal, and upon English coal carried coastwise, the Customs to collect the same, and appoint meters and weighers.

Duty was to be paid before breaking bulk, on the quantity of 'coal reported. If by measurement or weighing the cargo were found to exceed the quantity reported, the amount in excess was to be duty-paid by ' post entry.'

An added subsidy of tunnage and poundage on imports was granted for a period, to aid in furnishing an allowance for the king's household. This was subsequently continued, and made permanent as ' The New Subsidy.'

It was enacted that cases and dial-plates of English-made clocks and watches should not be exported without the ' works ' appertaining.

The law as to foreign alamodes and lustrings was amended. Their importation was restricted to the port of London, and even into London they might only be imported by special licence from the Commissioners of Customs.

An additional duty was levied on whale-fins, etc., the cargoes of the English Greenland Company paying only one-half of the new rates. This became a permanent impost, and powerfully protected the Company's trade.

The minimum legal weight at which packages of tobacco might be imported was fixed at 224 pounds net. Smaller packages were forfeitable. This, like the previously quoted regulation as to the legal content of spirit casks, was intended as a check to smuggling.*

An additional 15 per cent. *ad valorem* was levied on muslins and similar goods of the East Indies. The ' value ' to which the rate applied was the gross price realized at sale. This also became a permanent impost, as ' The 15 per cent. on Muslins.'

The wearing of East India silks and stuffs was prohibited. Their importation was restricted to London, where they might be landed and warehoused for exportation only. When thus exported they paid half the old subsidy rate outwards. Officers were deputed to inspect the East India Company's books and stock at stated

* Even at the present day there is a ' legal limit ' as to minimum size of imported casks of spirits, and ' weights ' of tobacco.

periods, and to prepare an account for each session of Parliament.

Meanwhile the Flemings, finding that their export trade suffered on account of the prohibition of foreign lace and cut-work under Charles II.'s Act, had prohibited English woollen manufactures. The English Parliament in response directed that the English prohibition of lace, etc., should cease three months after cancellation of the Flemings' prohibition of English woollens. Then Parliament repealed all duties upon English woollen manufactures outward, and provided that the ancient aulnage duties on cloth, which had been granted by Charles II. to the duke of Richmond and his heirs, should cease *on expiration of the grant in* 1724.

The collectors of customs at the outports were often in difficulties, the claims for bounties on exported corn frequently exceeding the amounts of official moneys available for their discharge.* They were therefore directed by an Act of 12-13 William III., when short of funds, to give each claimant of corn bounty a certificate of the amount due, which he might produce, with the debenture, to the Receiver-General of Customs in London, who might then pay the bounty out of the London moneys. It is not clear whether the claimant might employ an agent to do this, and probably many country merchants who exported small quantities would forego their claims rather than travel to London for their money, and risk being called upon to 'Stand and Deliver' on the way back. For at this time the roads swarmed with daring highwaymen, so that a special reward of £40 was offered by statute to anyone who arrested a road thief. (The highwayman's horse, pistols, and money, if unclaimed, became the property of his captor.)

In 1701 the minimum tonnage for vessels bringing foreign spirits was fixed at 15 tons. The trade in contraband spirits was steadily increasing. It should be

---

* The bounty system on exported corn was first instituted in 1689.

explained that the only real customs duties on foreign spirits were the old subsidy poundage, the impost on brandy, the French duty, and the Coinage ; but in addition to these there were heavy excise duties which, being payable on landing, were usually collected by the customs officers, although paid into the Excise account.*

Whilst diligently stiffening the import tariff, Parliament had lightened the taxes here and there upon native products. They had made Irish flax, hemp, and linen duty-free on importation. They had reduced the outward custom on English tin, and to balance this had increased the duties upon drugs imported in English ships, which under the Old Subsidy had enjoyed preferential rating. They had remitted the outward duty on English sail-cloth and bone-lace, and, as a necessary consequence of the bounty system, the outward duties on corn and bread. They had allowed a temporary drawback of the excise duty upon English malt, and prohibited foreign malt during the period.

Yet they had found time to complicate still deeper the provisions of the Plantation Acts, enjoining that ships lading or unlading at the Plantations should be subject to the Customs rules and searches as obtaining in England, and granting the Plantation customs officers powers accordingly. It had been thought that Plantation goods which had paid custom at the Plantations† might be exported thence without being first brought to England. Parliament made the matter clear by forbidding anything

---

* There was an additional duty payable upon foreign salt at landing, which was not really a customs duty, though collected by the customs officers. There were continual changes in the collection of many duties. Even the French duty on spirits was by 6 Geo. II. made an excise duty. An exact record of all these changes would only mystify readers. Some of the more advanced economists of the time ascribed the complications in collection to the villainy of legislators, whom they accused of wilfully creating hundreds of unnecessary offices, with no other object than the increase of their own political influence and scope of patronage.

† These would be goods carried from one colony to another (see p. 118).

of the kind. All commercial laws previously made *in the Plantations* were declared repugnant to the English Plantation Acts. The Treasury and the Commissioners of Customs were jointly empowered to appoint the Plantation customs officers. All ships trading with the Plantations were to be registered by the English collectors of customs, unless colonial-built, when they were to be registered by the chief Plantation revenue officer. The exportation of wool from the Plantations was forbidden.

The Navigation Act was strengthened. Masters of vessels going to the Fisheries (Newfoundland and New England) were ordered to carry a certain proportion of ' green men '—viz., men who had never been at sea as mariners. The collectors of customs were to obtain each master's declaration upon oath as to this, before allowing fishing-vessels to leave England. This was a laudable device towards increasing the stock of English mariners.

' The 4½ per cent. duties ' passed quite under control of the Commissioners of Customs. These duties had been granted to Charles II. upon all ' dead commodities ' exported from Barbadoes. They were usually collected in kind, and from the time of grant up to the ninth year of William's reign had been farmed. The goods collected under this tax, which since its institution had been extended to the whole of the Leeward Islands, were from the time of cession sent to London by the collectors of the islands, and stored in a separate warehouse. They consisted principally of sugars, and these were distinguished in the official memoranda as ' the King's sugars.' Two officials, the ' Husband ' and a Controller, supervised the warehouse. Thrice a year the 4½ per cent. goods were put up to auction. The sales (afterwards advertised in the ' London Gazette ') were without reserve, and if any parcel of goods failed to realize the value at which the collector had invoiced it the collector was surcharged.

Throughout the reign great exertions were made to put down ' owling.' Every owner of sheep living within ten miles of the coast in Kent or Sussex was required to furnish an account of his wool within three days after shearing. No inhabitant of Kent or Sussex, within fifteen miles of the coast, might buy wool without entering into bond not to export it. The price offered for English wool on the Continent must have been immensely higher than that obtainable in England, to induce the Kentish and Sussex men thus to brave the formidable penalties of the law forbidding exportation.

The inland impositions during William's reign were certainly severe : some of them appear grotesque. Not only were there taxes upon heads and windows, but *direct* impositions upon marriages, births, and burials. The tax upon widowers and bachelors, though it lacked the doubtful dignity that enshrouded most of the ancient impositions, was perhaps excusable, for the war had made marriageable men scarce. But what of the tax upon tobacco-pipes, ' for carrying on the war with France,' and the tax on hawkers and pedlars (collected by the most corrupt set of officials known to English history), which was appropriated to paying the interest of the transport debt incurred in the reconquering of Ireland ?

It is almost terrible to contemplate the progress of the taxes during this reign. They followed each other like billows sweeping in on a lee shore, and the silence with which the people regarded their advance is quite unaccountable. War and taxation, and the shouldering of their grievous results upon Posterity, were the chief objects of legislative energy. Be it noted that the war, which was begun with the avowed object of keeping out the Stuarts, soon became a mere crusade in defence of Dutchmen. Certain pamphleteers of the time did not scruple to express their opinion that the piling-up and subdividing, the re-sorting and re-complicating, of imposts, were the results of ministerial design—a threefold design : to favour the Dutch at the expense of English commerce, to provide opportunities for stock-jobbing and commissions, and to increase the ministers' powers of patronage. The first point of supposition was probably unfounded ;

the second and third seem plausible. Anyhow, it is evident that such religious and political advantages as accrued from the Glorious Revolution were extremely expensive benefits. The finger of the sedate little Dutchman was thicker than the loins of the Stuarts.

Anne's first Parliament was soon at work in the prevention of salt smuggling. Customs officers were empowered to board vessels ' hovering off the coast ' with salt cargoes, and compel them to come into port and unlade. It was enjoined that all foreign salt should be imported in bulk.

In 1703 additional tunnage and poundage were granted, at one-third the rate of William's ' New Subsidy.' This became a permanent branch of revenue as " The ⅓ Subsidy.' The importation of woollen manufactures was prohibited.

The Commissioners of Customs issued a quaint order, providing that one of their number should attend daily at the Bench Office in the Long Room of the London Customhouse, ' to ensure solemnity.' The ' Bench Officers ' were the higher indoor clerical patentees, and their deputies were very lazy fellows. The Board also decided that the recommendation of successors to vacant officerships in the outdoor branch should be vested in the Commissioner who might happen to be ' in the Chair ' at the Board Room when such vacancies were first made known.* Previously each Commissioner had held his own bunch of ports, and nominated successors to vacancies in his own district.

A Treaty of Commerce had meanwhile been concluded between England and Portugal, by which the Portuguese engaged to admit ' for ever ' the woollen goods of England, and the English to admit the wines of Portugal at such rates that the duty demanded on them should never be more than two-thirds that taken on French wines. The latter provision was to endure whether peace or war obtained between England and France. The English

* The Commissioners occupied the Chair week about.

preference of ' Port ' set in with the ratification of this
treaty.*

Additional tunnage and poundage were granted, at
two-thirds of the Subsidy rates, on all foreign wines, and
on all other foreign goods with a few unimportant exceptions. This became permanent as ' The ⅔ Subsidy.'
Thus it may be stated that on nearly all foreign goods
the duties were three times as much as those granted
in 1660. The special imposts on numerous articles must
also be taken into account, and the tremendous ' French
duties.'

In 1704 an additional impost was laid on spice, pic
tures, drugs, coffee, tea, chocolate, chinaware, white
calico and muslins, Indian dimity, and other cotton manufactures. This became permanent as ' The Additional
Spice and Picture Duty.'

A petition in duplicate reached the Treasury, one copy
being addressed to the Queen, one to the duke of Marl-
borough. It was from the merchants of London, stating
that some of the customs ' landing-waiters ' (officers who
took account of goods at landing) were Frenchmen, that
French goods were not properly excluded, and that the
landing-waiters made it a practice to work several ships
at once, so as to gain all the fees with a minimum amount
of trouble. Soon after, whether on account of the petition or no doth not appear, the Board of Customs directed
the London landing-waiters to desist from wearing swords
while on duty.

In 1705 the Commissioners, realizing that ' solemnity '
was as necessary in the Board Room as in the Bench
Office, directed that an ' instrument ' should be provided
with which to keep order. (The records are blank as to
the nature of the instrument.) Later the Lord Treasurer

---

* Said the blunt and heroic Borrow, in 1833 : ' The English,
who have never been at war with Portugal, who have fought for
its independence on land and sea, and always with success, who
have forced themselves, by a treaty of commerce, to drink its
coarse and filthy wines, are the most unpopular people who visit
Portugal.'

acquainted the Board that a person recommended for the post of collector of Milford was quite ignorant of customs work. After some discussion of this the Lord Treasurer announced his determination that none should be appointed to a collectorship 'unless bred up in customs business.' In the following year the Board enjoined that none should be appointed a 'tidesman' unless able to write. (The tidesmen were employed in boarding, rummaging, and watching ships, and tallying goods out and in.)

Before ending this chapter, a few extracts from a treatise published by one Charles Davenant, LL.D., may be profitably quoted. Davenant appears to have been at one time Commissioner of Excise. Why he left that department does not appear, but there are occasional bursts of peevishness in his book which seem to indicate that he would not have objected to return, if things could be made comfortable for him. He was dreadfully bitter against the Excise Commissioners, and never missed a chance of girding at them. Shortly after he published his treatise he was an Inspector-General of customs in London, and considered an authority upon revenue matters. He was a shrewd and observant man, but his 'tables of revenue,' like most of such statements, should be viewed with caution, despite his opportunities of consulting with the Receiver-General. He must have been a plucky and outspoken person : few, even now, would dare to attack the chiefs of an important department, to accuse them openly of incompetence and favouritism, and to suggest that their duties should be handed over to farmers.

Davenant charged the ministry with being hopelessly under influence of 'the wretched projectors and contrivers of deficient funds,' and with having under such influence formed funds in anticipation of the proceeds of various taxes, whilst having no definite conception of what the taxes would realize. He ridiculed the practice of conferences between high revenue officials and merchants. 'There is hardly a Society of Merchants,' said he, 'that

would not have it thought the whole prosperity of the
kingdom depends upon its single traffic. And at any
time when merchants come to be consulted their answers
are dark and partial, and when they deliberate in assemblies 'tis generally with a bias, and a secret eye to their
own advantage.' (That this statement was true as the
light of heaven no man of the world can conscientiously
deny.)

He likened the financiers of the period to the corrupt
ministers of Spain, who by their fostering of " funds " had
devoted the greater part of the Spanish revenue to the
payment of interest, and paralyzed and ruined a nation
once lordly and invincible. He boldly stated that it was
often to the advantage of corrupt officials that the nation's
affairs should be entangled, even as unjust stewards might
thrive under encumbered masters.

He denounced the system of encouraging the formation
of funded duties which barely realized the interest, and
left the principal a burden on the coming years, and
declared that a multiplicity of fund-holders meant ruin
to the rural interest, causing moneyed people to congre-
gate and abide near the centre of stock-jobbing. He
enunciated the unchallengeable proposition that it could
never be for the enduring public benefit that one class
should obtain an immovable hold upon the goods produced
by the rest. He recommended economy, peace, and
strenuous application to the discharge of liabilities, as
the surest means of making the new usurers ' quit their
hold.' (Better economic doctrine had never been
preached, and it would have been well for modern England
if Davenant's sermon had taken effect. But sound doctrine can only take root in sound minds, and at the time
most Englishmen who could read and write had gone mad
on stock-jobbing, and held that the world might be made
rich, not by productive effort, but by merely juggling
with the counters of wealth.)

It is foolish to believe that because an outspoken man
is inspired by a sordid motive there can be no truth in his

utterances. The most luminous and inspiring truths have been spoken by disappointed self-seekers. Readers may therefore applaud Davenant's doctrine, and assess the integrity of his motives by what comes after.

He attacked the Commissioners of Excise, and furnished most disconcerting statistics. He accused the Commissioners of having for years neglected to visit their officers, of discharging efficient gaugers to gain opportunity of installing favourites, and of engaging certain collectors who embezzled £25,000. He stated that there were men on the Excise Board whose fortunes made them above their work, and whose ignorance of revenue matters rendered them incapable of doing it, and showed that in spite of the huge increases in the excise rates the revenue was not so large as when Dashwood farmed the duties in 1680. He insisted that a regulated and judicious system of farming would be better than management by an incompetent Board, as the farmers would at least encourage energetic collection, and would not spend days in wrangling across a table ' over My Friend and Thy Friend.'

Among the many quaint hints furnished, one was conspicuous—viz., that the English disliked a variety of new duties, though they might answer with alacrity impositions with which they were acquainted, especially if not called upon to render the same " in dry money, out of the course of trade." (It is strange that so acute an observer failed to note that whenever a tax on commodities is altered someone who has an aptitude towards forestalling gets a splendid chance of plundering the public.)

Some of Davenant's figures may be interesting to modern observers of Commerce. For instance, he stated that the imports from the Plantations reached the annual value of £950,000, and that about two-thirds of these were re-exported. He displayed prophetic anticipation of a future American revolt. ' Wise countries never teach their colonies the art of war.'

In short, his treatise contained, amid many ingenious

statistics and some vagarious expressions, a deal of good material, and it may be read with profit even by the economists of the present day.*

LIST OF AUTHORITIES.

Permanent branches of revenue : 12 Car. II., c. 4 ; 14 Car. II., c. 11 ; 18-19 Car. II., c. 5 ; 2 W. and M., c. 4 ; 2 W. and M., s. 2, c. 4 ; 4 W. and M., c. 5 ; 5-6 W. and M., c. 20 ; 6-7 W. and M., c. 7 ; 7-8 Wm. III., c. 20 ; 9 Wm. III., c. 13 ; 9 Wm. III., c. 23 ; 9 Wm. III., c. 45 ; 11 Wm. III., c. 3 ; 7-8 Wm. III., c. 31 ; 8-9 Wm. III., c. 25 ; 2-3 Anne, c. 18 ; 3-4 Anne, c. 3 ; 3-4 Anne, c. 18.

Temporary imposts : 14 Car. II., c. 10 ; 1 Jas. II., c. 3 ; 1 Jas. II., c. 4 ; 1 Jas. II., c. 5 ; 1 W. and M., c. 10 ; 1 W. and M., c. 28 ; 1 W. and M., s. 2, c. 6 ; 8-9 Wm. III., c. 7.

Preventive measures : 12 Car. II., c. 25 ; 14 Car. II., c. 11 ; 2 W. and M., s. 2, c. 14 ; 10 Wm. III., c. 10 ; 12-13 Wm. III., c. 11 ; 9 Wm. III., c. 40 ; 1 Anne, c. 15.

Frauds : Treasury Papers, June 29, 1691 (on May 16, 1691).

Accounts : 2 W. and M., s. 2, c. 11 ; Board's Report to Treasury, August 31, 1692 ; 8-9 Wm. III., c. 28 ; 12-13 Wm. III., c. 10.

Exchequer trials : Hardress.

Departmental incidents : Treasury Papers, May 7, 1689 ; January 23, 1691 ; May 24, 1689 ; June 10, 1689 ; June 28, 1689 ; August 22, 1689 ; August 23, 1689 ; September 4, 1689 ; September 17, 1689 ; September 19, 1690 ; November 20, 1691 ; June 11, 1692 ; June 13, 1692 ; November 12, 1692 ; February 10, 1705 ; Sir William Musgrave's ' Memoranda.'

Protective measures and prohibitions : 12 Car. II., c. 18 ; 15 Car. II., c. 7 ; 12 Car. II., c. 32 ; 14 Car. II., c. 18 ; 14 Car. II., c. 13 ; 25 Car. II., c. 6 ; 25 Car. II., c. 7 ; 18-19 Car. II., c. 2 ; 25 Car. II., c. 2 ; 1 Jas. II., c. 19 ; 1 W. and M., c. 32 ; 1 W. and M., c. 34 ; 2 W. and M., c. 9 ; 3 W. and M., c. 13 ; 4 W. and M., c. 7 ; 4 W. and M., c. 10 ; 4 W. and M., c. 5 ; 6-7 Wm. III., c. 7 ; 7-8 Wm. III., c. 20 ; 9 Wm. III., c. 28 ; 9 Wm. III., c. 43 ; 11 Wm. III., c. 10 ; 11 Wm. III., c. 11 ; 11 Wm. III., c. 20 ; 7-8 Wm. III., c. 39 ; 8-9 Wm. III., c. 34 ; 11 Wm. III., c. 3 ; 7-8 Wm. III., c. 22 ; 10 Wm. III., c. 16 ; 10 Wm. III., c. 14.

Establishment : Patent Rolls, 23 Car. II., p. 2, m. 1*d.* ; ' Pepys' Diary '; ' Book of Rates,' 1671 ; ' The Royal Gauger '; ' Index Vectigalium.'

Privateers : 4 W. and M., c. 25.

Highwaymen : 4 W. and M., c. 8.

---

* ' Davenant's book is highly saucy . . . it was and is a hint to show everybody where they should be angry.'—*Matthew Prior to Stanyan :* 1700.

CHAPTER VI

THE SCOTS' CONTRIBUTIONS, AND THE GROWTH OF SMUGGLING

1707–1727

As this chapter opens at the period when the Act of Union between England and Scotland was planned and executed, a curt sketch of Scottish revenue history will not be out of place. There is nothing in the Scottish statutes to indicate that the customs returns were important, or that Scottish oversea trade, prior to the Union, was extensive or profitable. Ancient Scottish history undoubtedly contains elements of picturesqueness, even of grandeur. Many of the quaint statutes, notably those regulating the ' walpinschawingis,' the maintenance of bale-fires, the affairs of the Border marches and the Highlands, and the cleansing and safety of the old thatched cities, are deeply interesting. It is possible that the true Customs history of the rugged old land has not up to the present been comprehensively exhibited, despite the skill and industry of Scotsmen in research and compilation. No elaborate statement of Scottish revenue matters may be attempted here ; merely a rough précis of the more striking details. The task of amplification must be left to Scotsmen born, of whom there are many eminently capable, who may be referred encouragingly to the preamble of one of the Scottish Acts, worded thus : ' This nation hath continued now upwards of two thousand years in the unaltered form of our monarchical government, under the uninterrupted line of one hundred and eleven kings.'

In olden days there was no love lost betwixt Scots and English. Most of the Scottish revenue Acts were worded resentfully against the Southrons, and one or two of the English Acts disparaged the Scots. Overland traffic between the two countries seems to have been by mutual agreement confined to the narrow routes by way of Berwick and Carlisle (legal overland traffic, for there was occasional smuggling across the Border). There were other transactions which may scarcely be called ' traffic,' little ventures by the Scottish ' reivers,' by means of which English goods passed into Scotland, not only uncustomed, but without permission of owners. Sometimes these transactions were pushed beyond the bounds of endurance, and then a Norman king or a mail-clad Warden would come storming through the Debatable Land, with thousands of stalwart archers at his heels, each archer equipped with a six-foot bow and arrows of a cloth yard, and fire and sword would leave their traces across the hard, barren country, right up to the gates of Edinburgh. (The Scottish kings seem to have understood the Scottish deficiencies, for they were continually prohibiting the games of football and golf, and urging the country youth to practise at the butts.)

Most of the revenue laws were directed to the following ends :

1. The restriction or prohibition of English trade.

2. The confining of foreign traffic to the ' royal burghs,' or king's ports, such as Edinburgh, Dumbarton, etc. All these ports were on the south-eastern and extreme south-western coasts.

3. The compelling of foreign merchants to buy Scottish goods up to the amount of their Scottish takings.

4. The encouragement of the inbringing of bullion by Scottish merchants who had traded abroad.

5. The extensive importation of food material, and the discouragement of its exportation.

6. The establishment of a good understanding with the Flemings, who were the principal buyers of Scottish wool.

There appears to have been considerable doubt in the minds of most of the antiquarians who collected and transcribed the older historical records, as to the possibility of discrimination between the duties collected for the king and those levied as toll by the bailies of the various burghs. It appears that the privileges of the burghs were of extremely ancient origin. The dues collected by the bailies on merchandise brought in from the country were probably 'market impositions,' and in most cases they were levied after the goods had been sold.

It is doubtful whether the customs ratified by David I. were anything but burgh tolls on seaborne merchandise. A light tax was collected from each ship laden with corn or salt, and the cargo was subjected to trifling prisage. The tax was on the vessel, in account of her 'sett,' or privilege of riding at anchor in the haven. Each alien who brought wine, honey, or oil paid 'twal pennies' for his 'sett,' a duty of 4d. a tun on entry, and 4d. a tun on 'furth passing' (delivery). If his wine were 'tavarnyt' (sold to a taverner) the king had right of prisage. There were also slight taxes on 'fysschar schipps.' But it is inconceivable that these trifling money tolls were collected for the king, and it does not appear that the prisage of wine was at all extensive.

It is, however, quite evident that the king took custom on wool and skins outward, and that the origin of the tax, as in England, was immemorial. In the records appertaining to an ancient reign it is stipulated that the king shall have his dues of merchants passing by land and sea as in his father's day. Undoubtedly such wool as went by land to England was supposed to be customed before it passed Berwick, but it is unlikely that much went. The wool, it may with reason be assumed, would be of inferior quality —much like the 'rough wool' of the English shires north of the Humber. Yet there was a steady trade with Flanders, and it appears that David II.'s ransom was furnished out of the custom on Scottish wool, collected *in*

Flanders by certain Scottish burghers specially commis-
.sioned for that purpose.

In 1398 it was ordained that the statute made at Perth
during the previous year as to the paying of custom upon
English cloth imported, and upon Scottish cloth, butter,
horses, and cattle, should be ' payit as it wes ordanyt in þe
forsaid consail.' The burghers (of Perth ?) agreed to
pay certain dues, stipulating that their ' fredomes ' should
be preserved, that they should pay no more for wool, skins,
etc., outward than they had done in Robert II.'s time,
and that they should be free of the impost on salmon
(an export tax, usually applied with considerable rigour
to salmon bought by English traders).

The first plain account appears at the opening of the
reign of James I. (of Scotland). His export impositions
on cattle, sheep, and horses were 12d. in the £1 value.
Herrings paid 4s. per last if exported by Scotsmen, 6s. if
by strangers. There was an export duty on skins, woollen
cloth, and salmon, and an import duty of 2s. 6d. in the £1
on English goods.

In 1425 Scotsmen were forbidden to pass into Ireland
without special licence. If any person thus licensed
brought passengers with him on his return, they might
not land till permitted by the bailie of the port. This
was partly because many rebels against the Scottish king
had taken refuge in Ireland, and partly to prevent in-
cursions of ' the English Irishry,' who were held particularly dangerous. The statute explicitly stated that
nothing was intended in rupture of the friendship that
had long existed between Scotsmen and the native Irish.

James III.'s parliament decreed that none should trade
oversea unless he were a burgess of a king's port, that
craftsmen should not act as merchants, that no ship should
be freighted without a charter-party, that each merchant
carrying outward more than five lasts of goods should
render one ' sack ' to the ' Chaplains of the Nation,' and
that if he carried five lasts only, or less, he should render
half a sack. None was allowed to pass oversea as a

merchant unless he carried at least half a last of goods.

The practice with regard to the bringing-in of victual by foreign merchants was as follows : The strangers entered their goods at the tolbooth of the port, and the prices were fixed by agreement between the merchants and the port officials. The king's household was served ' with the best ' at the prices prescribed, and then the nobility had second choice. The remainder was sold to the common people. None might buy to sell again. As the port officials and the customs men frequently fleeced both merchants and ' common buyers,' it became necessary to proclaim the fixed prices at the market cross. (This Act applied particularly to Edinburgh.)

Unstable people were forbidden to trade abroad. Only ' famous and worshipful men ' were allowed to take goods to Flanders.

Towards the end of the century there was much smuggling, especially at Leith, and it was enacted that merchants landing goods at places other than king's ports should lodge at the principal taverns, and the tavern-keepers were held responsible that the merchants' goods did not pass uncustomed.

It was found that the collectors frequently took custom for the king first and for themselves afterwards, and a statute was issued prohibiting this. ' Quha that dois in the contrare to be punist as an oppressour and brekar of the Kingis law.'

A few years subsequent to the disaster at Flodden an Act was passed stating that for many years the districts near the Border had been wasted and plundered by English ' thevis and trators,' and that food was therefore at a great price. It was decreed that no Scot should send oxen or sheep to England, or victual, fish, or salt, but such Englishmen as were granted safe-conduct by the Scottish king might enter the realm and buy, paying in ' gold and siluir.'

In the sixteenth century Scottish merchants trading

abroad were bidden to carry passports.   Merchants going
to Flanders had to produce their passports to the Scottish
Conservator there stationed, and he was to keep the home
Government informed as to their manner of trading,
' vnder þe pane of tinsale of his office.'

War with England being contemplated, all Scottish men
of substance were ordered to furnish themselves with
' small artillery,' and all Scottish merchants from abroad
to bring home two hackbuts each, with a supply of
powder and metal.   This was just before the battles of
Halidon Rigg and Solway Moss.

James VI. (afterwards James I. of England) uttered
many revenue decrees.   He issued a ' Table ' to his
customs collectors (probably a rough ' Book of Rates ').
He created three extra ' King's Ports,' one at Lochaber,
one at Cantire, one at Lewis, and gave close attention to
the doings of both merchants and officers.

One of the Acts issued during his reign foreshadowed
so closely in its preamble the style of the 1611 English
' Book of Rates ' Ordinance that one is inclined to think
James dictated the preface, which stated that it was the
practice in all countries to impose customs, especially
upon strangers, and proceeded : ' It cannot be denyit
bot his maiestie is a free prince of a Souerane power,
haueing als grite liberteis and prerogatiues be the lawis of
his realme and priuilege of his crowne and diadame as ony
other king, prince, or potestate quhat-sum-euir.'   It
gave authority to the Auditors of the Exchequer to ' sett
down the A.B.C. of the custum,' and to fix values (issue a
' Book of Rates ').   The collectors were to ' uplift custum ' accordingly at the rate of 12d. in the £1.   The
nobility might import or export goods duty-free.

At this time James was anticipating the event that
was to make him monarch of a land where ' custum ' was
really worth ' uplifting.'   He was in secret and constant
communication with the audacious Cecil.   Still the old
spirit of hostility to English commerce was paraded.
Another Act stated that English cloth was ' unproffitable,

haueand onlie for the maist parte ane outwarde shaw [show] wantand the substance and strenth quhilk oftymes it appeiris to haue.' (It is likely there was some truth in this statement.) English cloth and English wares were accordingly prohibited.

In 1604, James being in possession of the English throne, certain Scottish Commissioners were appointed to confer with certain English Commissioners as to the best way of strengthening union betwixt the two countries. The preamble of the appointing Act ran : ' For sa mekle as it hes plesit his maist exellent Maiestie, acknawledging the unspeikable favour quhair-with the divine providence hath blissed him by the oft-wisched bot hardlie-expected cojunction of twa sa Ancient and lang discordent kingdomes . . . miracoulouslie accompleisched in the blude and persone of sa Rare ane Monarch.'

The eighteenth Parliament of this reign (1606) adjusted certain customs matters. The farmers of the Scottish customs were directed to keep a book of goods entered and shipped to England, and another of goods imported by sea from England. The English farmers were to keep similar books, and every year duplicates of the accounts thus taken were to be sent from Edinburgh to London, and from London to Edinburgh. It is evident that all shipments between the two countries were secured by bond, for the Act directed that the certificates in discharge of bonds were to be transmitted with the duplicates of account. Cockets for Scottish goods were to be granted to responsible persons only, ' not in poore menis names scarslie knawin in England.' Goods sent overland from either country were to be accompanied by certificates ; Scottish goods being certified by the farmers' deputies at Edinburgh, English by the farmers' deputies at Berwick or Carlisle. Goods might not pass by the waste lands (marches).

In 1641 it was enacted that the charge for taking a ship's report should not exceed 23s. 4d. Scots ; for issuing a cocket 40s. This was on account of extortions by collectors and report clerks. In the same year all ' extraordinary ' customs and imposts were declared illegal, and it was enjoined that goods which had been customed inward should be duty-free outward, ' as in England and Ireland.' It was also directed that the ' Book of Rates ' should be reformed. Many privileges were granted to ship-masters and merchants.

A system of Import-Excise was adopted in 1644, the duties being payable by the first buyer. Wine and tobacco were the principal foreign goods made liable. Certain inland duties were levied under the same Act. The rates were increased in 1649.

During the later years of the Commonwealth the West-minster Ordinance of Tunnage and Poundage applied to England, Ireland, and Scotland.

In 1661 a duty of 8s. Scots per gross was imposed upon foreign tobacco-pipes, to prevent money from leaving the kingdom !

In the same year a Scottish Navigation Act was passed. Its provisions were much the same as those of the English Act, except that ' Scots ' took the place of ' English ' in the clause dealing with the preponderance of mariners. English and Irish ships were to be accounted foreign, until the full benefit of the English Navigation Act should be extended to Scotland. The Act was not to apply to goods of Asia, Africa, America, Russia, or Italy, till Scottish mer-chants succeeded in establishing trade with those territories.

Later was issued a unique statute, providing that craftsmen might not import articles of the kind they manufactured. (Thus an armourer might not import swords, or a smith ploughshares.)

In 1663 certain merchants complained that the pro-visions of the Navigation Act were systematically in-fringed in the port of Glasgow by Dutchmen and other foreigners. The petitioners described themselves as on the verge of ruin, being unable to compete with their foreign rivals, who were encouraged and supported by many of the Glasgow people. Parliament enjoined that the Act should be enforced.

In 1689, at ' The Meeting of the Estates,' an embargo was put upon all vessels at the western ports, to prevent their passing to Ireland, and then being used to bring Jacobites to England and Scotland.

In 1695 it was found that the collectors of the import-excise of 6s. a pint on brandy had in some cases charged the retailers more than once. (Probably they had levied it on successive buyers of the goods, instead of confining it to the first retailer.) It was enacted that the tax should only be collected from genuine retailers, who were defined as ' Toppers,' keeping shops and taverns in which brandy was sold in small quantities for immediate consumption.

It appears that the distillation of rum from molasses was common in Scotland. The sale of this liquor was prohibited in 1695, on the pretext that it was ' a drug rather than a liquor,' and that its manufacture curtailed the distillation of spirits from malt, but in the following year the prohibition was repealed, as prejudicial to the Scottish sugar-refining industry. In 1698 the impost on brandy was transferred to the importer, and made a branch of the Customs.

Later Parliament reaffirmed prohibition of the exportation of wool, and forbade the importation of all foreign woollen manufactures. It also prohibited French wine and spirits, and all foreign silk and cotton goods, except goods of India and Persia imported in the ships of ' the Company of Scotland trading to Africa and the Indies,' plain stuffs for hoods and scarves, and materials for robes of ceremony.

These brief details may serve to illustrate the progress of the Scottish Customs revenue, previous to the Act of Union. The Articles of Union were agreed upon in 1705, by Commissioners nominated under the Great Seals of both countries. The Scottish Parliament ratified the Act early in 1706. It was provided that the two countries should be united on May 1, 1707, their armorial bearings conjoined, and their trade privileges made similar. Scottish ships were to be deemed British-built, provided that no foreigner shared in ownership. The ownership of Scottish vessels was to be attested to the Customs upon oath, and registers of shipping were to be kept at London and Edinburgh. The customs drawbacks, duties, prohibitions, etc., obtaining in England, were to be applied to Scotland. Patents and privileges were to remain undisturbed. The bounty on English corn, grain, meal, etc., exported, was to extend to similar Scottish goods. It was found necessary to add oatmeal to the list, and to provide that Scottish 'bere' should be rated as barley. Thus the English customs duties, together with the English system of Excise, in all their tangled and jumbled glory, were applied to a land in which the pound sterling meant a sum scarce sufficient to cover an English labourer's daily pay, and many a high-souled gentleman walked barefoot. Certain exemptions had to be made with regard to Scottish victual and salt, but they were temporary and trivial. The relative proportions of revenue were reckoned at something near the following figures :

			Customs.	Excise.
England	..	..	£1,350,000	£950,000
Scotland	..	..	£30,000	£33,500

The English coinage, weights, and measures were to be used, and a Mint was established at Edinburgh on the same lines as the London Mint.

The Parliaments were united, the Scottish members attending at Westminster, but Scotland was granted a separate Court of Exchequer at Edinburgh, with Exchequer barons as in England, and a separate Board of Customs Commissioners, also at Edinburgh, to control the Scottish customs. There was to be but one Privy Seal for the two countries. Scottish justices of the Peace were to be appointed under the Great Seal. The Scottish burghs retained their ancient liberties.

It is likely that the new scheme was viewed with sour

disapproval by the common people of both countries, and that, as usual, their wishes were not consulted. Scurrilous pamphleteers of the time did not scruple to express their opinion that the Scottish people suffered by the Union, being hit in their tenderest spot by the complicated English customs and excises.

After the Scottish customs had paid their share of the salaries of Exchequer and Session, and the expenses of collection, the net yield was but trifling. This was due to a trio of circumstances. Scotland was a poor country, not, like the Scotland of to-day, full of flourishing banks and roaring industries. The duties were loosely collected, and at some of the ports little or nothing remained after the ' salaries and incidents ' had been paid. Lastly, there was quite an enormous amount of canny smuggling— smuggling not conducted in the brazen, whole-souled fashion that obtained in Kent, Sussex, Hants, and Dorset, yet quite as effective in diminishing the revenue. The returns increased as the years rolled on, and then they were saddled with the bounties granted to the Scottish herring fishery.

From Scotland to Liverpool. In 1709, the port having greatly increased its business, and the Liverpool Corporation having granted four acres of land to furnish space for a dock, of which there was much need, the port being dangerous to enter, it was enacted that the land in question should for ever be devoted to the purpose assigned, and that the Corporation might during twenty-one years levy certain tonnage dues on ships coming to Liverpool, the proceeds to be devoted to the construction and maintenance of the said dock. The limits of the port were defined as the Redstones, Warrington, and Frodsham Bridges. The Liverpool customs officers were directed to withhold clearance till the dues were paid.

Parliament granted an impost, which became permanent as ' The Duty on Candles.' Later appeared another, which became permanent as ' The Duty on Pepper and Raisins.' Then came ' The Duty on Coals,' which included seven different duties on coals exported, and this also became permanent. With this impost was bracketed ' The Additional Duty on Candles,' also destined to become permanent.

The plague being prevalent at the northern European ports, ships from the Baltic were made liable to quarantine. This appears to be the first instance of a quarantine Act being deemed requisite to confirm the usual proclamation. Maritime justices were directed to set a watch upon all ships thus detained. The immediate administration of the Act was vested in the Customs authorities. (The Commissioners each received £200 a year extra for supervising the quarantine duties.)

Other fresh imposts were levied, all fated to become permanent. They were ' The Duty on Hides,' an impost upon hides, skins, parchment, vellum, cards, and dice ; ' The Duty on Hops,' an additional tax of 3d. a pound on foreign hops ; ' The Duty on Soap and Paper,' an amazingly tangled bunch of varying additional rates and duties, applying to foreign soap, paper, millboards, pasteboards, scale-boards, and various kinds of foreign linen ; ' The Additional Duty on Hides,' which varied with charming complexities the previous Hide Duty, and also embellished the rates on drugs and the duties on parchment, vellum, starch, tea, coffee, etc. ; and ' The Duty on Sailcloth,' an additional tax of 1d. per ell on the foreign commodity. Then came ' The Additional Duty on Coals.' Beside these were one or two fugitive imposts, which need not be described.

It was enacted that officers of customs should assist in procuring aid for vessels in distress. They were empowered to demand assistance from any man-of-war or merchant ship available, and to take part in regulating claims for salvage. If salvage were not paid they might detain ship and cargo. In disputed cases they might nominate justices to decide matters at issue. They were allowed to participate in salvage awards, and some of them soon found this privilege lucrative. The Customs administration of this Act was, as a rule, vested in the collectors of ports. The Act, which was issued on account of ' barbarous wrecking,' was to be publicly read four times a year in all seaport towns.

In 1711 a remarkable interview took place at the Treasury, the parties being the Lord Treasurer, the Chancellor of the Exchequer, and the Board of Customs. His Lordship recommended the Commissioners to take great care of the revenue, especially of the tobacco duties. He stated that he believed many of the officers of customs to be ' faulty,' and expressed a hope that the Board would apprise him if he happened to instal anyone who was unfit.

In 1712 the Board instituted a fund for pensioning superannuated tidesmen. A ' Receiver and Controller ' of the fund was appointed, and all moneys stopped from officers for misconduct were handed over to him.*

In 1713 an interesting case was tried in the Scottish Court of Exchequer. The English Prisage of Wine had been introduced into Scotland at the time of the Union, and appears to have been extremely unpopular. In the end a Scottish merchant named Gordon contested the legality of the imposition. He had imported a quantity of Spanish wine, and protested against paying the usual composition fee to the Prisage-holder, but he gave bond for payment if the decision went against him.

* During the infancy of the Superannuation Fund the allowance to pensioners was 1s. a day. Only ' preferable tidesmen,' who had served twenty-one years, who had no other means of subsistence, and were *over eighty years old*, were allowed to participate. The fund grew shaky in 1736, but was given a fresh start in 1741. In 1750 the Receiver, one Harrison, was charged with embezzling the moneys, and dismissed from the Service.

It was contended on Gordon's behalf that Prisage had not been provided for in the Act of Union, and that even in England it was merely 'an ancient usage indistinctly paid.' Sir James Stewart, the Advocate-General, appeared for the Prisage-holder. The judges were the Scottish Exchequer barons (Smith, Maitland, Clark, and Dalrymple). Their decree, summarized, ran thus :

'Prisage is an ancient prerogative, disposed at the time of Union in favour of certain subjects as a private right. It was never settled or established by any Act of Parliament in England itself, and there was no mention of it in the account of customs and duties given in by the English Commissioners at the time of Union, therefore it was not considered in the treaty.'

The barons accordingly directed that Gordon should be freed of his bond, and should 'go without day.' There was a good deal of rummaging amid the old records of English revenue in connexion with this case. Undoubtedly Gordon's courage deserved success, yet it seems likely a flaw might easily be found in the decision.

The official minutes of the London Commissioners of Customs show that the customs tidesmen employed on the Thames had rather a hard time. They were divided into two classes, 'preferable' and 'extraordinary.' Those in the preferable class were kept constantly employed, the pick of them in the Pool and on the quays, and a certain number of the seniors were stationed upon the sacred Customs wharf itself. These last were called 'piazza men.' The 'extraordinary' men were employed at a daily wage when required. The majority of the tidesmen were on 'boarding duty'—*i.e.*, kept in readiness at the London Custom-house, and drafted in bodies to Gravesend as required, to accompany ships from foreign up the Thames, and remain on board them as watchers till they were cleared. The records are full of curious things about these waifs of the river. There were at

Gravesend two taverns, at which the tidesmen were expected to lodge whilst waiting to be boarded. In times of fog or slackness the men often remained in these taverns for several days, and then the tavern-keepers were permitted to advance them money up to a specified amount. When news arrived of East Indiamen in the Downs a number of tidesmen were sent to Deal to be boarded on them. These men performed the journey from Gravesend to Deal on horseback, and were as merry on the way as Chaucer's Canterbury Pilgrims.

Once two of the tidesmen quarrelled, and one trounced the other. The Board fined the victor, and gave the fine to the beaten man. One afternoon a London tidesman went to sun himself upon the Tower Quay, lit his pipe, and made himself comfortable. The sentry on duty ordered him to put his pipe out ; the tidesman refilled it, and smoked harder than ever. The sentry summoned one of the guard, and the two soldiers attempted to enforce routine, on which the tidesman beat and overthrew them, and broke one of their firelocks. For this he was severely punished.

An extraordinary tidesman, being boarded on a ship in the Pool, neglected to apprise the river inspectors of the completion of the vessel's unlading. Why should he ? Her charge meant 2s. a day to him, and if he were cleared it might be a week or two before he was employed again. So he stayed on for eighty days after the vessel's discharge. The Board were extremely wroth with the careless inspectors who had permitted this, and made them pay the tidesman's wages out of their own pockets.

The tidesmen appear to have often suffered through the churlishness or inhumanity of shipmasters. They were in a way at the mercy of the captains of the vessels which they were deputed to watch, the captains being able to make things uncomfortable for them if they became officious. A master refused to allow his tidesman a place in which to sleep, and made him walk the deck for two days and two nights. The Board took the Solicitor-

General's opinion upon the matter, who decided that a prosecution would not hold. But the captain was not allowed to escape. There was a certain bounty called ' Portage,' which the Customs paid to masters of vessels from foreign, to induce them to make correct reports of their cargoes.* The Board made a practice of refusing this bounty when a master failed to report correctly, or otherwise misbehaved, and in the case mentioned they stopped it for ' obstinacy.' Once a master lost his portage for ' abusing ' a tidesman, and another skipper's bounty was stopped because his tidesman's ' trunk ' was stolen. One master gave his tidesman a dram, upon drinking which the unfortunate fellow went to sleep, and awoke no more. Apparently the case was not clear enough to warrant a prosecution, but the Board stopped the captain's portage.

The most interesting customs documents of Anne's reign are those kept at the Scottish ports, for they illustrate the effect of the Act of Union upon Scottish revenue practice. In 1708 the Scottish Commissioners of Customs were their Honours Dickson, Isaacson, Norman, Boyle, Rigby, Kent, and Fullerton. The collector and controller at Montrose were douce, earnest Scotsmen, rather overloaded with the responsibilities of the new system, and inclined to refer all doubtful matters to their Honours at Edinburgh. Their chief causes of worry were the drawback upon Scottish fish cured with foreign salt, and the high-handed proceedings of the Earl of Northesk, who was Deputy High Admiral, and looked sharply after his perquisites of wreck.

The Commissioners, whether they were Scotsmen or not, possessed in full the Scottish disinclination to rash-

* The captains of Danish and Norwegian vessels usually authorized the Customs to pay their portages to the ministers of the Scandinavian places of worship in London.

ness in giving advice, yet they were extremely desirous that there should be no chance of fault-finding by the English Treasury officials. They learned as fast as they could, meanwhile labouring to convince their subordinates that they would show little consideration if things went wrong. They received a deal of private information of contemplated smuggling, which information they promptly communicated to Montrose, with no result as regarded important seizures. Meanwhile the collector and controller lost no opportunity of informing the Board that it was impossible to protect the revenue in the Montrose district, especially in the neighbourhood of Arbroath, unless a few score soldiers were kept within hailing distance of the Custom-house.

The first question sent to the Board was to this effect : ' May the Admirall, who has salved goods from foreign, and taken a fifth as his share, be allowed to deal with them as he pleases ? He reffuses to export the prohibited goods, and he claims the ballance clear of duty.'

This question the Board referred to the Lord Advocate, and his answer was a miracle of ambiguity. It ran thus : ' The wrecked goods in excess of the fifth part are not liable, being meer casualtie. It hath been thought that wrecked goods are not liable to duty.' He then vaguely hinted that the admiral was in error as to the fifth part which he had retained as salvage compensation, but his expression of opinion was by no means lucid.* Meantime the Board dexterously made it apparent that they desired the officers to give the ' Admirall ' as little trouble as possible.

The officers were informed by the Board that Montrose merchants had entered French paper as Dutch, to avoid

---

* 3 Edw. I., c. 4 : ' Where wreck belongeth to other than the king, etc.' It is evident that the Earl of Northesk had taken the wrecked goods as droits, and, the owners having afterwards claimed them, he had handed over four-fifths, and kept the other fifth as salvage dues. In the condition of the law then, he appears to have been entitled to his fifth duty-free. The Advocate seems to have misapprehended both the law and the circumstances.

the 'French duty.' Later they were cautioned as to certain large exportations of tobacco on drawback at Borrowstoness. 'It has been thought,' wrote the Board, 'the merchant will run these goods after shipment.'

The Commissioners received 'A Book of Opinions' from their London brethren, and, perusing it, came to think that the Lord Advocate had gone wrong in his decision as to wrecked goods.

The officers were still puzzled over the salted fish drawback, and after much correspondence between Edinburgh and London instructions reached Montrose that some of the fish shipped on drawback were to be measured, so that an estimate might be formed of the quantity of salt used in curing. The officers were to certify to 'the dementions,' measuring from the bone of the fin to the third joint of the tail. 'You have herewith,' wrote the Board, 'the printed form of a codd, which is printed out by the letters A and B, according to which you are to governe yourselves.'

The Earl of Northesk claimed the wrecked cargo of a ship, and the officers sent queries to Edinburgh as to what duties they were to charge him. The Commissioners replied that they hoped there would be no dispute. The officers claimed *duty* on all the spirits salved, and detained such of the goods as were 'prohibited,' meanwhile asking the Board for further instructions. Not a word of instruction was received, but the Board's Secretary sent an ambiguous letter, hinting that the Board did not approve of the officers 'cavilling with the Lord Northesque or his doers,' and desired no further trouble in the matter. It appears that the Earl had made complaint in the proper quarter that he could not get his droits duty-free.

In 1709 the Board, having received 'relyable information' that the Montrose officers did not enforce the maritime regulations and duties applying to aliens, and that brandy was being smuggled into the port '1,200 anchors' (ankers) 'at a time,' sent the collector and controller a letter of warning, that ended thus : ' If a punctuall complyance be not given hereto, others will be appointed to succeed you who will make it their study and care to perform the same.'

Soon after another letter arrived from Edinburgh, commencing : ' We have certayn information that there is a very wicked practice in your precincts.' This, it appeared, was getting drawback at shipment on fish cured with foreign salt, and afterwards unshipping the goods and presenting them for drawback again, and yet again. The officers were directed to mark the casks in future, and to cut off the tails of the fish !

The Board sent the following instructions as to the details required in sufferances for carrying wine and tobacco coastwise. ' Specify of wine the casks prick't, made up, and upon the turn, of tobacco the quantity wet, funk'd, and dry rotten.'*

News came that a ship from the Plantations had gone ashore on the Orkneys, and that the islanders had stolen her cargo, the most valuable part of which consisted of 17,000 deerskins.

The Board sent a disconcerting letter, apprising the officers that French wine was being sold freely in all the Edinburgh taverns, and that it was thought to have been run at Montrose or thereabout. Other disquieting tidings followed, to the effect that Scottish captains were in the habit of taking fish to Bilbao, and then shipping French wine with the purpose of running it into England and Scotland, and that it had come to be known that other mariners were in the habit of shipping drawback goods in Scotland, pocketing the drawback, and then running the goods into England.

Undoubtedly the good citizens of Montrose, and others residing in the district, were guilty of some of the illegal

* ' Pricked ': spiled. ' Made up ': landed at a low ullage, and made up to a specified ullage by addition of wine from other casks. For instance, the last cask of a consignment might be expended in making up several other deficient casks. ' Upon the turn ': becoming sour. ' Funked ': offensive to the smell.

acts they were confidentially blamed for.   Extracts from the records of a later reign prove that most of the charges had good foundation.

We close our account of this reign with an enumeration of the Scottish ports, creeks, etc., from which it will be seen that a vast stretch of coast was left unguarded by the Customs.   The north-western portion of Scotland was a stronghold of lawlessness, the wild Highlanders and fisher-folk distilling their own whisky, settling their quarrels in their own time-honoured way, and no doubt occasionally welcoming the arrival of Dirk Hatteraick or Will Watch.   The customs stations most remote were Helmsdale on the east and Cantire on the west coast.

Ports.	Members.	Creeks.
Dunbar ..	Nil	Eyemouth, Coldingham, Cockburnspath, Skateraw, Tynninghame.
Preston- pans	Nil	North Berwick, Aberlady, Port Seton, Musselburgh.
Leith ..	Nil	Newhaven, Muirhouse Haven, Cramond.
Boness ..	Alloa	Queensferry, Blackness, Avon Water, Carron Mouth, Airth, Stirling, Clackmannan, Kincardine, Culross, Torryburn, Limekilns, Inverkeithing.
Kirkcaldy	Anstruther	Aberdour, Burntisland, Kinghorn, Dysart, West Wemyss, East Wemyss, Buckhaven, Methil, Leven, Largo, Elie, St. Monance, Pittenweem, Crail, Fife Ness, St. Andrews, Eden Mouth.
Dundee ..	Nil	Ferryport-on-Craig, Balmerino, Monifieth, Buddon Ness.
Perth ..	Nil	Earn Mouth, Inchture, Pow of Errol.
Montrose	Nil	Arbroath, Auchmithie, Lunan Water, Usan, Ferryden, Mathers, Johnshaven, Gourdon, Bervie, Tod Head.
Aberdeen	Nil	Catterline, Crawton, Dunnottar, Stonehaven, Skateraw, Findon Cove, Old Aberdeen, Newburgh, Slains, Boddam, Peterhead, Rattray Head, Cairnbulg, Fraserburgh, Rosehearty, Banff, Portsoy, Cullen.
Inverness	Nil	Garmouth, Lossiemouth, Burghead, Findhorn, Nairn, Alness, Cromarty, Portmahomac, Tain, Dornoch, Dunrobin, Helmsdale.

Thence the whole northern coast, with the western coast as far south as Knapdale, had no Customs supervision. The 'creek' most remote on the western coast was the Mull of Cantire.

Ports.	Members.	Creeks.
Campbel-town	} Nil	Mull of Cantire, Carradale Bay, Claonaig Bay, Skipness Point, Tarbert, Kyles of Bute.
Port Glasgow		Toward Point, Dunoon, Holy Loch, Roseneath, Dumbarton, Kilpatrick, Scots Town, Partick, Renfrew, Erskine.
	Greenock	Gourock, Cloch Point, Inverkip, Skelmorlie.
Irvine ..	Nil	Largs, Portincross, Saltcoats.
Ayr ..	Nil	Troon, Dunure Castle, Turnberry Point, Girvan.
Stranraer	Port-patrick	Ballantrae, Bay of Cairn, Scar, Loch Float, Drumore, Glenluce.
Wigtown	Nil	Burn of Monreith, Isle of Whithorn, Newton Stewart, Creetown, Gatehouse of Fleet.
Dumfries	Kircud-bright	Balmangan Bay, Balcary Bay, Entry of Ure, Eastside, Burbary Bay, Carse Thorn, Kelton, Cummer Trees, Annan, Entry of Sark.

The National Debt at the beginning of George I.'s reign amounted to several millions. The provision for the Civil List was at first less than that granted to Queen Anne, but it was speedily made up to £700,000 per annum, the extra money being yielded by 'The Aggregate Fund,' a new institution which combined several branches of Customs and Excise revenue, and two other inland duties.

The duty on coals in the port of London was charged with the maintenance of the ministers of fifty new churches. The churches had been built out of the proceeds of the same tax. ‘ The Duty on Wrought Plate ’ appeared, and became a permanent tax.

It was enacted that on account of frequent disputes between merchants and officers in dealing with wines found to be damaged, the ancient system of allowing the officers to remit the duty on damaged wine should be abolished, and that merchants should pay on all wines, good or bad, and receive an allowance out of the gross duties paid, or they might destroy the damaged wine, and be allowed a sum in compensation of freight charges.

Certain traders at once started manufacturing stuff, purporting to be damaged wine, in the Isle of Man, and bringing it to England so that they might destroy it, and gain an excessive ‘ freight allowance.’ To combat this it was enacted that damaged wine might be warehoused with the Customs, and sold for ‘ distillation into spirits.’

In 1719 it was found that much tobacco entered for exportation to Europe and granted drawback had been run into Ireland. Ireland was accordingly made ‘ foreign,’ as far as the drawback regulations obtained. (Later the Isle of Man was similarly dealt with.)

The Lord Warden of the Cinque Ports was directed to keep an eye upon the Deal, Dover, and Thanet pilots, who had used their pilot cutters for running goods.

‘ The New Duty on Apples ’ appeared (a tax of 2s. per bushel, which produced little revenue). It was probably intended to act as an instrument of prohibition. The tax on pictures, which, being included in the ‘ Spice and Picture ’ branch, had gained additional solemnity by being made ‘ perpetual,’ was amended. In its new form it stood as follows :

	£	s.	d.
On every imported picture of 4 square feet or upwards	3	0	0
On every imported picture of 2 or less than 4 feet square	2	0	0
On every imported picture of smaller size	1	0	0

The *ad valorem* duty on foreign books was made a tax *by weight :* 14s. a cwt. on all bound books imported.

(Evidently the authorities had lost faith in the artistic and literary discernment of the landing-waiters.)

The Crown acquired tenancy of the Wool Quay near the London Custom-house, for the purpose of warehouse accommodation. This quay had in 1432 been left by William of Sevenoaks, a London ' grocer,' to provide and maintain a teacher of grammar in Sevenoaks, and for the benefit of the poor there. The bequest was confirmed by Queen Elizabeth, and made a fund to maintain a free grammar school and an almshouse. The Crown now agreed to pay the Wardens of Sevenoaks, who were trustees of the fund, a sum of £2,500, and an annual rent of £550.

The weighing and garbling of imported tobacco were made subjects of a statute, and it was provided that tobacco might not be imported stripped of the stem, and that drawback should not be granted on exported tobacco-stalk. (The clause prohibiting stripped tobacco inward was soon repealed.) Throughout this reign there were many statutes against drawback frauds, and many readjustments of the Preventive laws. A writer on revenue matters has aptly remarked that the Customs regulations of the period were extremely formidable, ' from their many exceptions, and exceptions from exceptions—their many regulations, and regulations of regulations.'

The clause in the Act of Union stipulating that the Customs of England and Scotland should be under two distinct Commissions was annulled, and one Commission granted for Great Britain. (This system lasted till 1742, yet the English and Scotch revenues were still collected separately, and administered at London and Edinburgh by members of the joint Commission.)

An additional ' Book of Rates ' was issued. Since the grant of the Old Subsidy in 1660 many goods previously unknown had become articles of import, and as there was no mention of these in the old ' Book of Rates ' their values had been declared by the importers on oath. The new Act furnished rates of value for a number of them, and provided that if any articles not enumerated in either the old or the new list were imported collectors should be empowered to check the values declared, and if they thought the goods were undervalued they might buy them at the value stated by the importer, and pay him the same plus an extra 10 per cent. and the amount of the customs duties on the goods. The collector might then warehouse the goods for public sale. When the goods were sold he was to draw back the money previously expended, and the surplus, if any, was to go to the Sinking Fund. What would happen if the goods failed to realize the amount paid by the collector did not appear in the context.*

The additional customs duties on tea, coffee, etc., were repealed, and the goods made subject to a heavy excise tax. The duty on snuff was amended. Meanwhile home-manufactured silks had been granted an allowance on exportation, and the poundage outward on many British manufactures and products abolished. The duties on Plantation tobacco had been slightly eased. Old rags, linseed, and drugs used in dyeing, had been made duty-free inward.

In 1721 the Customs and Excise Commissioners were called up to the Treasury together. There may have been a dispute as to precedence, for the Customs Minute Books exultingly announce that the gentlemen of the Customs were ' called in first.'

The Board decided that gaugers, before being certified

---

* Legend has it that sometimes the collectors were duped ; for instance, that a merchant would bring in at one port a parcel made up of ' portions ' of an unrated article, and at another port the corresponding ' portions,' and declare both parcels at trifling values. The collectors would be afraid to buy the goods for the Crown, fearing that they would not get their money back, and would therefore assess poundage at the rate declared. Then the merchant would combine the two parcels. It may be that Legend is a lying jade on this point, for the two ' Books of Rates ' made up an exhaustive list between them, and the few kinds remaining unrated were not such as are specified in the tale.

to as competent, should prove that they were skilled in practical gauging as well as in ' working out contents in figures.'

A Treasury warrant was issued to provide £200 to furnish a regiment of soldiers with new shoes and stockings, to replace those worn out in chasing smugglers.

The Quarantine laws provided material for curious enactments by the Board. In 1722 it was enjoined that officers who in the prevention of smuggling boarded ships liable to quarantine need not perform quarantine in the same manner as the ships' companies. In the following year the Board granted the fishermen of Milton, Kent, a sum of money to compensate them for the loss of their oyster-fishing, which had been suspended while certain vessels performed quarantine in Stangate Creek.

The Weavers' Company of London approached the Board, and requested that officers might be appointed to seize ' prohibited apparel ' under the Company's direction. The Board complied.

Captain Thwaites, commander of the East Indiaman *Carnarvon*, succeeded in smuggling 880 pieces of silk and 1,500 pounds of tea. Afterwards information was laid against Thwaites, and on inquiry being made it was found that he had gone abroad with his vessel. On his return in 1724 action was taken against him, but there being some delay he managed to get his effects on board, and would have evaded prosecution again had the Board not called upon the East India Company to stop his ship. He was fined £2,800, and applied to the Treasury that the fine might be reduced. His petition was referred to the Board, and they refused to entertain it, stating they had proof that Thwaites had corrupted several of their officers.

The ancient system of sending tidesmen to Deal to be boarded on East Indiamen arriving in the Downs was discontinued, as the tidesmen were often rendered unfit for duty by sea-sickness. It was provided that certain persons of Deal, well accustomed to the sea, should be boarded in their stead.

About this time the Commissioners of Customs did several strange things. They had a fit of economy, and restricted the Bench officers' yearly allowance of stationery to eight reams paper and 6,000 pens. They issued a self-denying ordinance, stating that ' in order to a frugal management of the Revenue and an example to officers ' they would in future buy their own breakfast coffee, pay their own coach-hire, and purchase their own books and pamphlets, ' except the " Book of Rates," ' which had recently come out in new form under the editorship of Mr. Carkesse, Secretary to the Commissioners.

Jeremiah Gardener, an excise officer, being engaged on preventive duty at Blackstock, Suffolk, stopped a gang of smugglers who were carrying their venture inland, and demanded surrender of the goods. The smugglers replied with a volley of stones, upon which Gardener drew sword on them. They set upon him with cudgels, beat him cruelly, took his sword from him and cut off his nose with it, and left him lying in the road. Afterwards one of them returned with the intention of killing him. Gardener's affidavit on the matter stated that having crawled through a hedge he heard the smuggler pacing up and down the road searching for him, and that in the end the ruffian exclaimed, ' Ah, damn him, he is gone !' and then went off after the rest of the party.

During this reign both Parliament and the Customs Commissioners made desperate efforts to cope with smuggling, and to restrict the nefarious energies of corrupt officials. An Order in Council forbade the appointment of customs officers in ports near to their places of birth or recent residence. A process-server for wool frauds was appointed for Kent and Sussex. His salary was £120 a year, and he had to keep three horses and an attendant. Many riding-officers were appointed on the coasts of Kent and Sussex. Later, a few were appointed on the north-western coast, but most of these were subsequently removed to Essex. (Riding-officers are mentioned in the records as early as 1670.)

There was an immense amount of pilfering on London river, and the wharves and quays around the Pool were frequently harried by thieves. In 1716 three street-keepers employed by Christ's Hospital asked the Board of Customs to be allowed to watch the quays at night. The Board employed them, giving them 3s. 4d. a week each, and a reward of 5s. for every pilferer arrested and convicted.*

Disputes between customs and excise officers as to precedence in rummaging vessels were frequent. (The Excise had power to rummage afloat.) It was arranged that if a customs man were first on board he should be allowed to complete his work before an exciseman should search, and *vice versa*.

Meanwhile Parliament issued formidable acts of prevention. It was provided that vessels of less than 15 tons used in importing spirits should be forfeited, and that rum imported in casks of less than 20 gallons should also be liable to forfeiture. Goods found on a vessel in excess of report, and foreign goods taken in at sea by coasters, were made forfeitable. Vessels of 50 tons and under found ' hovering ' on the coast might be detained till the master entered into bond to proceed on his voyage. Later the legal tonnage for ships used in importing spirits was raised from 15 to 30 tons, and it was provided that ' hoverers ' found within two leagues of the coast might be compelled to enter port. In 1721 the tonnage for ships carrying spirits was raised from 30 to 40 tons, and on account of smuggling in large galleys, often rowed by twelve men or more, it was provided that any boat with more than four rowlocks found in the Middlesex,

---

* The subsequent history of this trio of thief-catchers should be instructive to all advocates of ' blood-money.' After a time their pay was increased, and they were directed to assist in pressing men for the navy. Later they were dismissed for conniving at frauds.

Surrey, Kentish, or Essex waters should be forfeited. Royal barges, ships' boats, and boats specially licensed, were exempt

The enactments aimed against operations from the shore were extremely severe. In 1719 it was enjoined that smugglers assembling to the number of eight or more, and 'hindering, beating, or wounding officers,' should be transported to the Plantations. In 1721 the number constituting 'an assemblage' was reduced to five. Smugglers were made liable to prosecution by 'capias,' directed to any magistrate convenient. On arrest they were to be called on to find bail for their appearance in the court from which the capias issued, and on appearing were at once to find security for the forfeitures and money penalties sued for.

The inducements held out to informers were alluring, and produced what at first appeared a huge outburst of sordid treachery. Most of the informations laid, however, related to transactions which had by lapse of time become immune from prosecution. In 1725 it was provided that in such cases the Crown might sue, but only for the duty involved, and that if the culprits were unable to pay the full rate the Treasury might effect composition. Action was to be taken in the Court of Record, London, for cases in England, Wales, and Berwick, in the Edinburgh Court of Exchequer for Scottish cases, and in the Dublin Court of Exchequer for Irish. The frauds on the Excise were as numerous as those on the Customs, though the quantity of goods involved was less. When excise officers made seizures the goods, if liable to inland duties, were held by the Excise, if liable to import duties they were handed over to the Customs. Officers of both customs and excise might detain goods *if they had suspicion* of their not having paid duty. The onus of proof that the goods had been customed lay with the owner, as it does even at the present day. (Officers might prosecute at their own charge, even if the Commissioners directed release of the goods.)

If officers entered into fraudulent understanding with importers they were liable to dismissal, and the owners of the goods to a penalty of treble value. Acquittal was promised to him who turned King's evidence. Yet the Act failed, and had to be amended.

The disposal of seized goods was regulated thus : Tea, coffee, and spirits were to be sold publicly at London and Edinburgh by the Commissioners concerned. A third of the proceeds was to go to the seizing officer ; the rest, minus expenses, was to be paid into the Exchequer. All seized tobacco was to be sold *by the Customs*. If the goods, being tea or tobacco, did not fetch a specified price, they were to be destroyed, the officers still being rewarded. Seized ships and boats were to be destroyed, or used by the Customs in the prevention of smuggling.

This Act contained a clause aimed directly at the customs officers, who, being first dealers with a widely dispersed traffic, had special opportunities of acting collusively. It provided that every customs officer who made a seizure should apprise an excise officer within forty-eight hours, otherwise any other customs or excise man might reseize the goods. Seized goods were not to be removed without an excise permit. This was severe on the Customs, but another clause implicated the Excise, providing that any officer of that department who dealt in tea, coffee, or spirits should be fined £50 and dismissed. Informers who supplied evidence in such cases were to be presented with the fine.

The more the fox is hunted the cleverer he becomes, and mountains of law may not prevail against winds that are favourable, nights that are dark, and fraudulent folk who are active and resolute. While the Rolls teemed with provisos and penalties, the art of smuggling was carried to a perfection previously unknown. For a full century from this date the revenue staff failed conspicuously in prevention. The contestants were unevenly matched. The population of the southern and eastern coasts of England, and of the south-eastern coast of Scot-

land, furnished thousands of turbulent men, eminently
fitted by Nature and inclination for the lawless trade.   It
must be borne in mind that the British lower classes, both
maritime and inland, were an entirely different race to
those of the present day.   Hardship, blows, and rough
company were their heritage.   The mob was a many-
headed monster to be fervently dreaded—a monster that
endured patiently many grievous inflictions, yet occasionally manifested its true temper ; not as now, by pro-
cessions and wordy tumult, but by wrecking palaces,
burning jails, and defying musketry.   He who would
realize what even rustics of that day were capable of must
read Somerville's ' Hobbinol '—read and believe, for the
author scarcely exaggerates except in burlesque of an
older literature of combat.   Glimpses of the British sailor
and longshoreman may be obtained in the pages of
Smollett.   Most of the men engaged in contraband
dealing had known the roughest of the rough life then
obtaining.   They were the best sailors and watermen in
the world—better far than the men of the Navy, many of
whom had been pressed from various sedentary occupations.

Against these shrewd desperadoes were pitted the
customs officers.   Little in the way of watching, chasing,
and capturing could reasonably be expected of the controllers, collectors, and searchers ; their training had been
utterly unfavourable to anything of the kind.   They had
their fees to collect and their involved accounts to check,
and such work rarely develops hardihood.   The riding-
officers were sometimes ex-cavalrymen, and had heard the
rattle of cold steel, but these had little knowledge of the
longshoreman's ways and wiles.   Others were men who
had been ' jobbed ' into the force, and were more likely
to make their rounds with as little trouble to themselves
as possible than to court danger and unpopularity by
being over-officious.   The ' sloop system ' of prevention
(certainly as ancient as the ' Old Subsidy ') was in some
ways admirable, yet often spoiled by the method of

equipment and manning. Some of the sloops were private ventures, the Crown paying the owners a sum towards maintenance and victualling, and in such cases it is conceivable that few risks would be taken with the vessels, and that petty seizures and savings on the allowances might be in vogue. The captains were not always men of sterling character, and sometimes informers were shipped as mariners. Anyone who has had actual acquaintance with the type knows that there is no more despicable character than your informer—a human rat with the nerves of a rabbit.

And the smuggler was quite a popular person. (Even now, when originality has been almost schooled and policed out of mankind, respectable folk, out of pure waywardness, occasionally attempt to defraud the revenue.) In the time of the Georges it was extremely profitable to live near the coast and be on confidential terms with one's neighbours. To be able to buy brandy at a third of the duty rate, and tea and tobacco at half-price, meant much to a man convivially inclined. And the liquor primed one the speedier, the tobacco was the more fragrant, the China leaf the more refreshing, that they were found in the outhouse at daybreak, and paid for at the back-door on the following night. Of course it was so. Stolen love is sweet ; so is smuggled liquor.

To illustrate fully the severe and searching nature of the preventive regulations, the determination of a large section of the king's subjects to evade them at all hazards, the unreliability of some of the collecting officials, and the nature of the work thrown upon the Board and Treasury by the complicated tariff, it will be necessary to furnish specimens of official correspondence. It must be understood that only one bundle of papers, taken almost at random, will be dealt with, and the period of time covered by them is very brief. They date from January to July, 1720, and undoubtedly they do not represent the total correspondence during that period between Thames Street and Whitehall. (Only a curt summary will be given.)

1. The Lieutenant-General in charge of the Leeward Islands complains to the Treasury of misbehaviour by the collector of St. Kitt's. The complaint is referred to the Board of Customs, the accuser and defendant are brought face to face, and the Board report the result of the investigation, as below :

It appears that a Creole named Drascon made affidavit that the collector employed him to buy uncustomed goods on board a vessel discharging at St. Kitt's. The collector produced an affidavit made by another person to prove that the purchase was made merely to find out whether there were uncustomed goods on board, that the articles bought were condemned, and that the ship was seized. The Lieutenant-General then urged that the goods were condemned and the ship seized as the result of after-thought, merely to screen the illegal proceeding. But the collector replied that he would have seized the ship earlier had not the weather been so rough that he was unable to go on board.

Drascon also made affidavit that the collector sent him to ' the French islands ' to buy wine and other goods, and transhipped the wine into a vessel for Europe, thus infringing the Navigation Act. The collector admitted trading flour for sugar. He pleaded ignorance of the law. He denied buying wine.

The collector was charged with offering to release a seized ship for 150 pistoles. He denied the charge.

He was further charged with commuting the $4\frac{1}{2}$ per cent. duties of sugar in kind for a money payment, and charging a shilling a tierce more than the monetary equivalent. He replied that he allowed certain merchants, for their own convenience, to commute the duties in kind, and charged the extra shilling for his trouble, as he had to use the money received in buying other sugars to send home ' for the king.'

Report : The Board consider the first three charges
not proven, but hold the collector blameable for commuting the duties in kind, and consider the practice likely
to lead to fraud.   They will warn the other collectors in
the Leeward Islands.

2. The Board inform the Treasury that it has become
a frequent practice to remove in boats goods which have
paid duty, and to lure the officers into seizing them.
Then action is taken for damages, and, as the case is tried
in the county where it has occurred, the jury are partial,
'being generally people concerned in smuggling, who
seldom fail of giving a verdict for the plaintiff.'   The
Board have therefore prepared a clause, which they beg
may be submitted to Parliament, giving power to the
Crown officers to claim that any such case may be tried
' in an indifferent ' (disinterested) ' county.'

3. The Board having in 1715 submitted a schedule of
values for certain goods as yet unrated in the ' Book of
Rates,' and having received no word as yet that it shall
be submitted to Parliament, suggest that certain of the
articles scheduled may at once be rated for poundage, to
counteract to some extent the existing ' evil practice of
swearing goods at different values ' (declaring unenumerated goods at insufficient values to escape a portion of
the poundage).

4. The collector of Bridgwater has reported to the
Board that a Hamburg ship went ashore near his port,
and that 370 hogsheads wine, 98 puncheons brandy,
12 hogsheads prunes, 36 casks resin, 1 hogshead indigo,
and 200 bags chestnuts, were salved, and secured under
Customs charge.   The master of the ship had no money
wherewith to pay the salvage claims, and his agent
applied for permission to sell a portion of the salved goods,
and to convey them by sea to Bristol for that purpose.
The rabble of the place prevented the shipment of the
goods, broke into the Customs cellars, and helped them-

selves to several casks of wine and brandy. The Board offer a reward for the apprehension of the rioters, and order two revenue sloops to repair to Bridgwater and defend the goods and the officers.

Attached to the correspondence is a doleful letter from the agent at Bristol to Mr. Earle, M.P., requesting him to use his influence in getting troops sent to Bridgwater. ' 50 or 60 men carried off 6 casks brandy . . . . We would have searched for it, but 40 or 50 villaines with Forks, Shovells, etc., opposed us, Swearing Bitterly they would " murder every soul of 'em." . . . The constables and tythingmen are among the greatest offenders. . . . In this Deplorable case what shall I do ?' (He referred to the unfortunate foreigners, who had been treated with great inhumanity by the rabble.) 'We cannot leave them to be Devoured by Beares.'

The Board suggest a troop of soldiers be at once sent.

5. The Board submit several clauses, to be embodied in a Preventive Act, to this effect :

(*a*) Promising pardon and reward to such as give information as to the obstruction of officers.

(*b*) Providing that brandy ships shall not lie nor hover within two leagues of the coast.

(*c*) Providing that when a vessel is detained for smuggling her officers shall be imprisoned for six months. Etc., etc.

6. A seizure of lace, muslin, and jewels has been made in a house. The owner of the house approaches the Treasury, stating that the muslin and jewels were left with him as pledges. The Treasury refer to the Board. The Board reply that they have returned the muslin and jewels, but will prosecute for the lace.

7. A London merchant approaches the Treasury. He imported 137 butts of raisins. The usual tare was 14 per cent. of the gross weight, but the customs officers insisted that 12 per cent. would be enough. The

importer then removed the goods to his private ware-house, being afraid that if tared on the quay they might be plundered. He still claimed the high tare, and asked the officers to go to his warehouse and tare one of the casks. They refused.

The Board report, upholding the officers. 'The permitting goods to be reviewed by officers after they have been out of their possession may be of ill consequence to the Revenue.' Therefore the importer must be content with the low tare.

(My Lords concur.)

8. Certain merchants approach the Treasury, praying an alteration in the method of paying drawback on exported cider and perry. (It was urged that the goods were sent abroad in small consignments so as not to glut the foreign market, that the drawback allowed was small, and the customs officials insisted on a separate debenture for each parcel shipped. This caused the merchants much trouble and expense. It was suggested that each merchant should take out one debenture per year, to cover his total annual shipment, and receive each year's drawback in a lump sum.)

Treasury refer to Board. Board report the patent officers and searchers are against the suggestion, as the method proposed will complicate their work.*

Minute : ' *Read*.'

9. Mr. Gravener, dismissed from the collectorship of Ipswich, approaches the Treasury. Board referred to.

(Gravener stated he had taken certain sums of money from merchants for attending their shipments of bountied corn at sufferance wharves and at other than legal hours, and that he was entitled to charge for such attendance.)

The Board reply that he had charged 10s. for each corn debenture and 6d. on every last of corn exported, and

---

* The proposal appears to have been business-like and reasonable, but readers must bear in mind that the patentees charged fees on *each* debenture.

that when a certain merchant refused to pay Gravener detained his vessel. ' No such instructions have been given by us.' Some slight recompense is due in such cases to the officers who actually execute the sufferance, but the collector should fix the sum. He has no right to charge for his own attendance. ' He cannot be a judge in his own cause.'

(Gravener stated that the merchant in question trapped him by insisting upon a receipt, and then sent the receipt to the Board; also that the merchant had a spite against him, because Gravener's father had tried to get the river made navigable from Stow to Ipswich, which was against the merchant's interest. Gravener also reminded the Treasury that when the Board dismissed the collector of Exeter for a similar transaction My Lords reinstated him.)

The Board reply that since Gravener's dismissal other charges have been made. He has been accused of extorting 4s. for every entry of goods inwards, and of charging a sufferance, in which several merchants took part, to each individual merchant; also with executing one bond for several transactions, charging the expenses on each transaction, and pocketing the surplus; also with extorting 5s. each from the captains of all colliers entering and leaving the port of Ipswich.

10. The Board, having received information from the Scottish Commissioners of Customs that great frauds occur in connexion with the Isle of Man, remind My Lords of a similar report sent from Thames Street on 18th February, 1718.

Minute : ' To be read at a full Board.'

11. The Board report as to charges of management in the port of London, stating that since the adoption of the new system of allowing for damaged wine and tobacco two out of the eleven surveyors in the port have not been required, and may be dispensed with.

Minute : ' Read. To be reconsidered another time.'

12. Presentment by Board to Treasury :

'Mr. Stanhope having by his letter of 19th Novr. last signified to us that your Lord^{pps} did agree to the Prosecution of E. Curll, Bookseller, for reflecting on this Board in an adv$^{t.}$ of the publication of a pamphlet intituled "The Present Management of the Customs," in such manner as should be advised by Mr. Attorney Gen$^{l.}$, a Prosecution has been commenced against the said Curll accordingly : But he having since attended us, and being desirous to make his submission for his said offence : We are willing, if your Lord^{pps} have no objection, upon his making his submission, that the Prosecution be dropped.

' J. STANLEY.
   J. PULTNEY.
   G. WALKER.
   G. D. PRINGLE.'*

Minute : 'Agreed to.'

(It may with safety be said that the above twelve papers are about a fair sample of the correspondence between the Treasury and the Board of Customs during the eighteenth century. Volume after volume might be filled with such matter—matter highly illustrative, not only of the revenue practice, but of the social condition of England—of the manners of the day, as well as of its customs.)

It is time to take a trip across the Border, to study a few incidents of Scottish smuggling ; afterwards to renew acquaintance with the controller and collector of Montrose,

* This was the notorious Edmond Curll, whom Pope made a butt of in one of the most obscene pamphlets ever printed. According to Sir William Musgrave's 'Memoranda,' the advertisement in question appeared in the *Daily Courant*. Curll in his day published much scurrilous and indecent literature, and on one occasion was set in the pillory for his pains.

and the ' Bide-a-wee ' Board at Edinburgh. First must be told the story of Dunbar of Thunderton.

In 1716, the collector of Inverness had a passage of arms with ' Dunbar of Thunderton,' Provost of Elgin County. It is evident that Dunbar, although a minister of the law, was not exactly a law-abiding person. Before describing the ' tuilzie ' between him and the collector a letter must be quoted, sent previously to Dunbar by one William Sutherland, a merchant who frequently acted as agent in smuggling ventures.

' I have ventured to order Skipper Watt, how soon it please God he come to the firth, to call at Caussie, and cruise betwixt that and Burgh-head until you order your boats to waite him. He is to give half of what I have of the same sort with his last cargo, to any having your order. It's not amiss you secure one boat at Caussie as well as the Burgh boats. The signall he will make will be all sails furled except his main topsaile, and the boats you order to him are to lower their saile when within muskett shott, and then hoist it again : this, least he should be surprised with catchpoles. He is to write you before he sails from Bordeaux per Elgin post.

' WILLM. SUTHERLAND.'

This letter was sent in 1710, and there is reason to believe that between that date and 1716 Dunbar continued to deal with Skipper Watt, and with other importers and receivers of smuggled goods. In 1716 the customs tide-surveyor at Inverness heard of a run, and, acting upon the information, traced seven hogsheads of wine to the cellar of William Crombie, vintner, of Elgin. He detained the goods, and summoned ' Dunbar of Thunderton ' to witness their seizure. That unreliable official attended, and he and the tide-surveyor placed their locks upon the cellar. The tide-surveyor then sent for Mr. Erskine, the Inverness collector, and told him what had been done ; whereupon Erskine, naturally anxious to view the seized goods, went to the Provost, and asked him to assist in unlocking the cellar. Dunbar declined (this interview took place late at night), and it is evident that the collector and tide-surveyor then foolishly went home.

Whether Dunbar really retired to rest does not appear, but it is likely that if he did it was not to sleep. On the following morning Erskine and the tide-surveyor revisited the cellar, and found that the customs lock had been broken, the Provost's remaining intact. They sent for Dunbar, who calmly took off his lock and admitted them. The casks were still there, but instead of good red Gascon they contained ' coloured water.' Then came the trouble, and it is necessary to quote some of the correspondence appertaining.

' *27th April*, 1716.

' Alexander Erskine, collector of Customs att Inverness, protests against Archibald Dunbar of Thunderton, Provost of Elgine, for all damage and loss that happened to seven hogsheads of rede wine, imbezled without payment of duty, and seized by Alexander Cummine, tyd-surveyor att Inverness, in the cellar of William Crombie, vintner, in Elgine, one of the keys of the said cellar being in the possession of the said Archibald Dunbar, and delivered to him by Alexander Cummine fforesaid, which key he refused to me, the said Alexander Erskine, on the 26th. att night, and next morning the hanging lock of the said cellar, of which the collector had the key, was brock off, and the other lock, of which Thunderton had the key, was intire and close lockt up, which he himself opened, and upon tapping, the fforesaid seven casks was found with nothing in them but water a little colloured with wine, whereas they were all left by the said Alexander Cummine ffull of good and sufficient rede wine upon his delivering up the key to the said Archibald Dunbar, and thereffor protests that he shall be lyable in the ffull value of the fforesaid seven hogsheads of rede wine, conforme to eighteen pound per hogshead, and also protests against the fforesaid William Crombie, vintner, ffor the value of the said wine imbezled by him and taken in without paying the duty, and also carried out of his said cellar and the casks ffilled up with water.

'ALEXANDER ERSKINE, *Collector*.'

It would seem that Dunbar and Crombie had been in such a hurry to remove the precious goods, and substitute 'coloured water,' that they had failed to extend due consideration to the matter of adjustment. Otherwise, it may be conceived, they would have broken *both* locks; and thus diverted suspicion from the person most liable to be suspected.

The collector also applied to Dunbar for a warrant to search the town, and a constable to assist and protect him. Dunbar refused point-blank, making his case look blacker than ever. The collector entered another protest :

'Alexander Erskine, collector of Customs att Inverness, protests against Archibald Dunbar of Thunderton, Provost of Elgine and Justice of the Peace of the County of Murray, ffor refusing me a warrant to search such houses, kilns, barns, &c. of the town of Elgine and adjacent places in that county, and refusing to give me a constable to goe along with me to search ffor wine imbezled out of the cellar of William Crombie, vintner, in Elgine, and other uncustumed goods, confforme to a Write of Assistance produced to him.

'ALEXANDER ERSKINE, *Collector*.'

He then reported the matter to Edinburgh, and Charles Eyre, Solicitor for the Scottish Customs, went to work with a view of having the Provost exchequered. Readers may be inclined to think that Dunbar was in a perilous position, but there were ways of settling such matters. The Provost consulted one Ludovic Brodie, writer to the Signet, and Ludovic took the only promising course. He interviewed Eyre more than once. The matter in dispute was one of wine, and it followed that a considerable quantity of wine was consumed while they were threshing the matter out. Let Brodie's letter to Dunbar after the final interview proclaim Brodie's method, and the pleasing result :

'Your affair with the Exchequer has bein advysed, and the bills are ordered to be redelivered, you paying the officers' costs who seized the wynes. Now the costs to them, according to the rules of Court, will be but about three or four guineas, besyde what may be claimed for information-getting, as to which Mr. Erskin seems not to demand anything for himself, but to referr himself to your discretion. This matter has stood the most drinking (and also some considerable charges) that ever I drunk in any other, for tho Eyre be a gentlemanie prettie little fellow yet he drinks like a devil, and I have had many sore heads with him. Wyseman will not deny but I desired him to buy or make such a brydle as would please you : if you do not plague him with your tongue you are in wrong to yourself and me, for he would not lose ane hour's drinking for all the bussieness in the world.

'Ludovic Brodie.'

Who 'Wyseman' was, and the meaning of the mysterious allusion to the 'brydle,' remain to be discovered, but it is possible Mr. Brodie wrote this with a wet towel around his head. The affair seems to have been adjusted in a manner likely to afford at least partial satisfaction to all concerned. Eyre had several rosy nights, Brodie ditto and got his 'charges.' Dunbar and Crombie got off with the good 'rede wine,' and the officers got their 'costs,' the collector probably coming off much better than the tide-surveyor. Dunbar, no doubt, was put to considerable expense, but it is probable the arrangement would lead to a comfortable understanding between Provost and officers, and that Skipper Watt would in future be able to run goods without fear of being 'surprised with catchpoles.' Small wonder that the returns of Customs revenue did little more than pay the cost of collection and the salaries of the judges.

In 1725 the collector of Montrose reported to the Scottish Board that the Montrose surveyor of customs had made a large seizure of brandy, etc., at Arbroath. The surveyor stated that finding that certain vessels, names unknown, had been ' hovering on the coast,' he procured a party of soldiers, went to Arbroath, patrolled the town all night, and in the morning searched and found the goods in question. The collector and controller in their report requested the Commissioners to use their influence towards procuring a detachment of soldiers to be permanently stationed at Arbroath. ' There are more goods run there than at any place on the coast.' Later a person named Dennison claimed that the seizure was due to private information furnished by him, and that he was entitled to a substantial share of the reward. This led to some very pretty fencing.

It was a practice amongst smuggling skippers, when freighting with contraband oversea, to obtain a bill of lading for Bergen, so that if whilst ' hovering ' to run their cargoes they were driven by stress of weather into a British port they might produce the document, and thus account for having on board a thousand or so ankers of brandy which, being under the ' lawful content ' of 60 gallons each, would be deemed illegal packages and liable to seizure. (At Bergen there was a Staple for all foreign goods taken into the Scandinavian realms.) Both the English and Scottish Boards were aware that this was usually mere fiction, for it had happened more than once that a ' hoverer ' had put forward this plea in port and been allowed to depart for Bergen, but shortly afterwards had been driven again by storm into the same port or one adjacent, when it had been discovered that there was no brandy left on board, except a demijohn or two in the captain's locker, and an ullaged anker in the forecastle. So when Captain Hamilton of the revenue sloop captured a ' hoverer,' and brought her into Montrose with her illegal cargo, and the master produced a Bergen bill of lading, the collector and controller referred the matter to Edinburgh. The Board directed that the master's plea should be accepted, that he should be allowed to depart, and that two customs tidesmen should be put on board to keep him company to Bergen, to see the cargo discharged there. One may imagine the smuggler captain's disgust at this inquisitorial proceeding. He left with his two tidesmen, and in due course the tidesmen returned safe and sound, and stated that they had carried out their instructions. Then they put in an appalling bill for expenses, which caused much correspondence between Montrose and Edinburgh.

The collector and controller, in a later message to the Board, gave a doleful description of the state of affairs in their district : ' The boatmen along the coast and the country people favour and assist the smuglers in carrying on their smugling trade so much that it is almost impracticable to an officer to get any intelligence from them, and when any poor man happens to bring an information to an officer he is afraid (if discovered) of his life, or at least of being obliged to leave this part of the country.'

In transmitting their account of the balance in hand for the month of December, 1725 (after paying certain charges), the collector and controller asked permission to retain the money and pay the officers with it. ' The amount,' said they, ' of this month is seldom enough to pay the officers.' The amount in hand was £42 odd.

Early in 1726 the collector of Newcastle informed the Montrose officers that a ship of Arbroath had been driven by storm into his port, that she had a large quantity of brandy on board, and that the master held the usual papers for Bergen. A week later the vessel entered the port of Montrose, and on being rummaged was found to have nothing in her hold but seed and old iron. The Montrose officers reported the matter to Edinburgh, but the concluding portion of their statement was unlikely to encourage the Board to proceed further in the business.

'We have questioned the sailors, but they are better taught than to divulge anything, either of the running of the goods or any other passage of the voyage, notwithstanding all the civil and discreet offers we can make them, they being a set of ingrain'd rogues. The master had the assurance to deny positively that he was ever within Tynmouth Bar.'

The officers at Kirkcaldy seized an ' open boat,' containing 60 bushels of smuggled salt. The sole occupant of the boat was a sturdy rogue, said to be Thomas Watt of Johnshaven. Thomas Watt ' furiously assaulted ' the Kirkcaldy officers, beat and overthrew them, triumphantly put to sea again with the goods, and escaped. The Board directed the Montrose officers to proceed to Johnshaven, and if possible arrest the valiant smuggler. The officers reported back to the Board the result of their efforts. They had been to Johnshaven, and failed to find Thomas, or his open boat, or his 60 bushels of salt. ' The only Watt in Johnshaven,' said they, ' is a shoemaker, and appears a poor silly fellow.'

Later one or two rather important seizures were made, in each case with the assistance of the military. The goods were kept for some little time in the warehouse of Montrose, and then sent per sloop to Leith for condemnation and sale, advised as to quantity, etc. The Leith officers examined them on arrival, and discovered the following discrepancies :

Montrose Advice.	Leith Re-examination Account.
1 butt brandy.	2 butts brandy.
73 full ankers brandy.	70 full ankers brandy.
1 ullaged anker brandy.	1 ullaged anker brandy.
25 full ankers geneva.	24 full ankers geneva.
1 ullaged anker geneva.	1 ullaged anker geneva.
A quantity of cocoa and treacle.	Largely deficient.
A quantity of tobacco.	38 pounds short of advice.
A quantity of coffee.	Slightly deficient.
A quantity of sugar.	Somewhat short.
A quantity of starch.	Largely deficient.
A quantity of currants.	7 pounds in excess of advice.
Four casks gunpowder.	No gunpowder.

The above are quoted from a Board's query on the matter. The collector and controller replied that possibly the goods had lost by leakage and drying during the voyage. They made no other attempt to account for the disappearance of three full ankers of brandy and one of geneva, for the transformation of one butt of brandy into two, or for the total evanishment of four casks of gunpowder. 'Never,' said they, 'were goods more carefully weighed and gauged, and shipped on the sloop that conveyed them. We can't understand it. We always have three locks on our warehouse.'

The balance for the Crown at the end of January, 1727 (after paying the quarterly salaries), was £2 19s. 10¼d.

The *Michael and Mary* of Holy Island was driven by storm into Montrose, and found to have on board a large number of half-ankers of brandy, a quantity of tea, and the usual Bergen bill of lading. The officers referred the case to the Board, and were directed to make the master enter into a 'hovering bond.'* The master complied. Seven months later the officers wrote to the Board, stating that having received no certificate of the landing of the goods at Bergen they still held the bond undischarged. No further correspondence on the subject is forthcoming, and it may reasonably be surmised that the sureties had absconded, and the vessel, with her rig and name altered, was 'hovering' again.

The balance for September, 1727, reached £182 odd, and the officers found themselves confronted with a new difficulty. They wrote : 'We cannot at present procure Bills on Edinburgh for remitting said balance.'

On October 6, 1727, a ship arrived from Philadelphia with 103 hogsheads of tobacco, legally entered for discharge at Montrose. This caused quite an official commotion. The sum due to the Crown at the end of the month was over £231. The officers asked the Board to allow them

* This was really a bond to refrain from 'hovering.' Convicted smugglers, on release, were often called on to enter into bond to refrain from smuggling, and this was called 'a smuggling bond.'

to keep a portion of this ' great balance ' in hand, as the importer of the tobacco had given them to understand he would soon be exporting part of the goods again, and asking for drawback. Thus it would appear that there was no accommodation for bonding tobacco at Montrose, and the importer had to deposit the whole duty even on goods that were soon to be exported.

The Board sent information that one Gillespie of Arbroath was about to make an illegal shipment of wool. The collector and controller replied that they were sending ' a trusty tidesman ' to assist the Arbroath tidesmen in seizing the goods. Lest the Board might become too sanguine of success, they added : ' Arbroath is so mobish a place that unless troops be quartered there it is almost impracticable to stop these frauds.' The trusty tidesman returned with news that the ships had left before he reached Arbroath.

Readers will no doubt have realized by this and previous quotations from the Letter Books that the Montrose officers were by no means equal to the exigencies confronting them. Later particulars will show that the exigencies were more formidable than they appear—that the collector and controller had reason to dread, not only the mob, but the magistrates.

Meantime the London Board had been kept busy, not only in devising schemes for the suppression of smuggling, but in dealing with complaints made by the public, in settling disputes between the customs officers and the excisemen, and in regulating the domestic economy of the Custom-house. The records are rich in amusing and instructive references, but here is space for a few only.

In 1714 a large fire broke out in Thames Street, which did great damage to the Custom-house.* The Commissioners laid a report before the Treasury, stating roughly the

* The Custom-house had been built after the Great Fire in Charles II.'s reign.

amount of the loss incurred, and of the expense sustained otherwise. The principal item of loss was the complete destruction of 232 hogsheads of sugar, which had been collected in the Leeward Islands as 4½ per cent. duties in kind, sent to London, and stored beneath the Custom-house. The value of these was stated as £2,780. 61½ gallons brandy and 18 gallons wine, being part of a seizure, had been distributed among the people who helped to put the fire out. The books and papers had been removed, but the Commissioners were unable just then to state the total expense of saving and housing them, or even the expense of temporary offices for the staff. But they uttered their minds upon the action of the Cloth-workers' Company, who had allowed them the use of the Clothworkers' Hall as a temporary refuge, and charged at the rate of £500 a year for the accommodation. (During the earlier stage of banishment the Commissioners themselves put up at Garraway's Coffee House.)

The London merchants petitioned the Treasury, objecting to the many holy-days observed by the customs officers, especially Shrove Tuesday, St. Swithin's, Holy Cross, and Wednesdays of Easter and Whitsun. They also requested that one Commissioner should attend in the Bench Office at 9 a.m. to sign cockets. The Commissioners at once agreed, and stated that if the merchants had approached them the Treasury need not have been troubled with the matter.

In 1725 the Board decided to allow a bonfire to be made upon the quay on Coronation Day. ' But,' said they, ' being apprehensive that a large bonfire would endanger the shipping, we direct our Housekeeper to make a moderate bonfire, not exceeding 40 faggots. He may give some liquor to the watchmen and others to drink the health of his Majesty and the Royal Family, as usual on such occasions, but he may not suffer firebrands to be thrown about or any squibbs fired.'

In 1727 a customs landing-surveyor and an excise officer were deputed to investigate the gauging of casks in the port of London. On the second day of inquiry trouble arose, it being discovered that the customs and excise methods of gauging differed. The merchants seem to have preferred the customs method, for they united in a complaint against the delay caused by excise gauging. Of course it does not follow that the customs gauging was correct because it pleased the merchants.

The Board issued an order that Swedish religious books, ' for the use of the Congregation in Pennsylvania,' should be allowed to pass duty-free.

It was the practice, when a new foreign ambassador arrived, for the Treasury to issue a warrant directing the Customs to ' extend every facility to the passing of his baggage.' He was allowed a certain quantity duty-free, and the Commissioners usually required him to furnish a schedule of the goods, and declare above his signature that they were for his own use, nor would they allow him to *import* goods duty-free afterwards. In 1720 Baron Discow imported ' a suit of cloaths,' and the Treasury enjoined the officers to ' use all civility and despatch consistent with law.' The officers reported that the clothes were embroidered, ' and cut out though not made up.' The Board of Customs thereupon directed a prosecution.

The king had to pay duty on his customable goods. The royal baggage on arrival was removed under seal to Whitehall, and ' the three senior land-surveyors ' attended to examine it. Stringent instructions were issued to collect all duties payable, and *two* officers had to be present whenever a package was opened. The Board in 1723 issued an order to the effect that His Majesty being expected to arrive from the Continent the river guard was to be strengthened ' to prevent running of goods,' and letters were sent to the chief officers of Kent and Essex, directing them to be extremely vigilant. When wine was imported for the king's use it was removed to Whitehall, being first entered on ' a Bill of Sight,' and officers were sent to gauge the casks and assess the duty. ' The Secretary of State's box ' was examined at Whitehall after arrival from foreign in 1715, the officers being particularly directed to charge duty upon any customable goods they might find in it.

Nor were the Commissioners childishly trustful of each other. They directed that whenever a package arrived from foreign for one of them the landing-officer dealing with it was to remove it to the King's Warehouse, and the Warehouse-keeper was bound to furnish a report of the matter at once to the assembled Board. Most of the Georgian Boards of Customs appear to have been aflame with zeal.

It should be mentioned that in 1724 Lord Poulet, one of the Exchequer 'tellers' or receivers, was called upon to account for £4,191 14s. 6d. which had been stolen from his office in the Exchequer.* (The deficiency was made good out of the Sinking Fund in 1729.) It appears that the thieves broke through the roof, and forced the lock off the end of one of the chests, thus creating an aperture, through which they withdrew five bags of gold. Four of these, and a portion of the contents of the fifth, they carried off, and left the broached bag lying on the floor.

LIST OF AUTHORITIES.

Scottish revenues before Union: Assisa de Tolloneis; Custum Portuum; Assisa Regis (David); Acts of Robert III.; Scottish Acts, 1424, c. 19, 22, 23; 1425, c. 18; 1466, 1-4; 1478, 5; 1493, 12-17; 1535, 25-32; 1540, 11-12; 1567, 63; 1581, 12; 1597, 'Act anent the Custumes'; 1597, 23; 1604, 'Commissioun for the Vnion'; 1606, 'Act anent the Customes betuix Scotland and England'; 1641, 127-150; Convention of Estates, January 31,

---

* This appears to have been the only theft of Exchequer money since the romantic feat achieved by Richard de Pudlicote early in the fourteenth century. The undetected thief who got off with Poulet's takings was a mere trifler, compared with Richard. Not only did the latter carry off £100,000 worth of gold and jewels, but he was assisted in his exploit by many of the monks of Westminster Abbey, and several of the officials of the Palace. The robbery was performed at dead of night, and the Palace mason assisted Richard and his associates in breaking through the wall of the Pyx Room. Much of the plunder was not recovered till months after the robbery.

1644 ; 1661, 92, 277, 310 ; 1663, 8 ; Warrant of April 16, 1689 ; 1695, Act 32 ; 1695, 70 ; 1696, 7 ; 1698, 42 ; 1701, 8, 9, 13.

Liverpool : 8 Anne, c. 8.

Permanent branches of revenue : 8 Anne, c. 5 ; 8 Anne, c. 12 ; 9 Anne, c. 6 ; 9 Anne, c. 12 ; 9 Anne, c. 13 . 10 Anne, c. 18 ; 10 Anne, c. 19 ; 12 Anne, c. 12 ; 13 Anne, c. 18 ; 1 Geo. I., s. 2, c. 23 (on 9 Anne, c. 17) ; 6 Geo. I., c. 11 ; 8 Geo. I., c. 20 ; 9 Geo. I., c. 19 ; 11 Geo. I., c. 7.

Quarantine : 9 Anne, c. 2.

Wreck : 13 Anne, c. 21.

Departmental incidents : Sir Wm. Musgrave's 'Memoranda' ; Montrose Letter Books ; Treasury Papers, July 16, 1727 ; Treasury Papers, vol. 261 ; Treasury Papers, January to July, 1719-1720 ; Customs Book, No. 15 ; Treasury Papers, vol. 252.

Establishment : Carkesse's Book of Rates, 8 Geo. I., c. 31 ; 9 Geo. I., c. 21.

Wine : 6 Geo. I., c. 12.

Frauds : 6 Geo. I., c. 21 ; 'Social Life in Former Days.'

Preventive Measures : 9 Geo. I., c. 21 ; 5 Geo. I., c. 11 ; 6 Geo. I., c. 21 ; 8 Geo. I., c. 18 ; 12 Geo. I., c. 28.

Temporary Imposts : 10 Geo. I., c. 10 ; 12 Geo. I., c. 26.

Protective measures and prohibitions : 8 Geo. I., c. 15.

CHAPTER VII

THE PERIOD OF FRANTIC RESTRICTIONS AND FEARLESS SMUGGLING

1727–1760

WHEN George II. ascended the throne, it must have appeared to some of his subjects impossible to invent many alterations in the tariff list. The latest ' Book of Rates,' although edited by the Secretary to the Customs Commissioners, had been an indescribable hotch-potch. Yet the revenue tables were to be rendered still more perplexing.

Imported wine-lees were made liable to duty as wine. Wine imported in bottle, or in casks containing less than 25 gallons, was prohibited, unless from the Levant. Lignum vitæ grown and shipped at the Plantations was freed of duty inward.

Amid uproarious rejoicing, the excise duty on home-made salt, and the customs surtax on foreign salt, were abolished. The collection of these imposts had been both inquisitorial and expensive, yet the pay of the collecting officers was continued for eighteen months from the cessation of the duties.

The bounty on British sailcloth was increased, and British gunpowder was bountied on exportation.

In 1732 the odious excise duty on British salt, and the customs surtax on foreign salt, were revived ' for three years.' Their renewal was tumultuously opposed, but the ministers were obdurate. The collectors were re-instated, as though the temporary remission had been a device towards securing them a holiday on full pay. (At the end of three years the duties were continued for seven years, and yet again, and yet again.)

To encourage British hat-makers, exportation of hats from the Plantations was prohibited, it being also provided that no plantation hatter should have more than two apprentices at a time, that no 'black or negro' should be taught the trade, and that no person in the Plantations should sell hats unless he had served full apprenticeship as a maker.

In 1729 the Customs Commissioners directed that goods of flotsam, jetson, and lagan were to be entered and duty-paid as though landed in the ordinary way.

In 1731 they directed that merchants who failed to enter their goods within the specified time should be sued for the duties payable.

It was found necessary to direct excise officers not to go beyond their stations to rummage vessels, and not to interfere with the customs rummagers.

The customs officers were instructed, when they suspected 'women of fashion' of carrying customable goods, to call in the services of a female searcher 'in whom they could confide.'

It appears that the eel-schuyts of Worcum, which may at the present day be seen lying in the Thames abreast of Billingsgate, plied between Holland and London in 1732. Duty was levied on the eels carried, at the rate of £3 a cargo.

The Custom-house Registers of 1732 stated the shipping belonging to the port of London as over 1,400 sail, navigated by nearly 20,000 men. 130 of the ships were from 300 to 500 tons, 83 from 200 to 300 ; the rest were under 200 tons, except one 'great ship' belonging to the South Sea Company, which was 750.

The Board of Trade informed Parliament that the Council of the American province of Massachusetts Bay, by passing an Act to encourage paper-making in the province, had seriously injured the British paper trade to the Plantations, that a duty recently levied by the State of New York upon imported negroes was undesirable, and that Plantation manufactures promised to compete formidably with those of Great Britain. Soon after more discouraging information was supplied. It was stated that large iron forges were being set up in New England, and that many ships built there had been sold to the French and Spaniards, being paid for in wines which were smuggled into the Plantations. Inquiries were made in consequence of these reports. The answers furnished were contradictory, every official questioned reporting according to the interests of his office.

The inland duty on coffee of the British Plantations was reduced from 2s. to 1s. 6d. a pound, and the goods were burdened with such a host of restrictions as to certificates, oaths of declaration, special markings, etc., that the planters would have been justified in resenting the remission.

To encourage the Plantation sugar trade, a duty was placed on all rum, sugar, and molasses imported into the West Indies from other parts of America, and all such goods sent from the 'other parts' to Ireland were to be landed in England during transit.

An alteration was made in the drawback on British refined sugar exported, leaving it as below:

	£	s.	d.
Rate during time of William and Mary	0	3	0
Increase during Anne's reign	0	1	0
Increase by this Act	0	2	0
Total drawback	0	6	0

Later the special 'French duty' on brandy from France was abolished, it having been extensively evaded by the importation of French spirits as Flemish, etc. Instead, an extra excise duty of 1s. per gallon was laid on imported 'single spirits' (spirits below a certain strength), and 2s. per gallon on 'double spirits.'

In 1736 the Board began to make arrangements for

the bonding of rum. Warehouses were to be provided at certain legal quays, the merchants interested to defray the cost, and the pay of the officers in charge. (Bonding was not legalized till 1742.)

The duty on arrack was amended. Previously arrack had been rated as an East Indian commodity, and its value for poundage had been the gross price paid at the East India Company's sales. The excise duties being payable as well, it had thus been rated higher than other foreign spirits.

The duty on woollen yarn from Ireland was abolished. The importation of books, written and printed in Great Britain, and reprinted abroad, was prohibited.

In 1739 the Stationers' Company undertook to pay the expenses incurred by the Customs in prosecuting importers of pirated books, and to reward the seizing officers.

In 1740 the Board enjoined that owlers should not be allowed to compound for penalties.

Rum and spirits of the Plantations were allowed to be deposited in warehouse on importation, the customs duty or Old Subsidy being first paid. Then bond might be entered into by the importer to pay the excise duties when he wished to deliver his goods for home consumption. The warehouses were to be supervised by the excise officers. The importers had to clear the goods within a specified time.

An additional tax was placed on foreign cambrics, and made a fund for bountying British and Irish linen. In 1745 ' The Additional Wine Duty ' was instituted, being an extra tunnage of £8 on French wine and vinegar, and £4 on other wine and vinegar. A loan of £2,000,000 was raised upon this tax, part to be by a lottery. During the reign there were about a dozen public lotteries in connection with national loans. And with all these lotteries and all this funding, Parliament issued statutes against private lotteries, stock-jobbing, horse-racing, gambling, and cursing and swearing.

French cambrics and lawns were prohibited importation, except if warehoused under bond to export within three years. The wearing of apparel made from these materials was also forbidden under heavy penalties.

The inland duties on tea, etc., were altered to 1s. a pound, and 25 per cent. of the gross price at the East India Company's sales. In 1746 'The Glass Duty' was established, being a bunch of additional duties on the various kinds of foreign glass. By 19 Geo. II., c. 27, it was provided that if a British ship arrived in a British port carrying foreign sails duty should be paid upon the sails. Later appeared 'The 1747 Subsidy,' an additional 5 per cent. poundage on all dutiable goods. The tremendous loan of £6,300,000 was raised upon it, and in connexion with this there seems to have been some tricky 'operating,' the courtiers and their friends trying to monopolize investment.

In 1748 a premium was granted upon Plantation indigo. By 22 Geo. II., c. 36, foreign embroidery and brocade were prohibited. In 1750 raw silk of the Plantations was made duty-free. A bounty was granted to British ships built for the herring fishery, being 30s. a ton per annum for fourteen years from date of building, provided they were decked vessels of from 20 to 80 tons. This act specified the limits of the herring-grounds, and the legal times of fishing. The Shetlands on the east and Cantire on the west were the northern limits. The fishing on the east was to commence not earlier than June 13, and the shoal to be followed not later than October 1. On the west coast fishing was to commence not earlier than September 1, and to end on December 31. The bounty money was to be paid out of the Customs revenue.*

Pig-iron from the Plantations was made duty-free, and bar-iron freed in the port of London only. (The latter privilege had soon to be extended to all British ports.) It was enacted that no mill for slitting iron, no plating forge to work with a tilt hammer, and no furnace for making steel, should be erected in the Colonies. (This

---

* In 1757 the bounty was increased to 50s. a ton.

Act, though passed by both Houses, was not put into execution.) The Irish parliament having bountied Irish sailcloth, and established a growing export trade, a duty equivalent to the bounty was placed on Irish sailcloth imported into Great Britain.

In 1752 two new permanent branches of customs were established—' The Duty on Linen Yarn,' and ' The Duty on Gum Senega.'

In 1758, it having been found that the owners of imported spirits which were liable to excise duties on landing frequently kept the goods on board ship for an unreasonable period, to postpone entering them for the Excise, it was enacted that such goods should be landed, entered, and the excise duty paid, within thirty days of importation, unless they were rums of the Plantations, in which case they might be bonded. The excise officers were permitted to take a sample not exceeding a quart from each cask, for the purpose of ascertaining the strength, and these samples were to be paid for by the Crown at the rate of 16s. a gallon. This last clause was soon found detrimental and repealed, and the official sample was limited to a half-pint without payment. The old practice of allowing the importer a duty-free sample of half a pint from each cask was reaffirmed.

In 1758 two of the Commissioners of Customs were directed to wait upon the duke of Newcastle, to discuss a scheme put forward by the Board of Trade for preventing revenue frauds in the Plantations. The Commissioners attended, but desired to be excused from considering the scheme, unless commanded to do so by the king, the Privy Council, or the Treasury. So the project was returned to the busybodies who had framed it.

During 1758 a royal licence was granted and a passport issued for the carrying of 800 bushels of oysters to France, ' for the Queen and Dauphiness.' This reads strangely, for at the time there was war between Great Britain and France. Besides, 800 bushels was a large order. Yet the record is clear on this point.

It was decided to employ a proctor at the Crown's expense to arrange for the appropriation of a quantity of Spanish silver, shipped by the collector of Charleston on board the *Winchilsea*, which vessel was captured by the French, and retaken by an English privateer. The amount originally shipped was 3,456 ounces, the amount restored by the privateer 1,736 ounces.

So many flagrant depredations were committed by British privateers that a committee of merchants was formed to inquire into the matter, and a customs solicitor was directed by the Board to attend the meetings, and render all assistance possible.

On account of an attempt upon the life of the Portuguese king, the officers of customs were directed to detain any Portuguese subject landing in Great Britain, and at once acquaint the Board. Later the order was qualified by an injunction that sailors need not be detained, and again to the effect that the order applied only to such Portuguese subjects as were 'scarred upon the cheek.'

Customs officers were directed to be vigilant in searching for escaped prisoners of war. If any were found they were to be sent ' to the nearest agent for such people.' The agents paid 10s. a head and expenses, in all cases of capture.

The quarantine regulations were strictly enforced. A man-of-war sent a boat's crew aboard a Levant trader to press seamen for the navy, and in consequence the man-of-war had to undergo quarantine.

It appears that tea was inspected as to quality. A quantity of tea from Deal (undoubtedly a contraband cargo seized) was ordered to be burned, it having been found ' dyed and adulterated.'*

Towards the end of the reign ' The Subsidy of 1759 ' was granted, another permanent branch, being additional poundage at 5 per cent. *ad valorem* upon many classes of merchandise, including tobacco, sugar, grocery,

* In 1761 a similar order was made in respect of a cargo seized at Exeter.

linen, paper, and spirits except rum. About this time appeared an Act allowing bonded Plantation rum a drawback on export of all the customs duties paid at landing, and remitting all the excise duties applying to such goods.

Undoubtedly at the end of this reign there was no citizen competent to act as a clearing agent for all classes of goods, and no customs official who thoroughly understood the whole of the Customs regulations.* The documents used in payment of duty were miracles of elaboration, with their numerous items of subsidies old, fractional, and new; of imposts, additional imposts, special duties, coinage duties, etc. The Plantation Acts bristled with exceptions and special provisions. The Coasting regulations were a monument of circumlocution. Every tax had a fringe of exasperating ramifications, even the Acts of bounty were clogged with bewildering formulæ.

The inevitable result of the huge burden of duties was increased smuggling, to combat which Parliament issued string after string of regulations, which we proceed to summarize. The first revenue law of 1729 was a concession to culprits, providing that in cases prosecuted by capias defendants might plead *in forma pauperis*. In 1732 an attempt at practical prevention was made. Three sixth-rate ships and eight armed sloops were sent to cruise in the Irish Sea, to prevent the exportation of woollen goods from Ireland to foreign parts. The captains were granted powers of search, and instructed to seize all vessels carrying Irish woollens not cocketed for the

---

* In 'The British Customs, with the Laws relating abridged and digested under Proper Heads,' a handbook compiled by Henry Saxby, of the Custom-house, London, which appeared in 1757, there are several remarkable paragraphs, conveying the author's declaration that all the previous compilers of similar handbooks had been guilty of many blunders. Specimens of the errors are given, and they are certainly flagrant. 'Although,' says Mr. Saxby, 'it is a disagreeable employment to animadvert on the errors of others, yet a just regard to improve and instruct necessarily requires that some few instances should be pointed out.'

stipulated western English ports.* In 1734 bitter penalties were prescribed against the landing of foreign hops prior to entry, and the carrying of foreign hops to Ireland without their being first landed in England.

The famous Act of Indemnity was issued in 1736. This was one of those odious revenue Acts peculiar to the time of the Georges, Acts which appealed to the baser villain. It indemnified all smugglers who might be mean enough to disclose their past offences, thereby implicating their comrades, and made the infamous process cheap and handy. (The plea of indemnity was to cost no more than 1s. 4d.) It provided against future offences by an enactment which for cold cruelty has never been surpassed. Persons pleading and subsequently offending were liable to prosecution for *both* offences, and if the offence quoted for indemnity carried the punishment of transportation the subsequent offence involved death without benefit of clergy. Three or more smugglers carrying firearms were punishable with transportation.†

* Later in this reign the privilege of importing Irish woollens was extended to every British port.

† The well-known Galley and Chater case furnishes a striking example of the deadly hatred felt towards revenue informers by the smuggling fraternity, of the fierceness and recklessness of many of the leading smugglers, and of the partiality and severity with which some of the judges interpreted the laws.

In September, 1747, a large quantity of tea was seized, and lodged in the Custom-house at Poole. On the night of October 6, 1747, a gang of armed smugglers attacked the Custom-house and carried off the tea. (Mr. Milner, later described by us as dismissed from the Service, was at this time collector of Poole, and was the first that gave evidence in the subsequent trial of Galley and Chater's murderers.)

The smugglers carried the tea inland, and on the way passed through Fordingbridge, Hants. One Daniel Chater, a shoemaker living at Fordingbridge, recognized a member of the gang named Dimer, and laid information at the Southampton Custom-house, in consequence of which Dimer was arrested and lodged in Chichester jail. It appears that one of the leaders of the gang, named Tapner, convened a meeting of the smugglers, and arranged for a night attack upon the jail, but, reckless as the men were, the arrangement fell through.

On February 14, 1748, the collector of Southampton directed one of the tidesmen of the port, named Galley, to accompany the informer Chater from Southampton to the residence of Major

Two or more armed smugglers carrying goods inland, or found within five miles of the coast with 6 pounds tea, or 5 gallons spirits not covered by permit, were to be deemed 'runners.' Persons 'lurking' within five miles of the coast were liable to be whipped and put to hard labour. Persons maimed in arresting smugglers were entitled to a reward of £50. Informers discovering two or more accomplices were entitled to £50 for each person convicted, and held free of their own offences. The law against 'hoverers' was strengthened, and the 'illegal limit' for transhipment of foreign goods at sea increased

---

Battine at East Marden. He gave them a letter which they were to hand to the Major. Battine was a J.P., and surveyor-general of customs for Sussex.

They set out on horseback, and on arriving at Leigh found it necessary to ask the way. Three villagers undertook to guide them, and brought them as far as Rowland's Castle. They all went into a public-house kept by a widow named Paine. Mrs. Paine became suspicious of Galley and Chater, and secretly apprised several smugglers living in the neighbourhood. The smugglers soon arrived, armed with whips, pistols, and knives, and managed to lure Chater out of the taproom. They proceeded to interrogate him as to his business, upon which the tidesman Galley came out and interfered. A fellow named Jackson struck Galley with his fist, and knocked him down. Then the gang took both the strangers into the house. Galley produced his commission, and announced that he was a king's officer. 'You a king's officer!' answered Jackson; 'we'll make a king's officer of you!'

Then the smugglers compelled the terrified men to drink, and it is likely they drugged them, for Galley and Chater fell asleep. Jackson and his comrades carried them into an adjoining room, and searched them. The letter was found, and it revealed that Chater was an informer.

The gang sat drinking for some time, and debating as to what they should do. First they decided to run both Galley and Chater across the Channel, and detain them in France, there being war at the time between France and England. Next they decided that the confederacy should subscribe for the men's keep, and detain them in England till Dimer had been tried. 'Then,' grimly suggested one of the gang, 'we will do unto them whatever is done to Jack Dimer.' But as the drink mounted they altered their minds, and resolved upon murder.

The ringleader Jackson went into the room where the men lay, and aroused them by slashing them with his whip. The poor fellows were driven into the road, and both of them tied upon one horse. It appears that many of the villagers came round, and some may have protested, for one of the gang drew a pistol, and

to four leagues from the coast. Revenue officers were privileged to oppose force to force, and entitled to bail if charged with maiming or killing offenders.

In 1745 a fresh Act of Indemnity was issued. In 1746 assembling to run contraband goods was made punishable 'by death as a felon.' Counties were made liable for offences committed within their limits. If goods were captured and afterwards rescued the fine on the county was £200. If an officer was beaten in the execution of his duty the fine was £40, if killed £100, but the county was held exempt if the offenders were convicted within

---

informed the spectators that if any man present uttered a word afterwards of the matter he would be sought out and shot down without mercy. Then away in the direction of Harting. It was already dark. The smugglers made one of the villagers lead the horse on which Galley and Chater rode.

As soon as they were clear of the village they made an on-slaught, and lashed the two unfortunates in a shocking manner. Jackson was especially vindictive, and urged his comrades on with shouts of 'Lick them, damn them, cut them, slash them, whip them!' He was very bitter against Galley, and in the end the poor tidesman fell into the road, and died of his wounds. His body was thrown across a horse in front of one of the smugglers, and the maddened cavalcade went on till they reached a public-house at Rake, kept by a man whom they knew. They compelled this man to show them a place where they might bestow the dead body. He took them to a fox-earth some distance away. A hole was dug, and the mangled remains were buried. Chater was conveyed to Trotten, and the party put up at a house kept by a notorious smuggler named Mills. Chater, who had been treated most brutally, was chained up in an outhouse hard by. All the smugglers living near who had been concerned in the attack upon the Poole Custom-house were sent for, and a council held. It was agreed that Chater should be put to death.

The man Tapner, who had proposed to rescue Dimer, was one of the new arrivals. He led the others into the outhouse, and bade Chater betake himself to prayer. While the poor wretch was praying one of the gang kicked him, and Tapner drew a knife and slashed his victim across the face. They led him to a dry well, and Tapner put a rope round his neck and hurled him down. They let him hang for some time, then cut the rope, and he fell. Thinking he might still be alive, they flung earth and large stones upon him. Then they went back to the tavern, and fell to drinking again.

It is of course impossible to urge anything in extenuation of such abominable brutality, yet there seems to have been some unfairness in the charge made to the grand jury by Mr. Justice Foster, when several of the persons implicated in the above

six months. If an offender failed to surrender within
forty days, and was afterwards captured, the person
capturing was entitled to a reward of £500. Strong
inducements towards official temerity were held out. If
an officer seized goods, and they were afterwards released
on action taken, the officer was exempt from costs,
provided that the judge considered there was 'probable
cause of seizure.' If an action for damages were won
against a seizing officer, and the judge certified 'probable
cause,' the plaintiff was entitled to no more than 2d.
damages. This Act contained one provision which

---

crime were put on trial the following year at Chichester, at a
special Commission of oyer and terminer, presided over by the
duke of Richmond. Justice Foster commenced by stating that
dangerous confederacies had been formed 'for robbing the
Revenue.' Like Duncan Forbes of Edinburgh (*vide* p. 235), he
invited every man of the jury to 'lay his hand upon his heart,'
and ask himself in what smuggling differed from robbery. (Yet
the prisoners were not on trial for smuggling, but for murder.)

Tapner was charged with 'choaking and strangling Chater with
a rope (of the value of sixpence).' Old Mills and his son were
charged with 'inciting, moving, stirring up, instigating, coun-
selling, persuading, and procuring thereto.' (This was a matter
of murder, and we think should have been as heinous a crime if
committed upon a miller and a tailor as upon a tidesman and an
informer.) Jackson, Cobby, Hammond, and Carter were also
charged with murder and participation. It is not exactly clear
why the learned judge should have delivered a long discourse upon
smuggling, and the revenue laws recently issued. Yet thus did he;
indeed, he spoke of little else. He stated that when armed persons
were assembled for smuggling, and one of them killed a revenue
officer, the whole assemblage were guilty of murder, though they
went out but to smuggle. And if, in striving to kill a revenue
officer, a smuggler killed one of his own comrades, the whole of
the smugglers present (except, of course, the dead man) were
liable for murder. Nor was this all. He insisted that all who
had advised or persuaded the smugglers to go a-smuggling would
also be liable for murder in the cases quoted. (Yet the men were
not tried for murder committed whilst smuggling.)

There can be no doubt that the prisoners richly deserved
hanging. They made little or no defence, and did not attempt
to question the witnesses. They were sentenced to death, and,
with the exception of the two Millses, their bodies were to be hung
in chains. Jackson had been ill before the trial, and died soon
after receiving sentence. The rest were hanged the day after trial.
Two of them, Cobby and Hammond, preserved an aspect of sullen
dejection. Tapner and Carter, when the hangman fitted the
nooses, reached towards each other and shook hands. The Millses

smacked of forethought, considering the difficulty of securing seasoned sailors for the King. It allowed smugglers to indemnify past offences by volunteering for the navy.

In 1750, on account of extensive smuggling of candles, soap, and starch, a legal limit for packages was fixed (224 pounds). In 1751 the tobacco trade from the Plantations was burdened with a host of maddening restrictions which need not be enumerated. In 1753 it was discovered that on account of the higher London rates on wine there had been a deal of fraudulent carrying of wine by land from outports to the metropolis, and it was

---

displayed not the slightest concern. All the men were turned off at the same time. The younger Mills was the first one noosed, and the hangman took some time in noosing the rest. During this interval Mills, who appears to have been a dogged and stubborn wretch, watched the process with evident curiosity.

The bodies of Jackson and the Millses were buried in ' a hole ' at the foot of the gallows. The rest were disposed of as follows :

Tapner's body was hung in chains on Rook Hill.

Carter's body was hung in chains on the Portsmouth Road.

Cobby and Hammond were exhibited in a fashion that reminds us of Tennyson's ' Rizpah.' They were suspended at Selsey Bill,

' That all the ships of the world might see them passing by.'

(Such a grim old England as it was !)

The most extraordinary point of the whole matter was that though the murders must have been known to many people, though the news must have travelled amongst the smuggling fraternity all over the south of England, the bodies were not recovered till several months after the crime. Undoubtedly this was due to fear of the smugglers, and it exemplifies clearly the power which a few armed and desperate men may wield over a scattered community.

The man Jackson was a notorious character. He was a native of Welsworth, Hampshire, and a smuggler of many years' standing. He professed the Catholic faith—if such a character may be held to have had any real religion. A relic was found on him after death, bearing this legend :

' Sancti tres Reges
' Gaspar, Melchior, Balthasar,
' Orate pro Nobis nunc et in Hora Mortis Nostræ.
' Ces billets ont touché aux Trois testes de S.S. Roys a Cologne. Ils sont pour les Voyageurs, contre les malheurs de chemins, maux de teste, mal-caduque, fievres, sorcellerie, toute sorte de malefice, et mort subite.'

enacted that ' outport wines ' brought to London should pay the extra duty at the place from which they were removed. ' London ' for the purposes of this Act included all places within twenty miles of the Royal Exchange. It was enjoined that velvets and silks imported should be sealed by the customs officers prior to delivery. The penalties of counterfeiting the seal were an hour in the pillory and a fine of £500. In 1755 the 60-gallon limit for casks of spirits was extended to all foreign spirits, even if reported for exportation. Tea above 6 pounds, imported in vessels other than those of the East India Company, was made forfeitable.

It should be mentioned that there were frequent riots to prevent the exportation of corn, bread being often dear. Throughout the reign there was much distress, and one of the latest freaks of Walpole's Parliament was a bloodthirsty Act against sheep-stealing, the offence being made punishable with death without benefit of clergy. Later, this cruel provision was extended to cattle-stealing.

The National Debt had been immensely increased, and the staff of tax-collectors had swelled into a small army— an army not overpaid officially, but tireless and insatiable in the collection of fees. Posts in the Customs and Excise were battled for with a fury that was intensely significant, and the sordid strife endowed all place-givers with far-reaching influence. It is probable that 20 per cent. of those able to read and write were either collecting taxes or clamouring to be thus employed, while most of the people with a few guineas to spare were on the look out for lottery results and dividends on public loans. Some of the more thoughtful writers of the period cherished forebodings of national bankruptcy. They had lost all faith in ministers, they suspected every professed patriot as a place-hunter. They referred to the pages of ancient history, and found warrant for their fears at every flutter of the leaves. Yet Britain was to sustain the rule of other Georges, to have vaster experiences of war and taxation; her debt was destined to assume proportions hitherto undreamt of, and to become impregnable as the everlasting hills, and yet she was to hold and even mend her place in the world. The croakers might have found solace in the contemplation of things around them. A magnificent record of naval and military achievements had been enrolled, the stock of illustrious poets, literary men, and inventors had been conspicuously augmented, and the lower classes, in spite of the imminence of famine, the press-gang, the stocks, the hulks, and the gallows, retained their old attributes of stubborn valour and broad humour. It was merry in England still. Even the tariff may not have been so dreadful in that day as it appears now to the student of Carkesse's 'Book of Rates.' The taxes may but have furnished food for laughter to that vast section of the community that never paid them.

It will be well to survey the regulations applying to Plantation commerce. Originally matters of revenue discipline in the Plantations had been left in a great measure at disposal of the surveyors-general stationed there. (Once one of these powerful officers forwarded to England a charge against a subordinate, and the Board made no inquiry. The officer accused was dismissed without being allowed to defend himself.) This method obtained up to 1740, and conduced to much injustice.

The Plantation collectors paid the wages of the inferior officers out of the receipts, but their own salaries were paid through their attorneys by the Receiver-General in London. The West Indian collectors submitted their accounts to the 'surveyor and controller' of Jamaica, the American collectors to the surveyor and controller of South Carolina. The surveyors-general were allowed a month to check the accounts, after which all the documents, with the moneys, were sent to London by the first available Government ship leaving. There appears to have been occasional difficulty in getting the accounts in, especially those of dead West Indian collectors, and in such cases the London Commissioners stopped the 'surveyor and controller's' salary till an attempt was made at clearing things up. In 1743 many frauds were detected in the Plantations, and one of the surveyors-general was dismissed.

The invoices furnished by Plantation collectors, which contained full particulars of the quantities, nature, and origin of goods shipped, accompanied the cargoes to which they related. When a Plantation cargo came to London, either for final unshipment or landing and reshipment for foreign, the invoices were sent to the jerquers at the London Custom-house. At an outport they went to the collector, and in either case if the out-turn did not correspond with the invoices the Board were at once apprised.

The doings of the East India Company at this period are extensively interwoven with Customs history. The Company's affairs were scrutinized closely by the Customs authorities, and there seems to have been need of vigilance, for the directors were always ready to exceed their charter privileges. In 1721 the Privy Council found it necessary to issue an order directing that the shipment of negroes by the Company, and the carrying of them direct to the Plantations, should be discontinued. In 1725 the customs officers employed at the Company's London warehouses complained of unfair dealings at the periodical sales. It appears that the system of 'sale by candle-inch' conduced to fraud. The Board amended the method of auction, and directed that no sale should be concluded until bidding had ceased. The Company's higher officials occasionally presumed upon the privilege granted of paying only half the duties at time of warehousing, and shipped goods thus partially duty-paid, claiming and receiving the full drawback. It was therefore provided that drawback should not be paid upon the Company's goods till the 'Collector Inward' had apprised the Receiver-General that the full duties had been rendered. The Collector was to endorse 'Secured' upon the debenture.

The Board distrusted the Company's maritime officials, and were never done with devising restrictions. As soon as it became known that an East Indiaman was in the Downs the official hive was astir, and great was the buzzing in the reaches of the Thames, and at the various legal quays. The ancient practice was to put eight tidesmen aboard in the Downs, to accompany the vessel to Gravesend. Later eight Deal men were used instead of tidesmen. In 1749 the practice was discontinued, and the vessel watched by a customs galley till she entered the Thames. The river officers were kept on the alert, and the Medway revenue sloops cruised in Sea Reach and the Lower Hope. At Gravesend 'head and stern boats' were posted, to guard the vessel by day and night. A tide-surveyor and eight tidesmen went on board, and at intervals during the night the tide-surveyor had to hail the head and stern boats, to ascertain whether their crews were keeping a good look out. Thus formidably occupied and beset, the vessel proceeded to her discharging place at Blackwall. (At the time there were no docks in London.)

The officers commenced to rummage as soon as the vessel was 'reported inwards.' All baggage and 'private trade' packages were unshipped into 'hoys,' and a special account of such goods was transmitted to the Customs Commissioners. The hoys were placed in charge of tidesmen, who accompanied them to the legal quays, where their cargoes were landed, and conveyed to the East India Company's 'private trade warehouses.' The keys of these warehouses were in duplicate, one being kept by the Company's warehouse-keeper, one by the customs officer in charge. By 'private trade' was meant goods brought on freight, and therefore not the

Company's actual property. The goods belonging to the ship's officers were put in the King's Warehouse.

The rest of the cargo was delivered into lighters from the ship, and each lighter was escorted by tidesmen to the quay where the goods were to be examined. After examination they were taken to the Company's warehouses in the vicinity of Crutched Friars, and the landing-waiters who had made up the account at examination delivered a duplicate of their list to the Company's warehouse-keeper, who at once entered the particulars in his ledger.*

Meantime the vessel was being watched, rummaged, and guarded,† as though her very ballast were gold-

---

* The Company made the customs landing-waiters a present of 30 guineas each ship.

† It may be instructive to compare the above with the following description of the methods used at the present time—to assume that a P. and O. steamer—say the *Macedonia*—arrives in the port of London, and proceeds straight to her berthing-place in Tilbury Docks. She has disembarked about two-thirds of her passengers, and landed most of their baggage, at Continental ports and at Plymouth. The rest go ashore directly she berths at Tilbury, or earlier by tender, and within an hour they and their baggage are clear of the Customs. A preventive officer and two or three ' rummagers ' go on board, and collect the dutiable goods brought by the officers and crew. If the owners of these goods desire to pay duty on them at once, the duty is taken and the goods are cleared. The larger parcels usually go to the baggage warehouse, and are cleared there. But if any member of the crew desires to keep his dutiable goods on board, for use during the outward voyage, they are placed, free of charge, under customs seal in the ship's storeroom, and when the vessel gets to sea again the seals are broken and the goods restored.

After the preventive officer has dealt with the ' stores,' he and his assistants rummage the vessel, or such portions of her vast fabric as they think fit. Partial re-rummages are subsequently made at intervals.

The *Macedonia* commences discharging directly she is alongside, and her cargo is tumbled ashore or into lighters with amazing rapidity. The Customs warrant for landing is a copy of the vessel's report, stamped in the Custom-house, and transmitted to the landing-officers, but a perfect entry must be passed for each consignment of goods before they may be examined and delivered. The duty-free goods are usually examined by the customs officers soon after the entries for them are received. A number of packages are opened and inspected to see that the goods are in accordance with the entry, and thus each consignment is rapidly

dust. Each tide-surveyor employed reported upon his brother tide-surveyor's conduct, and all the reports went to the Commissioners. Each day the ship was over-hauled from stem to stern, and the tidesmen who formed the watch were changed every week. As soon as a hold was cleared of cargo it was rummaged, and then placed under customs lock. Notices were posted on board, bidding all and sundry to beware of attempting fraud. Tidesmen stood constantly at the gangway, ordered to *search* every one who left the ship. The officers of excise came on board frequently, and, unmindful of the up-turned noses of their customs brethren, rummaged to

---

cleared and delivered. The *actual tally* of duty-free goods, and of such goods as are liable to low rates of duty, is furnished to the Customs by the dock officials, or the lightermen who receive the packages.

The higher-rated dutiable goods, such as tobacco, cigars, spirits, etc., are removed under customs lock to 'uptown' bonded warehouses. These, and goods transhipped for export without examination, are the only articles *counted* by the landing-officers. Now, if we suppose the *Macedonia* to have come from India or Ceylon, about one-third of her cargo will consist of tea. This huge quantity of dutiable goods goes by rail or lighter under lock to the City tea warehouses, and the first customs account of it is taken when it is brought to the warehouse scale to be weighed.

If the vessel is urgently required to load, as fast as a convenient portion of each hold is emptied of cargo the space is inspected and cleared by the preventive officers, and loading commences. Thus import cargo may often be seen going out at one side of the hatchway while export cargo is going in at the other, and by the time discharge is completed about one-third of the export cargo is shipped. Loading is performed as expeditiously as discharging. All 'bonded goods'—viz., dutiable goods shipped from bond—are swiftly examined by the customs officers prior to shipment. The vessel's requisites in the shape of wine, spirits, tobacco, etc., for use of passengers and crew, are also shipped from bond, and placed under customs seals, to remain thus secured till the vessel gets to sea. Such of the outward passengers as join in London go on board. The moorings are cast off, the dock tugs are in attendance, and away she goes fully loaded, having been in port, say, three weeks only.

The *Macedonia* is over 10,000 tons, and has accommodation for about 500 passengers, yet the clearance of passengers' baggage, and the 'searches' of the vessel, do not occupy in all much above a day's work of three or four customs officers. Compare this with the tremendous parade of search and guard in George II.'s day, on an East Indiaman of about 500 tons.

the best of their skill. The Board's concluding instructions upon the matter of East Indiamen were worded thus : ' And when all this is strictly performed and complied with, the ship is to be deemed and declared duly cleared inwards.'

There was a customs as well as a Company's warehouse · keeper for the general warehouses, and customs locks were on all the doors and outlets. The lockers were selected tidesmen, and the two seniors reported confidentially on the conduct of their assistants. The excise officers had free access, and checked all accounts and deliveries of goods subject to excise duties. The Company's method of account of receipts and deliveries was dictated by the Board of Customs. The Board's instructions as to sampling were painfully elaborate, yet the sampling officers were bidden to apprise Thames Street if they thought additional precautions necessary. The periodical sales were conducted with imposing solemnity, and under supervision of an army of customs and excise officers. When deliveries of private trade goods were required, the Company's directors granted a ' sufferance,' and sent their own selected officers to assist the Customs in examining the packages and supervising delivery. When a ship's officer wished to clear his stores from the King's Warehouse he had to apply to the Board, furnishing a full account of his goods.

It might reasonably be concluded that with all these precautions, the import vessel in a way corked and sealed by the Customs, watched on all sides from the time she was first sighted till she left the mouth of the Thames six months later, her cargo surrounded by officers till it reached the warehouse, then constantly watched though under lock, and every one concerned in the business spying and reporting upon his fellows, not one wisp of herba silk, not one ounce of tea, not one curio in porcelain, could escape custom. Be it borne in mind that the Company's directors were as eager as the Commissioners to suppress fraud, that they employed many supervisors for that purpose, and issued instructions almost as elaborate as those we have quoted. But nothing good ever came of circumlocution. The records show that smuggling was rife ; even the captains were frequently unable to accompany their ships outward because Exchequer proceedings were pending against them. In 1748 a number of customs officers were dismissed for conniving at export frauds committed by the Company's officials. Complaints from merchants who bought at the sales were frequent, and in 1756 the Board announced their opinion that the regulations governing the waterguard practice had been rendered futile by the instrumentality of the very officers who should have carried them out. Often there was great confusion over the payment of drawback, the Company having received the full amount, yet having only paid a moiety of the inward duty. Once the Collector of London was cautioned for *paying* debentures, instead of merely certifying to the account and leaving actual payment to the proper officer —the Receiver-General.*

It scarcely appears that the Commissioners were to blame. They sat aloof in Thames Street, doing the best that Commissioners could do, but knowing none of their subordinates except the higher indoor officials, and these latter really seem to have been victims of circumlocutory dementia. Whenever they got news of fraud or carelessness at the quays, in the warehouses, the Thames reaches, or at the outports and creeks, they meted out punishment to offenders, and then issued a few pages of fresh regulations. Now it is perfectly true that there was never yet an elaborate regulation contrived that practical men could carry out. Thus it must have been with the codes of instructions. The landing-waiters, tide-surveyors, and riding-officers, whether practical men or not, read

* Undoubtedly the vicious fee system was responsible for this. Payment of a sheaf of debentures meant a few guineas in fees to the paying officers, and thus the spectacle was presented of one civil servant complaining bitterly because another had intercepted his work.

them, shuddered at the penalties prescribed against disobedience, and, realizing that to comply would be impossible, at once started to devise dodges.

By the Letter Books of Montrose, May, 1728, it appears the collector and controller transmitted to Edinburgh the report of Roderick Pringle, tidesman, as to his treatment by the people of Arbroath, and suggested that troops should be stationed at that turbulent port. ' Our tidesmen,' said they, ' are so terrified to go on duty at that place for the insults given them by the inhabitants that unless some troops be quartered in that town there is no preventing their continued practice of smuggling at the very shoar.'

In 1729 the Arbroath tidesman sent word to Montrose that a large quantity of tobacco had been run. The Montrose officers provided themselves with a military escort, proceeded to Arbroath, and after search found a small quantity of tobacco abandoned in an open place. The Arbroath tidesman stated that though the smugglers passed close by him he was not able to recognize any of them. ' It was dark,' said he, ' and they were disguised.'*

Great news at last. The officers, assisted by the military, made a large seizure, and captured twenty-nine horses and fifteen carts. These were condemned, and the collector put them up for sale. There were no bidders, so he disposed of them ' to certain people at the appraised price of £15.'

(The officers excused themselves in their report to the

* It appears that smugglers, after a run, frequently abandoned one package, so that the officers finding it might be pacified and return home.   Of course this suited such officials as were not anxious to cross staves with a dozen scowling ruffians.   A flaming report was usually furnished, and the formula, ' We followed the track of wheels and found,' etc., seems to have been much in favour.

Board by pleading that the animals and vehicles were 'sorry truck,' but the Board waxed wroth, and censured the collector.)

This seizure made the next cargo of seized goods sent to Leith quite a respectable freight, amounting to 3,015 pounds of leaf tobacco, nearly 2,000 gallons of brandy, 8 gallons of canary wine, and 154 gallons of white wine. Sharpened by the Board's censure, and mindful of what happened with the last consignment, the collector wrote : ' All the casks have been filled to prevent imbezilment, and the goods are put free of all charges on board the sloop. We have paid the pilotage out and in.'

Trade was evidently growing brisker. The balance for one quarter in 1729 was £548 7s. 6d. ' But,' wrote the collector and controller, ' there is drawback due on a quantity of tobacco, which will exhaust most of this ballance.' It seems as though they hated parting with money.

Early in October, 1729, the officers of excise seized a large quantity of brandy, and placed it in the King's Warehouse for security. Shortly afterwards the Board received the following letter from the collector and controller :

'CUSTOM HOUSE, MONTROSE,
'11th October, 1729.

' HONOURABLE SIRS,

' This morning betwixt the hours of twelve and two the door of His Majesty's Warehouse was broke open, and 107 ankers of Brandy which was seized by the Excise Officers and one of the Quarter Casks of Brandy formerly seized by our officers, carried away.

' At two o'clock in the morning when the Guard came to relieve the two Centry's that were placed at the Warehouse door they found the door open, the Centry's gone, their muskets lying near the warehouse, and one of their Beyanats lying broke before the door, and no person to be seen near the Warehouse nor in the Street. The Sergeant immediately went and acquainted the Commanding Officer, who with a party came to the Warehouse and found it in the above Condition, nor no account what was become of the Centry's, and no person to be seen on the Street save a maltman whom he sent to the Guard. Thereafter the Officer came and acquainted the Collector, and they together went to the Provost's house to demand his assistance, but could get no entrance, so we went round the Town, and finding everything quiet and no person to be seen sent some of the Souldiers to the Links to patroall, when they found the two Centry's lying tyed neck and heel. The Officer asked them why they had left their posts, they told him that Fourteen or Fifteen men had come upon them with Clubs and other weapons and had knocked them down and tyed them in the condition they were found, and afterwards dragged them to the Links where they left them lying, but that they knew none of them—this is all they could say. Our officers with the Souldiers kept patroalling round the Town till the morning to prevent as much as possible the Conveying any goods out of Town, and this morning the Collector and Surveyor acquainted the Collector of Excise with what had happened, and they together went to the Provost and desired a Warrant for a General Search of the Town, which he refused, telling us that it was not an ordinary thing, and that he could not do it without calling a Council. We told him that did not relate to his Council, and so took a Protest against him, upon which the Collector as a Justice of the Peace gave warrant to the officers of Customs and Excise to search everywhere where they had any suspicion, but when they began their Search the Provost sent a Town Officer and carried off the Constable, which oblig'd our Surveyor and the Supervisor of Excise to go to him and ask his reason for taking away the Constable. He said he was an inhabitant in the Town and he would not allow him to officiate, and gave it them as his advice to take care of themselves. Upon this the Collector appointed a new Constable, and they began their search again, and when they came to the house of Baylie Murison there arose a Mobb of a vast number of People, so that the Collector was obliged to go and read the proclamation against Riots. This is all we can inform your Honrs. just now, the post going off, but we are affraid of little Success by reason of the night's coming on and almost all the Inhabitants against us, however we shall take all imaginable care that no goods be conveyed out of Town till Munday morning, and your Honrs. shall be acquainted next post.'

There appears good reason to think that the searchers were ' there or thereabout ' when they were preparing to invade Bailie Murison's premises. Further particulars were furnished on the ' Munday.'

'Custom House, Montrose,
'13th Octr., 1729.

'Honourable Sirs,
'We acquainted you by our letter of the 11th instant of our proceedings in relation to the Goods stolen out of the King's Warehouse. The Officers of Excise and Customs having demanded the Search of Baylie Murison's house and Shops he peremtorally refused, and called his Town officers to seize the Constable whom the Collector had appointed to act and carry him to prison, but the Souldiers protected the Constable, upon which the Mobb rose, but upon the Collector's reading the Proclamation the Baylie thought proper to call them to disperse. However this so terrified the Constable that he was ffrighted to act, not knowing whether a Single Justice's warrant upon such a juncture was sufficient for him. This with the night's coming on put a Stop to the Search, but upon application to the Commanding Officer he ordered Centry's to be placed upon the Baylie's house and Shops till this morning, when there was a Justice of Peace Court, where the Excise Officer who made the Seizure which was taken out of the King's Warehouse gave in a List of all the houses and places of this Town where he

had Suspicion the Brandy was Lodged to the Court upon Oath as the Law required, but the Provosts of Arbroath, Brechin, and Forfar with the Provost of Montrose (who as we understand had called them for that end) overruled the Court and refused the Officer a warrant after he had given his Oath, upon which James Scott of Logy and the Collector as two Justices of the Peace Showed their Dissent by Entring their Protests, as did the Collector of Excise protest against the proceedings of the Court in this matter as Illegal. Upon this we gave over any further Search, finding it impracticable to do any manner of Good, and some of the Excise officers fearing their Lives. The Collector of Excise is to lay all this before his Board, and we must humbly begg leave to lay before your Honours that if some notice be not taken of this matter the Officers of the Revenue in this District will have a difficulty to make good any Seizures or to protect the King's Warehouse.'*

It is apparent that the collector and controller were trying to whitewash themselves. Finding that they were involved in a dispute on legal points, they had allowed caution to disarm them, even with the law undoubtedly on their side, and were puzzled to invent excuses. ' The Officers *of Excise* and Customs having demanded the Search ' (' Excise ' first), ' Some of the *Excise* Officers fearing their Lives.' Probably the excise officers appreciated to the full the exigencies of their position, yet it is certain that the two old customs gentlemen were in considerable fear, if not of their skins, at least of queries from Edinburgh. If they had but thrown legal consideration to the winds, and pressed forward, protected by the soldiers, to the search of Bailie Murison's house, they would have been able to furnish warrant for their proceedings in the shape of 108 full ankers. He who takes no chances makes few seizures of contraband.

* It does not appear from the Letter Books that any action was taken by the Board.

In 1730 the Secretary at Edinburgh discovered that certain ancient revenue bonds of Montrose remained undischarged, and directed the collector and controller to investigate the matter. They did so, and the parties concerned refused to acknowledge their indebtedness. It appeared that when the rebels seized Montrose in 1716 the customs staff fled, and the Jacobites thereupon appointed one Skinner to the office of collector. The bonds mentioned, which were for security of certain coal duties, fell into Skinner's hands, and he raised about £20 on them. When the rebellion was over, the original customs staff were reinstated. The collector and controller laid these particulars before the Board, and intimated that there was little hope of recovering anything on the bonds. 'For,' wrote they, ' Skinner is long dead, and was broke before he died, and his family live on charity.' The matter was allowed to lapse.

In June, 1730, the collector applied for ten days' holiday. He stated that he had had no leave since March, 1727, and only ten days then. It is to be feared that he was not a brilliant official, but he stuck to his desk.

On May 18, 1733, the collector of Inverness sent the following lugubrious letter to the Scottish Board :

' Yesterday morning some ill-disposed villains have carried away the Custom House boat across the ferry, and with saws and axes have cut her in two by the middle, left the one half on the beach, and disposed of the other to the waves.

' The execution of this is owing no doubt to common people, but the contrivance to greater heads, and that it has been premeditated appears by the tools they had provided themselves with to perform it.

' 'Tis hard to tell where this will end. The warehouse has been twice broke open, the boat destroy'd, the Expresses from the outports stopp'd, and the Letters taken away, a Person under suspicion of being an Informer dreg'd across the Firth and his ears cut out, and hints every day given to myself to take care of my life ; in short, no part of the Face of the Earth is peopled by such abandoned villains as this Country.'

The letter proceeded in complaint that a promised revenue sloop had not appeared. ' I am in no small pain till she arrives, for I find the people here will stick at no kind of villainy whatsoever.'

This letter the Scottish Board transmitted to the Lords of the Treasury, and the covering report contained a remark which must have made my Lords stare : ' We confess we are not expecting a remedy. We are even at a loss how to propose the means.'

During the same year the English Commissioners of Customs apprised the Treasury of immense smuggling in Suffolk, Essex, Kent, and Sussex. Within twelve months 54,000 pounds tea and 123,000 gallons brandy had been seized, yet smuggling was steadily increasing. The cargoes were being run by ' well-armed gangs ' of desperate fellows, who had succeeded in intimidating both sheriffs and customs officers. One hundred and six dragoons were asked for, to assist 185 already supplied.

In 1736 the famous Porteous Riots took place in Edinburgh. One Andrew Wilson of Pathhead had been concerned in many smuggling enterprises, which had involved him in prosecution and heavy fines. Hearing that the Kirkcaldy collector was at Pittenweem, and in possession of a large sum of public money, Wilson, with three comrades, broke into his lodgings and robbed him. The theft appears to have been almost publicly conducted, and the thieves walked off with the spoil without the slightest hindrance. Later they were pursued, the money was recovered, and Wilson and one of his comrades were arrested, tried, and sentenced to death. While in custody Wilson, who was a powerful and determined man, contrived and secured the escape of his accomplice.

Captain Porteous, the commander of the City Guard, by his extreme officiousness and brutality had become unpopular with the folk of Edinburgh, and his proceedings in connexion with Wilson's execution excited them to fury. It appears that the citizens manifested their sympathy with the culprit by disorderly conduct directly the ceremony had ended, and Porteous thereupon ordered his men to fire upon the mob. Several people were killed, and many wounded. Porteous was arrested, tried in the High Court of Justiciary, and condemned to death. Many of the more wealthy citizens signed a petition recommending him to mercy, and Queen Caroline, in the absence of George II. on the Continent, granted respite. This caused great indignation amongst the lower classes of Edinburgh, and on September 7, 1736, an armed mob broke into the Tolbooth, dragged Porteous forth, and hanged him. Erskine, the Solicitor-General, appears to have investigated the matter, and from the tenor of his report it is evident that there was little likelihood of the active participants in the deed being discovered. No one was punished except the mayor, who by an Act of 1737 was disabled from holding office. It seems that the mayor had been over-cautious upon the matter of summoning troops to protect the Tolbooth; anyhow, the indignant authorities in London made him a scapegoat.

While upon Scottish matters, an incident of 1744 must be narrated, though it breaks the sequence of affairs. During that year one William Gordon ran a cargo of brandy and tobacco into the harbour of Spey, and landed it at various places along the coast. The Scottish Board came to know of this, and applied to the local justices to take a 'precognition.' The justices refused, alleging that they might be compelled to interrogate witnesses who would turn out to be implicated. The Board thereupon consulted the Lord President of the Court of Session, who sent the chairman of the local bench a tremendously solemn letter, which is here quoted.

' DEAR SIR,

' The Christmas holydays, which have emptied the town and adjourned the Board of Customs, have prevented my being able to write to you on the subject of your smuggling as I once thought I should ; but lest what I may write you after consultation with others should come too late for your meeting on the 15th inst., I have taken the part in the meantyme of dropping you this line.

' I have not been more surprised for a great while than when I heard that a majority of justices, at your last meeting, putt off the precognition on a doubt whether they lawfully could take information from the witnesses upon oath, and thereby, however innocent their intentions were, flung some cold water at least upon the enquiry.

' As to the doubt itself, I confess I am at a loss to guess on what it is founded : precognitions have at all times been taken on oath in Scotland, and hence the established practice in the Court of Justiciary of cancelling, at the trial, the oath formerly emitted on the precognition, before the witness emit his deposition in Court, if he desire it. No occult crime, however dangerous to the commonweal, or to the Crown, could be detected or punished, if witnesses were in the least backward, without a power, in those whose duty it is to enquire, to examine upon oath. And if the practice in English law is enquired into, no justice can commit, as they may in Scotland, upon a signed information only. The justice must examine the informant upon oath before he can issue his warrant, so that, as I apprehend the scruple is without any just foundation, I doubt not at your next meeting, after gentlemen have time to inform themselves duely, it will evanish.

' I cannot suffer myself to suspect that, considering

the notoriety of the mischief that smuggling does to this poor unhappy country, and the forwardness lately shewn, by all ranks of men, to express their detestation of it, and to bind themselves to one another and to the publick, by resolutions and engagements of honour, to discourage that villainous traffick, any gentleman or number of gentlemen, will in broad daylight, and in an open Court (whatever their connexion with, or tenderness for the unhappy smuggler be) be so impudently profligate as to attempt to screen the cutthroats of their country, and thereby expose themselves to the universal contempt and abhorrence of mankind.   Such an attempt requires more than an ordinary degree of courage and wickedness ; the guilty person cannot hope to remain unknown, the minutes of the court must record his infamy, nor is it to be expected by him that the character, which by such practice he may purchase, shall remain confined to his own country ; the common post can, by an extract from the minutes, convey his fame to Edinburgh, from whence it may be communicated to the whole kingdom.

' Now, tho for these reasons I hope you will be unanimous at your next meeting, yet, if contrary to my expectations, and very much against my wish, the smugglers should find protection, and the national justice, as well as interest, should be defeated, I hope you will be so good as to transmit the minutes, distinguishing how each justice voted, besides furnishing me as a private gentleman with information who I ought to detest and avoid as a scoundrell.   I may be able to inform my fellow-subjects, as far as that may be done within the laws, who they ought to look upon as enemies to their country.   Other rebukes they may possibly meet with, but it is not necessary to speak of that at present.   I write, you see, with great freedom, as I am very much in earnest, but what I have said are the dictates of my heart, and you are at full liberty to make what use you please of what I have wrote.   This mean, shameful course to destruction must be prevented, or our unhappy country must be undone. Make my compliments to everyone who can lay his hand upon his heart, and say he does not deserve the title of Rascal, and believe me to be, &c.,

'DUNCAN FORBES.'

A few extracts from the correspondence between Thames Street and the port of Boston may be of interest. Readers must picture the long stretch of coast under supervision, extending from Grimsby to Wisbech, the flat, dyked country inland, the North Sea with its chances of a quick run from the Continent, and the large and thirsty agricultural population of the Fens eager for cheap brandy and geneva. Ardent spirits were much in demand in Lincolnshire ; they were thought potent against marsh-fever and ague, and medicine more pleasant to the Fenmens' palates would be hard to find. To gratify an inherited liking, and benefit the constitution as well, what more popular pastime can be conceived ? No wonder the smuggler was liked, encouraged, and screened, when he was both cheap provider and family doctor.

In the play performed betwixt Boston and Thames Street the leading *dramatis personæ* were the Commissioners, very affable on paper, extremely forbearing with errant officials, and ever signing themselves with the gracious old formula, ' Your loving friends.' They seem to have been heart and soul in the prevention of smuggling. They had one or two indefatigable spies on the Continent, who kept them well posted as to the lading of illegal cargoes. Their secretary was Mr. Carkesse, a gentleman with literary leanings, who had compiled the most maddening ' Book of Rates ' known, and when information from the Continent reached Thames Street he transmitted it to Boston. The result as regarded seizures was not at all impressive. Some of the preventive men seem to have preferred interviewing informers after the fact to riding the bleak coast at night, and they sent on much information about ancient runs, a deal of which the Solicitor at London contemptuously dismissed as corrupt or inconclusive. Some of it, however, was manifestly sound, and showed that a large business was being done.

The collector and controller did nothing rashly. It may reasonably be assumed that they were of the average official type. They looked sharply after their fees, as most men in their position would. Once they quarrelled, and took to writing separate reports, till admonished by the Secretary.

A play is always the better for a whole-souled, persistent villain. The villain of the piece was Captain Jewell, commander of the revenue sloop. He appears to have been possessed by but two ideas. The first was that on that exposed Lincolnshire coast the weather was usually so rough that it was unsafe to put to sea ; the second that his sloop needed extensive and expensive repair about once a quarter. The bills he sent in for repairs would almost have defrayed the cost of a frigate. When queried on these points he stoutly maintained the correctness of his charges, and on one occasion actually discovered that he had forgotten an item of expense. The commanders of sloops had to keep journals, and occasionally the Board sent for the documents and checked them. Jewell was never caught tripping in that respect ; he had the gift of imagination, and could make startling records of work which had not been performed. It is likely that his journals were neat and well written, for he appears to have rarely ventured out into rough water.

The subordinate officers made many detentions of goods for informalities, for being brought coastwise without cocket, or with a cocket incorrect as to particulars, and other petty breaches of the regulations, and whenever, after due inquiry, such matters were cleared up, and found to have occurred otherwise than through official neglect, the parties in fault were directed by the Board to ' make reasonable compensation to the detaining officers for their trouble.' The amount of such compensation appears to have been settled privately between the detaining officers and the culprits.

Sometimes when seizures were made the London Solicitor informed the seizing officers that they might prosecute in the Exchequer at their own charge. This was usually ordered when the evidence was not conclusive. If the officers declined, the Solicitor sometimes directed prosecution 'at the Crown charge,' and in such case the officers were debarred from participating in the profits.

During 1733 the Board sent informations 'a many,' including news of a small Bridlington sloop loading contraband at Zealand to run between the Spurn Light and Bridlington, and of two Sunderland ships, one Whitby ship, two Newport ships, and one Chichester ship, loading tobacco and brandy at Dunkirk to run on the east coast. Boston failed to profit by the tidings.

In 1734 a quantity of silk was seized at Grantham by the excise officers, and handed over to the Customs at Boston. Samples were sent to Thames Street. Expert opinion was invited, and the goods were pronounced East Indian silks. The Solicitor directed that the goods should be formally seized by an officer of customs, and prosecuted in the Exchequer at the charge and for the benefit of the Excise.

Perhaps to stimulate Captain Jewell to action, H.M. ship *The Fly*, Captain Oates, was commissioned to cruise between Flamborough and Yarmouth, to prevent the exportation of wool from Lincolnshire to France, and the running of brandy and other goods. Captain Oates was directed to cruise diligently ; to visit all suspicious vessels, and in case of seizure take them to the nearest port and surrender them to the Customs ; to keep up correspondence with the Customs, not to search unnecessarily, to go into port only when necessary, to stay no longer than necessary, and to forward a copy of his journal once a month.

The officers seized *two and a half pounds* of tea *by information*, for that the retailer who owned it had offered it for sale without having an authorized room for the purpose, as required by law. The Solicitor directed as follows : ' If they have proof of this, let them prosecute under the Excise Act. If they have proof that the tea was run, let them also prosecute under the Customs at the King's charge. But if they have no proof, let them deliver it.'

The collector sent to London the annual account of Captain Jewell's seizures. The Board replied that the seizures were few and of small value, and asked if the sloop was often at sea with captain and mate on board, why more seizures were not made, and whether the sloop was really necessary. (That she was necessary there can be little doubt ; whether she was useful or not was easy to ascertain from the seizure list.) In response the collector and controller forwarded affidavits against Jewell, accusing him of embezzling seizures. He was directed to make answer in writing, and meantime the mate was put in command. The captain countered with an affidavit, stating that whilst trying to board a smuggling sloop he had been fired on. Evidently this cleared him, for he was soon in command again, and repairing his sloop. Soon the officers reported him for staying too long ashore. He was cautioned, and the collector was directed to ascertain whether he supplied his mariners with proper provisions. Mr. Carkesse urged the collector to be vigilant in his inspection of the men's food, hinting that it was possible to show good provisions at inspection and afterwards use bad.

Certain mariners on the sloop mutinied, and were discharged. The collector was instructed to have them pressed for the navy. (In equity it was Jewell who should have been pressed, but it is to be feared the navy would have found him not worth the trouble.)

In 1735 the Board directed the collector and controller to ascertain the course taken by smugglers in carrying goods overland from Lincolnshire to London, and in particular as to whether they passed by certain roads in Hertfordshire.

The collector asked the Board if he was to advance money to a troop of dragoons sent down to Lincolnshire to assist the officers.   Answer : ' No.   They will receive half the King's share of seizures made with their assistance.'

Repeated information was sent of vessels of Sunderland, Newcastle, Folkestone, etc., loading goods at Continental ports for running on the east coast.   One message spoke of six Folkestone cutters, each cutter carrying twenty-five men.

The Solicitor at London reported on a case submitted by the Boston officers.   A French vessel within the limits of the port had on board 400 half-ankers of brandy (illegal-sized packages) and she had illegally unshipped 80 gallons.   He directed as follows : ' If the vessel were really within the port limits, seize the illegal packages, but not otherwise.   Prosecute the runners of the 80 gallons at the Crown charge.   The vessel may not be seized, as she is of the legal tonnage.'

In 1736 an officer stationed at Grimsby granted an informal permit for wool, and in consequence of the informality the collector at Hull detained the goods.   The owner of the goods put in a claim against the Customs for £10 damages.   The Board ordered the Grimsby officer to pay it.

The Board received information of extensive smuggling between Boston and Lynn, and, thinking it possible this was due to negligence on the part of the sloop captains, directed that the Boston sloop should call at Lynn once a week, and the Lynn sloop call once a week at Boston. This must have been hard on Jewell, a man with a taste for snug anchorage.

Later there came information that at Zealand were three collier ships which had discharged their cargoes, taken in goods for running, and overstowed them with ballast ; a sloop that brought slates from Salcombe, and had freighted back with contraband ; about twenty smuggling *galleys* from Kent and Sussex busy loading ; and five other vessels full to the coamings specially for the Lincolnshire coast. The 'galleys' each carried ten men.

On July 31, 1736, the King's Warehouse-keeper in London, in transmitting a receipt for seized goods sent from Boston, endorsed the following memo on the document :

' We have hot sultry weather, which has thrown the populace into I don't know what sort of madness. For three or four nights past the Tower Guards and Militia have been up to prevent their Mobbing, which is not yet quieted. The popular resentment arises from the encouragement given to Irish labourers, who work for less money than the English.

' P.S.—Just shutting up the warehouse. Excuse haste.'

The collector and controller informed the Board that large runs were being made on the Lincolnshire coast by armed smugglers, whom the officers were powerless to oppose. The Board thereupon applied to the Admiralty, and two sloops were sent to assist the energetic and intrepid Jewell. Jewell at once took his sloop into harbour and started repairing her, and did not even employ his crew in watching the coast while this was being done. The Board received information of his proceedings, and censured him. They also censured the collector and controller for not looking after him.

Information reached the Board that goods for smuggling in England were brought from China to Sweden, shipped there by English Baltic traders, and afterwards run on the east coast. The collector of Wells apprised the Board that he had received information that the owners of a smuggling vessel recently seized at that port had bought another sloop and run a cargo between Boston and Lynn. The Board again censured Jewell, and directed the collector to examine Jewell's journal. The journal appears to have been quite in order.

In 1738 an order was issued that officers who made seizures with the assistance of the military were to furnish full particulars *on oath*, as complaints were made that the soldiers did not get their proper share of the seizure-money.*

Occasionally, in sending information of vessels loading contraband oversea, the Board furnished *the master's* name, but omitted the name of the ship. This appears to have been when the revenue spy who made the communication suspected that the ship's name would be ' painted out ' on departure, or a misleading name substituted.

The Board sent information of a boat expressly built in London for running goods. Though of great length, she had apparently only four rowlocks (the legal number), but was contrived so that she might be readily fitted with twelve. This boat had been taken oversea on board a smuggling sloop that carried a numerous company. When loaded the sloop hovered off the English coast, and the boat, with her additional rowlocks shipped, was used to run goods from vessel to shore. Later was sent a formidable list of vessels clearing outward for France and the Netherlands, and expected to smuggle on their return. These all cleared within three days, so the traffic in contraband must have been enormous. Four of the vessels belonged to Scarborough.

The Board issued a fresh stock of journals, new instructions to all the officers, and urgent injunctions to the collector, controller, and Jewell, to play the man and try to cope with the smuggling. (A note of despair is apparent in their repeated references to the illegal traffic. It is significant that the seizures were trifling, and there was scarcely any seizing of wool outward, though at the

---

* In the affidavits relating to these seizures, at all ports, the deponents end by stating that there has been no private arrangement or collusion between them and the military.

time there was an immense yield of wool in Lincolnshire, and it is scarcely conceivable that smugglers so active and resolute in running goods inward would neglect the outward avenue of contraband.)

Fresh information arrived of four smuggling vessels, and another troop of dragoons was sent to Lincolnshire and quartered at Wisbech. The particulars of information were as follows :

' The *Thunderbolt* runs her goods at the Old Chapel, Lynn Channel, the *Ann and Mary* on the Lincolnshire coast, the *Sugar Droger* to the north of Lowestoft, and the Dutch schuyt with the English skipper on the coast of Suffolk.'

At this period there were four riding-officers for the Boston district—one at Saltfleet, one at Wainfleet, one at Fleet, and one at Surfleet Bridge. There were also two riding-surveyors and one riding-supervisor.

In 1739 a sloop was seized, but not by Jewell. The crew and master escaped. The brandy and tea on board were ' prosecuted to condemnation ' in the Exchequer at the Crown charge, the sloop at the officer's charge. Certain other goods on board were prosecuted before the local justices. Soon after a riding-officer seized a horse loaded with tea, the rider escaping. The tea was prosecuted in the Exchequer at the Crown's charge, the horse at the officer's.

A smuggler in Lincoln jail turned approver, furnishing startling information. His name was Garrett, and he appears to have been a brazen and mercenary rascal. After implicating a number of people he informed Charlton, the officer in whom he confided, that he expected ' ten guineas down,' and if thus accommodated would give evidence of still larger transactions. The Solicitor in London advised that no reward should be tendered or even mentioned, and directed an inquiry into Garrett's character. The inquiry seems to have produced discouraging evidence, and the Solicitor promptly washed his hands of part of the matter, accepting the rest, and directing prosecutions. Below is a list of those against whom action was taken :

Jackson, an innkeeper of Hull, who had unshipped 515 gallons of brandy.

Bancroft, a tailor of North Somercoates ; Oliver, a mariner of Theddlethorpe. Each had been concerned in the unshipment of 300 pounds tea and 150 gallons brandy.

(Hubbard, a mariner of North Somercoates, had been concerned in both of the above transactions.)

Bancroft and Rossthorne, mariners of Saltfleet, who had unshipped 150 gallons brandy.

Baker, a mariner of Colchester, who had unshipped 400 gallons brandy.

Compton, a mariner of Hull, who had unshipped 250 gallons brandy.

Ombler, a mariner of Hull, who had unshipped 150 gallons brandy.

Burleigh, captain of the *Thunderbolt*, who had unshipped 3,500 pounds tea.

Bell, a mariner, who had unshipped 2,000 pounds tea.

Robinson, a mariner, who had unshipped 500 pounds tea.

The Solicitor's statement was interesting. He mentioned the grounds upon which smuggling *vessels* were liable to forfeiture. ' Carrying brandy and being below the legal tonnage ; carrying tea from a land where such tea is not grown.' Thus Burleigh's, Rossthorne's, and Robinson's sloops were liable to seizure—*when found*. The officers who might seize them should prosecute the sloops to condemnation in the Exchequer. If not prepared to do so, they must relinquish claim on the profits, and the Crown should prosecute. Hubbard's sloop was held not seizable, on a curious point. Since the date of the transaction quoted in the information she had been seized elsewhere for a more recent offence, and the Board had released her and accepted a sum of money from Hubbard in composition, he entering into bond to sin no more. Therefore his vessel was held not seizable, yet he was liable to prosecution. (The matter seems hard to understand, but thus said the lawyer.)

Soon after Garrett informed of one Patrick, keeper of the Spurn Head lighthouse, for unshipping 1,000 pounds tea. He also implicated the keeper of 'The Ferry in Lincolnshire opposite Holden Dyke in Yorkshire,' for 2,100 pounds tea. Then he asked again for ten guineas, promising that if he were given twenty he would implicate 'two men of fortune and estate,' who had lately run 1,600 pounds tea. All the above transactions took place within a limited period.

It is apparent that the excise officers did their work loosely. In 1729 an arrangement had been made between the two Boards that excise officers who seized spirits on the coast and placed them in customs charge should gauge and try the goods first, ledger the account, and obtain a receipt from the Customs. This had not been done, for in 1739 goods which had been thus handed over turned out at condemnation unaccountably different from the warehousing record, and on investigation it appeared that the excise officers had neither gauged nor tried them prior to deposit.

In 1740 Mr. Carkesse departed from his usual affable style, and addressed a few curt words of caution to the collector and controller, who had failed to make correct record of undischarged bonds for shipment of wool coastwise. They were directed to forward all bonds that had lain undischarged for six months. 'If you fail, you will be dismist. Your loving friend, CHAS. CARKESSE.'

Certain officers had been acting as appraisers of seized goods and ships, and in the usual fashion had appraised lightly. A reappraisement by trustworthy experts gave four times the officially appraised value.

Several smugglers arrested on Garrett's information were interviewed by officers, and became approvers. So many informations were forwarded that the Solicitor became restive. The officers began to strain the law in their eagerness to get awards. The Solicitor discovered

suspicious interlineations in some of the affidavits sent,
and some of the imprisoned smugglers accused officers of
using threats to induce them to give evidence. The
officers were warned by the Board to be extremely careful
in seizing for forfeiture ships with prohibited or uncustomed goods. ' Proof must be very clear, or the officers
may subject themselves to great damage.' Later came
a momentous order. ' Seizures have been made without
sufficient cause.' The collector and controller were
directed to inquire fully into all circumstances connected
with seizures, before taking the goods into warehouse,
and if the officers were unwilling to prosecute at their
own expense they were to be called upon to state why
they refused.

Captain Jewell transmitted the usual bill for repairs
to his sloop, and the Board sent it to be checked by a
competent and reliable person. The expert's report was
comic :

' It must be some extraordinary accident which the
Captain hath not mentioned that could occasion such
large Bills in so short a time after the Sloop's being
rebuilt. In October, 1739, she lost the Crown £142 7s. 1d.,
a very large sum for so small a vessel, and so soon after
to require £92 4s. 6d. for repairs only.' He then proceeded
to query :

' 1. The Joyner's Bill. 2. The Shipwright's Bill.
3. The Ironmonger's Bill. 4. The Cooper's Bill. 5. The
Ship-chandler's Bill. 6. The Smith's Bill. 7. The Sail-
maker's Bill. 8. Bread and cheese and beer for the workmen, amounting to £4 0s. 0d. 9. The Captain's own
expence, £34 17s. 0d.'

' And if I am not mistaken,' he went on, ' the better
part of the £10 charged for sails is charged twice.' Later
he wrote : ' As much Labour and Materials charged for
1½ years wear and tear as would almost build the
vessel.'

Jewell was directed to make his bill more reasonable.
After a struggle he abated an item, and got his money.

Like most inefficient revenue officers, when he did come to be concerned in a seizure he wanted more than his proper share of profits. He charged his cabin-boy for a share at mariner's rate, evidently intending to pocket the extra award; but his rascality was discovered, and the Board directed him to compensate the boy *out of his own share*. It is extremely improbable that the boy got anything, except an extra cuff whenever Jewell bethought himself of the failure of his trick.

In 1742 a petition was sent to the Board by two wool-dealers of Spalding, stating that Spalding paid a deal of revenue, that there were officers stationed there who were competent to supervise the weighing and shipping coastwise of wool, and asking that the town might be relieved from paying the heavy travelling expenses charged by the collector and controller of Boston, who insisted on seeing all parcels of shipped wool. The petition commenced thus : ' We do most humbly request on the behalf of ourselves and our country,' and requested that the deputy at Spalding might view the weighing and shipping coastwise of wool, the collector and controller of Boston making heavy charges, and often causing delay. ' We already pay 10s. 6d. for coquet, and 6d. for a permit for every parcell of wooll, a charge very burdensome.

' We crave that we may not under pretences suffer such impositions, or be further obstructed in our honest lawfull employment.

' John Skinner, Senr.
John Skinner, Junr.'

The collector and controller fought stoutly for their fees, quoting the Board's instructions of 1728 that the principal officers should attend the weighing; but the Board, who seem to have been eminently reasonable and practical, directed that the deputies at Saltfleet, Wainfleet, and Spalding should attend the weighing, thus depriving the Boston gentlemen of their fees and travelling allowances, and relieving the wool-merchants of much expense and delay.

The stolid rascal in command of the sloop, though more than her value had been charged as repairs within three years, had the effrontery to suggest that extensive alterations were again necessary, and to inquire whether the Board would be disposed to grant a large sum for that purpose. An expert was sent to survey this mysterious vessel, and reported that she needed no repairs at all. The expert found her at anchor, as usual. The collector thereupon ordered Jewell to put to sea. Jewell apparently considered the weather too unsettled, and calmly remained in port, nursing his frail shallop. The long-suffering Board thereupon dismissed him, stating that he had made no seizures of consequence during the whole term of his employment. It will be remembered that he had been shrewdly suspected of starving his crew, had been detected in trying to cheat them of their shares in award, and that once his company had mutinied. Yet when he was dismissed his mariners voluntarily went with him.

The new captain wrote to the Board, stating that he could get no men unless increased pay were offered. So far from consenting, the Board told him they intended to withdraw an extra allowance for victualling granted to Jewell in 1730, provisions having become cheaper, and if this did not suit him they would lay the sloop up. The captain at once procured men.

Quarantine was strict. The plague was at Smyrna, and on the arrival of the Smyrna fleet a watch was kept at southern ports, to prevent persons quitting the ships as they passed along the coast. The Board sent word to all ports that a Dutch vessel from Messina, with plague on board, had attempted to enter Plymouth Sound. On being ordered to stand off the master refused, and was at once treated to a broadside. He then bore away to the south-east.

An extraordinary bill for expenses was put in by

George Hall, riding-officer. Hall had been entrusted with the task of carrying what he called 'caipases.'* His account commenced thus :

'George Hall, Riding-Officer of Boston, his Bill of Charges to take Smuglers with Caipases, as Followeth.'

He charged two days' travelling expenses, at 3s. 6d. a day, for going into Norfolk to inquire into the 'Scircumstances' of two proposed sureties. He then charged two days spent in 'carrying Caipases.' Then his own and another officer's expenses in travelling to the Isle of Ely, 'to try and take Richd. Turrington, but could not find him.' Then a day's expenses for going into Northamptonshire, 'to try to take Anthony Walgrave and John Burke, but could not find them.' Again the same, 'but could not meet with them.' On the next day he went home, 'after trying to take ditto, but could not.' The next day, invigorated by the caresses of his family, he with a comrade went to the Isle of Ely, 'to try to take Richard Turrington, but could not meet with him.' Then they went home, charging another day's expenses, 'after trying to take Richard Turrington, but could not.' Again off to Northamptonshire. 'Tried to take Anthony Walgrave. Lay at Peterborough all night.' The next day they 'went after ditto, but could not meet with him.' On the following day they went home, 'after trying to take Walgrave and Burke, but could not meet with them,' and sent in a bill for £5 7s.

The bill appears to have been drawn up by an amateur notary. Hall *printed* his signature in the corner.

A Treasury order was issued in 1745, directing the customs officers to stop and examine all vessels going to or coming from Scotland, and send the Board account of their cargoes, and to allow no arms or military stores to be shipped coastwise without the Board's consent. This was on account of the rising under the Young Pretender.

* Carrying writs of capias.

An excursion southward will be a welcome change.   It appears from the Weymouth Letter Books, 1736, that the collector was in straits.   He had been queried frequently for errors in his account, the officers' salaries were in arrears, and he was desperately striving to explain quite inexplicable matters.   Referring to the 1733 accounts, he had to admit that the salaries and incidents for that year, ' though almost agreeing with the correct totall,' showed vast discrepancies ' in the severall branches,' and that scarcely any of the items agreed with the Controller-General's duplicate account.

Soon after he asked for leave, ' to settle urgent private affairs in Yorkshire,' and on his return was superseded. He wrote a letter to an official friend in London, and entered a copy of it in the Letter Book, evidently as his ' last speech and confession.'   It contained certain vague ' explanations ' of the errors in his accounts, and wound up thus :

' I had no intention of continuing here long, but I was injoyn'd to keep my design private, and therefore cou'd not be so free in communicating it to my friends.   I am a little surpris'd that I hear nothing from the Gentleman appointed to Succeed me, and as I am an intire stranger to him I wou'd be glad if you cou'd inform me in what way the Gentleman hath been bred.'

The new collector took up his appointment.   The staff of the port were as follows :

Warren Lisle, captain of the revenue sloop.   (Lisle appears to have been a brilliant officer.)

R. Henley, riding-supervisor.   (This gentleman was fifty-six years old, and was usually reported upon as one who took a deal of pains, and performed as much as could be expected from a man of his years.)

S. Templeman, land-surveyor (forty-six years old, and he and his two land-waiters were held ' very well quallified ').

E. Tizard, tide-surveyor.   (Tizard was sixty-seven, and efficient ' for a man of his years.')

T. Smart, tidesman and boatman ; and H. Morrish, extra hand. (' In an advanced age, yet hail men.')

There were six riding-officers, and once the collector handed the following memo. to Mr. Henley : ' You are to acquaint your men that if they do not exert themselves in preventing Frauds in their Respective Districts, and perform their Duty's with great care and diligence, the Honourable Board of Customs will provide otherwise for the Service.'

There were also waiters and searchers at various creeks and places adjacent, and one of these, named William Randall, who was stationed at Abbotsbury, distinguished himself in a peculiar manner. He made a large seizure of tea near Bexington, and his account of the same was scarcely satisfactory ; so the collector read him the Board's order of March 26, 1737, which provided that when a seizure was made and no one apprehended the seizing officer was to state full particulars on oath. Randall accordingly deposed that he found the goods concealed in certain hedges, that no person was near when he found them, that no boat or vessel was in sight, that no horses or carriages were near to the goods, and that he would be diligent in trying to discover the persons concerned. The tea was in fifty-eight oilskin bags (each two bags strung together and made up to resemble a mackerel-pot.) The collector was of opinion that the Sussex fish-buyers, who came into the county to procure fish for the metropolitan market, would have taken these goods to London.

In the following month the excise officer at Abbotsbury found 16 pounds of tea in Randall's house, and it appeared that this was part of the seized goods. Randall was then called upon to explain why he had kept the fifty-eight bags in his house during the whole of the night of seizure, instead of taking them direct to Weymouth and putting them in the warehouse. He replied that he left the tea in his wife's charge while he went to Weymouth to report, and bade her be careful ' not to embezzle the least quantity.' It would, he pleaded, have been dangerous to take the tea to the warehouse that night, as he had no assistance. The collector and controller in their report exonerated Randall, and put all the blame upon Randall's wife.

Mr. Carkesse sent twenty copies of the Act of Indemnity to Weymouth, and they were distributed thus : one to the mayor, one to each of the two bailiffs, one each to the land and tide surveyors, one each to the captain and mate of the sloop, one to Mr. Henley, one to each of his six officers, one to each of the two land-waiters, one each to two of the principal merchants, and the other two copies were kept in the Custom-house, 'for the upstairs officers or anyone wishing to peruse them.' Then the collector asked for six more copies, proposing to distribute them among 'the justices at large.'

Captain Lisle brought in *The Thomas*, of Galloway, with Irish wool and woollen yarn on board, intended for Nantes. As soon as the prize was moored her sailors ran away to avoid giving evidence. Two witnesses were procured from Ireland, who proved the shipment of the goods. The collector 'subsisted' them at 7s. a week each till the goods were condemned. Then he turned them adrift, and a few days later received instructions that proceedings were being entered against the master for the full penalty of £500. But the witnesses were not to be found, so the prosecution was abandoned.

One Colonel Horner, living near Abbotsbury, embarked in a smuggling transaction, of which the excise officers got wind too late to seize the goods, but not too late to serve a writ upon information received. The customs collector also went to work, and obtained vague information from the longshoremen who ran the goods for the colonel. They admitted bringing ashore four cwt. of tea and a cask of rum, and delivering the goods to the colonel's butler. 'But,' reported the collector, 'they refuse to make affidavit from fear of incurring the Colonel's displeasure. If suspena'd and compell'd to spake they will stand to what they have said.' The matter was left with the Excise Commissioners.

One Captain Cosart wrote to the Board, alleging that extensive frauds were carried on at Portland. The collector gave Captain Warren Lisle of the revenue sloop a reference, and the gallant skipper bluntly stated that he did not believe a word of the allegation. The collector and controller supported this denial, quoting Lisle's seizures, which had been numerous and important, and stating that if he had a reliable sloop ' he could not fail,' but that his vessel would not ' stay ' in a head sea, and therefore he had to keep his boats ' continually on the Scout, which,' said they truthfully, ' is one of the hardest services in the Customs.' They also expressed their reliance upon the riding-officers, five of whom, stationed respectively at Lulworth, Portland, Wyke Regis, Langton, and Abbotsbury, had each two dragoons as reinforcement. ' The Ill-Success,' said the officials, ' the Kent and Sussex gang of smuglers have met with on this coast, hath we presume driven them hence, having not heard or seen any of them in these parts for some time.' They reported also that the weapons used by Lisle's crew were rusty and unfit through constant exposure, and that new equipment was necessary. (The crew numbered sixteen, and each man carried a musket, a bayonet, a cutlass, and a pistol.)

Captain Lisle complained to the collector that Jonathan Hatton, one of his crew, had left him and shipped on an Ipswich schooner. The collector and controller sent for Hatton, and ' with offers of friendship ' pressed him to return, besides providing him with a new outfit of bedding, shirts, shoes, and stockings. After all this ' kindness ' Hatton refused to return, ' pretending that he had been insulted on board the sloop. We prest him severall times, but he would not be prevail'd on to discover the offenders.' It is evident that Hatton was an informer who had been taken on board as a member of the crew, and had found the work too hard and dangerous to suit him.

During a period of twelve days Warren Lisle made three seizures, amounting to 486 pounds tea, 102 gallons brandy, 72 gallons rum, 50 pounds coffee, and 4,120 pounds tobacco.

The Board called upon the collector for a statement of the method of dealing with bountied stuff of silk and worsted at shipment. The reply ran thus : ' In all silk stuffs mixed with worsted yarn the officers see that the warp is all mixed or twisted with silk, or that at least two-thirds of the ends of the threads are of silk, and that the same be obvious and apparent to their view, and that the silk therein used (to the best of their skill) is double the value of the bounty paid on the exportation of the manufactures.'

In 1741 an officer named Weeks was prosecutor in a smuggling case tried by the local justices. The case broke down, and the justices directed that Weeks should be prosecuted for perjury. He was convicted, and the collector urged the Board to support him in an appeal, ' or we shall never be able to carry on a penall prosecution more in these parts. Weeks,' said the collector, ' has been imprisoned with no other design than to deter every man from giving evidence for the Crown in future.'

In 1742 Warren Lisle chased a smuggling sloop so fiercely that her crew ran her ashore at Abbotsbury and escaped, and the riding-officer there seized her before Lisle could board. The seizure amounted to 200 pounds tea, 16½ gallons brandy, 5½ gallons rum, and 990 pounds tobacco.

A Guernsey vessel arrived with a French subject on board, The collector put a tidesman to keep close watch upon Jean Crapaud, ' in order to see that he does not stir from his quarters to view the town, or make any observation to the detriment of our shipping, as we lay open and exposed to the assaults of privateers.'

On May 28, 1744, the collector and controller sent the following report to the Board :

' We beg leave to acquaint you that this day arrived here from France in a Small Boat James Prescott of

Rochester in the County of Kent, mariner and late master of the *Sea Ranger* sloop of the burthen of 60 tons or thereabouts, with William Bagner a Saylor belonging to the mentioned vessell, who in her passage from Bideford laden with Oats for acc^t of Mr. Thomas Coxhead of Tower Hill London was taken this 9th inst. off of Bridport (on this Coast) by a French Privateer called *Le Subtil*, of 18 carriage and 6 swivell guns and 164 hands, whereof Joseph Fayle was Commander, and carried them into Sherbrooke* in France. Where after 12 days restraint in Prison these Two Men made their Escape, and by means of this Small Boat which they fortunately got Brought them safe here in Want of Everything for the support of Life. We have carefully examined the Boat and Men, and being fully sattisfied that what they relate are reall Facts we have let them go on their Lawfull occasions.'

A prosecution being entered against three smugglers, Beale, Elliot, and Chip, the collector intimated to the Board that it would be judicious to suspend proceedings. 'Chip is gone on board a Man-of-War, Elliot is delirious and often chain'd in his House, and Beale is so very Poore as hardly to have Bread to Eat.'

The Charming Molly arrived from St. Malo with 180 exchanged English prisoners on board. The officers rummaged her, and in certain artfully contrived places behind bulkheads found a large quantity of spirits concealed.

The Duke, a schooner of 40 tons, belonging to Cowes and bound for South Carolina, was captured 200 leagues west of the Lizard by a French privateer, carrying 20 guns and 200 men. The privateer captain put six hands on board to take the prize to St. Malo, and left with them one English sailor named White. The wind being south, and the weather thick, they failed to make the French coast. White persuaded them to let him navigate the vessel, and coolly brought her into Weymouth, where she was seized with her crew by the captain

* Cherbourg.

of the *Jamaica* sloop-of-war. The collector sent a flaming report to London, insisting that the customs tide-surveyor was the first to take possession of her.

During the entire period covered by the letters reviewed, the folk of Portland misbehaved sadly, plundering wrecks, assaulting and obstructing the customs officers, refusing to allow search of premises, and when proceeded against by the Exchequer disdaining to accept summons. The trouble was temporarily adjusted by the Portlanders paying the costs of the summonses, etc., and asking pardon of the officers in the public room of the Custom-house, Weymouth. A few days later certain sailors of the *Cholmondeley* revenue sloop came to Weymouth, and made affidavit that while attempting to seize goods run near Portland Castle the Portlanders ' grievously assaulted ' them, and carried off the goods. In his report of this the collector stated : ' And we further beg leave to assure your Honours that unless some speedy and effectuall method be taken to putt a Stop to the audacious and insolent Behaviour of these Islanders, no officer may with safety enter that Island to Execute his office. And we have reason to believe that on any ships in Distress comming on Shoar in or near the Island of Portland no officer of the Customs will venter to lay out all night in order to protect and defend such unhappy Sufferers and Guard their Goods, for fear of being knock'd on the head with a volly of Stones from the Islanders.'

A vessel of Amsterdam went ashore at Fleet soon after. She was stated to be a West India trader, but as she appears to have had ' a deal of money ' and little cargo on board, and to have carried 74 men and 24 guns, it is probable that she was a privateer. ' The Country People,' reported the collector, ' came down in Great Gangs and carry'd off what they could lay their hands on, in defyance of the officers.' Though the officers were badly beaten by the mob, they contrived to save some of the money. The conduct of the Dutch skipper and his crew was peculiar. They got ashore safe, but made no attempt to protect the officers in their efforts to save the treasure, nor did they lift a finger to help. Two of the sailors, while the mob were playing football with the officers' bodies, fought a duel on the shore with knives, which ended in one of them being mortally wounded, and then his comrades put him out of pain by beating him to death. The Dutch skipper made himself comfortable at a tavern adjacent, and when the officers went to tell him of their success in saving some of the money he blew a great cloud from his pipe, but no more. Not even a grunt of gratitude did he vouchsafe them, never a dram did he offer as ' medicine for their aching bones.'

A glance at the practice of the port of Cowes may be interesting. In 1749 the ' established ' staff consisted of a collector, a tide-surveyor, two landing-waiters, and a riding-officer. There were also the following ' incidental ' officers : a deputy-controller, three riding-officers, and two boatmen. There were thirteen tidesmen, all ' extraordinary '—viz., employed when required, at a daily wage. The total pay and ' allowances ' of the staff (including the ' incidental ' and ' extraordinary ' hands, who appear to have been constantly employed) amounted to about £1,000 a year.

The port was fairly busy. The drawback transactions were extensive, and sometimes there was not enough cash in hand to discharge the debentures. The Plantation trade assisted in keeping the port lively, Cowes being a convenient place of call for Plantation ships bound for the northern Continental ports. These vessels, under the Plantation Act, had to unship their cargoes in England, and afterwards reship them for the final ports of destination.

Wrecks were terribly frequent. Unowned wrecked goods were claimed by the Earl of Portsmouth, governor of the island, but most of the wrecked cargoes were salved,

and in such cases the collector, who under the Act of
Queen Anne held considerable powers with regard to
wrecked goods, did not fail to report himself to the Board
as ' aiding and assisting to the salvage thereof.' By the
Act quoted he was entitled to participate in salvage
money, and no doubt he came in for many a bright guinea
that way. The salvage claims were frequently disputed,
and then the collector, by authority of the Act, nominated
justices to decide. After the decision was announced it
was usual for the owners to make application through
the collector to the Board for permission to sell duty-
free as much of the salved cargo as would discharge the
award. In one case the skipper of a stranded Dutch
vessel agreed with an islander named Ratsey for £200,
to be paid down in case he got the ship off. Most of the
cargo had been jettisoned, and Ratsey succeeded in his
attempt, but the Dutchman proposed to delay payment
until the total salvage was assessed on ship and goods.
Ratsey entered a protest, and bided his time. Within
a very short period the award was made, and the justices
gave Ratsey his £200, with an additional *penny in the
pound* as interest due for the time he had to wait, and
£2 to compensate him for his trouble in protesting. This
roused the collector's ire, and he complained to the Board
that the additional sums were unfairly granted, but the
Board seemed indisposed to interfere.

The four riding-officers covered the whole of the coast
in their rides. Each ride extended about fifteen miles.
There appear to have been few seizures during the early
part of 1749, but the Board queried the collector as to
whether he had heard anything of extensive smuggling
in his district. He referred to the riding-officers and
tide-surveyor, and their reports were on the whole re-
assuring. Therefore he replied in the negative ; but it
is evident the Board had reliable information, for the
revenue sloops began to muster thick around the Wight.
This appears to have incited the officers to vigilance. A
small seizure of rum was made, and the boat carrying

the goods was seized as well. Some practical joker stole the boat during the night, and the collector reported the matter to the Board. The night after the report was sent on the boat was restored to her moorings, and the collector no doubt regretted his readiness with ink and paper.

The riding-officer at Niton saw two men landing a hogshead from a boat. He made for them, but they got the hogshead back into the boat, pushed off, and hailed him from afloat, asking if a couple of guineas would not be more in his way than a seizure. Said the collector suggestively in his report : ' They did not actually produce the money.' Finding the officer either too dull to apprehend their meaning or too virtuous to acquiesce, they put to sea again.

In 1751 the following letter reached the collector :

' SIR,

'One John Fleming has been so indiscreet as to take into his boat or wherry half-a-anchor of Gin, which some of your officers have seiz'd together with the Boat. As the Man has a Wife and Several Children, and the Boat his All, for want of which he must come chargeable to our Parish : We the officers of this Parish do Request the Favour of you to take the Man's Poverty and Family into consideration, and Order the Boat to be restor'd him, which will oblige many. Particularly

' Your most obedient Serv^{ts}.

' *Churchwarden*, WM. JOLLIFFE.

' *Overseers* {MARMADUKE BOOTFLOWER,
JNO. SKETCHLY.

' GOSPORT IN ALVERSTOKE PARISH,
' *2nd Augt.*, 1751.'

The collector reported favourably, and Fleming got his boat back. It appeared that Fleming had taken into his boat a female passenger from a passing Dutch ship, and the keg of gin had been thrown into the sea as a present.

One James Shotter was convicted of smuggling, and lodged in Winchester jail. His sons craved a composition, thus :

'*The Humble Petition of James Shotter and William Shotter.*

' Most Humbly Sheweth
' That your petitioners by supporting their Father with the Common Necessary's of Life during his confinement have expended all their substance and are reduced to the utmost Extremities that can possibly attend persons in such distressed Circumstances. That had not we his Sons out of our hard Labour now and then sent a small pittance to our Father he must long ago have perished through Want. That at the same time our poor Mother who is also very aged depends upon us entirely for her subsistence. That we have a very sensible and dutiful Concern for our unhappy Father, and were it in our power, of which God and all the World knows it is not, would willingly offer something by way of Recompence to the Government for his Great Offence. That we have hitherto lived in our Neighbourhood with the Reputation of Honest and Industrious Men. The Utmost we can do is to implore the Charity of well-disposed persons on the part of our distressed Father, and believe with their Assistance we may be able to offer to your Honours Twenty Pounds, if your Honours will be pleased to accept of that sum by way of mulct atonement for his past Offence.
' We humbly beg your Honours to take this our Petition into your Compassionate Consideration, and be pleased to let us know whether this offer in favour of our unhappy Father for whom our harts are bleeding will be accepted.'

It is to be hoped that readers will attribute the strained piteousness of this petition to its right source, the bad taste of the amateur notary. The collector's report stated that the Shotters were extremely poor, yet the official overcame the man, and a hint was inserted that a trifle was owing for expenses of prosecution. The Board thereupon claimed £30 as the lowest composition practicable. A genuinely pathetic letter from the old smuggler's wife announced that the £30 had been raised. Undoubtedly the money was made up by neighbours. The Crown and the lawyer were paid—even if an old dame's heart drops blood the lawyer must have his fee.

The commander of the *Savage* sloop was a man much unlike Captain Jewell of Boston. His name was Foley, and it is probable that he hailed from the Emerald Isle. He was a vigilant and successful officer, and made many huge seizures. Something of the sea-lawyer was in him as well; he was given to penning pompous dispatches, and seems to have imagined himself to be an extremely important person. Withal he looked sharply after Captain Foley's pecuniary interests, and no doubt spent much of his spare time in conning such Acts of Parliament as dealt with awards and shares in seizure profits. One of his seizures produced £524 odd on condemnation, and the collector paid one-third as captain and crew's share, upon which Foley nibbed a new quill and delivered himself of a bunch of quotations from the Act of Indemnity, proving beyond dispute that he was entitled to one-half the proceeds. He wound up thus :

' Pursuant to the Direction of this subsequent Act of Parliament . . . and if in Case it be doubted whether I am entitled to a Moiety or not I will readily submit the same to the decision of the Attorney-General, or any other person that shall be approved of by the Board of Customs, to whom I desire you will represent this case accordingly.'

Here is another of his messages :

' On the 10th inst. I cut my Cable in a Gale of Wind at Studland Bay, and gave chase to a Smugling Cutter called the *May Flower* of Rye, George Hemings Master,

which I took about two miles to the southward of Christchurch Head, and found in her 250 small Casks of Rum
and Brandy.

' I sent my master and seven men on board of her to
Rummage her effectually, and he is to deliver her with
all her furniture, to be proceeded against according to
Law, which I desire you will communicate to the Board
of Customs.

' I herewith send you a copy of the Orders my Master
is under for your information.

' I desire you will order the Casks to be carefully
Examined as soon as they are landed, and as they are
Leaky to give me leave to start the Liquor into Iron-
bound Hogsheads and Puncheons, which I will procure
at my own Expence, for it will be a very Considerable
Advantage both to the Crown and me.'

His orders to the master were explicit.

' Whereas the Smugling Cutter which was taken by
me,' etc.

The wonder is how he managed to pen all this in a gale
of wind, and how he came to write ' me ' after ' the
Crown,' and with a small ' m.'

There was a riding-officer, named Richard Rogers, who
was for ever getting himself ' obstructed ' and assaulted.
Here is one of his affidavits :

' To wit : Richard Rogers One of the Riding Officers
of the Port of Cowes in the Isle of Wight in the County of
Southampton maketh Oath that on the 27th day of
January last he had an Information that some Prohibited
and Uncustomed goods would be lodged in the Dwelling-
house of Henry Matthews, within the parish and Manor
of Godshill in the Isle of Wight aforesaid, Schoolmaster.'

It appears from the rest of the affidavit that Rogers
procured a writ of assistance and a constable, and ap-
proaching the suspected house met Matthews outside
the door. Matthews demanded the name of the informer,
and, failing to obtain it, put his back to the door, and
announced that if Rogers would enter he must first

prove himself the better man. He kept the officer at bay for some time, then stepped aside, and bade him ' Search and be damned.' On going into the room Rogers noticed that the back window had been removed. He searched, and found nought. Soon after Rogers' son, an alert youth of fifteen, told his father that while Matthews blocked the entrance several casks had been removed by the back window and put into the barn. Rogers thereupon made for the barn, calling upon the constable to follow, but that wary official promptly discovered that the barn was ' out of his jurisdiction,' and remained 'where he had a right for to be.' Matthews pursued Rogers, and seized him before he could enter the barn. Matthews' mother, an aged but spirited dame, also laid hands on the riding-officer, and assisted to drag him back ' into jurisdiction.' Rogers, who, like most of the other revenue officials, was a man of law rather than a man of hands, retired, and tendered affidavit.

Joseph Jerem, the constable, also made affidavit, and it is easy to perceive that evidence was dragged from Joseph Jerem against Joseph Jerem's will. He ended thus :

' The said Matthews left the place where he stood as aforesaid and bid the said Rogers search and be damned and thereupon the said Rogers went into the said room and when he came into the same said I see it is gone (or used words to that effect).'

But not one word from Joseph Jerem as to the assault outside the barn, that being ' outside his jurisdiction.'

It was not uncommon during the Georgian period—a period that opened many seductive avenues for mean knaves to wander in—for utterly unfounded information to be lodged against innocent people. In some cases this was done from motives of petty spite, in others to direct attention from the informer's own misdeeds. The following specimen was no doubt due to both incentives :

' Francis Morris of West Cowes Marriner and late Master of the *Prince of Wales* voluntarily maketh Oath that on or about the 22nd day of January, 1750, he did take on board the said vessel at Haverdegrace in France six Casks containing thirtysix gallons of brandy and Rum, one oilskin bag containing fiftysix lbs. of tea, one cwt. of burnt coffee in bottles, and two dozen lbs. of Soap, for and on account of Frederick Todd of West Cowes, and by him the said Morris put on Shoar,' etc.

This fellow Morris was a lying and malicious rogue. It turned out that on January 16, 1750, he had actually cleared with a cargo of salt for Shoreham, and that he did not return to Cowes till March 15.

Captain Foley reported that the cutter seized would be useful to him as a tender, and pompously proposed his intentions : ' Firstly ; I will take the cutter together with all her materials, and victual and Man her at my own Expence.

' Secondly ; I will keep the said vessel in wear and tear during the time I shall be commissioned,' etc.

He continued to ' Thirdly,' and ' Lastly,' making it apparent that though rather circumlocutory for a sailorman he was wide awake ; and in the end desired that his report might be laid before the Board, ' for their approbation and consent.' It is likely that about this time the gallant captain had to buy a new cocked hat, his head having become too large for the old one.

Later he again approached the collector. ' Having wrote to you on the 17th past, desiring you would report a proposal of mine to the Board of Customs : To which proposal I have not received any answer : I desire,' etc. In a postscript he commanded the collector to be expeditious in making up the seizure accounts. ' It will be an advantage both to the Crown and me.' But neither Board nor collector appear to have been much flustered by Foley's peremptory missives, even when it was announced that the Admiralty had directed him to bring to London the tea he had seized, amounting to $3,579\frac{1}{2}$ pounds. He made known his intention of ' arriving at the Nore in about six days,' and no doubt it irked his valiant soul that he could not pass up the winding reaches as some of the old plate-ship plunderers had done, with sails of silk, with hautboys playing and kettle-drums resounding, and lower his flag in response to a salvo from the Tower guns.

The riding-officer Rogers had another barn-door experience. On information he went, with neither writ nor constable, to the house of one Sanders. Sanders was from home, the barn was locked, and Mrs. Sanders inclined to believe her husband had the key with him. Rogers hardened his heart, and broke the barn-door in. ' In an empty cask ' within he found 227 pounds tea. For some reason or other the collector tried to screen Sanders, and wrote to the Board stating that he believed the man to be innocent. ' He is an inoffensive man, having scarcely common sense.' About this time Rogers' case against Matthews the schoolmaster was settled, Matthews paying five guineas as compensation.

During a terrible storm in January, 1753, the following ships went ashore on the Wight :

The Adrienne, of Bordeaux, laden with wine.

The Friendship, of Scarborough, laden with tobacco.

The Svend Hoolm, of Copenhagen, laden with staves and copper.

The Samuel, of Cork, laden with sugar, cotton, and ebony.

A Boston ship, laden with oil and turpentine.

A brigantine of Poole, in ballast.

A Dutch vessel, laden with wine and other merchandise.

All these became total wrecks. The Earl of Portsmouth secured thirty barrels of wine from the Dutchman, and these were put under Crown lock in Carisbrooke Castle.

Other wrecks were reported. The harbour was filled with vessels which had run in for shelter, and the collector was quite unable to provide tidesmen to watch on board of them. Soon after this Captain Foley returned to his cruising-ground, and signalized his arrival by a seizure of 1,823 pounds tobacco. The Crown warehouses were full to the very roofs with seized goods and wrecked goods, and the collector chartered private warehouses, and filled them up as well.

A vessel arrived from the Plantations, and her cargo was landed, the usual Plantation certificates were produced, and the goods reshipped on the vessel for Rotterdam. One of the parcels consisted of logwood, and this the master claimed as exempt from the restrictions upon Plantation goods, stating that it had been brought from Honduras to South Carolina to be put on board his vessel for Rotterdam. But he had no certificate of its place of origin, so the collector treated the parcel as Plantation produce, had it landed with the other goods, and demanded poundage on its reshipment. The poundage was paid, but the captain brought the necessary certificate next voyage, and got the money back.

Certain wrecked goods being liable to excise duties, the collector of excise desired to put them under excise lock. Full as the customs warehouses were, the collector of customs would not endure this encroachment upon his prerogative, but managed to squeeze them into the King's Warehouse. Then the excise officer attempted to put an excise lock on the King's Warehouse. The customs collector objected, and reported the matter to his Board. From which it may be gathered that rivalry between departments is no new thing.

The great Foley put his foot into it. Two of the customs tidesmen stopped Captain Foley's servant, who was carrying a package in the direction of his master's lodgings. The package contained six pounds tea. Foley wrote a flaming letter to the collector, stating that part of the tea had been bought of a grocer in Gosport, and that the rest was a present from brother officers. ' I was sending it to my lodgings to be dryed on a sheet, and I should be glad to be informed who were the officers that seized it.' The collector held on to the tea, and reported the matter to the Board. Foley's second letter on the subject was remarkably deferential. It does not appear that anything was done in the matter. But nothing could stop Captain Foley from making seizures. He pounced upon a parcel of coin, and got it forfeited as being illegally shipped for transmission to a foreign land. Directly after he made a great haul : 33 pounds tea, 37 pounds coffee, 264 gallons brandy, 90 gallons rum, 1,560 pounds tobacco, and 160 gallons wine.

An ancient longshoreman named Webster petitioned the Board from ' Winchester Goal.' (' Gaol ' was usually spelt ' Goal ' in those days, and indeed it was the inevitable goal of many.) The collector reported on the petition, stating that the petitioner Webster had served many years in the navy, and left with a very bad character ; that since his discharge he had pretended to be a fisherman, but really had been at the bottom of most of the smuggling in the locality, being assisted by his two sons, lads of thirteen and seventeen ; that the elder son had been smuggling ever since he was able, and was a most profligate young fellow ; and that Webster had been heard to boast of being worth £700.

Rogers the riding-officer got into trouble again. He went with another officer to arrest one Dyer on a capias. Dyer's wife and daughter, assisted by two yokels, assaulted and obstructed the officers. Dyer escaped, but was afterwards captured with others, one of whom was Matthews the schoolmaster.

A customs boatman saw a fisherman ' take up ' nine casks of wine, which had been attached to bags of ballast and sunk near the shore. The boatman would have seized the goods, but the wily trawler foiled him by announcing that he was about to take them to the Customhouse as wreck.

The three chief officers of the port had grown very keen after seizures. Mr. Godwin the tide-surveyor had returned 2,422 pounds of seized tobacco within the half-year, and Mr. Wilkinson the deputy controller 3,023 pounds, and the collector seems to have been anxious to distinguish himself as well. A sloop belonging to Dublin, and bound from Gothenburg to Oporto, put into Cowes, and it was discovered that she had fifteen tons of tea on board. By the letter of the law the goods were seizable, the tea being from a place not the land of its growth, the vessel not an East India Company's ship, and there appearing no likelihood of her having run in for shelter, as the weather had been fine for several days. Yet she could scarcely be deemed 'a hoverer,' for the tea was in chests each containing three cwts., and a hoverer would not have sailed into Cowes in fine weather and anchored near the shore. The three chiefs held council, and there is reason to think that they resolved to strain the law, being instigated thereto by the prospect of great gain, for if they succeeded in getting the tea condemned they would divide amongst them about £2,000. Anyhow, the collector sent Godwin to seize the tea.

The master of the sloop made no protest till the goods had been taken ashore and put under Crown lock. Then he came storming into the Custom-house, with witnesses to prove that on the previous night he had sent one of his crew to acquaint the customs watchmen with the nature of his cargo. His papers turned out to be correct, and it was found that he had entered harbour to obtain a new mast.

The collector at once penned a letter to the Board, and every line testified to the panic that possessed the writer. He described the circumstances under which he had made the seizure, using 'we' as often as possible, and making desperate efforts to thrust most of the responsibility upon Godwin. But in the end terror made him give himself completely away. He suggested in conclusion that perhaps a prosecution might hold, but stated that he and the others humbly relinquished their 'right title' to prosecute and their claim to reward, and surrendered said rights and profits to the Crown. He put the letter into the hands of his friend Mr. Gill, patent controller of the port, and Mr. Gill went express to London, crossing the Solent in the dark, chartering relays of post-horses, and running up a tremendous bill of expenses. Early on the following day Mr. Gill arrived at the London Custom-house.

The position was at once manifest to the shrewd gentlemen who sat in the room looking out upon the crowded river, and Mr. Gill was soon on his way back, carrying an order to the collector to release the goods, unless prepared to prosecute at his own risk. The collector sent back a doleful report. The master had refused to take the tea on board, and had communicated with the shipowners at Dublin. Mr. Godwin had made the tender of restitution, ' in presence of two witnesses,' but without avail, and had then retired, probably registering a mental vow never to seize tea again. The collector, in his letter, pleaded abjectly for protection, expressing a hope that their Honours would intervene. ' The master,' he wrote, ' seems quite litigious. We beg that you will defend us from damage, as we have done all in our power to avoid it.'

Later he wrote that he had personally tendered restitution, and had been repulsed. Again he wrote as to renewed tender, made ' in the most amicable manner,' yet again repulsed, although the new mast had been rigged, and the vessel made ready for sea.

Godwin, whose misdirected astuteness had been at the bottom of the bungle, collapsed under his manifold anxieties, and applied for a month's leave, ' to go to the baths.' And no doubt the collector prayed that the first bath Mr. Godwin took might end Mr. Godwin's tremors for good and all, and his chances of making any more seizures of ' tea in chests.'

Mr. Blennerhassett Grove, supercargo, arrived from Dublin, and allowed the tea to be put on board, ' but,' piteously stated the collector, ' he refuses to give any further indemnification.'

About this time there were many wrecks of tobacco cargoes, and when the wrecked goods were abandoned as unmerchantable the collector sent them to London for destruction. In May and June, 1755, he sent no less than 229,000 pounds of damaged tobacco, the freight per sloop amounting to £56 10s.

Mr. Godwin came back from the baths, and took to reporting tidesmen instead of seizing tea. He caught two unlucky fellows asleep when they should have been patrolling the deck and admiring the moonlit heavens. Richard Colebrook, charged with leaving his charge, going aboard another ship ' to drinking,' and being afterwards found asleep during his watch, answered thus, and his statement may have tickled the Commissioners :

' The charge I do not deny. I drinkt of a small mugg of Water, Sugar, and a little Rum * * * * to squench my thirst. To rest myself a little I set down on the main hatches where I chanced to fall on sleep. Gentle-men, if I am guilty of a Falt I must humbly ask Pardon. But Gentlemen, I was never the man to see the Govern-ment abused since I have been in the Employ, for I always act much to the Contrary, and I haterly wish I could serve it more.'

Michael Facey, charged with being found asleep on a hencoop during his watch, replied :

' I do hereby acknowledge that having a bad Legg I did set down on a Chest which was on deck. I very probably might take a Nodd, but was not sound asleep.'

(When an officer was accused the charge invariably concluded thus : ' To which matter you are hereby required to give a plain and distinct answer, avoiding all Scurrilous or Abusive Expressions.')

A poor wretch languishing in Winchester ' Goal ' for smuggling wrote a manly and affecting letter to the Board. He stated that he was starving, and that his wife was begging in the streets, and added that he had served in the navy. He prayed to be allowed to volun-teer for that service, and thus gain indemnity.

Mr. Godwin became more officious than ever. He cleared a Norwegian ship outward, and called upon the captain to pay duty on certain planks used for shoring the ballast. When the captain objected, Godwin seized the ship's dutiable stores (ten gallons brandy, which the skipper protested had been previously declared and passed). Godwin also reported that the Palatines (Germans), who shipped on the Continent for the Plantations, brought small kegs of spirits which they claimed were stores necessary for the voyage, and he suggested that the spirits should be landed and duty-paid before reshipment, as cargo for the Plantations. All this appears to have been pure litigiousness, to avenge himself by causing the collector trouble. The latter reported dead against Godwin in both instances.

A pilot wrote to the collector, stating that he conducted a Dutch vessel ' out of the Kneedles,' and the captain being short of money gave him a two-gallon jar of gin. This was seized from the pilot by the officers ashore, and they also detained his boat. He pleaded that the gin was for his own private use, he being ' troubled with the Gravel.'

In 1756 the collector, having allowed a year and a half to elapse, brought up the matter of the expense he had incurred in connexion with the abortive seizure of tea, and requested the Board to reimburse him. He furnished a statement, showing that he had paid in all £10 4s. 11d., which included Mr. Gill's posting expenses (£6 13s. 3d.) and an item of 5s. 2d. for ' nails and wood used in repairing the packages.' Unfortunately the records do not show whether he gained or lost his point, but it is evident he was not one to suffer tamely in pocket. Most of the memoranda in the Letter Books display the superior officials as sly fellows, ever on the look out for a chance of turning a penny, and regarding the Commissioners as champions pledged to stand betwixt them and the public whenever they might happen to overshoot the mark. It is improbable that either the controller or Godwin had subscribed to the expense, yet the collector thought it best to implicate them in the request for compensation.

'We hope your Honours will not let us be sufferers thereby.'

There was a new collector at Poole in 1758. His predecessor, Milner, had been dismissed for various malpractices, and had gone into partnership with a firm of Poole shipowners. Milner's dismissal had been mainly secured through the agency of the deputy controller, and it is plain that Milner and his new partners had resolved upon getting even with the deputy, if possible. Early in 1758 a sailor named Long, employed upon one of Milner's ships, furnished an affidavit, in which he stated that on coming into port he was approached by the deputy controller, who asked him if the captain had any brandy, and on being answered in the affirmative requested Long to obtain him five gallons at the cheapest possible rate. Long declared that he procured the brandy, and took it by night to the house of the controller's father. This affidavit, with the controller's reply, the new collector forwarded to the Board.

The controller stated upon oath that he did 'in a bantering way' ask Long if the captain had any grog left, and that his reason for uttering the jest was that the captain had been caught with 40 gallons. But the controller had to admit that his father *did* buy five gallons of brandy from Long, though without the controller's sanction. He declared that the whole business was 'mere trepanning,' and concluded thus: 'I now beg liberty to remark that this Long is a Brother-in-law to Glover (the Captain) who is in partnership with the late collector. They, in revenge for the discovery I lately made of Mr. Milner's malpractices, contrived this malicious Scheme against me, I being very creditably informed that they have given out that if this will not do they will endeavour to find out something else against me that I shall do, meaning to get me dismiss'd. So I find 'twill be necessary for me to exert myself against the late collector, by putting him in the Crown Office for collaring

me in my office in the month of January last. Having
proper witnesses to the Fact, which I thought to have
lain before the Honourable Board, but was not willing to
be troublesome.'

The Board very wisely took no notice of Long's affidavit, and the controller, perhaps with equal wisdom,
took no proceedings against Milner for the 'collaring.'
Milner, as will be seen further on, was an impudent and
determined fellow, who stuck at nothing to cause his
successor trouble.

The collector apprised the Board that four officers at
break of day found in Bitman's Chine a great number of
casks of spirits and bags of tea, with four of the crew of
the vessel from which the goods had been run standing
guard over them. One of the officers went to get horses
and a wagon, and soon after a number of country people
attacked the others, beat and bound them, and carried
off the goods. Officers were sent in pursuit, but without
success. The collector ambiguously stated : 'Should
have gone myself, but the Heighth of Plantation work,
and a sale at the Custom House.' A reward of £20 was
offered for discovery of the offenders. One Robert
Wilkins, of Sutton Mandeville, made an attempt at
securing this by an affidavit, but his information was bald
hearsay. He accused the following :

'Mark Chamberlain, who lives at John Goulding's at
the New Inn within the Parrish of Downton, and goes by
the name of "The old Man."'

'Isaac Gulliver, who is very often at the same Inn.'

In 1759 the collector, the controller, and the tide-
surveyor signed the following report to the Commissioners
of Excise :

'We apprehend ourselves indispensably oblig'd in vin-
dication of our Character to complain to your Honours of
the unwarrantable Liberties taken lately by Mr. Thomas
Ireland, the supervisor here, who in public company at
Wimborne declar'd that he would make a Reformation in
the Custom House at Poole. That he had been up in it,

and mark'd out a place where he would have an office built, by which he should save £500 per annum to the Revenue. We beg leave to assure your Honours he never was in this office on any such account, and that if he had he would have been properly turn'd down stairs. He told Mr. Keay, a Common Brewer of Wimborne, that the officers of the Customs at Poole were Smuglers, "and considerable ones." We humbly apprehend these Declarations carry a very severe reflection upon us as Principal Officers of the Port of Poole, and tho' we are sensible he was very drunk when he made them we humbly submit to your Honour's Determination how far that is an excuse for a Charge of this Nature.'

They went on to charge him with extorting £6 from the Vestry of St. James's, Poole, as a contribution towards his land tax, and furnished a certified extract from the parish register in corroboration. Then they asked that he might be made to apologize ' in the Publick Papers.'

But the supervisor was ready with an answer. Whilst flinging back a few vague hints that reformation was necessary, and one especially nasty hint about an irregularity in the entering of rum, he contrived to put quite a different aspect on matters. He denied that he was drunk at Wimborne, and implied that the customs officers had on several occasions obstructed him in the performance of his duty. He admitted that the Vestry made him a grant of £6, but proved that it had not been paid. ' I disdain'd to receive it.'

This roused the customs men's ire. They may also have been enraged that the Board of Excise referred the matter to the excise collector of the district. They returned to the charge, sarcastically pointing out that the grant was *made,* and that it was hard to tell whether Mr. Ireland would have ' disdain'd to receive it,' seeing that their charge was formulated before the time of payment had arrived. But the affair, like that between the controller and Milner's gang, seems to have ended in nought.

Readers must not think too harshly of the customs men whose sayings and doings are quoted. It was a corrupt age. Holy offices were sometimes traded, parliamentary seats often, subordinate official posts universally, and where jobbery rules in public business it is bound to influence private character. Probably most of the corporation officials, military and naval contractors, political agents, attorneys, and churchwardens of the day, as well as the civil servants, were almost as honest as men could be who desired to live at a little above the ordinary standard of expenses.

A curious list appears in Sir William Musgrave's notes on this period. It seems that even smugglers were occasionally smitten with genuine remorse for their misdeeds, and made anonymous tenders of 'conscience money.' The list is not extensive. It includes but nineteen contributions, extending over a period of twenty-six years :

In 1731, £3.   In 1734, 3s.   In 1736, £3 3s.   In 1737, £5 5s.   In 1738, £600 and £120.   In 1740, 20 guineas. In 1741, £58 10s.   In 1743, £7 8s.   In 1747, £100.   In 1748, £1 2s. 6d. and £31 2s. 9d.   In 1749, £3 3s.   In 1754, £7 11s. 8d.   In 1755, £30 and £3 17s. 6d.   In 1756, £40 10s.   In 1757, £25 and £4 13s. 6d.

It would be interesting to know what the 3s. signified. It may have been what some student of ancient revenue history conceived would be the reasonable duty on a tun of French wine. The subsidy tunnage on French wine was 3s. in Elizabeth's day, and the learned smuggler, having escaped George II.'s tunnage, which in London would be over £50, may have said to himself, 'Good Queen Bess's dues should be enough,' and sent in the Elizabethan tunnage. The 1747 contribution of £100 may have been a penalty, sent by some one who had on many occasions escaped it.

LIST OF AUTHORITIES.

Wine : 1 Geo. II., s. 2, c. 17.

Permanent branches of revenue : 3 Geo. II., c. 20 ; 5 Geo. II., c. 6 ; 6 Geo. II., c. 17 ; 7 Geo. II., c. 14 ; 15 Geo. II., c. 29 ; 18 Geo. II., c. 9 ; 19 Geo. II., c. 12 ; 19 Geo. II., c. 27 ; 21 Geo. II., c. 2 ; 24 Geo. II., c. 46 ; 25 Geo. II., c. 32 ; 32 Geo. II., c. 10.

Protective measures and prohibitions : 1 Geo. II., s. 2, c. 17 ; 4 Geo. II., c. 27 ; 4 Geo. II., c. 29 ; 5 Geo. II., c. 22 ; 5 Geo. II., c. 24 ; 6 Geo. II., c. 13 (same on 2-3 Anne, c. 9, and 9-10 Wm. III., c. 23) ; 12 Geo. II., c. 21 ; 12 Geo. II., c. 36 ; 18 Geo. II., c. 36 ; 22 Geo. II., c. 36 ; 21 Geo. II., c. 30 ; 23 Geo. II., c. 20 ; 23 Geo. II., c. 24 ; 23 Geo. II., c. 29 ; 23 Geo. II., c. 32 ; 33 Geo. II., c. 28.

Warehousing : 15 Geo. II., c. 25.

Puritanical measures : 7 Geo. II., c. 8 ; 13 Geo. II., c. 19 ; 12 Geo. II., c. 28 ; 19 Geo. II., c. 21.

Temporary imposts : 18 Geo. II., c. 26.

Excise duties : 31 Geo. II., c. 36 ; 32 Geo. II., c. 29.

Preventive measures : 5 Geo. II., c. 21 ; 7 Geo. II., c. 19, 9 Geo. II., c. 35 ; 18 Geo. II., c. 28 ; 19 Geo. II., c. 34 ; 23 Geo. II., c. 21 ; 24 Geo. II., c. 41 ; 26 Geo. II., c. 12 ; 26 Geo. II., c. 21 ; 28 Geo. II., c. 21.

Departmental incidents : Sir William Musgrave's ' Memoranda '; Montrose Letter Books ; Treasury Papers, 1733 ; Boston Letter File ; Weymouth Letter Books ; Cowes Letter Books ; Poole Letter Books ; ' Social Life in Former Days.'

CHAPTER VIII

1760–1787

IN reviewing the progress of revenue legislation during the first half of George III.'s reign, it will be unnecessary to specify every trifling amendment and imposition ; only the more important alterations need be noted.

In 1763 additional tunnage was levied on foreign wine and vinegar, and the ' leakage ' allowance was withheld except for wine imported direct from land of production. The latter provision was intended to counteract a practice which had become common of importing wine into the Channel Islands, coopering and filling the casks, and shipping them to the southern English ports, where the leakage allowance was claimed although the packages were landed full.

The duty on beaver skins imported from the Plantations was reduced to 1d. per skin, to encourage British hat-making. The outward duty was 7d. per skin.

Duties were laid on many articles imported into the American colonies. Much dissatisfaction ensued, but the imperial legislators took little heed. Wine landed in the Plantations was made liable to tunnage. Cockets were to be used for goods removed by sea from one colony to another.

The Plantation Acts had been evaded by masters calling at Great Britain with ' part cargoes ' of goods from foreign, shipping a few packages of British goods, and then under cover of the certificates for the latter landing the whole in the Colonies. It was therefore enacted that clearance should not be granted to any vessel bound for the Plantations from a British port, unless the whole of her cargo had been *shipped* in Great Britain. Irish horses, linen, and provisions, Madeira wines, and salt from any country for use in Plantation fisheries, were exempt from this restriction.

The law against hoverers was extended to ships cruising within two leagues of the Plantation coasts. Government vessels that made seizures in Plantation waters were granted preferential awards. All Plantation revenue officers absent from their stations were ordered to return at once on pain of dismissal. The Treasury directed the American governors to support the American revenue officers in the discharge of their duties. Several of the higher Plantation officials were on leave in England. They were ordered to place themselves under instruction ' in the business of their respective offices,' and on certificate being made of their fitness they were to depart at once. Their instructors were those eminently unpractical gentlemen, ' the patent officers of the port of London.'

Hemp and undressed flax from the American Plantations were bountied on landing in England. The bounty was to be £8 a ton from 1764 to 1771, £6 from 1771 to 1778, £4 from 1778 to 1785. It was to be paid by the collectors at ports of importation. If in any case the money were not forthcoming from the port receipts the Receiver-General was to pay it. The bounty was intended to secure a liberal supply of hemp and flax for naval use, and the Naval Commissioners had power to pre-empt the bountied goods. The customs officers at ports of importation were to examine the hemp and flax and satisfy themselves as to the quality. If after bounty the goods were not pre-empted, they might be sold in ordinary trade. If they were exported the bounty was to be returned.

(A vessel from the Levant, with the Algerian ambassador on board, was quarantined at Stangate Creek in 1761. The ambassador contrived to send a letter to the Secretary of State, complaining of detention. This caused much consternation, for in law all concerned, from the post-office people to the aristocratic officials who handled the letter on receipt, became liable to be sent to the Kentish marshes and rigorously quarantined. Needless to say, for once the law was evaded.)

Both the patent and deputed searchers of the port of London were reminded of their responsibilities, the Board stating that there were great frauds in connexion with the shipment of goods. (Many of the patent men reaped huge harvests of fees, and employed deputies and clerks to do the work of their offices, the said deputies and clerks being sometimes paid by the Crown 'out of incidents.' Whenever work became brisk, the deputies clamoured for extra assistance, and for many, many years they rarely clamoured in vain.)*

The Treasury complimented Mr. Temple, surveyor-general for the northern district of North America, upon his successful enforcement of the laws against smuggling. The higher Plantation officials were directed to furnish the English Commissioners of Customs with full reports of the character and capabilities of subordinates, and particulars of all cargoes shipped and unshipped, and the English Commissioners were to supply the Treasury with quarterly abstracts of the reports. All newly appointed Plantation officers were to be instructed by the London officers prior to leaving England, and their pay was to be withheld till they took up their employment. (The Custom-house records refer to a serious riot at Rhode Island, in opposition to one Lieutenant Hill, who acted for the Customs there.)

* The Bench officers (patent officers who actually attended in the Long Room) seem to have caused the Commissioners a deal of trouble. They were constantly being reproached for absence, disorderly behaviour, insolence to merchants, and rapacity. Much of the apparent lenity of the Board towards them was due to the fact that most appointments were the result of weighty recommendation, and each censure uttered by the Commissioners might offend some lordly patron.

The privilege previously enjoyed by South Carolina and Georgia of exporting rice to places in the eastern hemisphere southward of Cape Finisterre, without unshipping the rice in Great Britain, was extended to shipments to American ports lying southward of Georgia.

(Various interesting orders were issued to the British customs officers. They were directed to be vigilant in searching foreign vessels, especially those windbound in the Downs, for British seamen fleeing from the press, and to detain and send to the Secretary of State all sealed letters found on ships from abroad.)

The Attorney-General decided that customs officers were not empowered to enter the dwellings of 'private gentlemen' in search of contraband lace and embroidery, as the law was only intended to apply to 'dealers.' He gave no opinion as to the immunity or otherwise of 'private' plebeians, no doubt thinking that none but 'gentlemen' need be suspected of harbouring lace and embroidery. He also decided that duty might not legally be abated upon goods damaged by accident, so long as the owners had power to claim upon persons legally responsible for such damage.

Curious illustration of the laxity obtaining in the higher Customs was furnished by a Treasury letter, enjoining all newly appointed officers to take up their offices *within six months* after appointment.

In 1764 the Chairman and Deputy Chairman of the East India Company attended at Thames Street, and conferred with the Board upon the prevention of smuggling.

The Board issued new instructions as to dealing with effects of foreign ambassadors, etc. Each ambassador was to furnish schedules in duplicate of the goods he imported. One document went to the River Inspector, who witnessed the unshipment and landing of the goods, the other to the officers who performed the actual examination. The ambassador's agent witnessed the opening and searching of the packages, which took place in the King's Warehouse. The allowance of duty-free wine was one tun for an ambassador, two hogsheads for an official of ' inferior character ' (lower rank).   If there were any discrepancy betwixt schedule and goods, or the quantity of wine imported exceeded the above quantities, the Board were apprised.

Certain landing-surveyors were granted £120 each, as reward for discovering that various linens had been undervalued, and for ' extraordinary pains in considering the Irish " Book of Rates." '

Parliament levied stamp duties in the American Plantations, on the pretext that the Colonies should contribute towards the expense of government and protection.   The duties applied to almost all mercantile and legal agreements, to pamphlets, newspapers, almanacs, calendars, and advertisements, and to cards and dice.   The stamp duty on cards was 1s. a pack, on dice 10s. *a pair*.   On documents couched in other than English the duties were doubled.   Heavy duties were laid on indentures of apprenticeship, and formidable penalties enjoined against unlicensed retailers of wine and spirits.   These imposts were placed under the management of the British Commissioners of Stamp Duties.

An *additional* duty of 4s. per chalder was levied on coal exported from Great Britain to places other than Ireland, the Isle of Man, and the American colonies.

A bounty was granted to Plantation ' lumber ' suitable for shipbuilding, to be paid on landing in Great Britain. Plantation coffee was favoured by remission of part of the excise duty, and Plantation iron was allowed to be carried to Ireland without unshipment in Great Britain. But these grants were spoiled by odious provisions as to bonds, certificates, and affidavits.   The Plantation officers' fees, of which the colonists had complained, were directed to remain as settled by precedent, till they could be regulated by Parliament.   They were never regulated.

The bounty on British refined sugar outward was raised to 14s. 6d. per cwt. for loaf and lump sugars, and 6s. 4d. for bastard, ground, and candy.

Foreign-made silk stockings and gloves were prohibited from importation into Great Britain. If seized they were not to be burned, but sold by candle-inch for exportation.

The Board ordered that if a surveyor of the river rummaged any boat leaving an East Indiaman during the night, he should then call the crews of the 'head and stern boats' to re-rummage her, and if the crews made a seizure he should be shut out from the award. Of course this was a reflection upon the efficiency of the river surveyors. The Board would scarcely have issued an order so subversive of ordinary discipline had there not been grim reason.

Several peculiar grants of public money were made by the Commissioners. The deputy consul at Ostend received £100 for transmitting intelligence of illicit trade. The son of the late collector of Beaumaris received a gratuity of £20, ' on account of his long attendance in expectation of being provided for in the Customs.'

The superior officers at Gravesend were cautioned by the Board against undue preference in ' boarding ' tide-waiters (placing favourites as watchmen on comfortable ships). The Board also directed the tide-waiters not to take their wives on board !

It was provided that duties paid by the East India Company should be entered in the Exchequer books as a separate account.

The Board were directed by Treasury warrant to provide out of the customs £70,000, as purchase-money for the Isle of Man.

In 1766 the Plantation Stamp Act was repealed, and the next statute enrolled may be regarded as an expression of Parliament's displeasure at having had to yield to colonial disapprobation. The Act ran thus :

' Whereas several of the Houses of Representatives in his Majesty's Colonies and Plantations in America have of late against law claimed to themselves, or to the General Assemblies of the same, the sole and exclusive right of imposing Duties and taxes upon his Majesty's Subjects in the said Colonies and Plantations ; and have in pursuance of such Claim passed certain Votes, Resolutions, and Orders, derogatory to the Legislative Authority of Parliament, and inconsistent with the Dependency of the said Colonies and Plantations upon the Crown of Great Britain : May ,it therefore please your most excellent Majesty that it may be declared ; and be it declared by the King's most excellent Majesty, by and with the Advice and Consent of the Lords Spiritual and Temporal and Commons in this present Parliament assembled, and by the authority of the same : That the said Colonies and Plantations in America have been, are, and of Right ought to be subordinate unto and dependent upon the Imperial Crown and Parliament of Great Britain, and that the King's Majesty by and with the Advice and Consent of the Lords Spiritual and Temporal and Commons of Great Britain in Parliament assembled had, hath, and of Right ought to have, full Power and Authority to make Laws and Statutes of sufficient Force and Validity to bind the Colonists and People of America Subjects of the Crown of Great Britain in all Cases whatsoever.

' And be it further declared and enacted by the Authority aforesaid : That all Resolutions, Votes, Orders, and Proceedings, in any of the said Colonies or Plantations, whereby the Power and Authority of the Parliament of Great Britain to make Laws and Statutes as aforesaid is denied or drawn into question, are, and are hereby declared to be, utterly null and void to all Intents and Purposes whatsoever.'

Parliament continued to juggle with the Plantation trade, and issued a statute fixing legal ports in Jamaica and Dominique. This Act bristled with provisions as to single-decked ships, goods which might be carried, goods excepted for no apparent reason, methods of commerce in negro flesh and blood, and many other mysteries of traffic. It mixed up the commercial regulations of the

Colonies as a pestle blends ingredients, and was immediately followed by another statute that made confusion worse confounded. Attempts were afterwards made to explain and amend these perplexing Acts.

Three permanent branches were added to the British customs : ' The Duty on Exported Cambrics,' ' The Additional Duty on Italian Tiffanies, etc.,' and ' The Duty on East India Wrought Silk.'

The officers of the East Indiamen were told by the Board that if they were caught smuggling they would lose the privilege of importing ' private trade ' goods. The customs ' lockers ' employed at the Company's warehouses were enjoined not to accept food from the Company's officials, but to pay for it themselves and have their meals sent in.

More interesting grants. Mr. Venner, a surveyor, was given £65 as an encouragement to continue the compilation of a book called ' A Compleat View of the British Customs.' Two tide-waiters were given £5 each, as a reward for resisting ' frequent solicitations, and offers of bribes.'

The Board strengthened the Thames guard. (In 1770 they armed their London quay watchmen with cutlasses to prevent ' the frequent and daring attempts of the plunderers which infest the river.')

Corn became dear, and from 1767 to 1773 the exportation of corn, flour, and similar foodstuffs was prohibited. At certain stages of this period corn was allowed to be imported duty-free, and the privilege was occasionally extended to Plantation rice, sago powder, and vermicelli. ' Unenumerated ' Plantation goods were allowed to be imported into Ireland.

Resident Commissioners* were appointed in the American Plantations, to relieve merchants from the delay

* The new appointments were dated from 1767, and the American collectors were ordered to make up and close their accounts to date. The London ' Plantation Clerk,' Mr. Henry Hulton, was made one of the new Commissioners. See Patent Roll, 7 Geo. III., Part 5, m. 11.

caused by sending their applications on revenue matters to London. (The American collectors were at one time directed to pay their moneys to the Paymasters of the Forces in America, and take bills upon the Paymaster of the Forces in Great Britain, who had to make good the amounts to the London Receiver-General of customs.)

The East India Company were in arrear for customs duties to the amount of £180,000. They applied for time, and were granted a month's respite, conditional upon their paying down 6 per cent. on the moneys due.

The Treasury had purchased the Isle of Man in 1765,* and in 1767 a scale of duties was applied to the island, as below :

British spirits imported into the island from England	1s. per gallon.
Plantation rum imported into the island from England	1s. 6d. per gallon.
French wine imported into the island direct	£4 per tun.
Other wine imported into the island direct	£2 ,,
Bohea tea from England	1s. per pound.
Green tea ,, ,, ...	1s. 6d. per pound.
Coffee ,, ,, ...	9d. ,,
Tobacco ,, ,, ...	2d. ,,
Corn and grain, bountied in Great Britain ..	10% *ad valorem.*
Coal from Great Britain or Ireland ..	3d. per chalder.
Foreign hemp, iron, deals, and timber ..	5% *ad valorem.*
All other goods which had received drawback on exportation from Great Britain	5% ,,
All other goods from Great Britain or Ireland	2½% ,,
All foreign goods not previously mentioned	15% ,,

All linen imported had to be shipped in Great Britain or Ireland, and all glass and woollens in Great Britain. As the tariff shows, tea, spirits, coffee, and tobacco, had to be shipped *in England*, and the amounts of these which might be imported yearly were : British spirits, 50,000 gallons ; Plantation rum, 30,000 gallons ; tea, 25,000 pounds ; coffee, 5,000 pounds ; tobacco,† 120,000 pounds. All shipments of these articles were to be licensed by the

---

* The island had been a notorious smugglers' rendezvous.
† The quantity of tobacco allowed was afterwards at a much smaller rate.

Board of Customs, carried in British-built ships, and landed in the port of Douglas.

Manx wool and woollens might only be exported to Great Britain. Manx vessels were to be deemed British-built. Manx fishing-boats were to be registered, and their masters were to enter into bond to refrain from smuggling. An annual impost of 10s. was laid upon every Manx fishing-boat, and out of the proceeds the Government undertook to provide prizes for industry, thus :

	£	s.	d.
To the owner of the boat making the first herring-catch of the season	5	0	0
To the owner of the boat fishing through the greatest number of nights	10	0	0
To the owner of the boat fishing through the second greatest number of nights	7	10	0
To the owner of the boat fishing through the third greatest number of nights	5	0	0
To the owner of the boat fishing through the fourth greatest number of nights	2	10	0
To the owner of the boat catching most fish	10	0	0
To the owner of the boat catching the next greatest number	5	0	0
To the owner of the boat making the latest catch of the season	5	0	0
To the admiral of the fishing-fleet for his trouble	5	0	0
To the vice-admiral of the fishing-fleet for his trouble	3	0	0
To the water bailiff	20	0	0
To the champion weaver	6	0	0
To the second-best weaver	4	0	0
To the champion spinner	5	0	0
To the second-best spinner	3	0	0
To the manufacturer exporting most linen	10	0	0

The legislators renewed onslaught upon the Plantations. They imposed duties in the American colonies upon glass, painters' colours, pasteboards, strawboards, millboards, 'painted paper,' tea, and the various stationery papers. The paper duties varied from 3d. a ream to 12s. The duty on tea was 3d. a pound. Undoubtedly these were intended to lead up to the imposition of taxes much more comprehensive, but their ultimate results were the loss to England of a bunch of magnificent colonies, and the addition of about £100,000,000 to her National Debt. Indirectly they were the means of shattering her unequalled military prestige, and thus strengthening the hands of her immemorial enemy.

The new Plantation duties were to be paid in sterling English money. Masters were to report and enter their cargoes in and out, and furnish 'ship's content' at clearance. Formidable powers of search were granted to the customs officers, and, to facilitate search for uncustomed goods, it was provided that the Supreme Court of each colony should be competent to issue writs of assistance. A drawback was granted on Plantation coffee exported from Great Britain, and drawback was withheld from chinaware shipped in Great Britain for America. This last provision the legislators, in the eccentric fashion that was fast growing usual with them, soon thought fit to cancel, stating that it had worked quite contrary to their anticipations.

There is not much interesting matter in the minor British customs records for the year under survey. The patent searchers of London were directed to refrain from taking extortionate fees, and from being uncivil to merchants. An annuity of £9,000, payable out of the proceeds of the 4½ per cent. duties, was settled on the King's brother, the duke of Gloucester.*

The clerks in the Receiver-General's office were censured for extorting fees *from officers* on paying them their salaries.

The Board improved the pay of the tide-waiters, ' to obviate the distresses they are under by being obliged to borrow money at an exorbitant rate of interest for the support of themselves and their families, and to prevent their being under the influence of the captains of those vessels upon which they may happen to be boarded.'

A Mr. Samuel Vaughan attempted to buy the reversion

---

* In 1795 it was found that the duties were insufficient to meet the many charges levied upon them, and the duke was placed on the Aggregate Fund.

of a clerkship in the Plantation Courts.   It seems that the office had been previously traded, and the precedent thus furnished had encouraged Vaughan to put forward his application.   But the Ministry disliked his political record, and the duke of Grafton, who was Chief Treasury Commissioner, ordered him to be prosecuted.   This furnished the celebrated ' Junius ' with an opportunity of which he took full advantage.   He made public the particulars of an arrangement with Colonel (afterwards General) Burgoyne, by means of which the latter had been allowed to dispose of his patent office in the Customs to a Mr. Hine.   Nothing in the famous ' Letters ' is more remarkable than the malignant dexterity with which this counter-stroke was levelled.   The *coup* was effective. The prosecution of Vaughan was dropped, and though Junius reiterated his statement the duke remained silent. We furnish a few quotations from Junius's charges and challenges in connexion with this matter.

Letter 33, addressed to the duke of Grafton : ' Come forward, thou virtuous minister, and tell the world by what interest Mr. Hine has been recommended to so extraordinary a mark of His Majesty's favour, what was the price of the patent he has bought, and to what honourable purpose the purchase-money has been applied. ... Do you dare to prosecute such a creature as Vaughan, while you are basely setting up the royal patronage to auction ? . . . It is indeed highly to your interest to maintain the present House of Commons.   Having sold the nation to you in gross, they will undoubtedly protect you in the detail.'

Letter 34, to the same : ' I accused you of having *sold*, or permitted to be sold, a patent place in the collection of the customs at Exeter, to one Mr. Hine, who, unable or unwilling to deposit the whole purchase-money himself, raised part of it by contribution, and has now a certain Doctor Brooke quartered upon the salary for £100 a year. No sale by the candle was ever conducted with greater formality.   I affirm that the price at which the place was knocked down* . . . was, with your connivance and consent, paid to Colonel Burgoyne, to reward him, I presume, for the decency of his deportment at Preston. . . . With what countenance dare you appear in the royal presence, branded as you are with the infamy of a notorious breach of trust ? With what countenance can you take your seat at the Treasury Board, when you *feel* that every circulating whisper is at *your* expense alone, and stabs you to the heart ?'

Junius then challenged the duke to attempt to clear himself by bringing the matter before the House of Lords, or the Court of King's Bench, and ended with one of those curt, diabolic taunts with which he usually finished off a victim. ' My lord, you dare not do either.'

The duke was impressed by this concluding blow, and *did neither*. Soon afterwards he resigned his position on the Treasury Board, and we cannot help thinking that the dreadful assault influenced his action. A writer, signing himself ' Justice,' took up the cudgels on the duke's behalf. We reproduce a part of his letter.

' A place in the Custom House at Exeter becomes vacant. Colonel Burgoyne asks it of the duke of Grafton —he gives it. The colonel says, " I cannot hold it myself ; will you give it my friend ?" The duke consents—the colonel nominates—the duke appoints ; " but," says Junius, " the colonel set it up for sale, and actually received a sum of money for it." Be it so—he took a gross sum for what was given him as an annual income ; and who is injured by this ? If the duke of Grafton sold it, he is impeachable ; if he gave it to be sold, he is blame-able ; but if his Grace did neither, which is the fact, he is basely belied, and most impudently and wickedly villified.'

This defence was rather clever ; most pamphleteers of that day were clever. Yet it failed to convince. The duke had incited the attack on Vaughan, and then retired from it. Undoubtedly the duke had given the

* £3,500.

place to Burgoyne so that Burgoyne might sell it. Burgoyne had sold it. ' Justice's ' plea fell flat, and the denouncer triumphed. It could hardly be otherwise, for such was the denouncer's mastery of his weapons that even a foul stroke seemed fair, and a fair hit was irresistible.

Early in the following year Junius bestowed a parting slash. He taunted the ex-minister upon his withdrawal from the prosecution of Vaughan, and then dismissed the matter in a few masterly sentences. ' Your Grace is afraid to carry on the prosecution. Mr. Hine keeps quiet possession of his purchase, and Governor Burgoyne, relieved from the apprehension of refunding the money, sits down for the remainder of his life, *infamous and contented.*'

In 1769 the Coinage duty was made perpetual. Excise officers in Great Britain were empowered to seize and detain horses and conveyances used in the carrying of foreign uncustomed goods. A bounty of £25 in every £100 value was granted to raw silk produced in the Plantations and brought *to London*. The grant was to decrease periodically during three terms of seven years each.

The Board fined the Collector Inwards of London and his controller £60 each for having paid too much drawback, and also compelled them to make good a deficiency in their accounts.

The Receiver-General's clerk paid the salary of the patent searcher of Milford, who was in London on leave. For this little service the clerk exacted a fee of 6s. The Board came to know, and compelled the clerk's employer to return the fee out of his own pocket.

In 1770, on account of the volume of business, the London Commissioners agreed to breakfast together at the Custom-house.

An extraordinary incident is recorded. One Thomas, a landing-waiter, bequeathed £100, to be applied to the Old Subsidy.

The undermentioned officers of other departments had seats in the Long Room of the London Custom-house :

> The Collector of the Excise Office and his controller.
> The Collector of the Salt Office.
> The Receiver for the City of London.
> The Receiver for the Turkey Company.
> The Receiver for the Russia Company.
> The Receiver for the Trinity House.
> The Receiver for Lighthouses.

An ordinary ' weigher ' named Stone was deputed by the Board to examine tobacco on shipment, and the Commissioners thought so highly of him that they accepted his opinions in preference to those of the searchers, and even hinted that the Registrar-General of Tobacco might do worse than follow the guidance of this undeniable expert.

A yacht (and later a barge) were fitted up for the London Commissioners. (The barge was manned by ten stalwart oarsmen, and when the Board went afloat the whole water-side gazed admiringly. During winter the yacht cruised against the Kentish smugglers, but on April 1 it had to be ready and spick and span off the Custom-house. The regulations as to precedence were quaint. ' The Commissioner whose holiday it was on Friday ' might claim the yacht—not for Friday only : he might take her on the previous Wednesday morning, and enjoy her till the following Tuesday·night. Thus it seems that ' Friday off ' meant a week's holiday.)

Parliament repealed the new duties levied in the Plantations, in so far as they applied to glass, painters' colours, and paper, manufactured in Great Britain. The preamble of the repealing Act stated that the said duties on British goods had proved a great discouragement to commerce.

In 1771 the exportation of live cattle from Great Britain was temporarily prohibited, as imported cattle were duty-free for a period. 'White oak-staves' from the American Plantations were bountied, to encourage British cask-making.

In 1772 the East India Company's bond was put in suit, they being in arrear for duties owed eighteen months previously. Process was stayed on the usual deposit of 6 per cent. interest on the sum outstanding.

The London Controller-General was granted £190 a year to pay five additional clerks to bring up arrears, on condition that two years' arrears were wiped off per annum.

The Customs and Post-Office Secretaries were summoned to Whitehall, to confer with the Treasury upon a practice which had become common, of importing silks and lace through the foreign post. It was decided that goods thus imported were forfeitable.

A grant of £6 a year from the Customs to 'The Lecturer of Barking Parish' should be quoted.* (The London Custom-house was in 'the parish of Barking.')

The Board transmitted to the collectors certain instructions from the Admiralty with regard to the pressing of men for the navy. When men were taken from a merchant coaster by the captain of a man-of-war, the pressing officer had to put on board a sufficient number of trusty men from his own crew to assist in navigating the coaster to her destination. These had to leave the ship on her arrival in port, and present themselves before the collector of customs, who was directed to send them to another port to rejoin their vessel, or to maintain them until such vessel arrived. If they left by road to rejoin their ship he was to allow them 1d. a mile as travelling money; if they remained to await her he was to grant them 6d. a day as subsistence allowance. Moneys thus advanced were to be charged to and repaid by the Navy Board.

Great exertions were made to prevent the importation of infected animals, the cattle distemper prevailing

* This grant lapsed occasionally.

abroad. A copy of a letter from one Captain Fraser at
Dunkirk to Lord Weymouth was sent to Southampton,
in which it was pointed out that great quantities of eggs
were shipped from France to the southern English ports,
packed in straw which might have come from stables and
outhouses occupied by diseased cattle. It was enjoined
that all such straw should be burned.

The constables of seaport towns held ' press warrants,'
enabling them to arrest such seafaring men as might be
' lurking about,' and hand them over to naval commanders. The collectors of customs were empowered to
pay constables 20s. for each capture, with 1s. in addition
to reimburse the constable, who had to give the last-
mentioned sum as ' press-money ' to each man taken.
Moneys to be repaid by the Navy Board.

The Swedish Government required bills of health from
every vessel arriving in Sweden, and the British collectors were empowered to grant such bills to vessels
proceeding thither from Great Britain. One of these
documents is annexed to a Southampton Letter-Book.
It is quaintly worded, commencing thus :

' To all Christian People, To whom these presents shall
come : We, the Ministers of the Most Serene Prince, Our
Lord King George the Third,' etc.

The growing difficulties with the American colonists
appear to have influenced the Commissioners, for they
directed the English collectors to watch outward trade
to the Plantations, and if a ship cleared in ballast for
America to send full particulars to Thames Street ' by
the very first post.'

It seems that at this time the customs officers did not
try the strengths of imported spirits. The only customs
duty on spirits was the Old Subsidy, the rest of the varying
duties on ' single ' and ' double ' spirits being excise, yet
the Customs in most cases collected them. It is likely
that the excise officers tested the goods and assessed the
rates, and the Customs took the money, but it is tolerably
certain that the customs men always gauged the goods.

During 1772 the Commissioners of Excise suggested that their officers should be allowed to try the strength of all seized spirits sold, otherwise parcels of high overproof goods might be sold ' at a common price.' The Customs Board consented to allow the excisemen to sample and test one cask in five, ' but,' the document ended, ' they may not take the samples away.'

The duty on imported oak bark was reduced, to encourage the British tanning industry.

The East India Company were forbidden to build any new ships for oversea traffic till their total of shipping was reduced to 45,000 tons. (In the next year Parliament advanced the Company £1,400,000.)

A rigorous Act was issued against drawback frauds committed by Irish shippers, who entered goods for foreign, received drawback on them, and then relanded them, or ran them into Great Britain. Both drawback and ship were made forfeitable, and every person concerned was made liable to a penalty of treble the value of the goods. In all future cases of drawback shipments from Ireland both shippers and masters were to swear to the debentures, and if the goods were for Great Britain drawback was to be withheld till a certificate of landing was received.

The British system of bountying and customing corn, etc., was regularized in 1773. From January 1, 1774, when the price of middling British wheat reached or exceeded 48s. a quarter, the price of rye, peas, and beans 32s., the price of barley 24s., or the price of oats 16s., import duties were to cease on foreign corn and wheat-flour, except to the amount of 6d. a quarter on wheat, 3d. on rye, etc., 2d. on barley and oats, and 2d. a cwt. on wheat-flour. The price was to be estimated, as of old, in each county, and if the price at one port were at or above the specified rate, and at a port in another county less than the rate, corn imported at the first port might not be carried coastwise to the other. When wheat was at or above 44s., rye, etc., at 28s., barley at 22s., and oats at 14s., they might not be exported, but if under those prices they were allowed exportation, and bountied.

An additional duty was put upon foreign 'painted paper' (wall-paper, etc.).

The Board quoted a decision that goods shipped, and afterwards lost or damaged within the limits of a port, were not entitled to drawback.*

At this time the East India Company paid about £1,000,000 a year in customs and excise duties.

In 1774 appeared a statute, the preamble of which ran : 'Whereas dangerous Commotions and Insurrections have been Fomented and Raised in the Town of Boston in the province of Massachusetts Bay in New England by divers ill affected Persons, to the subversion of His Majesty's Government, and to the utter Destruction of the publick Peace and good order of the said Town, in which Commotions and Insurrections certain valuable Cargoes of Tea, being the property of the East India Company, and on board certain vessels lying within the Bay or Harbour of Boston, were seized and destroyed,' etc.

It proceeded to enact that all lading or unlading of goods within Boston Harbour, except stores for the troops or 'fuel for the inhabitants,' should be discontinued, and to endow the Admiral and the customs officers with power to compel any vessel nearing the coast to depart on penalty of forfeiture. It declared all charter-parties and bills of lading for goods to Boston void. The town was to 'make full satisfaction' to the East India Company, and 'reasonable satisfaction' to the revenue officers of Boston. (The difference between 'full' and 'reasonable' was not explained.)

The Act went on to state that when Boston had abased

---

* Observe the wretched lack of finality appertaining to legal decisions. In 1778 this opinion was set aside, and drawback allowed on goods shipped for Dublin and destroyed by fire before the vessel left Great Britain. In 1783 the Attorney-General decided that drawback might be paid on goods shipped, and afterwards damaged within the limits of a port, provided such damage was accidental, and the goods were thereby rendered valueless.

her mutinous crest, ' and not till then,' his Majesty would prescribe the limits of the port.

The Governor and Council of the State of New York were forbidden from assenting to any ' Act, Vote, or Resolution of the House of Representatives,' till his Majesty's troops had been supplied with necessaries as enjoined by statute.

The Act forbidding exportation of corn from Great Britain was temporarily relaxed, to allow of shipments to the Sugar Plantations (West Indies), to the Plantation fisheries (Newfoundland), and from Southampton to the Channel Islands.

The stock of tea in the East India Company's warehouses had grown so large* that sale within the specified time (three years from landing) appeared impracticable. The period was extended to five years, the Company being enjoined to keep the British market well supplied at a moderate price, otherwise the Treasury might withhold the privilege of exclusive importation of tea, and license other syndicates to bring tea from European ports.

Parliament issued a fresh statute against the disaffected colonists, providing that any person brought to trial for taking life in the maintenance of just authority might claim to be tried elsewhere than in the colony where the deed was committed.

Quantities of old and light silver coin of the realm, ' or coin purporting to be such,' were being brought into Great Britain. The practice was accordingly prohibited, and it was provided that such goods might be seized or searched for under Charles II.'s Act of Frauds. The standard of weight was 62s. to the pound troy, the standard of fineness 11 ozs. 2 dwts. pure silver, and 18 dwts. alloy.†

* Probably through stoppage of the trade with the American colonies.

† Compare these with the ancient standard, say, in Henry I.'s day, when the pennies were of pure silver, and 240 of them weighed a pound troy.

Parliament continued to apply restrictive and irritating legislation to the American Colonies. Originally the governors and their councillors had been appointed by royal patent, but in William and Mary's reign it was granted that the councillors might be chosen annually by the General Assembly. Parliament revoked this charter, and provided that the king should appoint the councillors by warrant, and that they should hold office during his pleasure. The governors were empowered to appoint judges, to make sheriffs without the Council's consent, and to forbid public meetings. Jurors were no longer to be elected, but appointed by the sheriffs. If the Colonies neglected to provide suitable barracks, the king's troops might be billeted upon inhabitants.

Several officers were sent from England to the West Indies, to investigate revenue matters, and their efforts secured the suspension of the collectors of Barbadoes and St. Vincent. The former was fined £1,500, and a cargo of sugar which he had collected under the 4½ per cent. duties, to send to England presumably for his own profit, instead of for deposit in the 'Husband's' custody for the Crown's benefit, was seized in transit. Both he and the St. Vincent collector were restored to duty, 'for a year on trial.' The bonds of several other Plantation collectors were put in suit, on account of large sums owing to the Crown.

The trade of the port of Liverpool had increased immensely. The Liverpool collector's bond for good behaviour was raised from £5,000 to £15,000.

The sum of £312 18s. 8d. was granted to pay expenses incurred by Emanuel Matthias, a revenue spy employed in collecting information on the Continent.

The port of Hull, which up to 1774 had been exempt from the laws* as to provision of legal quays, was deprived of the privilege, and empowered to provide a dock. The old Staiths, 'Thomas Walton's Shipyard,' and 'Rotten

---

* Elizabeth's Act, as amended by Charles II.'s Act of Frauds.

Herring Staith,' 'used,' quoth the Statute, 'from time immemorial,' were still allowed to be used for landing and shipment, on condition that they were fitted with proper quays.

A captain of a king's ship stopped a Newfoundland trader at sea, and overhauled her cocket. He found it to display an unratified erasure, and thereupon detained the ship. On inquiry being made, it was found that one of the London patent officers was responsible for the defect. What compensation, if any, was made to the shipowner and shippers may not be discovered in the records, but all the superior clerical officers known as searchers were called into the Board Room and admonished. The Attorney-General uttered an opinion upon the case, recommending that all erasures in customs documents should be made by drawing 'a strong line' across the superfluous item, the said line being ratified by the initials of the eraser and his check officer, 'agreeable to the ancient rules of the Court of Exchequer.'

Instructions were sent to all collectors that the brigantine *Industry* was on her way to England, conveying messages from the American rebels to sympathizers in England. Ships from the rebellious Colonies were to be closely searched for letters, and the Board were to be apprised of all vessels fitting out for America. The Plantation Acts were to be sternly enforced. Vessels going to America or the West Indies were to be rummaged closely, and the officers were to detain 'letters going to persons in the provinces actually in rebellion.' All persons coming from America were to be strictly examined, and their letters and papers sent to the Board. British officers carrying dispatches were exempt.

The old French duties, which had been continued in Quebec since its conquest by the British in 1759, were replaced by a new tariff. The French duties had been certain small levies on wine and spirits, and 3 per cent.

ad valorem on dry goods. The new duties were as follows :

Foreign spirits imported from Great Britain	1s. per gallon.
Foreign spirits imported from American Plantations	9d. ,, ,,
Foreign spirits imported from Sugar Plantations	6d. ,, ,,
British spirits	3d. ,, ,,
Plantation spirits imported from foreign ..	1s. ,, ,,
Molasses and syrups in British or Irish ships	3d. ,, ,,
,, ,, ,, other ships ..	6d. ,, ,,

The above duties were to be paid in sterling money, and the routes of importation were prescribed. The Receiver-General for the Provinces was to have custody of the receipts, which were to be applied towards defraying the expense of civil government, etc. Any surplus which might accrue was to remain with the Receiver-General, for disposition by Parliament.

Parliament recited the original conditions of Plantation trade—viz., that the Colonies should either export to each other, or send their goods to Great Britain, and should import via Great Britain (Irish linen, wine from Madeira and the Azores, and salt for the Fisheries, excepted). Then it forbade the disaffected provinces from trading with each other, or with the American Colonies that remained loyal. Thus they might only trade with Great Britain, Ireland, and the West Indies. Disaffection spread rapidly, and soon it was deemed necessary to apply the prohibition to the hitherto secure provinces of New Jersey, Pennsylvania, Maryland, Virginia, and South Carolina.*

* The Privy Council issued elaborate instructions to all newly appointed colonial governors. We furnish a précis. It must be understood that the instructions could scarcely be carried out in the American Colonies in 1775, but in the other Plantations they were rigidly enforced. Readers had best consider them as applying in full in the West Indies. These were the regulations of trade and revenue that a West Indian governor had to carry out:

1. The naval officers in charge of the various ports were to furnish security to the British Commissioners of Customs for the due observance of the Navigation and Plantation Acts, and to apprise the governor when this had been done. Custom-houses

The duty on rape-seed imported into Great Britain from Ireland for expressing oil was reduced, and it was enacted that ' rape-cake for manure ' might enter duty-free. Raw goatskins from foreign were freed of duty for five years, to encourage the manufacture of ' red leather.' The duty on foreign earthenware was increased.

Most of the troops on the Irish establishment had been sent to assist in the war with the disaffected colonists, and it was enacted that clothing and accoutrements for their use might be shipped in Ireland at will, provided a certificate from the ' Chief Governor of Ireland ' were produced at shipment. The bounty of 5s. a hogshead on imported flax-seed, provided in 1763 by the Irish Parliament, was supplemented by a similar grant from the British Parliament, to be paid by the English Receiver-General. This was to endure for two years.

---

might only be established at ports controlled by naval officers. The collectors were to reside at their places of employment.

2. No excuse for non-compliance with the provisions of the Navigation Act as to three-fourths British or Plantation seamen might be accepted, unless there had been loss from sickness, death, or foreign aggression, during the voyage. Spirits might not be exported from the Plantations to the Isle of Man.

3. William III.'s Acts prohibiting the exportation of wool, and the entrance into Plantation ports of foreign traders from places beyond the Cape of Good Hope, yet within the dominions of the East India Company, were to be enforced. If a foreign trader approached a port, the master was to be warned off, even if he pleaded distress ; and if he persisted in entering the Customs might seize ship and cargo, unless he could prove that he was bound for a foreign West Indian Plantation, and then he might be ' relieved,' and sent away as soon as practicable. He might not land goods.

4. All certificates as to goods carried under the Plantation Acts were to be closely scrutinized, and the bonds cancelled within eighteen months. The naval officers in charge might admit no person to bond until the collector approved the sureties. A close watch was to be kept upon inter-Plantation traffic, to see that the goods were really carried from one Plantation to another, and not to foreign countries.

5. Every three months returns were to be made to the British Treasury and Customs of vessels trading in the province supervised, with lists of the bonds appertaining. Invoices were to be sent in triplicate of cargoes cleared outwards, one invoice to go to the Treasury, one to the Board of Customs, and one to the collector at the British port of discharge.

In 1776 all trade with the rebellious colonists was forbidden. Ships engaging in such traffic might be seized. If taken into American ports they were to be handed over to the customs collectors. The crews were to be pressed.

The Declaration of Independence was issued. Adam Smith's ' Wealth of Nations ' appeared.

An extension of time was granted to the East India Company to dispose of their stock of muslins and calicoes, which had grown on their hands through stoppage of the Plantation trade.

The London Board tendered thanks to Sir John Frederick for his present of forty-four volumes of the Parliamentary Journals, and to Sir William Musgrave for his gift of ' a valuable collection of rare books.' One of the Board's solicitors made a compilation of the ' Laws of the Customs.' One thousand copies of this book were printed at the public expense, for the use of collectors

---

6. No European commodities might pass into the Plantations unless first landed in Great Britain. The cockets were to be inspected closely, it being thought that forged cockets were frequently used.

7. The collection of the countervailing duty on foreign sugar landed in the West Indies was to be supervised. Full particulars as to shipment and place of growth were to accompany all consignments of indigo from the Plantations to Great Britain, as the goods were granted a premium on landing. Planters and the public were to be informed of the regulations governing the legal weight of packages of tobacco. The sixpence per month from seamen's wages, for the support of Greenwich Hospital, was to be diligently collected.

8. The customs officers were to be supported and encouraged in the discharge of their duty, and allowed free access to the copies of the various Acts kept in public offices. Inefficient or neglectful officers were to be reported, and offending merchants prosecuted. In all trials as to ships, goods, or duties, the jurors were to be king's subjects, and this qualification applied to appointments of officials who served under the Treasury. If an official died, the governor might name a substitute ; the appointment to endure until confirmed, or until a new official was sent out by the home authorities.

9. Regular correspondence was to be maintained with the British Commissioners of Customs.

10. All Plantation by-laws repugnant to the Imperial Acts were to be made void.

and other officers. (In 1780 the author received £200 for his trouble.)

One of the London jerquers was charged with allowing his work to fall into arrear, paying many portages which he should have withheld, and acting corruptly in taking a fee of £200 for giving employment to a clerk. The first charge was dealt with by a severe reprimand. He was then surcharged to the amount of twenty-eight portages. He was acquitted of the charge of corruption, 'for want of proof.' Later the Board fined and censured him for neglecting to attend when summoned by them. He asked for leave 'to settle private affairs,' and failed to return. Dismissed.

The Board issued an order, that still remains in force, directing that officers going on leave should temporarily surrender their 'deputations' or 'commissions.' This was because certain officers while on leave had made improper use of the parchment scrolls.

In 1777 certain revenue cruisers under the command of Warren Lisle were supplied with carriage and swivel guns.

One Shafto, controller to the Receiver-General of Fines and Forfeitures, gave the Board much trouble. He had been allowed to levy 'poundage' on the awards made to seizing officers, and the Board thought fit to deprive him of this lucrative privilege, and grant him a salary instead. Mr. Shafto became indignant, and haughtily refused to accept the said salary. The Board therefore had it paid into the Exchequer. Shafto then demanded restoration of the power of levying poundage. The Board refused, and told him he would get no salary in lieu unless he 'made proper submission.' Shafto then memorialized the Treasury, and my Lords restored his right of poundage.

Meantime a new Receiver-General of Fines and Forfeitures had been appointed, at a fixed salary. As soon as this gentleman knew of Shafto's success he went to the Board, and demanded permission to levy poundage.

But the Board would not hear of it. Mr. Shafto went his extortionate way rejoicing, but the Commissioners had not finished with him. (In 1780 they caught him misbehaving, and stopped his poundage once more. In 1782 they caught him red-handed, and stopped his poundage for good and all; for they dismissed him, and then wrote the Treasury, suggesting that the office of controller of Fines and Forfeitures should carry no more poundage, so long as they remained in commission.)

The Admiralty granted commissions to privateers, empowering them to prey upon American commerce. Before proceeding to sea each privateer captain produced his commission to the collector at the port where the vessel fitted out. The collector thereupon inspected the vessel, and if he found her suitable for the work, and in accordance with the terms of her commission, clearance was granted.

The drawback on tea shipped from Great Britain to Ireland, which had previously been but a moiety of the duty paid, was made equal to the duty.

The captains of homeward-bound East Indiamen committed great frauds by unshipping tea, muslins, etc., into craft that met them at sea, and afterwards ran the goods at secluded places on the coast. Similar frauds were committed when the vessels left England, the runners meeting the East Indiamen in the Channel, and transhipping large quantities of foreign wine and brandy, which were thus conveyed to the East Indies without paying the usual British duties.

There was much fraud in connexion with drawback shipments generally, drawback bonds being illegally obtained, and the goods relanded after the drawback had been paid. It was therefore enacted that certificates of landing abroad should be produced for all drawback goods. The time allowed for production was six months if the goods went to Ireland or the Channel Islands, fifteen months if to any part of Europe, eighteen months if to Africa or the American Plantations, and thirty months if to ports within the boundaries of the East India Company's Charter. This provision was soon repealed, being found most inconvenient.

In 1778 extra tunnage was levied—£8 8s. on French wine and vinegar, £4 4s. on other wine and vinegar. This became permanent as 'The 1778 Wine Duty.' French, Spanish, and Portuguese wines were directed, on penalty of forfeiture, to be imported in casks not less than a hogshead.

Parliament attempted to conciliate the Americans. Cap. 12 of 1778 opened thus : ' Whereas Taxation by the Parliament of Great Britain for the purpose of raising a Revenue in his Majesty's Colonies, Provinces, and Plantations in North America has been found by experience to occasion great uneasinesses and disorders among his Majesty's faithful Subjects, who may nevertheless be disposed to acknowledge the Justice of contributing to the common Defence of the Empire, provided such Contribution should be raised under the Authority of the General Court or General Assembly of each respective Colony, Province, or Plantation,' etc. The Act continued that in future no tax should be imposed in North America or the West Indies, by King or Parliament, except such duties as might be necessary for the regulating of commerce, and that the net produce of these should be paid and applied for use of the colony in which levied.*

Cap. 13 was still more accommodating : ' For the Quieting and Extinguishing of divers Jealousies and Apprehensions of Danger to their Liberties and Rights, which have alarmed many of his Majesty's Subjects in the Colonies, Provinces, and Plantations of New Hampshire, Massachusetts Bay, Rhode Island, Connecticut, New York, New Jersey, Pennsylvania, the three Lower Counties on Delaware, Maryland, Virginia, North Carolina, South Carolina, and Georgia, and for a full Manifestation of the just and gracious Purposes of his Majesty and his Parliament, to maintain and secure all his Sub-

* A stillborn Act.

jects in the clear and perfect Enjoyment of their Liberties and Rights,' etc.

The king was empowered to appoint five Commissioners to treat with the Americans and inquire into their grievances. The Commissioners were enabled to order a cessation of hostilities, and to suspend the Act prohibiting Plantation trade and commerce, or any other Act relating to America which had been passed since February 10, 1763. They might also grant pardons and appoint governors. But the war was fated to continue to the bitter end.

Ireland's commercial fetters were eased. It was enacted that all Irish goods, except wool, woollens, cottons, hats, glass, hops, gunpowder, and coal, might be exported *direct* from Ireland to America or Africa, and that Irish cotton-yarn might enter Great Britain duty-free. The *full* privileges applying to British-built ships were granted to ships built in Ireland.

The East India Company's directors complained to the Board that the London customs officers did not attend at a sufficiently early hour, and requested that the landing-waiters might be ordered to work until two in the afternoon without going to dinner. (The Company's warehouses closed at two.) The Board granted this, subject to notice being given, so that the landing-surveyors could exercise close supervision.

The Board directed their Secretary to inquire closely into the antecedents of persons whom the Treasury might appoint to offices in the Customs, and to report if he found anything unsatisfactory, meanwhile withholding the commission of the grantee. (We are inclined to think that a stiffer-backed Board than this never sat around a carved table.)

An officer who had been dismissed applied to the Board to secure him repayment of certain moneys which he had lent to other officers, but all he got in reply was a reminder that trade amongst officials was against the rules laid down by the Exchequer.

The officers at Dover must have been either dull-witted or illiterate, for they were censured for admitting ostrich feathers to entry as French goods.

A Mr. Dwyer was appointed collector of a port in Jamaica. He entered into bond in the usual manner, received his commission, and proceeded to celebrate the occasion. The Commissioners revoked his appointment, and demanded return of his commission. Mr. Dwyer refused, and it was found that he had deposited the document as security for money borrowed. His bond was therefore put in suit, and the Board provided that in future, when a Plantation officer was appointed, his commission should be sent to the collector at port of appointment, and the newly made officer be told what ship it was going by, ' so that if he pleases he may accompany it.' It appears from the records that Mr. Dwyer's lapse occurred on March 17.

The captain of a privateer brought in a smuggling vessel which he had captured, and was told by the Board he might prosecute at his own risk, and if he got the sloop condemned he and his crew would receive two-thirds of her appraised value. Notice was sent to the collectors that this system should be adopted in all similar cases, and that privateer captains should be told that if they strained the law the Board would not protect them. (The Commissioners were always doubtful, and with good reason, of the honesty of bearers of letters of marque.)

That intrepid and vigilant seizing-officer, Warren Lisle, resigned his command—much, no doubt, to the delight of the Sussex and Hampshire smugglers. Why he resigned is not apparent. It is possible that he had gone a little too far, as such enterprising folk often do. Yet he may have resigned from other reasons, for we find by reference to the Treasury file that his son William was allowed to succeed him.

In 1779 the revenue cruisers on the south coast of England were manned and armed to the fullest extent necessary, and sent to the Downs, to await orders from the Admiral.

Up to this date small parcels of imported goods, the duty on which was less than 10s., had been allowed to enter free. The practice was discontinued.

Parliament levied a curious tax, being an impost of 5 per cent. upon *the produce* of all previous customs duties, import, export, and coastwise (after the usual discounts and allowances had been deducted). This was made permanent as ' The Additional Impost of 1779.' The produce of this tax, in the idiotic fashion then prevailing, was kept apart, and handed in separately, being appropriated to a fund for paying annuities and raising a lottery.

Certain provisions of the Navigation Act were explained by statute thus : All goods from Asia, Africa, or America, imported into Great Britain or Ireland, were to come direct. If raw goods were carried from Asia, Africa, or America, to Europe, and manufactured there, the manufactured articles, if brought to Great Britain or Ireland, were liable to forfeiture ' with ships and tackle.'

Cotton of the British Plantations, landed in Great Britain, was allowed to be exported duty-free, if carried in British-built ships.

Tobacco-planting was allowed in Ireland. The goods thus produced might only be exported to Great Britain, under the regulations applying to tobacco of the American Plantations. The Irish collectors were to deliver manifests with full particulars to all shipmasters conveying Irish tobacco to Great Britain, and send duplicates to the British Commissioners of Customs. On arrival at ports of unshipment the manifests were delivered to the collectors. The goods were liable to the same duties as Plantation tobacco. The packages were to be casks, chests, or cases, each containing not less than 450 pounds tobacco. The Act included Irish manufactured tobacco as well as Irish leaf.

In 1780 Irish trade to British Africa, British America,

and the West Indies, was placed on the same footing as British. It was enacted that goods might be exported from Great Britain and Ireland to any place in America that was under protection of the British arms. The Secretary of State was directed to apprise the British and Irish Commissioners* of Customs as to the ports thus available for trade, and the masters of ships proceeding thither were to enter into bond to land their cargoes at the places mentioned, the bonds being cancelled by certificates from the British naval officers in charge of the ports of destination. The trade was to be regulated by the British Commander-in-Chief in America.

The tunnage on French wine and vinegar was increased by £8, on other wine and vinegar by £4. This tax became permanent as ' The 1780 Wine Duty.'

Additional duties were levied upon foreign starch and hair-powder, and the exportation of copper was prohibited. The restrictions as to ' times and hours,' imposed by Charles II.'s and subsequent Acts upon the removal of wool by land, were repealed. These inquisitorial regulations had vexed farmers and wool-dealers, and played the mischief with the inland wool trade generally.

The public accounts were in a chaotic condition, and no department's books were more dolefully confused than those of the Customs, a circumstance that need cause no wonder, when the many divisions and subdivisions of duties, the bewildering discounts and allowances, the innumerable exceptions, and the absurd methods of entry and receipt, are taken into consideration. A Committee was appointed to investigate the national accounts, and to inquire into the management of the public departments.

That imbecile creature, Lord George Gordon, incited the lower classes of London to a series of outrages upon their fellow-countrymen. Many Catholic places of worship were plundered and burned, and those dreadful English Bastilles, Newgate, the Fleet, and the King's

* Note that there was a separate Board for Ireland (*vide* Chapter IX.).

Bench Prison, made heaps of smoking ruins. The rioters might have ended by burning London, but for the national failing. They proceeded to investigate the condition of the vintners' warehouses and vaults, and drunkenness overcame the ruffianism that had prevailed against stone ramparts and volleys of musketry.

During these riots great precautions were taken to protect the London Custom-house, and the 'Surveyor of Sloops' was directed to contract for 100 musquetoons for that purpose. The principal officials mustered their clerks, and enjoined them to be ready to defend the building if it were attacked. One of the said principals afterwards put in a heavy bill for expenses incurred, which bill the Board sent back, with the remark that the security of the gentleman's office was 'mainly his own concern.'

After the riots the Sardinian ambassador was allowed to import books and ornaments for his 'new chapel' duty-free. The old chapel had been destroyed by the rioters.*

During this year the Board cautioned the London jerquers, who checked the landing-waiters' books, against allowing their clerks to extort fees from the landing-waiters for passing their accounts.

The Board came to grips with one Wiggins, surveyor of baggage. Finding that Wiggins had various outside employments which interfered with his attendance at the King's Warehouse, they gave him a space of time in which to decide whether he would attend to his duties as a baggage officer, or resign the Customs and look after his other businesses. Wiggins took the full space allowed for consideration, and then went to the Treasury and

---

* See Horace Walpole's letter to Mann : 'Monsieur Cordon, the Sardinian Minister, suffered still more. The mob forced his chapel, stole two silver lamps, demolished everything else, threw the benches into the street, set them on fire, carried the brands into the chapel, and set fire to that. Poor Madame Cordon was confined by illness. My cousin Thomas Walpole dragged her, for she could not stand with terror and weakness, to his own house.'

obtained four months' leave. The Board refused to receive the Treasury warrant, stating that they had many times censured him for non-attendance.*

The baggage of the Lord Lieutenant of Ireland was ' allowed every facility ' in transit from London to Dublin. Officers were sent to his London residence to inspect and seal all the packages, and the customs men at Chester and Holyhead were instructed to pass the sealed goods without further examination.

Mr. Lutwidge, surveyor-general, inspected the port of Liverpool, and found that the collector had allowed a large quantity of dutiable foreign corn to be delivered duty-free. The collector was surcharged £2,496.

The Receiver-General paid £470 into the Superannuation Fund, being fines levied upon certain outport collectors.

The Board surcharged their ' housekeeper,' Mrs. Bridget Kelly, with a sum which she had expended in purchasing certain newspapers which they had not ordered. They also discovered that the keeper of the Coffee Warehouse, *and one of his lockers*, rented a portion of the warehouse, and they bade the two pluralists decide within six months which they would resign, the warehouse business or the Customs.

In 1781 Mr. Temple, who as surveyor-general of America had been specially rewarded for ability, was called upon to make good a large deficiency in his accounts. ' Plead within a week, or be proceeded against '—thus ran the injunction.

The clerks in the Secretary's Office presented a memorial against the special promotion of an officer to ' Western Clerk,' an office previously deemed a standing perquisite of the secretarial staff. The two leading protesters were suspended, one for six and one for twelve weeks, and the others were fined, the Board telling them that if they desired promotion they had best qualify themselves by becoming acquainted, not only with the

* In 1783 he was compelled to resign his office.

routine of outer work, but with all branches of customs practice, especially with the history of the 'Customs Laws, so as to be able to remind the Board.'

Two Commissioners conferred with the Secretary for War upon the matter of employing troops to prevent smuggling *in the neighbourhood of Croydon.*

The officers at Margate were enjoined to be vigilant in preventing artificers from leaving England.

A parcel of coin, amount £52,000, was allowed to be exported to Barbadoes, to supply a relief fund, the island having been devastated by a hurricane.

The Customs employed several solicitors, each solicitor advising upon a certain class of bonds, or upon matters connected with a certain number of ports. They were paid large salaries, and received liberal allowances for clerks and messengers. They were also granted sums of money annually for rent of chambers outside the Custom-house, and for coals and candles used therein, it being assumed that they frequently took their outstanding work home. The Board refused to continue the allowances for chambers, coals, and candles, stating that many other customs officials carried work home, yet received no extra grants. They also reminded the solicitors that many eminent lawyers contrived to support themselves in affluence upon fees earned under stress of competition, and to pay the rent of chambers and offices as well, while the customs lawyers had offices in the Custom-house, and clerks free of expense. Then these iconoclastic Commissioners reminded the solicitors of the heavy fees that enriched them, and bluntly adjured them to put their hands in their own pockets, for that the Revenue should no longer be burdened with their chamber-rents, coal bills, and charges for candles of expensive mould and material. Then the Board sent for the 'Auditor of Law Expenses,' and bade him pay particular attention to his work in future, so that he might be able to satisfy them that the large sums disbursed on credit of his certificates *were really due !* And they directed him, 'for his own more ample information,' to study and précis the Minutes relating to his office.

A fleet of eighteen East Indiamen arrived. The Board at once employed 174 extra customs watermen.

Parliament abolished the confusing discounts* allowed on customs duties, and considerably relaxed the provisions of the Navigation Act. A heavy impost was laid upon foreign verdigris, and 'smalt blue' was made duty-free.

It was directed that the prices of corn, whether for bounty or duty, in Kent and Essex, should be regulated by the London price, which was to be published weekly in the *London Gazette*, and certified to by the collectors of London and of Kentish and Essex ports.

An additional duty of 1¾d. per pound was laid on tobacco, and of 4s. 8d. per cwt. on sugar. The proceeds of these imposts were to go to the Sinking Fund. British refined sugar was granted a handsome additional drawback on exportation, and tobacco an added drawback equal to the increase in duty.

In 1782 an additional 4d. per pound was levied on tobacco, and 8d. on snuff. The rate value for brandy was abolished, and the customs† duty on that article made £8 8s. per tun, which included the Coinage duty. The new duty was liable to the 5 per cent. impost on net proceeds. Additional duties were placed on salt and beeswax, and to crown the whole an additional 5 per cent. was levied on the produce of all duties, the previous 5 per cent. excepted.

It was provided, 'for the better securing the freedom of elections,' that no revenue officer should vote at parliamentary elections, under penalty of £100 and loss

---

* This rendered the old 'Books of Rates' useless, and Messrs. Frewin and Sims, of the Customs, were ordered to prepare a new 'Book of Rates.'

† The French duty remained, and it must be borne in mind that besides the customs duty on spirits there were nine different branches of excise duties. The total excise on 'double spirits' was nearly twice the excise on 'single spirits.' At most ports these duties were collected by the Customs.

of office, but officers might retain the power of voting by resigning their appointments prior to the date on which the Act came into force. Thus it is evident that Parliament did not wish to disconcert people whose votes were worth more than their offices.

An Act was passed empowering the king to treat with the Americans for peace, and to repeal by letters patent any Act relating to the American Plantations.

To prevent British ships from passing into the possession of the king's enemies, it was enacted that they might not be sold to persons residing abroad, without special licence for each sale, and that the master or owner of any British ship trading foreign should give bond not to sell his vessel to foreigners. If a British ship were sold to a British subject the old bond lapsed, and a new bond had to be entered into by the purchaser. The bonds were to be at the public expense.

There had been some misapprehension as to the application of the Tobacco-planting Act to Scotland, and the point in doubt was consequently made clear by statute. It appears that tobacco had been cultivated extensively beyond the Border. The Scottish supervision must have been very slack, for it was found necessary to provide explicit regulations as to the method of taking Scottish tobacco to account for duty. Future planting was prohibited, but the standing crops were allowed to be gathered. Each planter was to account to the nearest collector of customs for the tobacco grown by him or in his possession, furnishing the amount of the current crop within three months after gathering. The goods were to pay the same rates as Plantation tobacco, and they might not be removed to England except by sea.

It was enacted that no office newly granted by patent in the Plantations should be executed by deputy.

A large quantity of tea was stolen from one of the East India Company's London warehouses, and the Attorney-General decided that the Customs could not claim the duty involved, as the goods had not been exposed for sale.   This appears a challengeable decision, for one of the conditions under which the Company were allowed to warehouse goods was that they should keep the goods in safe custody.

The learned gentleman had no scruples as to advising enforcement of the regulations, when he was asked as to the legal method of dealing with a crop of tobacco grown in Yorkshire.   He advised that the excise officers should procure the co-operation of the local justices, and arrange for the destruction of the young crop, and that if the grower gathered it in spite of them the Customs Board should proceed against him for a penalty of £10 *per rod* of land from which the crop was gathered !

The Committee of Account queried the Board of Customs as to why the customs accounts were in arrear. The Board made a telling statement as to the difficulties they lay under in dealing with the patent officers.   Thereupon my Lords of the Treasury stopped their previous practice of granting long and frequent holidays to the patentees, and decided to refer all future applications for leave to the Board of Customs.

The Board had for a long time been empowered to levy dues on vessels lying at Custom-house Quay, and the collection seems to have at first been leased to a high customs official.   The system of leasing was discontinued, and they appointed a manager of the business, giving him 5 per cent. of the takings.   The Margate hoys discharged and loaded at this quay, and the Board seem to have thought little of the Margate trade, for they instructed their manager to turn the hoys away if he could secure the custom of the Ipswich packets.

The Treasury directed the Board to prepare a scheme for consolidating the customs taxes.   A committee was formed, consisting of the Solicitor, the controller-general's principal clerk, the deputy Collector Inwards, and the deputy Collector Outwards.   They were instructed to begin by drawing up a list of such titles of goods, expressed in the old 'Book of Rates,' as had become obsolete. The Board spoke highly of their Committee, but informed the Treasury that, 'on account of the intricacy of the computations,' there was little chance of a scheme being got ready for the ensuing Session.

The Plantation collectors were instructed to procure 'good bills' for remittance of such balances as were not transmitted in kind or in bulk silver, and were told that if their bills were 'protested' they would be charged with the sums at issue, plus interest. It was arranged that whenever a Plantation collector was dismissed or removed for misconduct his successor should, before departing from England, be called into the office of the London controller-general, informed of his predecessor's irregularities, and cautioned against repeating them. The controller-general was to endorse the certificate of the new collectors' qualifications with a statement that this had been done.

Messrs. Frewin and Sims produced their new 'Book of Rates,' and each compiler was rewarded with £100. The book was published by Longman, and it seems to have sold well. In 1784 Longman paid £153 7s. 6d. into the hands of the Collector Inwards.

The Customs Committee appointed to arrange the consolidation of duties were directed to prepare a new 'Book of Duties and Drawbacks,' 'disregarding fractions.'* Thereupon Messrs. Frewin and Sims came forward, and stated that they had evolved a plan of consolidation. They were directed to proceed with it, and promised £500 each if the result were satisfactory

The Treasury and the Board had a dispute over the ex-collector of Rochester. That gentleman had been dismissed for misconduct. He contrived to incite the Treasury into reopening his case, and they called on the Board for a copy of the proceedings. The copy was sent, and accompanied by a manly and remarkable statement.

---

* The net duties in previous ' Books of Rates' had been carried out to minute fractions of a penny.

The Board declared that the ex-collector had not served with ' high integrity ' for twenty years, as in his application to the Treasury he had stated, but had during that period been guilty of many gross irregularities. They described the official method of adjudicating upon such cases, and protested that they had always used great care in investigating them, weighing every point of evidence as closely as possible. The concluding portion of their statement deserves literal reproduction :

' The Commissioners cannot recollect a previous instance of the Treasury having influenced the decision of the Commissioners in these cases, and it is sincerely to be wished that the Treasury may in future adhere to so salutary a rule, because the Board, having no means of rewarding, if they are deprived of the power of punishing, will lose every kind of control over their officers, and the effect of such relaxation will be immediately felt at the Exchequer.'

The salaries of the customs boatmen were adjusted, the Board quoting a Treasury warrant of 1684-1685, which enjoined that the boatmen's pay should be ' a competent and congruous subsistence.' Under the new scheme it was made £30 a year in England, £25 in Wales.

A merchant's clerk apprised the Board of certain clandestine dealings contemplated by his employer. The information saved the Revenue £532, and the Board gave the informer £100.

The following is an exact copy of an order issued to the officers (as quoted in the memoranda) instructing them as to the approved method of distinguishing flour from starch on importation :

' Put it into a tumbler of water which if Starch will sink to the bottom and form a hard Substance, and if Flour will turn into Paste and may be drawn into a kind of string like doe* and further by Starch being much whiter than Flour.'

The ' Officers of the London Burning-Ground ' were

* Dough.

fined for allowing a seized cutter to lie in ' the Condemned Hole ' with her sails unbent.

In 1783 an extra tide-waiter laid information against certain customs officers who had connived at extensive smuggling from the *Rochford,* East Indiaman. He received a reward of £40, and was superannuated with a yearly pension of 16 guineas.

The Commissioners set to work to curtail the expenses incidental to the domestic management of the London Custom-house. They discovered that the official House-keeper, Mrs. Kelly, had made a practice of claiming all the partly used candles and selling them, realizing private profit thereby to the amount of £150 a year. This was stopped, and boxes were provided, in which the candle-stumps were deposited every morning, and kept under lock till the receptacles were full. Then ' the Controller of the Housekeeper ' had to weigh the candle-ends and return them to the chandler, who had to allow for them in his bill.

It appears that Mrs. Kelly received an allowance of £215 per annum, to enable her to keep twelve servants, but the notable dame had only kept eight, and one of these had been paid in candle-ends and broken victuals. She was ordered to keep the full complement of servants in future, and to pay them proper wages.

She was also told to refrain from selling the cinders, the Commissioners shrewdly suspecting that in such secret traffic coal might pass as well as the charred residue. All cinders were to be collected, ' and carefully used again.' The Secretary was ordered, no doubt much to his disgust, to direct the scavenger to clear the ash-hole every third day.

The Board's order upon these important matters was emphatic. It began : ' Notice is hereby given to the Housekeeper in the most solemn manner,' and proceeded, ' The Housekeeper surely cannot imagine that the same plea of precedent would justify collectors, who hold under the same sort of grant as herself, in converting the public money to their own use, and yet the loss is equal, whether officers deprive the Revenue of the money, or of the candles that cost money.' Of course this was simple and honest reasoning, and it is to be wished that such homely truths were oftener uttered. Yet the Board might have been a little easier with Mrs. Kelly. They need not have ended with : ' She would have been made sensible to her cost that her plea is inadmissible if the Board had ordered her to be prosecuted for her misdemeanors.'

Then the Commissioners went into the matter of ' chips.' The yearly charge for chips with which to light the fires was £28, and the Housekeeper admitted that only £14 worth had been used. She had also ordered ' mould candles ' for use in her private apartments, and had unduly profited by charges for supplying pens, ink, and paper at the sales of condemned goods. She seems to have been a notable lady, with an admirable knack of here and there turning a penny. Though the grave gentlemen in the Board Room came down with more than Roman firmness upon her secret profits, it is evident they found her indispensable.*

The keeper of the King's Warehouse was charged with breaking open a package addressed to the Queen. Acquitted, but told to inform the Secretary whenever packages arrived for members of the Royal Family, so that the Secretary might apprise the Board of Green Cloth.

The landing-surveyors were told to enjoin their subordinates ' to behave soberly, civilly, and with good manners towards each other, as well as to merchants.'

---

* Mrs. Kelly was a great favourite. She merely supervised the deputy Housekeeper occasionally ; indeed, her office was, in the main, a lucrative sinecure. Two or three years later the Commissioners increased her ' chip-money ' from £14 to £55, and her allowance for cooking their breakfasts and furnishing attendance from £110 to £150. In 1798 her daughter, Miss Eleanor Kelly, was allowed to succeed her, receiving the full emoluments of the office. Miss Eleanor appears to have been an interesting lady, and to have infused considerable gaiety into the domestic arrangements of the Custom-house. It is even stated that she occasionally gave balls in the Long Room.

The Treasury appointed a collector at Senegambia. The Board returned the warrant, stating that the appointment was unnecessary.

There were three classes of ' searchers ' : the patentees, their deputies, and the ' deputed ' or ' controlling ' searchers. The last-named officers were appointed by the Board, while the patentees were of course granted their privileges by the Treasury, and employed deputies at will.* During 1783 the Board reminded the deputed men that they had no legal right to take any money as fees from merchants, except such ' satisfaction ' as the merchants might give them for extra attendance, and that they were expected ' not to be a clog upon public business, but a check upon the patent officers and their deputies.' They were told to report at once to the Board any irregularities committed by the deputies or patentees, and that if they failed in this they would be deemed participators.

A large seizure was made in the house of the Bavarian Minister, and his secretary, Mr. Hellerhof, was prosecuted and committed.† One Burdett, an army officer, assisted in making the capture, and the Board rewarded him with 50 guineas. The customs men concerned also offered to

---

* The Board appear to have always grudged the Treasury officials their power of appointing patentees. Here is a passage in a letter on the subject, sent to the Treasury in 1694 : ' But for Patent offices, the Com^{rs}. have alwayes look't upon them as bountyes, in the hands of the Crowne or y^r Lord^{pps}, being generally bestowed upon persones with power to execute by deputy, and therefore the Com^{rs}. have alwayes been passive and easy in the transaction of these grantes, not thinking it became them to enter into consideration of the meritts or services for which they were bestowed.'

† It is likely that the real culprit was the Minister, Count Haslang. See Horace Walpole's letter on the Gordon Riots, 1780, which proclaims that Haslang had for many years been suspected of smuggling : ' Old Haslang's chapel was broken open and plundered, and, as he is a prince of smugglers as well as Bavarian Minister, great quantities of tea and contraband goods were found in his house. This one cannot lament, and still less as the old wretch has for these forty years usurped a hired house, and though the proprietor for many years has offered to remit his arrears of rent, he will neither quit the house nor pay for it.'

reward the gallant ensign out of their shares, but he declined, stating that he was satisfied with the Board's gift.

The Attorney-General's opinion was taken as to whether the Customs Board had authority to compel their patent officers to render obedience to orders issued for the public benefit. He remarked that proceedings might be taken to repeal the patents, which appeared to be 'a clog upon the administration of so large a branch of the public service.' Notice was sent to the patent officers that the Board would take proceedings if any future misconduct occurred.

The Bristol officers refused to clear a French vessel with goods for the United States. In this the officers appear to have been wrong. They were set right by a letter from the Privy Council, explaining that though under the old Acts vessels might not trade from Great Britain to the American Plantations, they might now trade from Great Britain to the newly recognized American Republic. Clearance was granted.

The Treasury directed that all loyalist refugees from the United States might land their effects in Great Britain free of duty.

It was provided that any person liable to a revenue penalty (sum less than £500) might clear himself by furnishing one seaman and one soldier. If the penalty were higher he might clear himself by providing two seamen and two soldiers.

The directors of the Bank of England approached the Board, complaining that large quantities of coin of the realm were clandestinely exported. The Board issued special instructions to the officers.

The *Wasp*, revenue lugger, Captain Beer, after a bloody and desperate conflict, captured a smuggling lugger called the *Cow*. The Board wrote *pleno jure* to Captain Beer and his crew, complimenting them upon their conspicuous gallantry.

The first-fruits of the labours of the Commission of

Public Account were made apparent in an Act that must have caused temporary discomposure in certain official circles. 'Whereas it appears from the Reports made by the Commissioners appointed to examine, take, and state the Publick Account of the Kingdom, that in the Receipt of His Majesty's Exchequer there are several useless, expensive, and unnecessary offices, and that the Emoluments arising from other of the offices in the said Receipt of Exchequer are become excessive, and that the mode of Paying the officers by Allowances, Fees, and Gratuities is inconvenient both to the Publick and to Individuals,' etc. It was directed that the offices of the Chamberlains, the Tally Cutter, and the Usher, should expire on the death, surrender, forfeiture, or removal of the holders.

A cheque receipt was to replace the tally method, on the death of the Chamberlains. There was a quaint provision as to the lapse of the Usher's office.* His successor had been named prior to the investigation, therefore he was to succeed to the vacant office when the Usher died, and keep it during life. The Teller's ' Second Clerks ' were adjudged superfluous, but they were to retain office till their respective superiors' interest determined.

When the holders of the offices of Auditor of Receipt, Clerk of Pells, Tellers, or Chamberlains died or were removed, the ' Fees, Gratuities, Allowances, Perquisites, and Emoluments ' were to be bestowed in paying the inferior clerks employed by the Auditor of Receipt, Clerk of Pells, and Tellers, who succeeded them. Any surplus left was to be divided thus : one-third towards the expenses of his Majesty's Civil Government ; two-thirds to the Sinking Fund. The officers succeeding to the posts were to be paid salaries : good salaries. The Auditor was to get £4,000 a year, his Chief Clerk £1,000, the Clerk of

---

* Horace Walpole held the patent of this office. See his published statement, produced after the Committee queried him. Horace was also quartered on the London Collectorship Inwards (Customs).

Pells £3,000, his Chief Clerk £1,000, each Teller £2,700, each Teller's Chief Clerk £1,000. The rent-free houses previously allowed to the Auditor, Tellers, and Usher were to pass to the Crown as their tenants vacated office. The daily hours of labour in this venerable and picturesque Court were four in winter and five in summer. There were many holy days, and it is likely that about 800 hours per year would be considered decent attendance.

Much of the tobacco that during the previous year had been grown in Scotland was found not worth the duty, and the Scottish Commissioners were empowered to buy it for destruction, paying not more than 4d. a pound.

To encourage the cultivation of coffee and cocoa in the West Indies, the British excise duty on those articles was lowered by two-thirds.

In 1784 an additional duty was placed on candles, ' not of wax or spermaceti.' ' To encourage British Hat-making,' the exportation of hare-skins and coney-skins was prohibited, and foreign goat's-hair was made duty-free. Additional customs duties were levied on foreign tiles and bricks, and an additional excise duty on home-made bricks. The duty on imported wax was increased. An impost was levied on certain kinds of foreign paper.

Yet occasionally there were signs of a broader spirit moving in revenue matters. The vexatious Aliens' duties and the one per cent. Mediterranean tax were repealed. The ' Aliens' Custom ' was about 480 years old, and the Mediterranean tax about 120.

A curious adjustment of the tea duty followed, it being changed to 12½ per cent. on the gross price paid at the East India Company's sales. The new duty was to be paid to the Company by the buyers. The Company were to make up the account within thirty days after conclusion of each sale, and pay the duty collected into the hands of the Receiver-General. The Company were enjoined to at once put upon the market 5,000,000 pounds of tea, and soon afterwards another 2,500,000 pounds, after which the sales were to be held at least every quarter.   The goods were to be sold without reserve to the highest bidder, the bidding to advance at 1d. per pound.   Maximum 'putting-up' prices were prescribed for the first four sales, as below :

Bohea, 1s. 7d. a pound ; Congo, 2s. 5d. ; Souchong, 3s. 3d. ; Singlo, 3s. 3d. ; Hyson, 4s. 11d.

After the four sales were completed the goods might not be *put up* at prices exceeding the prime cost, plus freight, importation charges, and lawful interest from time of landing.   This seems an impracticable proviso, but be it remembered many parliamentary enactments of that day proved abortive.

The Company were to keep enough tea in stock for one year's public consumption, and to buy back at prime cost all sold tea left in warehouse.   The reasons put forward for the change were the excessively high price of tea, and the success of smugglers.

To counterbalance the loss caused to the customs revenue by this reduction of the tea duty, that unpopular inland imposition, the window tax, was increased, and the additional moneys thus obtained were to go into the Customs Receiver-General's account.   If the sum thus forthcoming more than made up the deficit, the surplus was to be paid back to the Excise.   The duty on foreign coffee and cocoa was increased under this Act, and the previously existing inland duties upon those goods repealed.   It is hard to see what good purpose was intended to be served by such abominable complications. The idea dominant with the disposers of revenue seems to have been to keep as many tills as possible, to have as many clerks as possible, and to toil unwearyingly in devising fresh methods towards obfuscation.

The two 5 per cent. imposts on the proceeds of duties were removed from West Indian rum for two years. Additional duties were then placed on raw silk imported, lead exported, on foreign hats and caps, and on gold and silver plate.

In spite of the Attorney-General's decision of the previous year, the patent officers continued to misbehave, and were censured by the Treasury.

The Commissioners conferred with the directors of the East India Company upon the prevention of smuggling, and certain sly tricks performed by the Company's warehouse officials, especially their conspiring to keep prices low at the sales of ' private trade ' goods. The Board directed that when passengers landed at outports from East Indiamen their baggage should be sent under seal to the King's Warehouse in London, in order that assessment of the proper duties might in all cases be secured. About this time a Treasury warrant was issued, empowering the Company to import tea from Copenhagen and other Continental ports, to an amount not exceeding 3,000,000 pounds.

The searchers at Gravesend were censured for taking exorbitant fees, and charging 2s. 6d. as ' boat-hire ' whenever they visited a ship.

A quantity of provisions arrived from Hamburg for the king, and the Treasury directed that they should be delivered duty-free. The indomitable Board declined, stating that no proper proof had been furnished that the goods were for the royal household, and that previously whenever the Board of Green Cloth had applied for such goods the duties had been demanded and paid. They referred the Treasury to ' the ancient usage,' as applied to King George I. on his arrival, and stipulated that if this were to be departed from, and the goods delivered duty-free, the officers of the royal household should send some responsible person to clear them, instead of a common broker. Strange Commissioners, indeed, were these Thames Street worthies—now haggling over chips and cinders, then standing to their guns with the pertinacity of the gallant and unconquerable sailors of the period, defying my Lords of the Treasury, and suggesting that the king should pay duty on his caviare and sausages !

In 1785 the riding-supervisor at Dartford stopped a messenger who was conveying dispatches from Dover to the Spanish Embassy at London, and treated him rudely. The officer was censured, and ordered to apologize to the Spanish ambassador.

Two officers made a large seizure of East India goods. The case went before the Exchequer barons, who allowed the prohibited articles to be exported, admitted the rest to entry on payment of the ordinary duty, and refused to allow the seizing-officers' expenses. But the Board, believing the officers to have been in the right, gave them as a reward the amount of duty received on the goods.

A number of officers were informed against for conniving at fraud. The Commissioners had a notice posted at the London Custom-house to the following effect : ' All persons making complaint against any officer of this revenue are desired to do the same in writing, and at the foot thereof to mention the place of their residence, in order that recourse may be had to them from time to time to substantiate the said complaints.'

The salaries of the following London officers were stopped from January 29 to July 6, their accounts being in arrear : the Collector Inwards and his controller, the patent surveyor, the patent surveyor-general, the Examiner in the Long Room, and all their deputies and clerks.*

The French ambassador complained of depredations committed on the French coast by English revenue cruisers. Two commanders were charged, and one of them was dismissed.

The East India Company owed £923,000 Customs duty, and deposited £400,000 to stay proceedings.

The various customs collectors were ordered to search all bays, rivers, creeks, inlets, and boatbuilder's yards,

---

* Of course the salaries were merely nominal. The Board could not stop the collection of fees.

within the limit of their respective surveys, and to seize all boats of illegal build thus found.

The London searchers were warned against absenting themselves from duty on trifling pretexts. The Board informed them that such conduct did not become officers who held such an important trust, and on whose certificates the Revenue disbursed annually over £2,000,000 in drawbacks and bounties.

The Solicitor for Bonds and Criminal Prosecutions 'obtained an order' from one Commissioner to defend 'Justice Addington' from an action. The rest of the Commissioners, on hearing of this slip, waxed furious, and ordered him never to act thus again, but to ask sanction of a full and competent Board, and warned him that if by acting otherwise he caused the Crown to be saddled with expenses they would make him pay them out of his own pocket.

The collector at Cape Breton, Newfoundland, was one Mr. Uncle. His controller, when error led the Lieutenant-Governor and Council of the colony to suspend his coadjutor, did take it upon himself to appropriate the fees of the office. The Board investigated the affair, restored the collector to duty, and suspended the controller till he returned Mr. Uncle's fees.

An appalling statute appeared, regulating the importation and warehousing of tobacco—a statute full analysis of which is neither practicable nor desirable. Only tobacco grown in Ireland, the British American Plantations, the United States, and the Spanish and Portuguese dominions, might be imported. The ports at which tobacco might be landed were specified : London, Bristol, Liverpool, Lancaster, Cowes, Hull, Whitehaven, Greenock, and Port Glasgow. Sampling regulations were introduced, and no doubt these were judicious, for they are in existence at the present time. All imported tobacco was to be warehoused.

A Commission was instituted, to inquire into the system of fees in public offices, to 'examine into abuses,' and to report as to possibilities of improved methods of business. The departments to be overhauled were the Treasury, Admiralty, Board of Ordnance, Secretary of State's Office, Paymaster of Forces' Office, Secretary for War's Office, Naval Treasurer's Office, Naval Commissioners' Office, Customs, Excise, Sick and Wounded Seamen's Department, Tax Commissioners' Office, Stamp Commissioners' Office, Salt Commissioners' Office, Postmaster-General's Office, Land Revenue Department, Woods and Forests, Hackney Coach Commissioners' Office, and Hawkers and Pedlars Commissioners' Office. It would be interesting to know whether the officials of the Sick and Wounded Seamen's Department levied fees,* and, if they did, who paid them.

For some reason not apparent to ordinary minds, Parliament thought fit to remodel the new tea duty. Instead of £12 10s. per cent., as enacted in 1784, it was made £5 per cent., and £7 10s. per cent., the first portion to be under the Customs, the second under the Excise.

In 1786 an additional duty was placed on foreign deals and battens.

It was enacted that all captains arriving from foreign ports should produce manifests, and when shipping goods on drawback enter into a personal bond not to reland them, and that no ships subsequently built outside the king's dominions should be deemed British. even although owned by British and British manned.

The four latest imposts on wine, amounting in all to £32 8s. per tun on French, and £16 4s. on other wines, were repealed, together with the two 5 per cent. imposts on proceeds (as far as these last applied to the four wine imposts), and in lieu an impost of £35 14s. per tun on French and £17 17s. on other wines was established, and placed under the Excise. The £35 14s. and £17 17s. were, of course, in addition to all duties levied on wine up to 1745.

---

* They did, and some of the fees seem to have been for peculiar services.

About this time the legislators began to shake the revenue items this way and that. Certain customs branches went to the Excise, and certain excise and stamp duties to the Tax Commissioners.

For the present adieu to the tariffs. As the opening of the next chapter will show, things had become utterly unendurable to the public. But it appears that the British commercial mind had for years been pondering a return to simple methods, and the consolidation of the Customs was at hand.*

The rest of the administrative history of the period covered by this chapter is principally connected with official derelictions. Here are a few for the year 1786.

It being found that a cargo of barley transhipped for London had been charged with the ' low ' duties when it should have paid ' high,' the Collector Inwards (Sir Banks Jenkinson) and his controller were surcharged with the difference.

The London collector of coal duties and his controller were suspended, and all their clerks dismissed. The controller was told to occupy himself during suspension in learning the duties of his office.

Instructions were issued to collectors that when receiving seized goods from the captains of revenue cruisers they were to make each captain furnish a certificate that he had thoroughly searched his own vessel, the Board having reason to apprehend that seized goods were frequently embezzled by the sailors.

The collector, the deputy controller, the deputy searcher, and the tide-surveyor, at the port of Chepstow, were dismissed in a batch. Dismissal also overtook the commanders of the revenue cruisers at Poole and Yarmouth. A number of London officers were dismissed for conniving at frauds on board East Indiamen. During the period from 1760 to 1787 the Commissioners used the

---

* Towards the end of 1786 Messrs. Frewin and Sims produced schedules of rates for the new scheme, and it was ordered that the Inspector-General should be supplied with an account of the gross produce of the customs duties.

broom strenuously. They were lenient with subordinates who had committed trifling errors, but once they got a fair hold of a hardened sinner they made an example of him.

It must be understood that only such cases of dismissal have been quoted as illustrate the habits of the time, and the exigencies of revenue administration.* It appears that the Commissioners of the period were conscientious and independent, and that nothing would have suited them better than to have power to dismiss most of the insufferable patentees, to abolish the wretched fee system, and to render the ' Book of Rates ' understandable by ordinary men.

Before passing to purely preventive matters, mention must be made of a few strange incidents connected with the Superannuation Fund. The Fund had become a permanent institution. All the officials contributed to it, and it was enriched by grants out of fines, special awards, etc. Only such officers as had reached the age of sixty, and had subscribed for ten years, could be pensioners, and if after they became pensioners it was found that they had other means of subsistence they were at once struck off the list.

In 1776 a pensioner living at Hull was struck off, it having been found that he had ' an estate of £100 per annum.' In 1780 a pensioner (of course over sixty years old) was struck off because he had joined the army, and during the same year another venerable scapegrace was disqualified because he had taken service on board a privateer. In 1784 John Partridge, a native of Deal, was struck off for having become a leader of smugglers, ' frequently going as Captain on board the smuggling shallops.' In 1785 a pensioner living at Poole was dis-

* During the last six weeks of 1772 the Commissioners dealt with seven successive cases of smuggling by officers of the East India Company, connived at by customs officials. During the first nine months of 1773, they adjudicated upon fifty-eight similar cases. Many officials were dismissed, and many others saved themselves by treachery.

abled from further benefit because he had ' sold the king's sails.' All which goes to show that the Customs service produced some hardy veterans.

During the period covered by this chapter the senators exercised themselves frequently in devising schemes for the prevention of smuggling. These must be dealt with as briefly as possible. The ' legal tonnage ' for vessels carrying spirits and tobacco was increased, and the restrictions with regard to hoverers were intensified. Ships from foreign, entering the port of London, were prohibited from being moored ' at the back-doors of masters' houses,' or near riverside taverns, while waiting to go alongside the legal quays.

In 1778 the Board of Customs made a strange proposal to the East India Company. They suggested that the pilot-boat which was sent out to meet each homeward-bound East Indiaman should carry ' a complete crew ' for the vessel, and that the original crew should be removed from the ship and put ashore. All this was to be done before the vessel entered the lower reaches of the Thames. They insinuated that by constant practice the relief crews would become extremely skilful in navigating East Indiamen ' through the narrow channels of the river,' and that this would be of advantage to the Company. Then they revealed their real motive, hinting that the method suggested might put a stop to ' the atrocious smugling ' that prevailed. But the Company, probably conceiving that their pilots, not their mariners, were responsible for the safe navigation of the Thames, declined to entertain the proposal.

In 1779 a biting statute was issued, in consequence of smuggling by ' gangs of daring and dissolute persons armed with offensive weapons.' It made ships forfeitable for having on board brandy in illegal packages, or when, not being over 200 tons, they carried any *goods* which became forfeitable. The Act against boats with more than four rowlocks, which applied to the south-eastern counties only, was made to include all boats with more than six oars in the other counties, tow-boats of Bristol excepted. Excise officers were granted still wider powers of seizing goods afloat, and justices were enabled to fine jailers for allowing smugglers to escape. Smugglers were made liable to be pressed for the army as well as the navy. All foreign thread lace was to be stamped by the Customs at the end of each piece, and was forfeitable if found unstamped.

In 1781 out came an Act levelled against fraudulent traders rather than hoverers and runners. It provided that a ship's captain caught smuggling should be liable to forfeit his wages to the shipowner, and pay the ship-*owner* treble value of the goods seized, besides paying the Crown penalties. If mates or seamen were caught, the shipowner might sue them for 10s. a pound for all tea smuggled, and 10s. a gallon for spirits, besides keeping back all their wages, and if the offence were committed during time of war he might then send them aboard a king's ship for three years. (Well might Sir Samuel Romilly say, ' I have examined the codes of all nations. Ours is the worst, and worthy of the Anthropophagi.')

In 1784 it was enacted that a ship should be forfeitable for hovering within four leagues of the coast for the purpose of running goods. Boats built for running and found hovering were made forfeitable, even with no cargo on board. Vessels found ' within the limits,' carrying weapons beyond two carriage-guns of 4 pounds calibre, and two muskets to every ten men, were made forfeitable, Government vessels and ships from ' distant places ' excepted. Any person shooting at a revenue vessel or officer, or wounding an officer, was made liable to ' death as a felon, without benefit of clergy.' Revenue cruisers might fire upon vessels that refused to bring to. Many other severe provisions were included in this Act.

Yet, in considering these terrific statutes, it should always be borne in mind that they were carried out by other than twentieth-century methods. Such laws would indeed be terrible now, when men have forgotten how to defy danger and endure pain, and the law is unerring in pursuit of criminals. The bark of the old statutes was worse than their bite. The skill of the smugglers increased as the penalties became more formidable. Many of the contrabandists were desperate fellows, and their determination in combat was so great that the officers usually shirked an encounter. Then the justices around the coast were often inclined to favour the free-traders—men whom they had in youth fished, sailed, and played with. Even if convicted, the smuggler might make an attempt at compounding, and the Treasury officials were often willing to accept part of the money penalty, rather than lose all. True, the smugglers might be pressed, but many of those who were sent aboard men-of-war succeeded in escaping, and were soon back at the old trade. It does not appear that the grim laws were plied viciously. The customs solicitors, though anxious, as we have shown, to saddle the public with their office expenses, were just and able lawyers, who weighed and sifted evidence as though it were dust of golden ore, and would touch no ' shaky case.' It would be hard to find men more merciful than the Commissioners. The most daunting thing, after all, about the old revenue laws is the display they furnish of their framers' knowledge of human villainy. Those dreadful plots against comradeship, that incessant prompting to mean betrayals ! Small wonder that a humorist of the period said : ' There should be no such thing as King's Evidence. The villain who tenders it should be hanged head downward !'

Once more to the practice of the outports, and the doings of the hardy contrabandists. It is a pity that direct literary touch cannot be established with the latter. Unfortunately they kept no letter-books ; the only official documents to which smugglers put their mark were petitions for mercy, offers of composition, professions (usually false) of poverty and penitence, and occasional epistles of treachery. Referring to the Letter

Books of Poole, it is apparent that the ex-collector Milner was still inclined to do his best to get the officers into trouble.

The collector reported that Milner's son-in-law borrowed £500 from Captain Pinney of Poole, and gave as security a bill upon effects. Payment was required and refused, so Pinney took possession, and called a sale. Milner thereupon put in a claim to part of the effects, stating that they were the property of his own son, 'who,' blithely interjected the collector, 'recently broke out of Jayl in this town.' Pinney met the claim with derision.

Now, part of the pledged effects consisted of twenty-eight casks of wine, bought at a sale of condemned goods during Milner's term of office, and these were stored in Milner's garden. Pinney called the two customs surveyors of the port to his assistance, and proceeded to take possession of the wine, but Milner sent for a cooper, and ordered the said cooper to stave the casks. This was done, and

> ' Down ran the wine into the road,
> Most piteous to be seen.'

Then, and not till then, the two surveyors thought they had better have refrained from accompanying Pinney, whence the collector's report. The collector tried his best to gloss over matters. He stated that he made the report simply to justify the officers, who had acted 'inadvertently out of Compassion to the Distress'd [Pinney] and not with any presumptuous Design. Mr. Milner's Conduct,' he wrote, 'is very extraordinary, and full of Cruelty and Revenge.' But the Board neither interfered with Milner nor openly blamed the officers.

In 1761 three riding-officers made an important seizure on information. They also made a private arrangement with the informer that he was to receive out of the proceeds a guinea for each hundredweight of tea, and three shillings for each keg of spirits. After making the seizure they tried to beat him down, but he put his case in the hands of a local attorney. Then the officers offered him 25 guineas. The informer referred them to his lawyer. They appealed to the collector, who reported the case to the Board, and the Board compelled the officers to fulfil their promise.

A riding-officer and two excisemen came upon a gang of smugglers and train of horses, carrying tea. The officers charged boldly, and succeeded in cutting a number of packages adrift. Then the smugglers attacked them, and mauled them badly, finally riding off and escaping with about two tons of tea. ' Mr. Glynn the exciseman,' said the collector in his report, ' was beat in the most Cruel manner about the Head with his own Pistol, which the Smuglers took from him by force. It is doubtful whether he will live or dye. The Riding-officer has been ill ever since.' A country gentleman living near assisted the wounded officers, and the collector, in his report, praised the gentleman most effusively, especially commenting upon the fact that he took Glynn into his house, ' and washed his wounds with rum.' All which was beyond doubt praiseworthy, yet the plain duty of any law-abiding man ; and still it seems that the collector was immensely surprised that the like should be done— indeed, he kept on lauding the good Samaritan in an extraordinary fashion.

An anonymous letter reached the Board, accusing the collector of granting certificates to sailors that they were men of the Customs, thus enabling them to escape the press. The Board queried the collector, and the latter referred to Captain Milligan, an undeniable Irishman, who had charge of the press-gangs. Milligan stated that he had never found any such certificate on any seaman whom he had stopped, and concluded his statement thus :

' The information in my Oppinion is False and Scandalous, and the Villain that Sett it on Foot ought to Lose his Ears.'

The officers, in their eagerness to make profitable seizures, sometimes ran astray. The tide-surveyor and his crew went aboard a Guernsey trader in Swanage Bay, and seized several casks of brandy. It is probable that the casks were not legally liable to seizure, for the surveyor made no attempt to detain the master, and did not report the seizure till after the vessel had left. Then he stated that he found the casks 'in a boat.' The collector discovered the facts to the Board, intimating that the officers 'humbly prayed to be forgiven their indiscretion.' The Board cautioned them.

Three customs boatmen, named Barns, Phippard, and Harvey, seized sixty-five kegs of spirits at Swanage. The goods were found by 'creeping'—viz., searching in holes and gullies along the coast, where the smugglers often stored their 'truck' till it could be carried inland. On the same night two riding-officers found four kegs, and left them with the boatmen, so that the latter might take the whole to Poole on the following morning. The boatmen stored the kegs for the night in their watch-house at Swanage, and during the process of housing two kegs mysteriously vanished. The boatmen seem to have concluded that it was best to keep their own counsel about this, and in the morning they set out for Poole, conveying sixty-three kegs of their own, and four kegs of the riding-officers' seizing. Carriages were not plentiful at Swanage, so they hired a wagon and a dung-cart.

Vehicles more suitable were procured when they arrived at Southhaven, and the wagon and dung-cart proceeded back to Swanage. But when the boatmen arrived at Poole, only sixty kegs could be tallied into the warehouse. The collector gave them 'a reference,' and their reply deserves clear reproduction.

'The Sixty Three Casks of Brandy and Rum that were taken up by us in Swanidge Bay we deposited that night in the watch house. Next day we loaded the same in a Waggon & Dung Plow & do believe the same Number of Casks were put in that Carriage but when we delivered them Three Casks were a-missing & what became of them We can give no Account. We have been to severall Places enquiring about them especially to those People who owns the Plows that brought them. They say they know nothing about Them and never meddled with Them. We assure you we kept by the Plows & never left them till deliver'd. How they should be gone we can't think if t'was not when they were taken from the Carts at Southhaven. As to the 2 kegs we know not anything about or what became of Them To the Truth whereof we are ready to make Oath Witness our Hands this 8th Day of Decr 1761.

> ' JOSEPH BARNS.
> PETER PHIPPARD His X Mark.
> RICHARD HARVEY His X Mark.'

The statement, viewed along with the collector's report, is rather misleading, with its complications of carts, plows, and wagons, its inaccuracies as to the real number of casks found, put in charge, and beyond ken. The collector reported on the statement with considerable sardonic force.

' Why they should conceive the Casks were lost at Southhaven sooner than at any other place we can no otherwise account for than by informing your Honours that at Southhaven there is a Publick House.'

Further inquiries were made. The collector interrogated the driver of the wagon, who stated that when the casks were transferred at Southhaven he asked Joseph Barns if they were right as to number, and Joseph answered, ' All is well.' The driver of the dung-cart was questioned, and stated that he asked Peter Phippard if his lot were right as to number, and Peter answered, ' All is well.'

The collector sent another report, stating his belief that after thus ejaculating impressively ' All is well ' the boatmen went into the public-house and fell to drinking, and while they were thus engaged seven casks were stolen. No doubt his surmise was correct.

The collector and controller got into trouble through illegally selling damaged tea to a grocer, and afterwards reconsidering matters and refusing delivery. The grocer became litigious, and the dismayed officials reported themselves to the Board, stating that though the tea was only worth half the price they had charged for it, the grocer refused to receive back his money, or to consider a tardy hint that they would give him a few guineas to boot. There was something in this business that is hard to understand. The Board, to save the officers from the exposure of a lawsuit, allowed them to deliver the tea.

In 1762 several ships which had been to Newfoundland arrived at Poole, with news that the French had taken St. John's. They had landed part of their goods, which consisted of drawback and bountied articles, and consequently their cargoes and manifests did not agree. The officers asked the Board for special instructions ' on this melancholy occasion.'

A tidesman charged with being drunk and assaulting a shipmaster named Linthorne made a singularly fluent defence, which ended thus :

' I humbly hope that the blameable part of my Conduct in this affair will be imputed to a sudden absence of Reason and impulse of Passion which all Mankind are or may be subject to. I have neither malice, envy, or Ill design against Mr. Linthorne, and I hope that his heart is as free from those detestable qualities with regard to me.'

A Newfoundland ship, liable to the provisions of the Plantation Acts, landed and reshipped at Poole a cargo of salt fish for Oporto. After she was discharged at Oporto her certificate of landing was sent to Poole in the usual manner. The quantity landed and reshipped at Poole had been 3,228 quintals ; the account of landing at Oporto showed 2,710 quintals. The collector reported to the Board, suggesting that the certificate should be accepted and the bond cancelled, as the Portuguese quintal was larger than the English, and the Portuguese officers had appropriated a number of the largest fish, the customs fees there being paid *in kind*.

The following have been extracted from the Southampton Letter Books of a few years later :

In 1768 the Board sent to Southampton copies of three depositions, made in France by masters of foreign vessels, and transmitted by the French Minister to the British Secretary of State. They were to the following effect :

1. The captain of a Danish vessel reported that while passing through the Channel he fell in with two English shallops, each carrying eight men, who came alongside, and boarded him on either quarter, pistol in hand. They drove the crew below, and by menaces compelled him to give up all the money he had, amounting to 200 livres.

2. The captain of a Dutch vessel reported an encounter with the same pirates. They boarded him, brandishing axes and pistols, beat his crew, searched him by force, and stripped him nearly naked. They took all the money they could find, besides fourteen bottles of wine and two half-ankers of brandy.

3. Another Dutch captain recounted his experience. The same pirates boarded him, took all his money and provisions, and maltreated his crew.

Soon the Board sent copies of three other depositions made by Dutch skippers. The same methods had obtained, the sailors being beaten and driven below, and the captains compelled to surrender all their effects. One Dutch skipper had the temerity to object, and to hint of an imaginary Dutch man-of-war not far away, that would make things hot for the pirates, but one of the Englishmen ' gave him a back-handed blow in the face,' drove him into the cabin, and stole his pipe and tobacco-box, while the rest helped themselves to his wine and geneva.

Directions were given by the collector that the revenue cruisers should look out for, and if possible apprehend, these imitators of John Wilcock of old, but there is no word of success.

The seizures at Southampton were numerous and important. One parcel returned for condemnation included 5,956 pounds tea and 1,603 gallons spirits. The tea was burned ; the spirits were sold. The appraised value of the tea was 2s. 6d. a pound ; of the spirits, 6s. a gallon.

In 1769 a sloop called *The Harvest* loaded in London for British possessions in Africa, and afterwards ran part of her cargo near Southampton. The goods were seized, and the ship was detained. The owner applied to the Board to have his ship released so that she might continue her voyage. The Board declared her forfeited, but allowed her to complete her voyage, the owner to give security that he would then return her for condemnation. Later the vessel was reported as wrecked. The owner absconded, and the surety became bankrupt.

Information was received that six Irish wherries had left Dunkirk laden with goods for running on the south coast of England. The revenue cruisers were instructed to keep a sharp look out.

A seizure of ' 12,000 Chip Hats ' and a quantity of annatto was made on information. The Board instructed their solicitor to prosecute the chip hats to condemnation in the Exchequer. The annatto was declared not dutiable, yet forfeited by being imported in contravention of the Navigation Act.

Captain Collingwood, of the revenue cruiser *Tweed*, inquired of the Board as to the amount due to him and his company on account of a large seizure of brandy. The Board replied that one-third only of the net proceeds would be awarded, unless he succeeded in capturing the smugglers concerned.

An officer stationed at Jersey seized two sloops, apparently without sufficient cause ; for an action was entered against him by the owners, and he was made liable to pay £65 as damages. The collector at Southampton, who had control of the revenue officers in the Channel Islands, reported the matter to the Board, and stated that the officer's household goods had been seized in satisfaction of the award. He was directed to pay the £65 out of the port moneys in hand.

The collector was instructed to caution all officers who might seize vessels that when the vessels were condemned they were not to appropriate them and substitute others. It appeared that ships appraised at a high price had been privately disposed of, and old and worthless craft sent to the burning-ground in their stead.

On account of great frauds committed in the trade between Southampton and the Channel Islands, a Mr. John Major was allowed to fit out a vessel of 100 tons and a ' tender ' of 50 tons, to cruise in the neighbourhood of Jersey and Guernsey, and along the English coast as far as the Rame Head at Plymouth. This venture, as will be seen, turned out disastrous for Mr. Major.

There appear to have been many mistakes and informalities in sufferances granted for coastwise goods, and these were usually attributed by the traders to oversight on the part of their clerks when entering the goods for shipment. In all cases the goods were detained till the Board's decision was made known, which usually followed the old lines, directing release ' on a reasonable satisfaction being made to the detaining officers.'

A small vessel left London for Southampton with 15 hogsheads of bonded tobacco, covered by the usual coast dispatch. The surveyor of the London coast-waiters, evidently a person prone to subtle imaginings, got to thinking that these goods might be run during the voyage, and that the vessel might then proceed oversea, take in similar packages, and land and warehouse the new packages at Southampton under cover of the coast dispatch. It is not clear how anything could be gained by such a complicated move, or how it would be easier to run goods removed for warehousing than to go oversea in ballast, procure a cargo, and run it offhand. For it is clear that the run would occur at some unfrequented place, and its success depend upon the absence of the riding-officers. If the riding-officers found the vessel landing her bonded cargo they would seize it, just the same as if it had been brought direct from oversea. Perhaps the surveyor had remoter contingencies under contemplation, for he put a private mark on each package, and apprised the Board, who thought it worth while to transmit the information to Southampton. When the vessel arrived the casks were inspected, and the private marks could only be found on one or two, and in those cases they were incomplete. The Board directed the collector to send the tobacco back to London in charge of an officer, in order that the packages might be examined by the ingenious person who had marked them. The affair seems to have ended in nought.

The surveyor-general of Hants and Dorset, one Fiennes Eddowes, overhauled the port of Southampton, its 'members,' and its 'creeks,' and found fault with many things. He was especially severe upon the collector and the controller of Cowes, who had made it a practice to keep back large sums 'to pay salaries and meet exigencies,' and had failed to record the nature of the said claims and exigencies. He found that since his last survey there had been three occasions upon which over £2,000 at a time had been thus retained, eight retentions of over £1,000, and seventeen of over £500. Thus it appears that the officers exceeded their prerogative upon twenty-eight quarterly occasions, and that the surveyor-general's visits were at intervals of seven years at the very least (most likely ten). Fiennes Eddowes also observed that too many extra tidesmen were employed, some of whom had been placed by the collector on board a sloop owned by him, to cruise in pursuit of smugglers for the collector's private advantage in the way of seizure awards. Thus the public had been paying men in order that the collector might benefit.

Goods which had been improperly entered had been put right as to entry, and the extra duties taken, without the Board's cognizance. Improper bonds had been used to cover the exportation of corn to Jersey. Seized *prohibited* goods had been sold for home consumption, instead of for exportation. Mr. Eddowes also intimated that he suspected the coal-meters of fraud, as coals shipped at Cowes frequently turned out unsatisfactorily on discharge. Casks of exported tar had been granted bounty without being gauged.

He severely censured both collector and controller, and then went through the district, awarding censures at most of the stations.

In March, 1770, a warehouse hired by the collector of Southampton to accommodate a seizure made by one of the revenue cruisers was broken into during the night, and three casks of brandy were carried away.

Two London officers visited the port in consequence of private information, and made a large seizure of smuggled hops.

The Board transmitted the Attorney-General's opinion upon the matter of imported train-oil of Newfoundland. In spite of the numerous provisions of the various revenue Acts, or perhaps in consequence of their extreme elaboration, the regulations do not appear to have been systematically administered, and the Crown lawyers were frequently called upon to clarify the faculties of the officers at various ports. Below is a decision upon the vexed subject of exemption of oil from duty.

' I think the only Oil which is exempted from Duty is Oil taken and imported in British ships which do but in part belong to British owners, not such Oil when the rest of the property of the Ships belongs to Americans or Dutchmen. It is not a British ship unless it is entirely a British ship. I am therefore of opinion that Oil taken and imported in Ships belonging in part to Americans and in part to English, on whichever side the Majority of Owners is, cannot be imported duty-free,' etc.

This may have conveyed illumination to the collector of Southampton, yet ordinary minds will make neither head nor tail of it. It is scarcely probable that the South-ampton clerk transcribed it incorrectly, for it was intended to remain in the records as a reference in case of doubt. No doubt it was rarely referred to, and the collector and his successors jogged along as best they could, hoping that all would be well, and that Mr. Fiennes Eddowes would refrain from prying too deeply into their accounts of 'Oil and Blubber.' Evidently the Attorney-General desired that they should, for he added a note thus : ' But if the Merchant has been led to Trade upon the faith of such practice it is fit such faith should be kept.'

One hundred bales of chip hats were seized on a vessel from Dunkirk, condemned, and sold for £517 15s. There-upon arose a squabble about the shares due to the various seizing-officers.

An inhabitant of the district sent an extraordinary letter to the Lords of the Treasury. It commenced thus :

' MY LORDS,

' I beg leave to inform you that there are two Bays or Arms of the Sea on each side Christchurch Haven in Hampshire that are constantly frequented by a most daring crew of Smuglers who appear to hold all the Revenue Laws in Open Defiance.'

It went on to recommend that a troop of dragoons should be sent to Christchurch, and stated that at the time of writing the smuggling cutter was lying in Christ-church Bay, *flying his Majesty's colours !* This amazing epistle was signed ' Richard Hughes of Wick near Christchurch.'

News came to Southampton of a Dutch ship cruising from port to port in the Mediterranean. She had put into Malta with her master and fourteen sailors dead of plague, and only twenty-three survivors. The Grand Master of the island had her towed out to sea. She tried to enter Tunis, but the Bey refused to admit her. She entered Naples, and was driven to sea again, and the Italian officers of health placed sentries along the coast

to prevent the survivors landing.   The various British
sloops and men-of-war were apprised, and directed to keep
her out if she appeared on the British coast.   What
became of this plague-smitten craft in the end ?   Was
she found derelict at sea, her deck strewn with rotting
corpses ?   The story of Vanderdecken seems a pleasant
tale, when the possibilities of this ghastly cruise are
considered.

Southampton's record of seizures is imposing.   Below
is a list of seized goods and appraised values for the
quarter ending June, 1770 :

				£	s.	d.
239 gallons brandy	..	..	..	71	14	0
166 ,, rum ..	..	..	..	49	16	0
54 ,, geneva	..	..	..	16	4	0
256 pounds tea ..	..	..	..	28	16	0
				£166	10	0

Another parcel during the same period :

			£	s.	d.
230 gallons brandy					
207 ,, rum	..	..	390	11	0
43 ,, geneva					
2,386 pounds tea					

Another during same period :

			£	s.	d.
388 gallons brandy	..	..	219	6	0
343 ,, rum					

Another during same period :

			£	s.	d.
518 gallons brandy	..	..	260	8	0
316 ,, rum ..					
34 ,, geneva					

In addition to these, there were parcels of dimity,
muslin, linen, and flowered lawns, and a host of petty
seizures of various kinds of goods.   The total appraised
value was £1,343 12s. 2½d., and the Exchequer and
solicitor's charges on proceeds amounted to £27 17s. 1d.

Tidings were sent to the Board that Mr. John Major,
who during the previous year had been appointed to cruise
on the coasts of Guernsey and Jersey, and to sweep the

Channel free of smugglers as far as Plymouth, was a prisoner in Guernsey Castle, on account of two risky seizures which he had made. Mr. Stiles, a customs officer of Portsmouth, was sent to Guernsey by the Commissioners, to inquire into the case and to desire Major's 'enlargement,' in order that he might appear before them. Stiles was to draw upon the Southampton collector for expenses.

Later news came that both of Major's ships were ashore, and in a state of wreck. The Board desired the collector to send 'a trusty tidesman' to Guernsey with a letter, instructing Stiles to dismiss the mates and mariners. From a reference in a subsequent memorandum it appears that Major was also dismissed.*

Irregularities having occurred in compositions effected between officers and informers, the Board issued orders that no officer should compound an information till the full particulars were made known to them. The licence issued by the Exchequer Court authorizing a composition was to be attested on oath, sent to the Inspector of Prosecutions, and by him transmitted to the Attorney-General. From this it would seem that the Exchequer officials had been in the habit of granting such licences at the private request of the officers concerned.

Instances had occurred of commanders of revenue sloops appropriating part of the seizure awards due to mariners. The Board recited the legal rates of award, and enjoined that the captains were not to stimulate their men by promises of money. Said the wary Commissioners, being no doubt fully aware of the dangerous influence of blood-money : ' It may invalidate their testimony in case there should be occasion to make use of them upon a Tryal.'

The Irish smugglers appear to have been very daring. An advertisement by the Irish Commissioners of Customs

---

* In April, 1775, a Mr. ' James ' Major was appointed commander of a revenue sloop at Stockton. It is possible this was the same man. In 1779 he was convicted of threatening to kill Sir William Musgrave, one of the Commissioners.

reached Southampton, offering a reward for the capture of certain ' fellows ' who had murdered a revenue officer, attacked ' the King's Barge ' in the Bay of Dundrum, and captured and plundered the *Pelham* cutter at Beaumaris. Further news came of their doings. They were stated to be in the habit of making four voyages yearly to Dunkirk. They had four ships, well manned and armed, and the little squadron was commanded by one John Connor (called ' Jack the Bachelor '). The ships were classed thus :

A small cutter carrying six carriage - guns, besides swivels and small-arms. Two large cutters with eight carriage - guns each, besides swivels, etc. A large schooner-rigged wherry with six carriage-guns, etc. The captains were Thomas Field, Thomas Knight, John Creenan, and the redoubtable Connor. Several of the smugglers were described in picturesque fashion :

' Jack the Batchelor. A low-set fellow with a small stoppage in his speech. About 35, etc.

' Patrick Bawn, one of his crew, a middle-size well-made fellow, a Flatt nose, about the age of 36.

' Patrick Farren, a middle-size fellow, a little mark'd with the Smallpox, about the age of 30.

' Nicholas Kean, a middle-size well-made fellow, a Fresh complexion, about the age of 48.

' Thomas Field. He is a set well-made fellow about the age of 44.'

A series of quarrels took place at Southampton over seizure-money, always a fruitful source of dispute among revenue officers. An officer accused the collector of apportioning awards unfairly. The Board investigated the circumstances, rectified matters, and rebuked the collector.

About this time there were many large seizures on the coast. In most cases the smugglers escaped, sometimes after severely beating and wounding the riding-officers.

An advertisement of a gang of famous housebreakers,

who were attempting to escape from the country, was sent to Southampton, and the officers were directed to scrutinize all passengers outward.

The peculiar hostility between customs and excise officers was exemplified twice at Southampton in 1773. A customs officer complained that an exciseman had boarded an incoming vessel and commenced to examine the passengers' baggage prior to the arrival of the customs men. Soon after there was another dispute as to priority of claim to search. The Customs Board recited the ancient regulation on the matter : ' He who gets there first has first rummage.' There can be no doubt that the excisemen were fond of encroaching.

The captain of the *Anson* revenue cutter, foreboding a run at a certain spot, landed his crew, and placed them in ambush. They remained there through the night, hearing nothing and seeing nothing, and at daybreak he directed them to go on board the vessel. Just as he was abandoning his post, down came several riding-officers at full gallop. (It appears that while the *Anson's* crew were watching for a run, the riding-officers had been watching them.) The officers entered a stable hard by, pulled down a panel or two, and hauled forth 250 bags of tea. Upon which the *Anson's* men vociferously asserted their claim to participate in the seizure, and the claim was met with equally vociferous derision. So the riding-officers went off with their booty, and the captain of the *Anson* took his crew before the nearest justice, and piled affidavit upon affidavit, claiming that had he not watched all night the tea would have been carried off by smugglers. His claim, backed by a sheaf of depositions, went up to the Board, and met with the ill success it deserved.

A document was transmitted from London to Southampton, furnishing details of a concealment discovered on board a small vessel.

' He therefore renewed his search, and the better to enable him to discover any concealment, he admeasured the Distances of the Bulkhead above and below the Deck.

In comparing this Distance from the forepart of the Mast to the inside of the Stem upon Deck with that below the Deck, he found a difference of 3 feet. On pursuing this Discovery it at Last appeared that a false Bow, in every respect imitating the real Bow, had been built up within Board 3 Feet from the Inside of the Stem. This consequently left a vacancy between the false and real Bow which in this little Vessel was so considerable as to contain 750 lbs. of tea, and sufficient for 3 cwt. more,' etc.*

In 1775, the Mother Country being at war with the American colonies, a sharp look out was kept for vessels bringing intelligence to sympathizers with the Rebellion. A letter from the Treasury was sent to Southampton by the Board, stating that information had been received that a vessel, supposed to be an ' advice boat ' from America, had passed Cowes during the night, and landed a person who at once set out for London, and that the vessel, after cruising off and on for a space, departed and was seen no more. The commanders of the revenue sloops were urged to vigilance in searching all vessels suspected of the like, and directed, did they find American letters on board, to seize them and detain the ships concerned.

A riding-officer and two boatmen, in attempting to make a seizure on the coast, were terribly beaten by smug-

---

* The document went on to describe in stately periods the various devices incidental—a false ' apron,' a false ceiling, false breastworks, delusive planks, entrance between bitts and stem, and the iron ring of the admitting trap ' tarred over and let in.' All which may have at the time seemed very wonderful; but he would be a poor customs rummager who failed to discover such a device on board a vessel little larger than a modern dingy. Anyone who has seen a skilled rummager at work in one of the vast engine-rooms of a modern liner, crawling through the maze of bilges, exploring the ' columns,' threading all the manholes of the screw alley, groping in the oil-tanks, smelling his way beneath the enormous boilers, winding in and out amid the complicated machinery, and ending by stripping to the waist, and burrowing amid the coals in the bunkers, to emerge at last with a few pounds of ' hard ' sewn up in canvas, will have a better idea of the art of searching than can be gained from the above.

glers. The famous Captain Warren Lisle, most vigilant and determined of seizing-officers, was directed to interview the wounded men, and afterwards do his best to discover the offenders. (Some of this gentleman's exploits have already been narrated, and readers may be assured that he really ' did his best.') There is a peculiar sameness in the accounts of coast seizures, occasionally broken by details which possess a sameness of their own. Either the officers seized the goods and the smugglers escaped, or the officers were beaten within an inch of their lives and the smugglers carried out their run. It would seem that the latter occurred whenever the officers attempted to make arrests.

An honest shipmaster brought into Southampton 28 hogsheads of wine which he had found floating in the Channel, and surrendered them to the collector. It was a risky thing to do, for it is likely that if he had been boarded ' within the limits ' by one of the revenue cruisers protestations of honest intention would not have availed him. The collector sent an account of the goods to the Admiralty.

The following letter reached Thames Street :

CHRISTCHURCH,
' 13th Sept.

' GENTLEMEN,

' I most Humbly beg Leave to acquaint you that James Noyce, one of the Custom-house officers at Christchurch, does at this time carry on the trade of a Collar-Maker as usual before he was an Officer. Whereby I am greatly injured in my Business as a Collar-Maker, and my Family deprived of Subsistence. Your Humble Petitioner therefore craveth your kind Relief, as he is informed it is not usual or Legal for King's Officers to Carry on any Business.

' Your Honours' most obedient and most
humble Servant,
' JOHN WHITE.'

The Board directed instant inquiry, with a view to restraining James Noyce from unfair competition with his neighbour.

A fellow arrested for receiving 600 gallons of smuggled brandy wrote to the Board, stating that he lodged the goods in his outhouse at the request of certain seafarers, who told him they had landed them because their ship was in danger. He pleaded the usual small wife and large family, and expressed a hope that his extreme humaneness might not be counted as a crime. None can with certainty measure the extent to which he may have been thus spiritualized, or decide whether it was the cause of his adding that if proceedings against him were stayed he would at once betray his comrades. Insincerity and inherent treachery were apparent in every line of this epistle, which the writer called his ' ingenious [ingenuous] confession.'

The Board sent a memo. to the collector, lucidly defining the main points of the Plantation Acts, thus :

1. All Plantation goods not specially excepted, intended for foreign ports, were to be brought to Great Britain, landed, examined, taken to account, the duties paid, and the goods reshipped. If British goods were to accompany them, the Plantation cargo was to be thus dealt with before the British goods were shipped.

2. All British goods not specially excepted, shipped in Great Britain for the Plantations, were to be duty-paid before shipment ; and if any excepted British goods were to accompany them, such goods were not to be shipped until the dutiable cargo had been put under hatches.

The Board alluded to a practice prevailing at certain ports of evading the regulations quoted under (1) by making a rough computation on board, and charging a certain sum as duty without insisting upon the goods being landed. They forbade the continuance of this practice. It is astonishing that such a method could ever have been ventured upon in the teeth of the formidable statutes, and evident that in remote ports the collectors did almost as they chose.

In 1781 the Treasury received the following letter from Dunkirk, and sent it to the Board :

' I think it the duty of every Friend of his Country to think seriously of the trade now carried on with our Enemies and at Dunkirk, by several large Cutters belonging to Folkestone and Hastings, authorized by letters of Marque from England, and passes from France.'

The letter went on to particularize ships, owners, masters, and equipment. The goods run were tea. There was Captain Thomas Wood, with his ' deep-waisted ' cutter of 200 tons, carrying sixteen carriage-pieces and forty men, and he usually ran his cargo between Dunwich and Orfordness. The vessel's rendezvous was at Folkestone, and her owners were Proveau and Pinfold. Proveau was a Frenchman living at Dunkirk ; Pinfold an Englishman living at Folkestone. There was Captain Robert Tapley, with his 180-ton cutter, carrying fourteen guns and forty men, and he usually ran his cargo in Cornwall. There were Solomon Bevel and Marks Bayley, who jointly navigated a 200-ton cutter carrying fourteen guns, and ' ran ' between Beachy Head and Shoreham. There was also Anthony Warman of Folkestone, with his cutter of 90 tons.

The Board transmitted this picturesque information for the enlightenment of the Southampton officers. It will also enlighten readers. They will perceive that often the bold patriot who asked for letters of marque had three strings to his bow. If he fell across a French merchant ship, he towed her into an English port and claimed prize dues. He was also in the confidence of the French authorities, and for a consideration supplied them with tidings of the movements of the British fleet, and the general state of affairs in southern England. And he smuggled whenever a chance offered. Other little tricks were at his command ; he carried criminals, both French and English, clear of the eager claws of Justice. Thus his vocation was both profitable and exciting. It is likely, after all, that he would lean a little to the side of the land of his birth, and that some of the information that he furnished to the French would be profoundly misleading. And during his spells ashore at Folkestone, as he sat carousing with his comrades, no doubt his favourite toast was, ' Here's luck to long wars and high duties !'

The captain of one of the revenue cruisers applied for letters of marque. Allowed, but the revenue not to suffer by the indulgence. No compensation if his ship were damaged in fight, unless the fight were with a smuggling vessel. Not to leave his station on pretence of engaging the enemy. Thus he could do little privateering unless the French ventured within the limits of his station.

The excise officers seized a quantity of wine in a ' warehouse ' belonging to a person who horsed the road-wagons travelling between Southampton and London. The Customs Board were of opinion that there were no grounds of prosecution, unless the excisemen could prove that the jobmaster received the wine, knowing it to be contraband.

The following order was communicated as an incentive to heroism : ' On account of great increases in the Size and Force of smugling vessels, accompanied with such violent Outrages that in Defiance of all Law they have the Audacity not only to carry on their illicit Designs in Sight of the Revenue Cruisers, but whenever they have approached within a certain Distance have actually fired into and threatened to sink them, and that in such case the Mariners engaged in our Service have frequently refused to bear down and Repel their Attacks, alledging by way of Excuse that no Provision is made towards their Support in case they should receive an injury therefrom,' etc. The Board promised an annuity of £10 to any revenue mariner who might lose a hand or foot, or receive any serious injury, in such encounters, and to pay surgical expenses if he were only slightly wounded.

Soon after this the widow of a Southampton riding-officer who had been murdered by smugglers received an annuity of £15, and a yearly allowance of £2 10s. for each of her children under the age of fifteen.

The owner of a brick-kiln at Fawley approached the Board, stating that he had been 'continually teased and threatened' by the customs officers of Portsmouth and Southampton, who had told him they would seize any bricks shipped coastwise by him, unless he took out a cocket for every shipment. He pleaded that the vessels employed were very small, that the cocket expenses would, in all, amount to about 40s. on each consignment of about 10,000 bricks, and that he could not carry on his business under such conditions. 'If I have to do this it will ruin the brick-kiln.' 'As to Bricks, no man can say that ever a Cargo was Smugled, as they would not pay the very Freight to carry them abroad.' He stated that the Isle of Wight brickmakers were allowed by the Board to ship bricks coastwise with a 'sufferance' only, costing but 2s. per consignment.

Mr. Charles Clapham, Chairman of the Committee of Yorkshire Woollen Manufacturers, informed the Board that a foreigner had been detected in attempting to export a machine lately invented for spinning wool, and a model of another machine for preparing wool for spinning, and that there was another foreigner residing in Leeds, and engaged in the secret exportation of 'press paper,' an article used in the finishing of woollen cloth. The Board sent a memo. to Southampton, urging the collector to do his best in discovering such exportation.

The Italian silk merchants of London complained to the Treasury that their silks, imported from Italy via Ostend, had been detained as quarantinable. At this time imports from the Mediterranean coast of Italy were liable to quarantine, the plague prevailing in Turkey, etc.; but the silk merchants pleaded that their goods were manufactured in the interior of Italy, and taken overland to Ostend for shipment, and that therefore they had 'no communication ' with the Levant. The Treasury thereupon freed such goods from quarantine, and the Board apprised the various collectors to that effect.

A smuggler who had been pressed informed the Board of an old smuggling transaction in which he had been concerned, and asked to be released from his ship in order to give evidence against his comrades. But the customs solicitor stated that the men informed upon could not be found. So the informer had to remain, and unwillingly defend his country.

A communication from the Privy Council reached Southampton, to the effect that the plague raged in Servia, and that ' a new distemper ' had broken out in Belgrade. ' It begins with a wen on the throat, and death follows after three or four days.'

The *Rose* revenue cutter, the master of which had been recently granted letters of marque, captured the *Fox*, a well-known smuggling vessel, after a fierce engagement, in which the *Rose* was so badly damaged that, after being temporarily patched at Southampton, she was sent to London to lie up for repairs. The appraised value of the *Fox* on condemnation was £1,450.

The collector received a copy of certain correspondence between Sir William Hamilton at Naples and the Earl of Hillsborough. The former, in a letter dated July 31, 1781, conveyed intelligence of a startling kind. He stated that a vessel from Smyrna, with a foul bill of health, after being driven away from Ancona, had been quarantined at Venice, and her crew taken into the lazarette ; that another from Alexandria, with pestilence raging on board, had been conducted to Corfu by a Venetian ship, and that during the voyage her captain and three mariners escaped ; also that a Venetian vessel infected with plague had been burned with all her cargo at Malta, and her crew lazaretted. A Swedish vessel with plague on board had been driven away from Venice, and was adrift in the Mediterranean, and many other plague-smitten Levant traders were cruising in those waters. The king of Sicily had given orders that all Levant traders should be kept at a distance, and that the cavalry guard along the coast should be doubled to prevent the landing of infected persons. The British ambassador at Constantinople also wrote, stating that the plague was 'raging with dreadful fury' at Salonica. The collector apprised the captains of cruisers and the preventive staff generally.

A memo. from the Treasury arrived, embodying an extract from a letter sent by Lord Hillsborough. ' Intelligence has been received at my Office that it has become a capital trade on the coast of Kent and Sussex to build and sell to the Enemy cutters which are used as privateers by them, and that a Considerable Quantity of Cannon and Ammunition is carried from that Coast to France.' It went on to repeat information of forty pieces of cannon which were said to be lying concealed on the Kentish shore, and intended for the use of the French. It concluded, ' Will get further information of this.'

The collector issued an advertisement as below, offering a reward of £100 for the apprehension of certain persons who had rescued smuggled goods : ' Whereas, on Friday the second Day of this Instant November, A Large Seizure of Brandy was made by several of the Officers belonging to this Revenue in the Parish of Christchurch, Hants, & whilst the said Officers were endeavouring to convey the same to a Place of Safety a Daring and outrageous Gang of Smuglers on Horseback, to the number of 12 and upwards, some of whom had their faces black'd & were otherwise disguised, Armed with Blunderbusses, Muskets, Pistols, & other Offensive Weapons, forcibly & violently assaulted, beat, and wounded the said Officers, & carried away the said Seizure,' etc.

The Board issued an order as follows :

'Custom House, London,
' 5th Jan. 1782.

' The enormous Increase of Smugling, the Outrages with which it is carried on, the Mischiefs it Occasions to the Country, the Discouragement it Creates to all fair Traders, and the prodigious Loss the Revenue Sustains by it,' etc. The Board announced that they were ' Desirous to give a Great Cheque to this National Evil,' yet they were much dismayed at the officers' want of success in making captures, and believed that this ' defect ' would not have been ' if the Instructions and Orders given by this Board had been duly Observed.' ' We therefore enjoin you carefully to peruse those Orders, And the fresh Set of enlarged Instructions herewith sent.'

Yet large quantities of goods were occasionally captured. The Southampton record for the second half-yearly term in 1781 was striking. One seizure consisted of 3,305 gallons brandy and 1,620 gallons rum ; another of 85 gallons brandy, 70 gallons rum, 251 gallons geneva, 92 pieces muslin, and 7,563 pounds tea. There were also many small seizures, and the total appraised value was £3,854 14s.

The Attorney-General's opinion upon the matter of a husband's responsibility for his wife's contraband ventures was quoted in a Board's letter. It was to the effect that if the wife smuggled without her husband's privity she might be proceeded against summarily before justices. The husband need not be summoned, but in the information and proceedings the woman should be described as ' A.B., the wife of C.D.,' etc., and if she were convicted the justices might distrain on the husband's goods, unless there were a return of *nulla bona*, in which case the wife might be committed.

One of the revenue cruisers attacked the *Kite*, a smuggling cutter of 100 tons, belonging to Folkestone. After a long engagement the *Kite* beat her off, and escaped. A few days later the Portsmouth revenue cutter and the ' Excise cutter of Cowes,' while cruising in company in Sandown Bay, sighted the *Kite*. Being afraid to attack, they signalled for assistance to a Government cruiser that was near, and the latter, in company with the cutters, bore down upon the Folkestone vessel. The

smugglers thereupon took to their boats, landed in Shank-
lin Bay, and escaped. On boarding the *Kite*, the officers
found three of her crew in the forecastle, desperately
wounded. Her cargo had been run, except a few gallons
of spirits. It turned out that during the previous year
she had gone under the name of the *Union*, and had been
captured, condemned, and afterwards restored to her
owners, they paying a heavy fine. She had then been
altered and renamed, and her captain had actually succeeded in getting her approved as a privateer. The
letters of marque were found on board by the officers.

It may be well to conclude this chapter with a comprehensive review of the general condition of the Customs
at this interesting period. Evil indeed had the state of
the ancient department become. The bad old systems
of specialization of duties and cherishment of sinecures
constituted a serious menace to the trade of the kingdom.

London possessed about three-fourths of the import
trade, Liverpool one-eleventh, Bristol one-seventeenth,
Hull one-forty-sixth, and the balance went to sixty-nine
minor ports. About three-fourths of the sum expended in
drawbacks and bounties was paid in the port of London.
It was not uncommon for about a dozen of the minor ports
to show deficits, the expenses of management greatly exceeding the gross receipts. Usually these deficits occurred
at ports where not a penny was disbursed as drawback or
bounty.

Each outport throughout the kingdom had been certified since the Restoration, under the terms of an Exchequer commission, as a place approved for the transaction of import and export trade. When an investigation
was held with regard to this in 1783, the commissions
granted to Minehead, Chepstow, Gloucester, Llanelly,
and Scilly could not be found.

Forty-four revenue cruisers, carrying in all 1,041 men,
and costing between £40,000 and £50,000 annually,
guarded the coast from Berwick to Land's End, and occa-

sionally some of these were directed to scout between Ireland and England. Twenty of the cruisers were ' on the Establishment ' ; the others were run ' on contract,' and often the contractor was a customs official. The contract system, especially when managed by collectors as a private venture, was found to work badly. The largest and best-armed cruisers plied off Colchester, Dover, Sandwich, Deal, Rye, Southampton, Cowes, Poole, and St. Ives. The guard was strongest from Margate to Poole.

The principal ' seizing ports ' were London, Yarmouth, Harwich, Dover, Sandwich, Southampton, Cowes, Plymouth, and St. Ives. The value of the seizures made at London was about one-third of the total. In one year (profitable both to smugglers and seizers) the London return of the value of seized goods was over £60,000. In the same year Dover returned £13,000, Cowes £10,000, Plymouth nearly £9,000, Sandwich £6,500, Southampton nearly £7,000, Harwich nearly £7,000, Yarmouth nearly £5,000. The west-countrymen had improved but little on their ancient reputation, for St. Ives returned nearly £11,000—nearly treble the gross revenue produce of the port. Yet certain goods might be bought freely by coast-dwellers, at prices amounting to little more than one-third of the duties to which the goods were liable. So huge and industrious was the force engaged in contraband that the smugglers suffered by competition, and often had to ' undercut ' prices.

The systems of account and collection were preposterous. The number of ' branches '—for every duty was kept apart—ranged between ninety and one hundred. Of these, five were Plantation duties, and between twenty and thirty repealed duties, the latter figuring in account because many of the claims under them had not been fully answered. Each branch was a fiscal puzzle. There might be a dozen varying rates of duty on one article, each rate involving a separate computation. The number of branches was increased in every Session, for if Parliament took one duty off it speedily added two or three new ones. The correspondence between the outport collectors and the London Board was voluminous and bewildering, for the officers were continually asking for information upon points of revenue law and practice, and this may account for the scarcity of visits by the Commissioners. The officer who was an accurate computer of duties in one or two branches was esteemed a treasure. Tables of net duties published for the guidance of merchants and officials were often misleading, and the erroneous calculations influenced collection many years before they were detected.* It must be borne in mind that the duties were computed to remote fractions.

The central account was in a hopeless muddle. The various outport collectors sent the net produce of their ports to the Receiver-General in London, using bills and notes as instruments of remittance. The London takings reached the Receiver-General in gross, usually in the form of money or bonds. The Plantation collectors remitted their balances in bills or bullion. (The proceeds of the 4½ per cent. tax were, as previously stated, mostly remitted in kind. But this was a separate branch entirely, and in our accounts of Plantation returns we ignore it. It produced about twice as much as all the other Plantation duties put together.) Certain expenses of home and colonial management were paid by the Receiver-General out of the Plantation receipts.

When remittance was thus made, an account of the same, with a statement of the deductions, if any, made from the gross receipts, was sent to the Controller-General. That official compiled an annual return, in which the Receiver-General was charged with the total of sums advised, and this went to the 'Auditor of Imprest.' The Receiver-General furnished for the same period an account of receipts and disbursements, and sent it to the same office of audit. The accounts were from January 6 in one year to January 5 in the next—

* Note particularly 'Crouch's Survey of the Customs,' considered an infallible mine of reference for many years.

both dates inclusive—and puzzling accounts they were, for it should be stated that not only were the receipts under the various branches kept apart, but an attempt was made to apportion in similar fashion the expenses of collection.   The headings of the various columns were venerable formulæ, and would appear to have been contrived with a view towards mystification.   When these circumstances, with the brief hours of employ, and the general drowsiness prevailing in ancient Government offices, are taken into consideration, none need wonder that the accounts were usually presented for audit when about two years overdue.   Then the Auditor of Imprest got to work, and what did he ?   Merely checked the casts !   The two accounts never agreed, but that did not trouble the scrutineer.   Even if they had agreed, it would have proved little, for the Auditor, not being a customs official, was quite ignorant of ' the practice.'   He knew not the methods of receipt of duty ; he did not understand the system of computation used for any separate rate on any article in any branch ; the amounts stated as incurred for salaries and incidents might be excessive, but he knew not how to detect an overcharge.   So he sat quiet, checked the casts, and never called for a single minor voucher.   His audit was a solemn farce.

As to collection.   There were five collectors in London, seventy-two at the outports, twenty-six in the Plantations.

The London collectors or cashiers paid in the bulk of their takings during the current year, *always reserving a portion*.   For instance, the Collector Outwards (the duke of Manchester) instructed his deputy to bank a large sum of public money in the principal's name.   Occasionally the deputy drew a portion and paid it into the Receiver-General, but it is observable that after such withdrawal he invariably banked a sum larger than that withdrawn, and thus the patentee's balance throve steadily upon public money, till certain Commissioners of Account interfered.   It does not appear that the moneys thus reserved were actually *appropriated*, but the practice of ' keeping a bit in hand' was general. The Receiver-General had no power of detecting, neither had the Controller-General, except by observing that the receipts as a whole were falling off. When a collector's account was rendered, the casts were checked, and no more. The Board had little power of intervention. The patentees who dominated the various offices of receipt were practically independent of the Commissioners. The latter might stop a patentee's salary if they came to know that he was acting to the prejudice of the Revenue, but it does not appear that they had any power to push investigation. They might not scrutinize his books or check his cash.

At the outports many accounts of dead or dismissed collectors remained unliquidated. The outport books were clogged with records of these ancient liabilities. Many of the duties unaccounted for belonged to branches that had since been repealed, and they had been computed by methods which had passed out of ken. The current accounts were bemuddled. A collector might have paid in every penny of net duty he had handled, and still have undischarged accounts of his own, so mysteriously did receipts, drawbacks, allowances, and bounties, cross and intermingle.

The Plantation business was still worse. It appears that the accounts were never passed in the Exchequer, so hopelessly imperfect was their condition. Balances a century old were still 'depending.' As previously stated, the remittances were in bills and bullion. Often the Receiver-General let the bills lie unrealized for long periods. But one construction can with reason be placed on such conduct—viz., that the person on whom the bills were drawn recompensed him for the delay. One year, though the Board had stopped the salaries of a number of colonial officials for misbehaviour, the colonial and home charges of management swallowed all the gross Customs produce of the Plantations, except £4 7s. 8¼d. Yet the Receiver-General paid into the Exchequer on account of the Plantations for that year over £5,000! It is probable that he realized on his stock of unpresented bills, yet by no means certain ; for on another occasion, when the charges exceeded the gross produce, and he was unable to complete payment of the home management, he made up the deficit by appropriating a sum from a British Customs branch. It is apparent that so long as a tolerable amount was paid into the Exchequer yearly no one was troubled as to outstanding matters and cash balances.

It may cause surprise that the collection of Plantation customs was continued when the net proceeds were so insignificant (rarely amounting to £5,000 a year). But it must be remembered that the Plantation collectors administered the Act of Navigation, and the laws regulating Plantation commerce. The takings really formed a 'Commercial Police Fund,' the ' police ' acting as guardians of the Imperial interest, collecting maintenance in the form of customs duties, and transmitting to the Imperial Exchequer any trifling balance that might remain. Nor must the extent to which the colonies contributed towards their own embarrassment be measured by the ' gross produce ' of the Plantation customs. The officers took fees and extorted ' gratuities,' and these did not appear in the account.

The Scottish Receiver-General made a practice of withholding even larger sums than his fellow-accountants in London, although the Scottish return was in all respects eminently unsatisfactory. During one year the English gross produce was over £3,700,000, and the Scottish barely £250,000. So heavily did salaries and local bounties bleed the Scottish total that the net produce was little over £90,000. Two years later the Scottish Receiver-General transmitted to the Receiver-General in London, to be paid into the Exchequer, a sum for the year amounting only to £60,000. When the returns were so trifling, the Scottish cashier should have known better than to keep back occasionally a sum of £40,000 or £50,000. What would have been thought of the collector of Bristol, where the gross return often approached that

of all Scotland, if he had kept back half of the net proceeds ?

The Coinage duty, both in England and Scotland,
failed to meet the expenses of the London and Edinburgh
Mints, and the deficiency had to be made up out of the
Supplies of the year. The Exchequer officials never
knew what these yearly grants amounted to.

The ' manning ' of the higher customs offices was both
costly and defective. Most of the more lucrative posts
were held by people of rank, who never performed any of
the duties, but entrusted them to deputies. In many
of the offices there were no duties to perform. All these
' employments ' were secured by patents granted by the
Crown. Some of the endowments were ' for life,' some
' during pleasure.'

There were three other methods of appointing officials.
The Treasury appointed by Constitution or named by
warrant. The Chancellor of the Exchequer might appoint by warrant. The Board of Customs appointed
inferior officers by commission or order.

The sinecurists endowed by royal patent named their
own deputies, in some cases subject to approbation by the
Treasury. We may take the ' patent customer ' at the
outports as representative of the obsolete type of office,
the ' patent searcher ' as representative of the radically
useless.

It has been stated in a previous chapter that when
Customs farming was finally abolished in 1671 a new staff
of collectors and searchers appeared at the outports,
but the old ' customers and searchers ' were allowed to
remain. Thus arose the system of having a collector, a
controller, and one or more searchers, to do the actual
work, and a patent customer with a controller, and a
patent searcher as well, to do little or nothing but pocket
salaries, fees, and gratuities.

The patent customer did absolutely nothing. His
deputy collected the principal's perquisites and his own,
and sent the principal's share to Bath, Brighton, London,

or wherever the principal might happen to be. Sometimes the patent controller acted as customer's deputy ; sometimes the patent controller was non-resident, and had a deputy of his own. Sometimes the *actual* collector acted as deputy to both patent customer and patent controller. The patent controller, when resident, pottered a little with the ' coast bonds ' (quite a superfluous exercise, for the actual controller also dealt with those documents, and duplication was unnecessary), and sent certain quarterly accounts to the Controller-General, which were never inspected on receipt, but tied up in bundles and put away. The patent searchers did absolutely nothing. Their deputies collected fees and gratuities.

Some of these sinecurists lived abroad, and whenever an inquiry was held into the matter of emoluments it was found difficult to trace the absentees. Yet it is certain the deputies knew where their patrons resided, or they could not have remitted the emoluments. It would appear that they were instructed to forget addresses, except when forwarding the spoil.

Sometimes a patentee held several sinecures, and sometimes, for cheapness, two or three patentees employed one deputy among them. These arrangements illustrate still more vividly the utter uselessness of both patentees and deputies. About 150 of these officials were quartered upon the outports, and so vigilant were some of the deputies in collecting fees that small trading contracts were frequently abandoned because the Customs exactions would have swallowed all the profits. It was not uncommon to postpone the departure of one of the many coasting ' hoys ' because the freight was insufficient to answer these wicked impositions.

In one year the gross Customs produce of the port of Cardiff was but £54, which proves that Cardiff was a quieter port than the Cardiff of to-day. Of course there was a large deficit, for the salaries and incidental expenses of the actual collecting staff amounted to several hundreds. Yet the patent customer's takings were £504, his deputy acknowledged receiving £23, the patent controller took £332, and the patent searcher £162.

The returns from Carlisle were trifling, yet during one year the patent customer's perquisites were £343, the patent controller's £211, and the patent searcher's £185.

(Note that the bulk of the above was collected from coastwise traffic, or from export transactions that yielded no revenue except to the patentees.)

Extremely profitable to patent officers was the ancient port of Chester. In one year the patent customer received £1,593, his deputy acknowledged receiving £103, the patent controller received £766, and the patent searcher £1,323.

Averaged, the fees taken by patent customers at outports were to the customers' salaries as 10 to 1 ; those of the patent controllers and searchers 12 to 1. And none of these officials did a stroke of useful work.

It had been a practice since the days of yore to issue ' port-books ' to the various outports. These were forwarded periodically by the Remembrancer of the Exchequer, but for many, many years scarce any use had been made of them. Sometimes certain items, previously recorded elsewhere, were entered, and the books returned to the Exchequer as of old, but in most cases they were thrown aside when received by the outport men, and never handled more. The Remembrancer kept an account of the books sent out and those returned, but though the output was huge and the return diminutive he never queried for the balance. Why should he ? He had his allowance for transmission, and the Exchequer Usher (Horace Walpole) made a handsome profit on stationery. So the dreary fraud went on, year after year, though Commissioners of Inquiry raged and protested. It should be mentioned that had the books been regularly used and returned they would have served no practical purpose. The entries would have been mere duplicates or triplicates of entries which in themselves were valueless.

It appears that all the actual collectors of revenue at the outports were nominated by Treasury Warrant. Record has already been made of one appointment of an incompetent person, and of an arrangement between the Lord Treasurer and the Board of Customs that the latter should in future apprise Whitehall of any similar slip that might occur. Yet it is evident that this was but a fleeting reform, for many years later the Board were practically impotent in that respect. They merely inquired, whenever a new collector was named, whether he had been previously dismissed from the Customs! If he had, they returned the warrant. But they could go no further. If he had not been dismissed, they had to appoint him at once, and at his leisure he entered upon the important office, without the slightest official instruction in its duties. It might be found, after he reached his port, that he was quite ignorant of Customs work, and either unable or unwilling to learn. And yet when the Treasury approved a landing-surveyor, a landing-waiter, or a coast-waiter, the Board had power to place the nominee under instruction.

There were many useless officials in the port of London, and some of them were extremely expensive to the public. It must be stated that a Commissioner of Customs, although his office was no sinecure, had no Customs emolument except his salary, and an allowance for the extra work entailed by administering the quarantine regulations. There were nine Commissioners, each of whom received £1,000 a year, and £200 as 'Quarantine allowance.' Judging from the memoranda, they had to perform a deal of intricate and often distasteful work.

In the secretarial department were eighteen clerks, supported by salaries, fees, allowances, and gratuities.

In the legal department there were six solicitors, with salaries, allowances, and law fees (*vide* p. 310).

There was a gentleman named Poyntz, who was 'Inspector of Prosecutions.' He dealt with informations, and the king's share of the proceeds of seizures (*vide*

p. 344). It appears that he had little to do, and much for doing it. ('Heavy has been, and still is, the expense to the public of this useless office'—*Report of Messrs. Anguish, Roe, etc.*) He had held his post by patent since 1741. During the ten years from 1772 to 1781 inclusive, his annual perquisites averaged about £3,700. But when, in 1781, the Board were empowered to amend the application of the king's share, his yearly takings dropped to a little over £1,400. He then petitioned the Treasury, stating that he had made his future arrangements under the impression that his income would remain at the high figure. This, though he admitted that the takings had risen immensely since the date of the patent. And the Treasury granted compensation. The Great Commoner's son signed the Minute of grant, thus establishing another record of what Junius had once called the 'benefit of complaining.'

There was an office called 'The Receipt of Fines and Forfeitures from the Outports.' In 1777 the principal was dismissed. He owed the public over £20,000, about half of which was subsequently recovered from his estate. In 1782 his successor was found to be in arrear to the amount of £7,500. The public lost over £4,000.

There was an officer called 'The Customer of Cloth exported and of Petty Custom outward.' The outward cloth duties had long been abolished except on white woollens, and Petty Custom outward was no more. During ten years, from 1775 to 1784 inclusive, the duties collected on white woollens averaged about £64 a year. The fees and gratuities taken by the 'customer' averaged £76. For, though Petty or Aliens' Custom had lapsed, this patentee still collected fees, etc., from alien exporters.

Nearly all the more profitable offices were sinecures. The patent Collector Inwards received in all over £2,700 a year, and the patent Collector Outwards over £2,100. Neither of them ever attended. The Surveyor of Subsidies and Petty Customs, whose occupation had long ceased, made £1,850 a year. He had nothing to do, and a deputy and a clerk to help him, whose perquisites amounted to £180.

In the three offices mentioned below the work was done by deputies and clerks. The principals did not attend, but their perquisites were collected and transmitted by the underlings, and amounted to the following sums :

	Per Year.
Supervisor of Receiver-General's duties	£660
Registrar-General of British Ships	690
Inspector-General of Imports and Exports ..	780

The two patent searchers at Gravesend, who never went afloat, and rarely even saw the river, divided between them £1,200 a year. The Registrar of Seizures made about £500 a year. He was one of the unemployed.

The established officers who really went on duty and performed useful work also charged fees and received gratuities. Some of the memoranda of receipt are extremely suggestive. For instance, the Receiver-General, in addition to many other fees and gratuities, took during one year over £100 as 'compliments on salaries and debentures.' This meant that officers, when taking their salaries, and merchants, when cashing their drawback certificates, left small sums on the counter as presents to the lordly paymaster. When duties were paid to the various receivers, it was the practice for the payers not to take change for an odd sixpence. No doubt they were equally polite when cashing debentures.

The Receiver-General's chief clerk charged the owners of whalers 10s. 6d. each, whenever he 'marked their papers' for the Greenland Bounty. The chief Teller in the Pay Office had a fee of £250 for paying the London Establishment. His assistant usually received about £25 as ' New Year's gifts from inferior officers.' Another clerk had £10 a year in gifts from patentees, and six guineas in Christmas-boxes from the tradesmen who supplied the Custom-house with coals.

There was an office called ' The Receipt of Great Custom outwards.' There had been no collection since the abolition of the outward wool and lead duties, yet the officers continued to draw their salaries, and levy fees on coastwise traffic.

The Long Room officers were divided into four classes. Class 1 dealt with export and import business. The fees collected in this department were to the salaries received as 5 to 1. Class 2 dealt with imports only, and the fees were as 4 to 1. Class 3 dealt with exports only, and the fees were as 18 to 1. Class 4 — the jerquers—merely checked books and warrants. In this branch the salaries exceeded the perquisites, for the latter could only be collected from shipmasters who were paid portages, and ' inferior officers ' whose landing-books had been certified.

The Usher of the Long Room rarely attended. His clerk and deputy did the work, which consisted principally in collecting fees on the various oaths made to bonds, manifests, etc. The Usher had 2d. for ' every oath outwards.' The deputy had 6d. for every transaction necessitating one to three oaths, and 1s. on four to six. Then came the clerk, and took fees on the same scale as the deputy. Thus a single oath cost 1s. 2d., of which the Usher had 2d., the deputy 6d., and the clerk 6d.

The landing-waiters made about £220 a year each in fees and gratuities—nearly three times the salary of their office. Their ' gratuities ' were for attending at ' sufferance wharves ' to supervise work which should have been performed at the ' legal quays,' and for working after or before the legal hours.

The gaugers were appointed by the Treasury. Usually they received 3d. a cask from merchants, and 7s. 6d. for every 100 barrels of tar gauged. Their gratuities were about double the amount of their salaries.

The chief patent searcher's official income, after paying his deputy, etc., was about £500. The five patent under-searchers did better still. Only one of them attended. He paid no deputy, and his takings amounted to about £900 a year. The other four were sinecurists. Each of them employed a deputy at £160, and pocketed about £740.

The officers who attended at the East India Company's warehouses received many gifts of tea and spices, besides ' compliments,' Christmas-boxes, etc.

There were sixteen ' Land Carriage officers,' and a surveyor to direct them. Their work consisted in hanging about inns in London and Westminster, for the purpose of peeping into carriages and stables, to ascertain whether uncustomed articles were conveyed under the seats or concealed amid the straw and hay. So far as can be ascertained, they collected no fees, nor does it appear that they made any seizures.

Besides the officers specified, there was an army of coast-waiters, tide-waiters, boatmen, constables, door-keepers, and messengers. We find from the Board's memoranda that these had often to be rebuked for trying to extort illegal fees and gratuities. The large staff of river inspectors, surveyors, etc., appear to have subsisted principally upon salaries.

The laws were still in existence forbidding officers to take more in fees than the amounts prescribed by Parliament. Yet many of the fees were ' of usage ' only. It had been repeatedly directed that tables of fees should be posted at the various ports, and lists of transactions which were exempt. The first direction was occasionally complied with ; the last never. The officers, especially at remote ports, charged almost at will. Extra dispatch could in most cases be procured by augmenting gratuities. Occasionally one officer would collect the fees for several transactions, and divide them among the officers concerned, and often there was a squabble over the division.

Another grievance of which the mercantile public complained bitterly was the delay caused by the brief ' clerical hours ' and the numerous customs holidays. The Long Room hours at this period were from nine till noon. The jerquers attended from nine till three. The searchers attended from nine till four, and took two and a half hours for lunch. Outside, of course, the working day was much longer. There were forty-five customs holidays in a year, commencing with ' Circumcision ' and ending with ' Holy Innocents.' The ships from foreign usually arrived in fleets, and there was much delay when a couple of holidays occurred during one week (sometimes on successive days).

But there were premonitions of reform. Various committees of inquiry had pried into the dusty corners and mouldy crannies of the Revenue departments, and the maritime branch had not escaped its share of overhauling. The Board of Customs clamoured louder than ever for wider powers of control, reward, and punishment. The official atmosphere was stirred with whispers of consolidation and retrenchment. Consolidation was at hand, though it was not destined to confer lasting benefit. Retrenchment was about to be attempted—attempted cautiously, and not always in the quarters where retrenchment was most desirable.

LIST OF AUTHORITIES.

Wine : 3 Geo. III., c. 12.

Protective measures and prohibitions : 4 Geo. III., c. 9 ; 4 Geo. III., c. 15 ; 4 Geo. III., c. 26 ; 4 Geo. III., c. 27 ; 5 Geo. III., c. 12 ; 5 Geo. III., c. 45 ; 5 Geo. III., c. 48 ; 6 Geo. III., c. 12 ; 6 Geo. III., c. 49 ; 6 Geo. III., c. 52 ; 7 Geo. III., c. 30 ; 7 Geo. III., c. 2 ; 7 Geo. III., c. 41 ; 7 Geo. III., c. 46 ; 9 Geo. III., c. 38 ; 10 Geo. III., c. 17 ; 11 Geo. III., c. 37 ; 11 Geo. III., c. 50 ; 12 Geo. III., c. 50 ; 13 Geo. III., c. 43 ; 14 Geo. III., c. 19 ; 14 Geo. III., c. 5, 11 ; 14 Geo. III., c. 39 ; 14 Geo. III., c. 42 ; 14 Geo. III., c. 45 ; 14 Geo. III., c. 54 ; 15 Geo. III., c. 10 ; 15 Geo. III., c. 18 ; ' Instructions to Guy Carleton ' (Canadian Archives) ; 15 Geo. III., c. 34, 35, 37 ; 15 Geo. III., c. 45 ; 16 Geo. III., c. 5 ; 17 Geo. III., c. 27 ; 18 Geo. III., c. 12 ; 18 Geo. III., c. 13 ; 18 Geo. III., c. 55, 56 ; 19 Geo. III., c. 48 : 19 Geo. III., c. 53 ; 20 Geo. III., c. 46 ; 20 Geo. III., c. 55 ; 21 Geo. III., c. 16 ; 21 Geo. III., c. 50 ; 22 Geo. III., c. 71 ; 23 Geo. III., c. 79 ; 24 Geo. III., c. 21 ; 26 Geo. III., c. 40.

Departmental incidents : Sir William Musgrave's ' Memoranda '; Poole Letter Books ; Southampton Letter Books ; Fifteenth Report of Sir Guy Carleton's Committee.

Permanent branches of revenue : 5 Geo. III., c. 35 ; 9 Geo. III., c. 25 ; 18 Geo. III., c. 27 ; 19 Geo. III., c. 25 ; 20 Geo. III., c. 30 ; 20 Geo. III., c. 52 ; 21 Geo. III., c. 16 ; 22 Geo. III., c. 28 ;

22 Geo. III., c. 39, 61, 66 ; 24 Geo. III., c. 11 ; 24 Geo. III., c. 24 ;
24 Geo. III., c. 36 ; 24 Geo. III., c. 46 ; 24 Geo. III., c. 49, 51, 53 ;
26 Geo. III., c. 42 ; 26 Geo. III., c. 59.

Isle of Man : 7 Geo. III., c. 45.

Excise Duties : 9 Geo. III., c. 6.

Frauds : 12 Geo. III., c. 55 ; 17 Geo. III., c. 41.

Temporary imposts : 13 Geo. III., c. 67 ; 21 Geo. III., c. 32 ;
24 Geo. III., c. 18.

East India Company : 14 Geo. III., c. 34 ; 24 Geo. III., c. 38 ;
25 Geo. III., c. 74.

Hull : 14 Geo. III., c. 56.

Quebec : 14 Geo. III., c. 88.

Privateers : 17 Geo. III., c. 7.

Preventive measures : 17 Geo. III., c. 41 ; 18 Geo. III., c. 40 ;
3 Geo. III., c. 22 ; 19 Geo. III., c. 69 ; 21 Geo. III., c. 39 ;
24 Geo. III., c. 47.

Tobacco : 19 Geo. III., c. 35 ; 22 Geo. III., c. 73 ; 23 Geo. III.,
c. 75 ; 25 Geo. III., c. 81.

Accounts : 20 Geo. III., c. 54 ; 25 Geo. III., c. 19.

Officers : 22 Geo. III., c. 41 ; 22 Geo. III., c. 75.

Treaties : 22 Geo. III., c. 46.

Exchequer : 23 Geo. III., c. 82.

Repeal of ancient duties : 24 Geo. III., c. 16.

CHAPTER IX

THE various branches of Customs revenue were ' consolidated ' by the thirteenth statute of the twenty-seventh
year of George III.'s reign. The Act opened with a
statement that was certainly unchallengeable :

' Whereas the present mode of charging and computing
the several duties of Customs and Excise, and other duties
under the management of the Commissioners of Excise in
England and Scotland respectively, is in many instances
intricate and complicated, and productive of much embarrassment to the persons who are to pay the same, as
well as of great perplexity in the Accounts of Public
Revenue,' etc.

The Act provided that from and after May 10, 1787,
the existing customs and excise duties should cease, and
be replaced by new duties, and that the said new duties
should not be subject to discount. The drawbacks were
also to cease, and be renewed in other form.

The separate Boards for England and Scotland were
maintained, and enjoined to keep separate accounts of
revenue. The methods of prevention and prosecution
survived, and all goods previously duty-free continued
exempt. The hours of lading and discharge, the officers'
fees, and the official hours of attendance, remained unaltered. The bounties on exported goods endured. The
restrictions upon French commerce were removed. A

slight alteration was made in the method of abating duty on damaged goods, it being provided that the amount of abatement should be settled by ' two indifferent* merchants.' The bounty called ' Portage,' payable to masters who reported their cargoes satisfactorily, was abolished. Nearly all the regulations annexed to the old ' Book of Rates ' were repealed.

Under the new method the duties on all goods, except coal, might be bonded—*i.e.*, payment might be postponed until the merchant required his goods for sale, he furnishing security. The East India Company were to pay their customs when due,† instead of, as before, paying them in gross at stated periods. In order that customs moneys might reach the Receiver-General as early as possible, the duties collected in London were to be paid in on day of receipt. Drawbacks and bounties payable in London were to be disbursed by the Receiver-General ; at outports the collectors might pay. The Act stated that under the previous system many collectors had applied moneys taken as duty to the wrong ' branches,' and that their accounts remained ' unsettled and unliquidated,' and it directed that all such erroneous accounts should be promptly closed.

By the new system the duties upon most articles, instead of being levied as percentages upon value, were expressed in definite sums. The principal exceptions were the rates on the East India Company's goods (which in most instances were *ad valorem*, duty being computed as a percentage on the gross prices obtained at the periodical sales) and on unenumerated goods. Unenumerated goods were to be assessed as to value according to importer's or exporter's declaration, but the collectors were still empowered to buy them if undervalued.

The new duties, drawbacks, etc., were expressed in six schedules, as below :

Schedule A included the duties inward and outward upon most articles, and the drawbacks payable.

* Disinterested.　　　† As soon as possible after sale.

Schedule B included the duties and drawbacks upon the East India Company's goods.

Schedule C included the duties and drawbacks upon goods distinctively French.

Schedule D included the duties and drawbacks upon 'other unenumerated goods'—*i.e.*, articles that varied much in quality, and therefore could not be safely charged with specific duties.

Schedule E included the duties outward on unenumerated goods.

Schedule F included the excise duties, drawbacks, allowances, and bounties.

All customs, excise, and inland duties were to be carried to one fund, called 'The Consolidated Fund.' The Coinage duty was abolished, and the Treasury were empowered to issue a sum of £15,000 annually out of the customs receipts, towards the maintenance of the Mint. Denizens and aliens paid the same duties, but telling advantages were granted to certain goods brought in British-built ships. As of old, the wine duties were lighter at outports than at London.

The rates on French goods were considerably lessened by the new Act. To give an idea of the enormous burdens that had been gradually piled upon French trade, and the large reduction considered necessary, we quote the tunnage at various stages of the period extending from 1611 to 1787. The rates given are those levied at outports, upon wines imported in British-built ships, for sale, and filled at landing. Up to 1782 the rates are 'denizens' duties.'

French Wine, the Tun of 252 Gallons.

	£ s. d.		£ s. d.
1611	2 0 0	1787	25 4 0
1725	48 11 8	Excise duty ..	17 17 0
1774	64 11 8		
1782	90 3 10	Total	43 1 0

We now furnish the duties on a few other familiar articles. When at any period used there was a discount allowed for ready-money, or a preferential rate for goods brought in a British-built ship, or a preferential rate for denizens, we deduct the discount, and select the preferential rate. Thus we quote the *lowest* net duties payable. Fractions rejected.

Candles of Tallow, per Cwt.

						£	s.	d.
1600	..	.. Not on list						
1611	..	.. Not on list	1774	..	..	1	4	1
		£ s. d.	1782	..	..	1	6	2
1660	..	.. 0 1 4	1787	..	..	1	12	8
1725	..	.. 1 2 8						

Venice Soap, per Cwt.

			£	s.	d.				£	s.	d.
1600	..	..	0	1	8	1774	..	..	1	19	6
1611	..	..	0	3	4	1782	..	..	2	2	0
1660	..	..	0	2	10	1787	..	.. Not on list
1725	..	..	1	16	6						

Currants, per Cwt.

			£	s.	d.				£	s.	d.
1600	..	..	0	1	6	1774	..	..	1	2	1
1611	..	..	0	4	10	1782	..	..	1	2	2
1660	..	..	0	5	8	1787	..	..	1	3	4
1725	..	..	0	16	1						

White Unrefined Sugar, not of Plantations, per Cwt. (Plantation Sugar was preferentially treated.)

			£	s.	d.				£	s.	d.
1600	..	..	0	3	4	1774	..	..	1	15	6
1611	..	..	0	8	4	1782	..	..	2	3	4
1660	..	..	0	6	11	1787	..	..	2	5	6
1725	..	..	1	0	10						

Refined Loaf Sugar, per Cwt.

						£	s.	d.
1600	..	.. Not on list						
1611	..	.. Not on list	1774	..	..	4	2	1
		£ s. d.	1782	..	..	4	14	6
1660	..	.. 0 16 1	1787	..	..	4	18	8
1725	..	.. 2 8 6						

Leaf Tobacco, not of Plantations, per Pound.

	£	s.	d.		£	s.	d.
1600	0	0	4	1774—Spanish ..	0	2	3
1611	0	1	4	French ..	0	6	8
1660	0	0	5	1782—Spanish ..	0	2	11
1725—Spanish ..	0	1	6	French ..	0	8	2
French ..	0	5	10	1787—All leaf tobacco			
				not of Plantations	0	3	6

Leaf Tobacco of Plantations, per Pound. (Irish-grown=
Plantation.)

	£	s.	d.		£	s.	d.
1600	0	0	4	1774	0	0	6
1611	0	1	4	1782—From place of			
1660	0	0	1	growth ..	0	0	10
1725	0	0	4	1787	0	1	3

Apples, per Five Bushels. (The duty was levied per one or three
bushels. The duty on five bushels is given to effect comparison
with the earlier rates, which were so low that the poundage on
a single bushel cannot conveniently be quoted.)

	£	s.	d.		£	s.	d.
1600	0	0	1	1774	0	10	4
1611	0	0	1	1782	0	10	10
1660	0	0	1	1787	0	11	8
1725	0	10	4				

White Salt, per 40 Bushels of 84 Pounds each.

	£	s.	d.		£	s.	d.
1600	0	1	4	1774	0	9	10
1611	0	1	4	1782	0	10	10
1660	0	1	3	1787	0	11	5
1725	0	8	6				

Before comparing the duties on wheat, we must re-
capitulate the conditions governing rates. From 1600 to
1787 there was a specified ‘ plenty price ’—a standard
(varying occasionally) which indicated full garners and a
plentiful supply of bread. In 1600 and 1611 the ‘ plenty
price ’ did not affect the import duty, but when the
standard was exceeded wheat might not be exported.
In 1660 and afterwards, when the ‘ plenty price ’ was
exceeded, the import duties were lowered. For instance,
under the Consolidating Act of 1787, when wheat was at

less than 48s. a quarter, the import duty was £1 4s. 3d. ;
when it was at 48s. or more the duty was but 6d. The rates
quoted for comparison are those levied when wheat was
at the ' plenty price ' ; therefore they are the _highest_
duties payable.

Wheat, per Quarter of Eight Bushels.

		£	s.	d.				£	s.	d.
1600	.. ..	0	0	4	1774	..	..	1	1	9
1611	.. ..	0	0	4	1782	..	..	1	3	1
1660	.. ..	0	1	10	1787	..	..	1	4	3
1725	.. ..	0	19	9						

Below is a comparison of the 1782 and 1787 duties on
certain other goods :

	1782.			1787.		
	£	s.	d.	£	s.	d.
Wax candles, per pound	0	1	1	0	1	8
Hard soap, per cwt.	2	2	0	2	4	0
Soft soap ,, ...	1	15	8	1	17	5
Hay, per load of 18 cwt.	0	10	6	0	11	0
Hops, per cwt.	5	13	4	5	18	10
Thrown silk, dyed, per pound of 16 ounces	1	1	6	1	4	9

It will be observed that the tendency of the new Act
was to increase rates, except on French goods. In comparing the seventeenth century duties with those of the
eighteenth, it should be taken into account that the value
of money decreased during the 187 years under survey.
This should also be borne in mind when the annual proceeds are compared. It will now be useful to state the
amounts paid into the Exchequer, from Customs, at
certain stages during the period extending from 1600 to
1787.

*The net yearly Customs revenue during the reign of

---

* This was never intended to be a statistical treatise, yet great
pains have been taken in comparing tables furnished by previous
writers who dealt largely in figures. It would seem that
many of the tables given by them are misleading. They have
occasionally misapprehended returns, through confusing the
amounts stated as ' Net Produce ' with the amounts actually
paid into the Exchequer. It is difficult to explain the difference

James I. can rarely have approached £200,000. During Charles I.'s reign revenue matters were immensely confused by the squabbles between king and Parliament, and thus it is unsafe even to guess at returns. Proceeding to Commonwealth times, we find in Thurloe's collection an estimate of a year's proceeds of Customs and Excise, and from this we assume that the average net Customs return under the Protectorate was about £450,000.

In the early part of Charles II.'s reign Sir Philip Warwick held that though the rates and scope of taxation had increased the proceeds were less than under the Commonwealth. Davenant maintained that towards the end of the reign Customs and Excise produced about equal amounts, and he quoted the Excise return as about

---

between 'Net Produce' and 'Payments into Exchequer,' as shown in the old customs tables of proceeds, but an attempt must be made to display an annual account.

The 'Gross Receipts' from each branch were shown and totalled, and the total represented the 'Gross Produce.' From this was deducted the amount of 'Payments,' made up of drawbacks, bounties, salaries, and incidents. The residue was the 'Net Produce,' but the exact amount of this was not paid into the Exchequer. A considerable sum, made up of 'Debts decreased in Money,' 'Debts decreased on Bonds,' and 'Moneys overpaid,' was added to the 'Net Produce,' and another large sum, made up of 'Debts incurred in Money,' 'Debts incurred on Bonds,' and 'Overpayments decreased,' was deducted. Thus in one year the actual 'Payments into Exchequer' might greatly exceed the 'Net Produce,' and in the following year the 'Net Produce' might exceed the 'Payments into Exchequer.' It would be possible to quote instances in which a statist has mixed these varying returns, yet called one series of results a table of actual payments, and another a table of net products.

The sums quoted from 1700 to 1787 in the present treatise are taken from a Parliamentary Return furnished in 1869. This may be approximately correct. Yet one thing is certain : the Parliamentary Return renders no exact information as to the growth of the revenue year by year, for the East India Company were often in arrear to the extent of hundreds of thousands of pounds, and made up the deficiency in a subsequent year. The revenue officials who acted as receivers in London and Edinburgh were also in the habit of withholding large sums, as has already been stated. Therefore it has been deemed best to make comparison at intervals of *ten* years, comparing 1732 with 1742, etc.

£500,000 per annum. It is likely that the average net Customs yield under Charles did not exceed £450,000 a year. (See p. 118 of this treatise, in which the return of 1680 is stated. That return was, of course, much larger than the yearly product at the beginning of the reign.)

After 1688 taxation increased immensely. Population had also increased since the time of the Commonwealth, and the Navigation and Plantation Acts were held to have assisted English commerce. Yet the Customs return for the four years ending in 1692 was only about £2,800,000—say £700,000 a year. From 1692 to the end of William's reign four permanent branches of Customs and one complete Subsidy were added. In 1702 the return was about £1,470,000.

During Anne's reign ten permanent branches and a Subsidy—made up by the combined ⅓ and ⅔ Subsidies— were added. In 1712 the return was about £1,481,000.

From 1713 to 1722 two permanent branches were added. Return for 1722, £1,490,000. Return in 1732, £1,690,000. From 1733 to 1742 Sir Robert Walpole was at the head of public affairs. Return in 1742, £1,280,000 only. From 1743 to 1752 the Glass Duty, a Subsidy, and several permanent branches, including the ' Additional Wine Duty,' were added. (This last came out in 1745, and though there was much wine-drinking about that time, the 1746 return was but £1,017,000). In 1752 the return was £1,630,000. A Subsidy was added in 1759, and the return for 1762 was £1,820,000. From 1763 to 1772 several permanent inward and two outward branches were added. Return for 1772, about £2,500,000. From 1773 to 1782 several important branches were added, and two imposts, each of 5 per cent. on proceeds. Return for 1782, about £2,900,000.

During the latter part of the period traversed, export duties had been removed from many kinds of British goods, and the systems of drawback and bounty had been extensively remodelled. It is likely that in 1782 about

£2,000,000 had been taken from the *gross* receipts to meet debentures under the above heads. Still, £2,900,000 appears a paltry return.

It is evident that the fiscal experimenters were slowly learning better doctrine. The Consolidating Act was not a dazzling effort, yet it was a step in the right direction. It was received with acclamation, especially by merchants. Even the increased duties were for the time overlooked by the rejoicing community ; for it was a blissful change to be able to ascertain the duty on a parcel of goods by a single computation, instead of struggling through a dozen. The saving effected in stationery alone must have been great, and little may justly be said against any measure that dethrones circumlocution.

Further increases were soon deemed necessary. Additional duties were levied on foreign glass, and placed with the Excise.

It was enacted that foreign goods liable to Excise duty should be entered with the Excise within thirty days after report of ship. A clause of this Act stated that foreign spirits had for many years been tested by ' Clarke's Hydrometer,' that the instrument was not accurate, and that experiments would be made with a view towards securing a more elaborate test. Another clause empowered excise officers to administer the oath necessary on the exportation of goods liable to drawback.

The next Act of the Session provided that any cutter, etc., belonging to the king's subjects, and found within four leagues of the coast, having a bowsprit of a length more than two-thirds that of the vessel, should be forfeited. All seized goods sold at the King's Warehouse were to be stamped before delivery. Every boat plying within four leagues of the coast was to have its name lettered on the stern. The *customs* duty on geneva, which under the Consolidating Act had been 5d. a gallon, was made equal to the customs duty on brandy (9d.).

The Board directed that East Indiamen should not be allowed to come into the channels of the Thames near

London, but should anchor in Long Reach, and that their cargoes should be reported within twenty-four hours of reaching Gravesend. This was intended to prevent smuggling. The directors of the Company arranged to send a fleet of hoys to Long Reach whenever one of their vessels arrived, to bring her cargo to London. The East Indiamen were to be strictly watched while at their new anchorage, and their ports and scuttles secured each night under joint locks of the Crown and Company. The Board found occasion to censure their river inspectors, who had thrown obstacles in the way of this scheme.

The Board requested the Commissioners of Excise to order the excise officers not to gauge imported spirits unless a customs man were present, and not to deliver the goods unless with customs cognizance, and intimated that if the request were not complied with they would direct the tide-waiters to watch and follow all such goods to their destination.

It appears that the regulated quantities of rum and sugar allowed for consumption in the Isle of Man were shipped at Liverpool. Up to a certain date in each year the Liverpool collector received tenders from merchants who were desirous of supplying the goods, and on the date specified the Board apportioned the trade equally among the merchants who had tendered.

The deputies of the late duke of Manchester (Collector Outwards) were permitted to retain office pending the issue of orders from the Treasury. The Board empowered them to continue the allotment of fees collected, ' keeping the same proportion for themselves as of old.'

Much friction was caused by the inquisitorial enforcement of the taxes upon wearing apparel. The Board advised their officers to be tactful, and to discriminate between clothing worn by passengers and clothing imported unaccompanied. The order concluded, ' This will save our time; which may be more usefully employed than in deciding constant applications.'

Hannah Randall was granted a gratuity of £30. It

appears that she had given evidence against several customs officers who had been charged with conniving at fraud on board the *Deptford* East Indiaman.

Customs ' guard-boats,' each with six boatmen and a ' sitter,' were stationed at Sheerness, Whitstable, Sandgate, Eastbourne, and Bridport, to prevent smuggling.

It was proclaimed by the Board that certain errors, which had for many years acted to the prejudice of the revenue, had been discovered in Crouch's ' Survey of the Customs,' a handbook previously much esteemed.

The department became convulsed on the matter of American corn. Sir Joseph Banks, President of the Royal Society, communicated with the Treasury as to the ' flying weevil ' and the ' Hessian fly,' insects that had seriously damaged the wheat crop in the United States. The correspondence, in which several American experts took part, is too extensive to quote in full, yet it is extremely interesting.

It appears that the Hessian fly was first observed at Staten Island in 1776. The Hessian auxiliaries landed about the same time, and to this coincidence the insect owed its title. Sir Joseph Banks refused to believe that the fly was taken over in the baggage of the Hessians, but the colonists cherished that idea. A letter to General Washington from Colonel Morgan, of the American army, was quoted, stating that the writer witnessed the first passage of the pest across the Delaware. ' It travelled,' said he, ' like a cloud, neither water nor mountain impeding its progress.'

The fly attacked the young wheat when first sprouting in autumn, and appeared as a caterpillar, which afterwards became fixed in chrysalis between blade and stalk, emerging as a fly about the end of the year. Observers were undecided as to whether this fly survived, or laid eggs which endured the cold of winter; but they were unanimous as to the invisibility of the eggs, if eggs there were. A similar caterpillar appeared in spring, and preyed upon the plant. The ravages committed by this insect were described as dreadful and resistless. It annually devastated the province of New York, part of Connecticut, and the borderland of New Jersey, and threatened the entire corn-land of the United States. Doleful indeed was the tone of the American advices : ' Unless means be found to impede its progress, the whole American continent will be overrun. Were it to reach Great Britain, it would be the greatest scourge that island ever experienced. Were a single straw containing the insect, egg, or aurelia, to be carried and safely deposited in the centre of Norfolk in England, it would multiply in a few years so as to destroy all the wheat and barley crops of the whole kingdom. There cannot be so atrocious a villain as to commit such an act intentionally. To us it appears unlikely that any means within the bounds of human wisdom will be found to destroy the fly.'

Certain methods had been tried, such as rolling the wheat before the first autumn frost, dressing the land with lime and ashes, sheltering the young plant with seaweed or straw, etc. All were unavailing, but it had been found that a particular kind of wheat (the ' yellow-bearded ' variety) was impregnable.

Danger to British agriculture from the assaults of the flying weevil was the burden of the next missive from the naturalists. The insect was described as a minute moth, ' much like that infesting woollens.' Its eggs produced a tiny caterpillar, that preyed upon ripe wheat. The moth differed from the European weevil in possessing wings and immense energy, and attacking wheat in the field as well as in the rick. This horrid pest first appeared in Carolina, and then travelled northward, following the extension of wheat-farming, and rapidly becoming acclimatized in the colder regions. Sir Joseph Banks feared that it might be brought to England in American corn cargoes. He had discovered it ' as a worm ' in many samples of American corn, but always dead, and he prescribed an experiment by means of which the customs officers might detect it. The experiment was but the ancient method of throwing the corn into water, and scrutinizing such grains as floated. ' In some may be found the worm, or the husk of its chrysalis, or the mere shell with excrement which the insect has left.'

In consequence of these disquieting reports, American corn was forbidden customs entry. There is record of the stoppage of a cargo from the United States. The corn was destroyed, and the rest of the goods were landed and placed under Crown lock. Later an outrageous order was issued, to the effect that wheat infected with flying weevil might be ' applied to the use of the navy.' Subsequently this was countermanded, and instructions were given that the infected wheat should be ' ground down at the ports where the same was imported.'

Edward VI.'s Act, prohibiting the exportation of white ashes, was repealed in 1788.

The laws prohibiting the exportation of wool, except the regulation that wool might not be housed within ten miles of the sea in Kent and Sussex, were repealed, and fresh prohibitive provisions enacted. The exportation of live sheep from Great Britain and the Channel Islands was forbidden. Persons exporting wool were made liable to a penalty of 3s. for every pound of wool. Wool carried coastwise without entry was made forfeitable.

Another Act provided for the regulation of the African slave-trade. Only a certain number of slaves per three tons of the vessel's capacity might be carried, unless they were children or below a certain stature. When a slaver arrived in the West Indies the master was to make a declaration before the Customs that all legal conditions had been complied with, and the customs officers were to inspect the vessel and count the slaves.

All surgeons of slavers were to give bond before clearing outwards for Africa that they would keep an authentic journal of the voyage, which journal was to be produced to the Customs at first port of arrival. No vessel was to be cleared outwards as a slaver unless she carried a duly qualified surgeon. If the master, on arriving at the West

Indies, could satisfy the Customs that not more than 2 per cent. of the slaves had died during the voyage, he was entitled to a reward of £100, and the surgeon to £50.

Two Commissioners of Customs in England and one in Scotland were appointed to inquire on oath into Customs emoluments, and to report to the Treasury.

An Act of 1789 repealed certain clauses of the Consolidating Act relating to tobacco and snuff, and placed new duties on the articles. It enjoined that after a specified day in 1789 customs entry of tobacco should be confined to goods from the American Plantations and the United States, and tobacco grown or produced in Ireland, or in the Plantations belonging to the Spaniards and Portuguese. The legal tonnage for tobacco vessels was fixed at 120 tons, and the legal weight for a package of tobacco at 450 pounds net. American tobacco might only be imported from the United States, or the British-American Plantations, in American and British built ships. The British ' tobacco ports ' were re-defined : London, Bristol, Falmouth, Liverpool, Lancaster, Cowes, Whitehaven, Hull, Greenock, Leith, and Port Glasgow.* All tobacco from the United States was to be accompanied by a special manifest, to the correctness of which the master was to make oath. The hatches of all tobacco vessels were to be locked down by the Customs, except during hours of work. The Board were empowered to appoint places for the mooring of tobacco-ships, and to provide warehouses for bonding the goods. The exportation of tobacco to the Channel Islands and the Isle of Man was made subject to special licence by the Board, and limited to a certain quantity per year. All persons employed in tobacco warehouses were to be licensed. Certain articles used in ' imitating ' tobacco were quoted : walnut, hop, and sycamore leaves. It was directed that a permit should accompany all removed tobacco.†

---

* Newcastle-on-Tyne was added to the list in 1791.

† Part of this Act deserves quotation : ' If any tobacco, tobacco stalks, Spanish, Returns of tobacco, Tobacco stalks for Tobacco Stalk Flour, Snuff work, Tobacco stalk Flour, or Snuff,

The Act also provided that all tobacco of four pounds weight or upwards, removed after 5 p.m. or before 7 a.m. in winter, or after 7 p.m. and before 5 a.m. in summer, should be liable to forfeiture, together with all boats, carriages, or horses used to convey it. The Act also prohibited the hawking of tobacco, and rendered forfeitable all roll tobacco produced for exportation, and containing more than 20 per cent. of water or foreign ingredients. It recited the old proviso that no customs officer who made a seizure should be entitled to reward, unless he had given notice of his capture to an excise officer, and it reaffirmed the right of excise officers to board and rummage vessels. This terrific statute contained 173 clauses.

Another Act removed the outward duty from unwrought tin exported to any place beyond the Cape of Good Hope, and hinted that the trifling relaxation might benefit British commerce to a marvellous extent. Exporters of tin were to furnish security at ports of shipment that the goods would be landed according to entry outward. The bonds were to be discharged as follows :

If the goods were to be landed in China, by a certificate from the chief supercargo officiating there for the East India Company.

---

removed under Colour of any permit, shall be seized, or if any Action shall be brought by the Owner or Claimer of any such Tobacco, Tobacco stalks, Spanish, Returns of Tobacco, Tobacco Stalks for Tobacco Stalk Flour, Snuff Work, Tobacco Stalk Flour or Snuff, against any Officer or Officers of Customs or Excise, or any Person acting in his or their Assistance, for such seizure of any such Tobacco, Tobacco Stalks, Spanish, Returns of Tobacco, Tobacco Stalks for Tobacco Stalk Flour, Snuff Work, Tobacco Stalk Flour, or Snuff, the proof that such Tobacco, Tobacco Stalks, Spanish, Returns of Tobacco, Tobacco Stalks for Tobacco Stalk Flour, Snuff Work, Tobacco Stalk Flour, or Snuff, being such Tobacco, Tobacco Stalks, Spanish, Returns of Tobacco, Tobacco Stalks for Tobacco Stalk Flour, Snuff Work, Tobacco Stalk Flour, or Snuff, as is or are mentioned in such permit, although such Tobacco, Tobacco Stalks, Spanish, Returns of Tobacco, Tobacco Stalks for Tobacco Stalk Flour, Snuff Work, Tobacco Stalk Flour, or Snuff, shall appear to have been kept in the Officers' Books or Account of the Stock from which such Tobacco, Tobacco Stalks, Spanish, Returns of Tobacco, Tobacco Stalks for Tobacco Stalk Flour, Snuff Work, Tobacco Stalk Flour, or Snuff, was or were removed,' etc.

If the goods were to be landed in the East Indies, by a certificate from the Governor or Council of the Company.

If the goods were to be landed at a place beyond the Company's jurisdiction, by a certificate from two principal merchants.

In all cases the certificates were to be forthcoming in Great Britain within thirty months from date of bond.

Inquiry had been resumed as to the flying weevil and Hessian fly, and copious information had been furnished to the Privy Council by Phineas Bond, British consul at Philadelphia. All the papers on the matter were laid before Parliament. On November 28, 1789, the Privy Council advised the king to revoke the prohibition of American corn.

It had been usual, whenever duty was overpaid, to adjust the matter by allowing the payer to export goods duty-free up to the amount of excess. The Board abolished this clumsy method, directing that over-entry certificates should be granted, and the overpaid moneys returned.

Comprehensive instructions were issued to the gaugers. Casks of wine and spirits were to be gauged by both Customs and Excise on importation, there being heavy excise duties on both classes of goods. 'Standards of allowance' were prescribed, varying according to the types of cask, but the gaugers were directed, whenever the casks had ' copped bouges, indented bung-staves, squeezed quarters, or dished or buckled heads,' to consult upon such distortions of shape, and then submit their decision for the landing-surveyor's approval. It would seem that the casks in which wines and spirits were imported were of much the same ' standards of content ' as those used in recent times—say down to 1880.* For instance, the standard content of a port pipe was shown as 137 gallons.

* Within the last twenty or thirty years the standards have in many cases been departed from. Port pipes may be found to hold 125 gallons, and brandy puncheons 130. Brandy hogsheads may be met with that contain 65 gallons ; in fact, standard construction is the exception, not the rule.

The wine gallon contained about 231 cubic inches, and 137 gallons old measure would be about 114 modern. But the prescribed standards of allowance show that the casks were thinner and of better shape than those now used, the sherry butts especially. The method of recording measurements was similar to the modern system, the length, head, bung, wet inches, full content, and liquid content being ' razed ' upon the front head ; but the spirit ullages were cast out to the gallon, instead of to the tenth part of a gallon. The customs gaugers were enjoined to be courteous and friendly with the excisemen, ' studying on every occasion to preserve that harmony and good understanding between the officers of both departments that is so essential to the Publick Service.'

Other instructions were issued, specifying the conditions under which vessels seized for smuggling might be sold for ' breaking up.' Buyers were to dismantle their purchases under customs supervision, separating planks, unhinging rudders, unshipping windlasses, removing sternposts, and then sawing through the keels in three equidistant places.

Both Customs and Excise Commissioners issued instructions that whenever a ship arrived with a cargo of spirits the first officer going on board should dip all casks stowed above the hatches, and record the wet inches in the ' blue book.' If a customs man were first, the first excise officer visiting the ship was to check the wet inches by redipping, and *vice versa*. It appears that many casks thus carried had been found almost empty when landed on the quays.

All the London jerquers were censured for irregular attendance.

An expert named Betts was appointed to estimate the values of imported violins and violoncellos, and particularly enjoined to report upon previous valuations, the Board being desirous of preventing illegal combination betwixt officers and importers.

One Valentine Green was allowed by Treasury warrant

to import, duty-free, certain copies of pictures, produced at Dusseldorf.

The Board directed that no sufferance for landing foreign goods should be granted to any London wharf ' below Brown's Wharf near Hermitage Bridge on the north side of the Thames, and St. Saviour's Dock on the south side,' and that no foreign goods, except iron, should be landed above London Bridge. Several notable places were exempt from the former restriction—the King's yards at Deptford and Woolwich, the East India Company's wharves at Blackwall, and the Greenland Dock. At certain wharves both coastwise and foreign goods might be landed if kept separate. These were Irongate, Watson's, Hawley's, and Brown's on the north side ; Chamberlain's, Cotton's, Hay's, Beal's, Griffin's, Symons's, Stanton's, Davis's, and Eustace's on the south. At Carrington's, Hogarth's, Scott's, Meriton's, and Topping's foreign goods only might be landed, and the packages were to be examined ' on the open quay.' The only two places above-bridge approved for the landing of foreign iron were Dyer's Wharf and the historic Steel Yard.*

The Board apprised the Treasury that the Tobacco Warehouse on Tower Hill was not large enough to accommodate all the tobacco imported into London, and they had therefore been compelled to hire additional accommodation.

The Treasury called for quarterly returns of the fees taken by the London Collector Outwards (the duke of Manchester's heir). The London jerquers were again censured for non-attendance. (Their prescribed hours of employment were from nine to three.) It was discovered that certain returns required from the indoor customs officials in 1788 had not been furnished (1790).

* Later Harrison's and St. Katherine's Wharves were granted sufferances for foreign goods, and the Carron Wharf for iron. Although the Hanse Leaguers had lost nearly all their old trade and political influence, the famous Steel Yard remained in their possession till well on into the nineteenth century. In 1853 the premises were sold for £72,000.

Orders were issued that no officer, except one of the solicitors, should quit his work to attend at the Treasury, without first acquainting the Board.*

The East India Company fell behind with their payments, and were ordered to deposit £15,000 per cargo on the duties in arrear.

The Board decided that too many tide-waiters per ship were allotted as watchmen, and reduced the numbers thus :

On ships with wine cargoes, from three tide-waiters to two.

On ships with tobacco cargoes, from five tide-waiters to four.

On short traders (Continental packets), from four tide-waiters to three.

On ships from Hamburg, from four tide-waiters to three.

On ships from the Levant, from four tide-waiters to three.

This alteration effected a saving of £2,480 per annum.

It is evident that the provisions of the Navigation Act were as charitably administered as of old. A cargo of cotton and mahogany imported from the United States, ' yet not the growth thereof,' was allowed to be entered and landed. Instructions were given that all similar cargoes might be privileged for a period, till the merchants became fully aware that such goods were prohibited.

It was enacted that from and after August 1, 1790, any subject of the United States might settle in Bermuda, Quebec, or Nova Scotia, and carry his effects and negroes thither in British ships free of duty, provided that the value of the effects did not exceed £50 for each white person and £2 for each negro.

Another Act directed that all foreign tobacco for home consumption should be duty-paid on the weight ascer-

* This appears to have been intended to suppress visits by the higher officials, who frequently pestered the Treasury with private schemes.

tained at delivery, and that none should set up a tobacco factory within five miles of the coast, except at 'a tobacco port.'

Additional excise duties were placed on foreign spirits, to be paid before landing, unless secured by bond.

An extra customs duty of 2s. 8d. per cwt. was levied on sugar. A separate appropriation was made of the moneys arising from this impost. The first year's produce was to go to the Consolidated Fund, and afterwards the proceeds were to be applied to paying the interest on a loan of £1,833,000. Thus the bad old system was revived.

Parliament repealed a number of Acts dealing with the duties and restrictions on corn. It also repealed Charles II.'s prohibition of forestalling and engrossing. The second clause of the new Act commenced : ' Whereas it will be for the Benefit of the People of this Kingdom that the Circulation and Trade of Corn should be free from all improper Restraint.'* The Act, by its ' Table A,' provided that wheat, when under 44s. a quarter, might be allowed a bounty of 5s. on exportation. Table B prohibited exportation when the price reached 46s. Table C specified the quantities of British corn that might be shipped from various ports and to various places.

The duty on foreign wheat was fixed at £1 4s. 3d. when the price was under 50s. a quarter. This was called ' the High Duty.' When wheat was at 50s. or under 54s. it was liable to a rate of 2s. 6d., ' the first Low Duty.' When at 54s. or over the rate was 6d., ' the second Low Duty.' But upon wheat from Ireland or the Plantations the High Duty was leviable only when the price was under 48s. ; the first Low Duty when at 48s. or under 52s. ; the second Low Duty when at 52s. or over. ' Regulating prices ' were also specified for barley, oats, etc.

---

* This may have been brought about by Adam Smith's statement in ' The Wealth of Nations ' that the restraint of engrossing was undesirable. Plain people who have read of the ' cornering ' that afterwards took place may be disposed to question the accuracy of Adam Smith's judgment in this particular case.

Corn might be bonded on landing, and on delivery from warehouse for home consumption it was liable to the duty payable at time of such delivery, and the first Low Duty as well. A vessel laden with corn, and arriving at a port where the price was low and the High Duty in force, might depart with her cargo to another port where the price was higher and the duty lower. The maritime counties and chief ports were districted with regard to the proclamation of price, as below :

1. Kent, Essex, Sussex, and the City of London.

2. Suffolk and Cambridgeshire.

3. Norfolk.

4. Lincolnshire, and East and North Ridings of Yorkshire, including Hull.

5. Durham and Northumberland, including Berwick.

6. Cumberland and Westmoreland.

7. Lancashire and Cheshire.

8. The counties of Flint, Denbigh, Carnarvon, Merioneth, and Anglesea.

9. The counties of Cardigan, Pembroke, Carmarthen, and Glamorgan.

10. Gloucestershire, Somerset, and Monmouthshire.

11. Cornwall and Devon.

12. Dorset and Hants.

13. The counties of Fife, Kinross, Clackmannan, Stirling, Linlithgow, Haddington, Berwick, Roxburgh Selkirk, and Peebles.

14. The counties of Dumfries, Wigton, Ayr, and the Stewardry of Kircudbright.

15. The counties of Argyle, Dumbarton, Lanark, Renfrew, and Bute.

16. The counties of Caithness, Sutherland, Ross, Inverness, Cromarty, Nairn, Elgin, Banff, Aberdeen, Kincardine, Forfar, and Perth, with the Orkneys and Shetlands.

The prices regulating duty in District 1 were to be those quoted at the London Corn Exchange, Mark Lane. Every corn-factor had to make a weekly return to an appointed inspector, who then apprised the London collectors of customs. In Scotland the prices were to be fixed by juries convened by the sheriffs. Each jury was to consist of two freeholders, two farmers, and other 'reputable men.' No buyer of corn might sit as juryman.

'The Controller of the Great Customs of Wool and Leather,' whose office must have been a sinecure of long standing, was granted three months' leave, 'on account of derangement of his mind.'

Correspondence took place between the Board and the Treasury as to the Receiver-General's bond, and it was decided that the amount of security should at least equal the average weekly sum paid by him into the Exchequer, and that no one of his sureties should engage for more than £10,000. The 'average weekly sum paid into the Exchequer' was stated at £70,000.

The Customs 'Conscience-money' from 1771 to 1791 was £949, which included one sum of £400, one of £300, and one of £210, the balance being made up by petty contributions.

It had been the practice, when a subordinate official was found unworthy of further employment, to 'desire' his principal to dismiss him. The Receiver-General, being 'desired' to dismiss one of his clerks, took no notice of the message, and the Board called upon him for an explanation. He replied laconically that he had not been 'ordered.' The Board then *commanded* him to dismiss his underling, and provided that in future all directions to dismiss should be peremptorily worded.

In 1792 the allowance to 'The Lecturer of Barking Parish' was reinstituted. The Board paid the costs and damages incurred by certain officers of Bristol, who had been proceeded against in the public courts for searching a house without cause or warrant.

Certain moneys, which had been taken as fees in offices where the patents of the original holders had lapsed and not been regranted, were paid into the bank to the account of two of the Commissioners, pending further directions as to disposal.

The lands and effects of the deceased collector of St. Vincent were confiscated, on account of frauds previously committed by him. His widow made ' claim of dower,' and was granted £40 per annum ' as full compensation.'

The Receiver-General's right of fees was abolished, and he was granted a yearly salary of £1,500,* and an allowance of £480 for clerks and messengers. (In 1793 the ' allowance ' was cancelled.)

One of the inspectors suggested that duty should be charged upon the calico used as wrappers for the bale goods imported by the East India Company. The Board concurred, and gave him a gratuity of £500.

Certain new wharf privileges were granted. Dundee Wharf, Wapping, received a sufferance to land coastwise goods. Lucas and Spencer's Wharf was made a legal place of discharge for ships employed in the whale fishery. A sufferance was granted to an alien, Mr. Moses Ancona. He was allowed to land marble of his own importing at Pedlar's Acre,† on condition that he paid a customs watchman to guard the goods.

In 1792 Parliament reduced the excise duty on candles by $\frac{1}{2}d.$ *a pound.*

It was enacted that the drawback on Plantation sugar, and the bounty payable on sugar refined from Plantation muscovado and exported, should cease when the price of imported raw sugar was over 60s. per cwt., exclusive of duty. This was to endure for a period, then the price annulling drawback was to be 55s. per cwt., again for a period, and then the annulling price was to be 50s. The Clerk of the Grocers' Company of London was to gazette the price of the imported raw article. Sugar and coffee from countries other than British possessions might be

---

* His fees amounted to about £1,000 a year.

† In Lambeth, near Westminster Bridge. The site was left to the parish of Lambeth in 1504 by a pedlar, on condition that the testator's effigy should be painted upon one of the windows of Lambeth Church.

warehoused for exportation free of duty, if carried in British ships. Thus Parliament undid the work of the simplifiers of tariffs.

An Act was passed relieving the coasting trade of Great Britain from the heavy expenses previously imposed by the regulations as to cockets, bonds, and stamp duties on the same (*vide* p. 363).

It was provided that the exportation of naval stores, such as pig-iron, bar-iron, hemp, pitch, tar, resin, turpentine, cordage, masts, yards, oakum, sheet-copper, etc., might be prohibited by royal proclamation or Order in Council whenever prohibition might seem necessary.

The exportation of wheat, wheat-flour, bread, and biscuit was forbidden for a period, and the king was empowered to prohibit the exportation of potatoes and of all kinds of corn, and to permit the importation of corn at the Low duties. Thus the recent Act regulating duty by price was for a time nullified.

The next Act was levelled against aliens. ' Whereas a great and unusual number of Persons have lately resorted to this Kingdom, and much Danger may arise to the Publick Tranquillity unless due Provision be made in respect thereof,' etc. Shipmasters were to furnish the Customs with particulars of all aliens carried, and the customs officers were to ascertain the aliens' names, occupations, etc., and to grant each alien a certificate if his record were satisfactory. The officers might detain arms, etc., brought by the strangers. The king might, by Order in Council, prevent all aliens other than merchants from landing in Great Britain. Each alien who was allowed to land received a passport signed by a chief magistrate. On reasonable suspicion warrants might be granted for the search of houses occupied by aliens. Ambassadors, and aliens not above fourteen years old, were exempt from this Act. If an undesirable alien were banished, and returned, he was liable to transportation. If, after undergoing his sentence, he made another attempt, he became liable to death without benefit of clergy.

Great Britain had declared war against her old enemy France, and many people believed that one of the chief reasons of quarrel was that the French revolutionists were bent upon the conquest of Europe and the suppression of all taxes. Yet one might assume that the English people, after a century's experience of the inseparableness of war and taxation, should have known better ; that they should have realized that no nation can even attempt to subjugate a continent unless it charges its own resources recklessly to provide the means ; and that if the tremendous effort succeeds, the result will certainly not be a total abolition of imposts.

The spirit of Parliament was soon made manifest. An Act was passed providing that any person who should supply, or assist in supplying, the French with arms, ammunition, naval stores, coal, iron, lead, copper, Bank of England notes, bullion, corn, or victuals, without royal licence for the same, should be ' deemed a traitor,' and suffer death.

Another Act provided that drawback might be allowed on wine shipped for the use of naval officers, up to a specified quantity per year, varying from six tuns in the case of an admiral to half a tun in the case of a lieutenant. (Most of the old admirals were sturdy drinkers, and fond of treating their subordinate officers ; still, 1,512 gallons a year was a liberal allowance.) It was provided that Plantation and American tobacco might be shipped duty-free for the use of naval seamen. After being warehoused at importation, the goods might be removed to Rochester, Portsmouth, or Plymouth, re-warehoused with the Customs, and then issued duty-free as provided.

Parliament still further complicated the Plantation Acts. But one of the numerous alterations need be quoted. It was provided that Plantation goods which had been imported into Ireland might afterwards be brought to Great Britain in British or Irish ships, if accompanied by a certificate.

It was also enacted that vessels condemned for smuggling might be sold for use as privateers.

The Board discovered that a person who had been sworn in as an established tide-waiter had been engaged for many years in 'practices detrimental to the Excise Revenue.' They dismissed him.

The Treasury authorized the Board to grant letters of protection against impressment to lightermen employed in conveying bountied or drawback goods for shipment, the document to be the same as granted to the sailors on board revenue cruisers.

The revenue lawyers withdrew from a prosecution for smuggling, the Crown costs being paid by the defendant. Then they apprised the seizing officers that they might continue the prosecution if they wished. Needless to state, the officers failed to profit by the permission.

The Treasury asked the Board to furnish a list of notorious smugglers who were in confinement or under prosecution, to the end that they might be excluded from the scope of a general pardon that was contemplated.

In 1794 the Collector Outwards was directed to obtain from shipmasters, when they reported their cargoes, an account of the places where their ships were moored, and to placard it for the information of merchants and officers. At this period the Thames near London Bridge was terribly crowded with vessels. The legal quays were overcharged with goods, and the Board were compelled to extend the quay privileges to many ' ordinary wharves.'

An additional excise duty, payable before landing of goods, was levied on foreign spirits. The previous additional duties, and the additional duties on sugar, were made perpetual. An additional duty was placed on foreign bricks.

The duties on foreign paper were repealed, and fresh duties levied *by weight*, instead of by ream as before. The duty on foreign-bound books was increased. It was provided that the Board might reward officers for seizing pirated books. Additional duties were placed upon foreign glass.

Fresh preventive regulations were added to the already formidable roll. It was enacted that any cutter, lugger, etc., belonging to the king's subjects, that was found, provided with arms and ammunition, within the limits of any port or four leagues of the coast, might be seized and made forfeitable, unless licensed by the Admiralty ; and that any rowing boat of a specified length, and having planks not of a specified thickness, should be similarly liable. The limits within which hoverers might be seized were redefined by a series of imaginary straight lines, cutting off sections of the indented coast, thus :

' A straight line from Walney Island to the Great Orme's Head.

' A straight line from Cromer to the Spurn Head.

' A straight line from the Mull of Galloway to the Point of Ayr in the Isle of Man,' etc.

British slate, stone, and marble, carried coastwise, were made liable to coastwise duties, and the duty on Guernsey granite was made *ad valorem*.

Cap. 68 of 1794 strengthened the Navigation Act.

In 1795 additional duties of excise were charged upon foreign wines, at the rate of £30 a tun on French and £20 on all other wines. Wines previously duty-paid, but found upon excise survey to be still in the hands of dealers, were liable to this impost. Additional excise duties were placed on foreign spirits. Soon after this additional excise duties were placed on tea, at the rate of 7½ per cent. of the gross prices obtained at the East India Company's sales, and other imposts upon cocoa and coffee. Additional customs duties were put upon oranges, raisins, waste silk, and various kinds of wood, and the export duties on coal and rock-salt were increased.

During this year and the next there were several applications by customs officers for permission to absent themselves from duty in order to join the various fencible regiments. A tide-surveyor went to the Bedfordshire

Militia. A tide-waiter received six months' leave at the request of the colonel of the West London Militia, the colonel stating that he required the tide-waiter to assist in ' forming the regiment.' A landing-waiter was allowed by Treasury Order twelve months' leave, to act as adjutant of the Lancashire Militia. An acting patent searcher was granted leave, ' to attend his military duty.' An established waterman was allowed six months' leave, in order that he might qualify as a pilot, pilots being urgently required ' for the public service.'

The regulations as to the breaking-up of vessels condemned for smuggling were amplified. Read in their new form, they convey a sensation of ferocious solemnity. The ballast, masts, pumps, and bulk-heads were to be taken out, the decks ripped fore and aft, the beams sawn asunder, the bottom planks ripped off, the keels cut into four pieces, and the stern-posts into three. Boats condemned were to be cut through the thwarts, the hulls sawn into four parts athwartships, and the stems and sterns into two.

The Customs Housekeeper complained to the Treasury of the high price of provisions, and requested an increase in her allowance. The Treasury referred the request to the Board, stating that they were not prepared to admit that the rise in the price of provisions was other than temporary, yet if the Board wished it the allowance might be made. The Board allowed £100 a year extra, to be expended in paying increased wages to the servants.

A customs doorkeeper behaved unbecomingly to one of the Commissioners, and was suspended. The Secretary was told to ' exhort the doorkeepers and messengers, in the most solemn manner, to observe proper behaviour in their several stations.'

Sir Jamieson W. Gordon and a Mr. Charlton had been joint patent collectors of Newcastle-on-Tyne. Mr. Charlton died, and his partner made application to be allowed to receive the emoluments of the two situations. This cool proposal was negatived.

Earl Spencer and Mr. Thomas Grenville, who had been on a mission from the king to the emperor of Germany, were allowed on return to bring a butt of wine each duty-free. The Countess of Mornington was allowed a number of patterns of French dresses duty-free, giving security to return them abroad within three months.

The river inspector was ordered to repair to the Downs, and keep a watch upon the West India fleet, as soon as news reached London that the ships had been sighted. The Board issued fresh orders as to the surveillance of East Indiamen, stating that they were resolved to dismiss any watchman or officer who, ' whilst guarding the gang-way, neglected to search any person who might leave the ship.' The watchmen put to guard East Indiamen were furnished with great-coats, lanthorns, and *rattles*.

It appears that the Board had been asked to assist in drawing up a scheme for improving the port of London. The Thames at this time was often dreadfully crowded, especially when any of the merchant fleets arrived. Plunder and smuggling were rampant, and the need of better accommodation for shipping was urged by all classes of the water-side community, except the hardy rogues who profited by the existing confusion.

Extra duties of excise were laid on imported tobacco, being 4d. a pound extra on Irish, Plantation, and American goods, and 1s. a pound on other tobaccos. It was provided that tobacco might be shipped from warehouse duty-free, for use of soldiers on board transports.

The drawbacks and outward bounties on sugar were reduced.

A ludicrous statute appeared in 1796 : ' Whereas it is expedient for the more effectual preserving and en-couraging of the manufacture of blacklead melting-pots in this country to reduce the duty payable on the importa-tion of foreign blacklead,' etc. The Act reduced the duty in question to 1s. a cwt. It almost seems as though Parliament imagined that from the date of enactment blacklead melting-pots would be turned out as plentifully as horse-nails, and that if afterwards the high rate on blacklead were re-enforced every maker of melting-pots would soon be begging by the wayside.

The clauses of the Consolidating Act of 1787 that dealt with the landing of foreign goods were recited, and the statement that all foreign goods landed otherwise than in the presence of the proper officer of customs were forfeitable was reaffirmed. It appears that the overcrowding of the legal quays was partly due to the slackness of officers, who had neglected to enforce their prerogative of placing in the King's Warehouse all foreign wine not entered within twenty days after report.

The provisions of Charles II.'s Butter Act were recited and strengthened.

Parliament brought out a string of new imposts, levying additional customs duties upon wine, at the rate of £30 a tun on French and £20 on other wines, and additional duties on sugar (2s. 6d. a cwt. extra on Plantation and East India sugars, 5s. on others). The extra duty on Plantation sugar might be drawn back if the goods were exported. Loaf sugar refined from Plantation muscovado and then exported was granted an additional drawback of 4s. per cwt., and other sugar refined from Plantation muscovado an additional drawback of 2s. 6d. An impost of 10 per cent. upon the produce of all customs duties was applied to brimstone, hemp, unwrought iron, and staves, imported from Europe, and a similar impost of 5 per cent. to all other foreign goods.*

Certain provisions towards commercial reciprocity between Great Britain and the United States were expressed in an Act of 1797, being principally as below :

1. American goods in American ships were to be liable only to such British duties as applied to other merchandise imported in British ships.

2. American raw produce imported in American or British ships was liable only to such British duties as

---

* The excise tax on dogs appeared about this time.

applied to the raw produce of British possessions imported in British ships.

3. American leaf tobacco imported in American or British ships was liable only to the duties on leaf tobacco from the British Plantations, plus 1s. 6d. per 100 pounds.

4. The same British bounties were to be paid on goods exported to the United States as were paid on similar goods exported to the British Plantations.

5. As British ships trading in the United States paid heavier American tonnage dues than American ships did, it was provided that such American ships as traded in Great Britain should pay tonnage dues equal to the excess. If such tonnage dues on an American ship in Great Britain were withheld more than three months after her arrival, the British Customs might seize and sell the ship, deduct from the proceeds the tonnage dues and the expenses of detention, and give the residue to the shipowner.

6. American vessels might trade freely with British possessions in the East Indies, on condition that they carried all goods shipped in the East Indies *direct* to the United States.

After all this toil towards equalization, the Americans continued to impose certain heavy duties on European and Asiatic goods taken to the United States by British ships. Therefore, and notwithstanding the provisions expressed above under 1, 2, and 3, an impost of about 10 per cent. was laid upon American goods brought into Great Britain by American ships. This contradictory provision was intended to endure till the Americans repealed their extra duties upon British-carried goods.

The Act contained an extradition clause, providing that the respective Governments should surrender refugees charged with murder or forgery.

Another Act provided that the captains of privateers should keep journals, and produce them at the request of any collector of customs, or of any master of a ship of war or revenue cruiser. A false entry in a journal was punishable with a fine of £500, and this harsh penalty attended various infractions. The Act was necessary, yet it may have had little restraining effect upon the redoubtable rogues who went a-privateering.

An additional duty of 3d. a pound was placed on warehoused pepper, and made payable when the goods were delivered. A second impost was levied upon the proceeds of customs duties—import, export, and coastwise—not to apply to tea, sugar, wine, tobacco, olive oil, and calico, or to the proceeds of the previous imposts of 10 and 5 per cent.

It will be apparent that the taxes had been largely augmented since the issue of the Consolidating Act, and that the tariff was sliding into the toils of complication. It should be stated that some little attempt had been made towards ease in certain remote branches of revenue ; for instance, lime, limestone, and *manure* had been granted exemption from the coastwise regulations, and Plantation arrowroot, linseed-cake, and rape-cake, imported in British ships, had been made duty-free.

The vessels of all friendly nations were empowered to trade in the British East Indies, subject to the approval of the East India Company's directors.

The customs staff of the port of Liverpool was increased. The Treasury directed the Board to reward the customs staff of Milford and Pembroke, and the masters and mariners of the revenue cruisers stationed there, for vigilance and zeal ' in the defence of their country.' A collector, a controller, and two landing-waiters were appointed at the newly acquired colony of Demerara. The collector received £70 a year as salary, the controller £50, and the landing-waiters £35 each.

Certain privileges with regard to customs examination were extended to manuscript of the late Sir William Jones, Orientalist, on its arrival in England from Bengal. Sir Gilbert Elliott, late viceroy of Corsica, was allowed to import a tun of port and a tun of sherry duty-free.

A tide-surveyor stationed at Portsmouth was desirous

of producing a scheme for preventing the embezzlement of naval stores. The Board gave him permission to employ his spare time in this pursuit, 'under the supervision of the Admiralty.'

In 1798 a wine debenture was laid before the Board, signed by a person *not known to the Commissioners*. The Board censured the Examiner of wine duties.

A collector and controller were appointed at Montreal. The collector's salary was £80 ; the controller's £70.

During this year the port of London was crowded with vessels from the West Indies, loaded principally with rum and coffee. The Board allowed these vessels ten days beyond the usual time allotted for discharge.

It was enacted that vessels liable to quarantine should hoist quarantine signals on meeting other vessels at sea, or on coming within four leagues of a British coast. It was also directed that foreign glass should be forfeited unless imported in packages weighing not less than 5 cwt., and stamped on the outside with the word 'Glass.' Foreign glass was to be specially reported.

An additional duty was levied on foreign salt.

The Aliens Act was amended. No alien might leave the kingdom unless he carried a passport signed by a Secretary of State. The passport was to be produced to the Customs at port of departure. After it had been signed by the collector, the bearer had to produce it to the captain of the ship in which he was about to embark.

Exportation of British spirits to the Isle of Man was prohibited, and the Board of Customs were empowered to grant licences for the importation into Douglas of foreign brandy 'from any place,' at a duty of 3s. per gallon, up to an amount not exceeding 10,000 gallons per year. The quantity of tobacco previously allowed to be imported into the island had been found insufficient, and it was provided that British ships licensed by the Board of Customs might carry tobacco thither, from Great Britain, to the amount of 60,000 pounds per year, at a duty of 6d. per pound, and wine 'from any place ' to a yearly quantity of 70 tuns, the wine being liable to the Manx duties and an added £8 a tun. The Board might also license Manxmen to import live sheep from Great Britain to the number of 100 per year. Each importer of sheep was to announce his intention a month beforehand. No cloth or cotton yarn were to pass into the island except from Great Britain. Cotton yarn or cloth produced in the island were to be duty-free in Great Britain. The Treasury might under special circumstances authorize the Board of Customs to license larger quantities of goods than those specified. The conditions of the above Act were to endure until 1801.

That peculiar impost, the Convoy duty, was instituted during 1798. No vessel was to sail from Great Britain without convoy, under penalty of £1,000. If a vessel, sailing under convoy, were wilfully navigated so as to separate, her master's share of insurance was to be void. Coasting vessels, ships trading to Ireland, ships licensed by the Admiralty, ships not registered, and the vessels of the East India and Hudson's Bay Companies, were exempt. To recompense the Government for its unwelcome protection, small duties were levied on certain imports and exports, in some cases by weight, in others by value, and trading ships were made liable to tonnage duties, varying from 6d. per ton on vessels trading with Ireland to 3s. per ton on vessels trading with the East Indies.

Later it was enacted that any of the king's subjects who during the continuance of the war visited France, or any place under French occupation, or corresponded with the French Government or anyone in France, should be liable to death without benefit of clergy, unless they held licence from the king thus to travel or correspond. This made the smuggler's vocation extremely perilous, yet smuggling prevailed the more.

Cap. 86 of 1798 caused commotion in the Customs. It stated that certain offices, usually granted by letters patent, and often executed by deputies appointed by the patentees, had become unnecessary ; that such as were vacant should at once be abolished ; and that such as were occupied should cease when they became vacant. The officials affected were the Inspector of Prosecutions, the Inspector of the books of the Patent, the Surveyor-General of the Customs and Subsidies of the port of London, the Patent Customers at the outports, and the Keeper of the Books and Entries for the port of London.

Other offices were deemed partly useful, with a stipulation that the Board might by permission of the Treasury provide otherwise for their occupation, or combine two or more of them into one. These were the offices held by the Registrar-General of trading Ships, the Inspector of the outport collectors' accounts and vouchers, the Controller of the Customs in London, the Collector of the Subsidy of Tonnage and Poundage in London, an official rejoicing in the complicated title of Collector of Customs of Tonnage and Poundage outward in London and Keeper of the Cocket Seal, and another known as the Chief Patent Searcher of the Customs in London ; together with the controllers at all outports, the patent searchers at outports, two patent searchers at Gravesend, five under-searchers in London, nineteen king's waiters in London, and four king's waiters in Bristol.

It was further provided that certain offices, when vacated, should be granted no more, unless at pleasure of the Board and the Treasury ; that if it were decided to refill them the Board might fix the salaries appertaining, but that whenever one was totally abolished the clerks and deputies affected might receive compensation. Whenever one of the abolished offices was revived, the Board were to apprise Parliament, stating reasons for the revival. So far as we have been able to trace, none of them was revived, so that it may be taken that early in the nineteenth century the crowded quays, and the corridors of the Custom-house, were illuminated no longer by the occasional presence of the following stately figures :

The Receiver for Sales of Condemned Goods, the Receiver of the King's share of fines and forfeitures from outports, the Controller of the same, the Accountant of petty receipts, the Customer of Cloth and Petty Custom in London, the Controller of Pretermitted Customs, and the Examiners of outport books. Most melancholy to relate, the three venerable gentlemen mentioned below also disappeared, and the golden links that had connected the department with hoary Eld were shattered for ever.

The Collector of Aliens' Custom in London.

The Collector of Customs of Hides, Woolfells, Lead, and Tin, and Keeper of the Cocket Seal to that office belonging.

The Controller of Customs of Hides, Woolfells, Wool, Lead, and Tin, and of the Subsidy of Three Shillings for every Dolium, and of Twelvepence for every Pound in the Port of London.

(It is likely that for many years no merchant had found it necessary to approach the last-named Illustrious One by letter, which was fortunate, paper being dear.)

The office of Collector Outward in London had been granted in 1782 to the duke of Manchester. The patent had not been perfected, yet the Act continued the emoluments of the office to the duke's sons as though such perfecting had taken place. It was provided that the office should be maintained till the informal lease expired ; the Board to appoint persons to execute ' the necessary duties.' When the lease expired, the office was to be abolished. Therefore it appears—

1. That the office was *unnecessary*.

2. That it was granted, as a lucrative sinecure, to wealthy nobles.

3. That the grant was informal.

4. That the expensive grant was continued despite the informality.

5. That, in order to cloak the proceeding, deputies were to be maintained to perform ' the necessary duties.' Who paid the deputies ?

The salt duties were repealed, and new duties levied.

The Scottish excise on salt was less than the English, and when Scottish salt came into England the extra English duty had to be paid. Exported home-made salt was allowed a drawback of the excise duty. Bounty at varying rates was allowed on 'exported dried cod, ling, or hake, in length 14 inches from the bone in the fin to the third joint in the tail,' on the same fish 'wet,' on salmon, white herrings, red herrings, 'clean shotten' red herrings, dried sprats, pilchards, and beef or pork cured with duty-paid salt. The importation of salt from Ireland, the Channel Islands, and the Isle of Man, was prohibited.

In 1799 new duties were imposed on the East India Company's goods. These were peculiarly arranged. A slight *ad valorem* duty was levied on the goods at import, payable when they were warehoused, but the Company might postpone payment by entering into bond. Such goods as were afterwards exported had to bear the convoy duties on shipment. Goods sold for home consumption were liable on sale to the convoy duties, and to new duties payable by purchasers, the said new duties vastly exceeding those previously levied. Below are given a few of the alterations :

	Previous Duties.			The New Duties.		
	Per Cent.			Per Cent.		
	£	s.	d.	£	s.	d.
Arrangoes, on sale price	31	13	4	53	9	1
Chinaware	47	10	0	109	8	6
Cotton manufactures	50	0	0	122	4	5
Cowries	31	13	4	53	9	1
Drugs, manufactured	40	0	0	78	11	5
,, unmanufactured	31	0	0	51	14	10
Japanned ware	49	10	0	119	10	9

This Act was stated to be in encouragement of East Indian trade.

Imposts were levied on imported sugar, and the drawbacks and bounties on exported sugar reduced. The export duty on coffee was increased.

Another Act increased the bounty on exported pilchards.

American goods brought by the ships of nations in amity with Great Britain were allowed to be warehoused, and afterwards exported free of convoy duty.

It was provided that Matthew Boulton, a Staffordshire engineer, might export machinery for erecting a Mint at St. Petersburg, and send English workmen to erect the same, notwithstanding the previous Acts forbidding the exportation of labour-saving machinery and the foreign employment of British artificers.

It was provided that Levant goods might be admitted, by Order in Council, even if brought in ships without clean bills of health. The convoy duty on British goods exported to the Levant was reduced.

The crowded condition of the river Thames and the legal quays had been alluded to in an Act of 1795. Cap. 69 of 1799 (local) commenced : ' Whereas considerable disadvantages to the trade of the Port of London arise from the circuitous course of the river Thames round the tract of land called the Isle of Dogs,' etc. It provided that a canal might be cut from Blackwall to Limehouse Hole, under control of the Common Council of London. The moorings in the Thames from London Bridge to Bugsby's Hole, previously leased to Lord Gwydyr, were also to pass under control of the Common Council, the holder being compensated. The Council were to supply new moorings, under supervision of the Trinity House.

The second part commenced : ' Whereas the ships in the West India trade frequently arrive in large fleets, and occasion great crowding, Confusion, and damage, and their Cargoes, being carried in lighters to the legal quays, cause upon the said quays great obstruction, and are exposed to pilfering,' etc. It proceeded that certain persons whose names were specified had agreed to form a company, with a capital of £500,000, to be called ' The West India Docks Company,' and to construct docks. After completion of the docks, dividends were not to exceed 10 per cent. The Trinity House were to approve the Dock-Masters, and were also to approve a Harbour-Master for the port of London. For twenty-one years all goods coming direct from the West Indies were to be landed in the new docks. Tobacco might be unshipped at the dock quays, and removed thence, without examination, to the King's Tobacco Warehouse. The Board of Customs, if satisfied at any time that the docks were full of shipping, might allow West Indiamen to discharge at the legal quays on the riverside. Outward-bound West Indiamen were to be loaded either in the docks, or in the river below the Blackwall entrance to the Canal.

All vessels docked were to be expeditiously unloaded, and then, if not intended to be loaded at once, were to be removed to the river. In recompense of the concession to the public convenience, the king was allowed certain tonnage dues on all ships coming to the port. These dues were to be paid in at the Custom-house. It was provided that the Treasury might advance money out of the Consolidated Fund to purchase land as site for the docks, and the residue of the Crown tonnage dues, after the expense of the river moorings and the salary of the Harbour-Master had been defrayed, was to be applied to repaying the moneys thus advanced by the Treasury. The dock rates were specified. The Common Council of London were empowered to charge transit dues for vessels passing through the Canal. The customs officers were empowered not to allow vessels concerned to enter inwards, till such dock or transit dues had been paid.*

---

* Soon afterwards an Act was passed authorizing the construction of a tunnel, wide enough for the passage of cattle and carriages, under the Thames, from Gravesend to Tilbury. This scheme proved abortive. The estimated cost was only £50,000! The stoppage of the works appears to have been due to an inrush of water and a mysterious fire, which destroyed the steam-engine and woodwork connected with the undertaking. The fire was thought to have been intentionally ignited, the blame being by some cast upon the authors of the undertaking, by others upon the Gravesend watermen.

In 1800 an additional excise duty at the usual rates was placed on foreign spirits. The total excise duties on foreign spirits after the passing of this Act were :

	Per Gallon.			Per Gallon.	
	£ s. d.			£ s. d.	
Single spirits from the Plantations ..	0 6 11	Double spirits from the Plantations ..	0 13 4
All other single spirits ..	0 8 5	All other double spirits ..	0 16 5

The customs duty was payable as well.

At the end of the preceding chapter was furnished an account of the general condition of the Customs department immediately prior to the passing of the Consolidation Act of 1787. As no further information in detail will be submitted with regard to the English Customs in this volume, it may be judicious, at this stage, to furnish another general review.

The benefits conferred by the Consolidation Act were vast, and the commerce of the country increased in consequence. The average annual net produce of the Customs, from 1789 to 1796 inclusive, was about £4,150,000. The cost of collection, compared with the *gross* receipts, was about 6¾ per cent.

The gross produce of 1796, after being decreased by a charge of £1,457,352 for drawbacks, allowances, bounties, etc., and nearly £400,000 for ' charges of management,' yielded a ' net produce ' of over £4,500,000, the highest return made up to that date. Out of this ' net ' nearly £40,000 was devoted to certain Scottish purposes, over £850,000 to ' bounties for encouraging national objects,' over £26,000 to bounties for naval seamen, and the residue, amounting to £3,612,676, was paid into the Exchequer. It should be mentioned that the return included the Scottish customs, but the Scottish contributions were still remarkably small. For instance, in 1782 the gross produce of English and Scottish customs had been in the proportions of about 15 to 1.   In 1796 the proportions were as below :

England and Wales : gross produce, £6,118,391.
Scotland :   ,,   ,,   263,511.

= say 23 to 1.

The value of English imports had increased from £11,650,000 in 1783 to £21,000,000 in 1796.   Exports had increased in value from £13,900,000 to over £29,000,000.

There were about 1,200 articles rated for duty—900 by rate, the rest *ad valorem*.   The amount raised on 1,040 of the 1,200 articles taxed failed to realize a total of £100,000 a year.   Several new special branches had been added since 1787, and experts had already begun to talk of a reconsolidation.   Certain reforms had been effected in the practice of the department.   The Receiver-General in London had been directed to make up his accounts every Saturday, and to pay the moneys into the Exchequer every Wednesday.   Thus he was no longer able to retain large sums of public money, nor were the various London collectors able to bank to their own accounts the outstanding proceeds of customs duties.   But it appears that the Receiver-General at Edinburgh still neglected to forward his remittances promptly, and sometimes kept back large sums, amounting to more than a quarter of the gross annual produce of the Scottish Customs.*

Many abuses remained.   The Plantation balances had not yet been passed in the Exchequer.   Though many of the patent offices had been abolished, the idiotic and expensive practice of issuing port-books was still pursued.

---

* A Committee of Finance, that sat during the concluding years of the century, made a startling pronouncement upon the tactics of this official.   'The compensation,' said they, 'which the Scottish Receiver-General may be entitled to ought to be by salary, not by profit derived from the use of the public money.'   It appears that Mr. John Campbell thought nothing of retaining for long periods sums amounting to £50,000 or more, though he gave security for but £25,000.   The Committee recommended that an effective officer should be put to fill the post, at about half Mr. Campbell's emoluments.

It had been recommended by Committees of inquiry that the Prisage, Butlerage, and Duty on Coals should be taken from the grantees and re-vested in the Crown, and the Board of Customs had supported the recommendation, but the reform had not been effected. The Auditors of Imprest still dealt with the Customs Annual Accounts, but it is apparent, from a scrutiny of the documents, that the auditing had become effective.

Selected Commissioners of Customs had visited the outports, and noted the evil influence of the customs charges upon coastwise traffic, the disastrous results of a system that entailed expensive bonds and sufferances upon almost every incident of mercantile intercourse betwixt creek and creek. Reform had been effected, and relief afforded to the quaint and homely coastwise trade.

Forty-six useless and expensive offices had been abolished, and many others would lapse on the death of holders. The ideas that the method of bonding duties should be amplified, that fees and gratuities should be done away with, that the system of appointment by patent should be limited, and that effective officers should be promoted by seniority, were fast coming into favour. But the preposterously brief ' clerical hours ' and the huge list of holidays endured.

Many of the revenue cruisers were still run ' on contract.'

Although forty-six offices had ' fallen in,' and many others had been abolished by the Treasury and the Board, the staff had increased in numbers on account of the great increase of commerce.

Some historians seem to have been of opinion, with regard to the tremendous naval, military, and disbursive efforts of the British people at this period, that ' all these things had to be.' Though the framers of statutes erred occasionally, their intentions may have been laudable and patriotic, for every care was taken that British ships were manned by British mariners, and it is certain that agriculture was not despised, as it came to be in mid-Victorian days. The older legislators longed to make Britain supreme in trade, yet strove, as far as their abilities allowed, to enable her to grow sufficient corn to feed her people for a space if her fleet failed to protect her.

Once more across the Border. It appears from the Montrose records that on May 3, 1787, the Commissioners of Customs at Edinburgh had to blame both themselves and the Montrose officers for failing to reward certain soldiers of the 7th Regiment of Foot, who had assisted in making seizures. The Scottish Board rectified matters by allowing the soldiers a sum out of the king's share, and the Montrose officers had to disburse a like sum out of their own receipts.

The Board also blamed the collector for not seeing that the reports of foreign ships were properly made out. Manifests had reached them in which the amounts of goods were stated in figures instead of words, and the cargoes described as consisting of packages, ' contents unknown.'

On May 9, 1787, the Board forwarded copies of the momentous ' Consolidating Act ' and the Tables appertaining, and blandly yet curtly threw all responsibilities of administration upon the collector and controller. ' We order you carefully to consider these, to the end that you may in every respect comply with the directions therein contained, as no excuse will be received for your not doing so.'

An excise officer made a seizure of 1,125 pounds tobacco, and 2,446 pounds tobacco stalks. He was awarded 3d. a pound on the tobacco, and 1d. a pound on the stalks, with a sum for expenses—in all £26 11s. 1d.

Later the Board sent certain instructions as to the Consolidating Act. Goods upon which the duties were reduced by the Act, carried in ships arriving before

May 10, 1787, were to be charged with the old duties, and the Board would afterwards return the difference. (This would apply to few except French goods. No instructions were given as to how other goods thus brought were to be dealt with ; but no doubt they would be liable to the increased duties.)

The collector of Dumfries had gone astray in dealing with Scottish salt removed to England. The inland duty on Scottish salt was less than on English, and such salt when removed across the Border had to pay the difference between the two duties. He of Dumfries had left it to the English officers to collect the difference on arrival of the goods, whereas he should have taken it before the goods left Scotland. The Board apprised the Montrose officers.

On June 28 the Board sent a copy of a letter received from the Treasury. Scottish officers of customs had been charging their countrymen illegally. They had taken certain coastwise fees which had lapsed of yore ; they had charged fees for dealing with parcels of goods of less than £5 value, and doubled the legal fees on shipments of coal. The Board ordered these malpractices to be discontinued on pain of instant dismissal, irrespective of rank of offender. A copy of the order was to be displayed at the Custom-house, and the officers were to sign it, ' that they may not pretend ignorance.'

On July 12 word was sent that the collector of Aberdeen had allowed a ship from Leghorn to discharge her cargo without performing quarantine. The Montrose officers were warned not to transgress thus. ' Only the fidelity and general good behaviour of the collector and controller of Aberdeen saved them from being dismissed. This will avail no officer in future.'

The London Board apprised their Edinburgh colleagues of a recent decision by the Attorney-General as to the conditions under which a British-born person might become an American citizen. ' Very difficult questions,' quoth the lawyer, ' may arise in consequence of the independence of America, but if I understand the present question it is whether a man born in Great Britain, and not resident in America at the time of grant of her independence, can make himself a subject of America. I am of opinion that he cannot. The man is a British subject, and may not legally command an American vessel in a British port.'

A startling exposure of official slackness occurred at Ferryden. To convey an accurate idea of the matter reference must be made to the regulations dealing with the lading and unlading of coastwise coal. All such coal was supposed to be accurately measured at shipment, and the quantity thus ascertained was reported at place of discharge. The duty was paid in a lump sum, and then the coal was measured out. If it proved to be less than the quantity paid on, there was no remission of duty, it being assumed that the master had landed part of the coal during transit, but if it proved to be more, a ' post entry ' had to be passed for the quantity in excess, and the extra duty made good.

There was a brisk trade in coal between Sunderland and Ferryden. At Sunderland the coal was measured in per Newcastle chalder, but at Ferryden it was measured out per Winchester chalder, and it must be borne in mind that the Newcastle chalder was almost twice as large as the Winchester measure. It appears that the Sunderland skippers merely reported so many ' chalders,' without specifying the kind of chalder used. It follows that each cargo should have measured out almost twice the quantity reported and duty-paid, and that in each case a post entry should have been passed for a sum almost equal to the duty originally deposited. Strange to tell, the years had flown by, and colliers a-many had come and gone, yet no post entries had been furnished. The customs tidesmen at Ferryden acted as coal-meters, and the landing-waiters were supposed to supervise them, and to tally the measures in the official books. When a cargo was discharged, the account was made up, and the books went to the collector at Montrose. He checked the records, initialled the duty accounts, and closed each transaction. How came it that the cargoes invariably turned out according to transire, when the great chalder was used at shipment, and the small one at discharge ?

The answer is that at Ferryden the coals were merely measured *on paper*. The landing-waiters winked at the tidesmen's misdeeds, and cooked their own accounts. The Sunderland skippers said nothing, and thus matters had proceeded for years and years, the Sunderland trade thriving, and Ferryden gradually increasing in importance as a place for the landing of English coal. It is scarcely probable that the officers were bribed. Coal-measuring is dirty work, and no doubt it was mere consideration of personal convenience that led to the practice of accepting the reported quantity as correct. The Ferryden officers did not know that the great chalder was in use at Sunderland, and the Sunderland skippers were not the men to enlighten them.

One day a new tidesman, named David Fettie, was appointed to the duty. He insisted on actually measuring the coals, and a huge post entry had to be called for. The same thing occurred with the next cargo measured by him, and the Montrose collector at once communicated with the Sunderland customs officers. Then the entire business was laid bare, and the collector reported matters to the Commissioners at Edinburgh, who sent back a demand for the last few years' coal-books, and it is conceivable that when they arrived the Commissioners scanned them dubiously, noting the extreme symmetry of the tallies, and the absence of grimy finger-marks. The further inquiry went, the worse did matters appear. But it seems that the magnitude of the considerations involved stayed the hand of Authority. The Board censured the tidesmen and landing-waiters, and gave the collector and controller weighty warning. The letters conveying the censure occupied many pages, therefore they may not be reproduced, yet are well worth reading, one bears some evidence of having been composed by the great political economist who was at that time a member of the Scottish Board. They were solemn productions, yet coloured by one humorous passage, levelled at the landing-waiters, who had stated in defence that they were kept too busily occupied with the foreign trade to be able to apply themselves to supervising the discharge of coal cargoes. But the Board had observed that though the landing-waiters had not had time to attend, they had collected the fees incidental. And therefore they adjured them, while the foreign trade remained brisk, to abandon the coal-measuring fees in favour of people like David Fettie.

Information was sent from Edinburgh of a Pittenweem sloop which had gone to Flushing, and been sold there to a smuggling syndicate. The command of the sloop had then been granted to a foreigner, and her original captain had thought it worth while to ship in her as an ordinary seaman. She took in a cargo of brandy, and ran the greater part of it at Tweedmouth, but was driven off by a gale before she could complete discharge. Then she returned to Flushing. During the voyage she was challenged by a revenue cruiser, and made answer that she was from Hull with timber. The cruiser thereupon let her pass. Who sent this information? It must have been some one who took part in the run.

A most extravagantly worded letter reached the Scottish Board, accusing the collector's clerk at Montrose of illegal connivance. It commenced, ' In the course of my nocturnal perambulations I observed a piece of business which I was somewhat surprised at,' and went on to state that the collector's clerk deliberately sent the customs boat on a wild-goose chase, and then with two boatmen assisted certain friends of his to run a large quantity of contraband goods. ' Many such things happen. The officers seldom make seizures, and then but small ones, and from people not in their confidence. More villainy is carried on and contrived by that clerk and his adherents than by all the revenue officers in Scotland.'

The Board appear to have attached little importance to this, thinking it likely that the letter was from some pompous scoundrel desirous of stepping into the clerk's shoes. It was signed ' An Observator.'

During 1788 many seizures of goods concealed on board regular traders were made at various ports, and the Board directed that shipmasters should be warned that in all such cases proceedings would be taken to condemn the ships as well as the goods. ' Hitherto,' said the Board in confidence to their subordinates, ' we have refrained from doing so, thinking that the concealments may have been encouraged by the improper lenity, negligence, or connivance of officers.'

The seizures at Montrose during one quarter reached the following amounts :

1,643 pounds tobacco, and 1,122 pounds tobacco stalks, captured by Customs.

1,605 pounds tobacco, and 1,099 pounds tobacco stalks, captured by Excise.

John Watt, customs boatman at Montrose, attempted to seize certain carts conveying tobacco across ' the Links,' and the smugglers treated him to a pistol-shot at short range. Later the Board granted payment of a doctor's bill, amounting to £8 19s. 6d., for ' extracting a Bullet from the Belly ' of the said unlucky John, the doctor protesting that he had made the bill ' as reasonable as possible.'

It was a Scottish revenue practice to pay drawbacks and bounties to agents as well as principals. The Board directed the Scottish collectors to conform to the English practice of paying the allowances to principals only. Later, at the advice of the Lord Advocate, and application of the Glasgow merchants, they allowed the old system to continue, with certain qualifications.

The officers at Montrose made a curious seizure of unreported goods, the parcel consisting of a few dried tongues, a piece of salt beef, a ham, and a pot of pickled eels. The Board allowed the ham and tongues to be delivered on payment of duty. The beef and eels were compounded for by payment of 5s. 6d. per £1 value.

The amount of tobacco seized during the quarter ending April, 1789, was as follows :

Customs : 8,359 pounds tobacco, and 2,187 pounds tobacco-stalks.

Excise : 2,607 pounds tobacco.

The Board issued instructions to amend the oath used by manufacturers who desired to remove tobacco 'from warehouse to mill,' it being thought that the terms of the oath in use were not sufficiently solemn. The words, ' as he shall answer to God,' were therefore interpolated.

It having been discovered that some of the Scottish officers, on exchanging or resigning offices in favour of others, received large sums of money for the concession, the Board directed that all parties to such transactions should make oath, as in England, that no money had passed between them.

In 1790 an order was issued by the Privy Council authorizing the capture of all ' straggling seamen ' fit to serve in the navy. Sir George Holme, ' regulator of the Impress,' requested the Scottish Board to order the captains of revenue cruisers to detain the crews of all smuggling vessels fallen in with, and communicate with the head Impress officer at Leith, who would then take steps to secure the culprits for his Majesty's service.

The collector sent to Edinburgh his yearly ' Account of Ages and Capacities ' (a return specifying the age, official attainments, and private character of each officer employed under him). In this he gently insinuated that certain tidesmen, including the two who for years had so unsuccessfully checked the output of coal at Ferryden, had a habit of crooking the elbow overmuch. In return he received a sharp rap o' the knuckles. The Board commented upon his statement that he reported princi-pally from hearsay, and told him it was his business to see all the port tidesmen every day, and those at the creeks frequently, ' so as to be able to report their real behaviour.'

He was to caution the tidesmen concerned that unless they refrained in future they would be dismissed, and in his next report to state whether the land-surveyors, landing-waiters, and coast-waiters were ' sober men.'

The captain of a Greenland trader back from the whale fishery claimed the usual voyage bounty, but the Board refused to allow it, as he had not carried the prescribed complement of ' green men.'

Mariners of Greenland ships were exempt from press, and collectors had power to grant them ' certificates of protection.' Tidings reached Edinburgh that the certificates were often granted to others for a pecuniary consideration, and the Board called for a return of all documents of protection previously issued.

Two landing-waiters at Port Glasgow had made it a practice to underweigh sugar. An invoice of two cargoes thus improperly weighed came into the possession of an officer at Greenock, who sent it to the Glasgow collector. The collector reported the matter to the Board, but his report was diffident in tone, and absurdly partial in defence of the offenders. The Board sent a Mr. Osborn to investigate, and so many and remarkable were his discoveries that the Board dismissed the two landing-waiters, and censured the rest of the staff, being particularly severe upon the controller. A full report of the case, with the Commissioners' remarks, was sent to all the Scottish ports.

If a case of the kind occurred in modern days, the port concerned would be provided with a completely new staff. But in 1790 appointments were usually the result of aristocratic recommendation, and it was a risky proceeding to cancel them. This may account for the leniency shown, and for the lengthy report, which filled many pages of the Montrose letter-book, and in elegant language bewailed the condition of affairs. Such gentle yet cutting censure, such stately moralizing, such impressive admonition, had never before appeared in official manuscript, even above the signatures of the Scottish

Commissioners of the period. The report was unsurpassable in detail ; the complicated matter was unravelled and displayed with real literary skill.

It was made plainly apparent that the dismissed officers had carried on fraud for a considerable period, with the knowledge and to the great pecuniary benefit of the Glasgow sugar merchants. They had reserved a means of defence by weighing the casks before they were coopered. In most cases the packages were brought to the scale in a damaged condition, as landed from the importing vessel. They were then underweighed, and afterwards coopered ; and thus the culprits were enabled to put forward the plea that portions of the sugar might have escaped after weighing and before or during repair, and that the addition of staves and hoops might have increased the gross weight, and have suggested to the merchants the possibility of increasing the net on the invoices, the customs tare being of course inscribed upon the casks. But the plea, though in a way plausible, did not avail. It was evident, too, that the officers underweighed for lucre, and made the underweighing proportionate to the extent of reward given by the respective merchants concerned. In some cases the discrepancies amounted to a few pounds only on each hogshead ; in others to hundreds of pounds.

It was curious, too, that whenever the casks were flagrantly underweighed the landing-surveyor, whose duty it was to check the weighing at intervals, and to record the times at which he checked, did not subscribe his initials against the packages selected, although it was afterwards proved that he had gone through the ceremony of reweighing.

It was also strange that when Mr. Osborn visited the port, and called for the incriminating invoice, the collector had to admit that he had restored it to the merchant concerned. And when Mr. Campbell, the said merchant, was asked for the invoice, he stoutly refused to surrender it, and actually convened a meeting of the Glasgow sugar merchants, all of whom as stoutly pledged themselves to furnish no information to the Crown. The collector and controller, too, had never troubled themselves with superintending the outdoor work, and on this matter the Board pointed out to them that it was their duty to see that the practical customs business was properly carried on. The collector was let off lightest, ' being a young man and new to customs work,' which statement, when the growing trade of Port Glasgow is taken into account, should be admirably illustrative of the qualities then considered necessary to fit one for occupation of an important collectorship. It is a pity that want of space forbids full discussion of this remarkable official document, remarkable equally for its majestic literary qualities, the dignity of its official doctrine, the dexterity of its deductions, the mildness of its punitive prescriptions, and the illumination it sheds upon the revenue methods of its day.

Little mention of the Irish Customs has hitherto been made in this treatise, but, as the Union of Great Britain and Ireland will be the subject of the opening pages of the second volume, the first may be profitably concluded with a brief history of Irish revenue, and a few extracts from the Irish records.

It appears that prior to the conquest of Ireland by Henry II. the revenues of the Irish monarchs were allotted at the meetings of the National Council. The Church was free of all taxes, and it is likely that the royal impositions were light and cheerfully rendered. The petty chiefs were empowered to exercise purveyance, and to billet warriors upon their subjects. After conquest by the English most of the Norman feudal impositions were introduced, but there is reason to believe that little revenue was collected in the districts remote from English occupation.

The Irish Exchequer was located at Dublin early in the thirteenth century, and for a considerable length of time the Irish Treasurer accounted to the English Exchequer for his receipts. The Irish revenue officials were appointed by the English king.

There is little worth recounting in the statutes till the time of Edward IV., when it was enacted that if hides or ' other staple merchandise ' were carried from Ulster into Scotland without payment of ' the custom of the Cocket ' the goods should be forfeited.*

The next statute prescribed that every merchant trading from England to Ireland should bring 100s. worth of bows with every £100 worth of merchandise, Ireland being ' desolated of bows.' (This would appear to imply that poundage was levied on imported goods.†) Later it was enjoined that hawks carried out of Ireland should be liable to a special impost, ' besides poundage.' (Thus it is evident that poundage was levied on exported goods.) The rates of the impost were as follows :

On each goshawk	..	..	..	1 mark.‡
,, tiercel	..	..	..	½ mark.
,, falcon	..	..	..	10 shillings.

The Irish Lord Treasurer was empowered to appoint the customs officials.

A later statute (14 Hen. VII., c. 1) provided that all Acts existing in England for punishment of controllers, collectors, and searchers who misbehaved should apply in Ireland.

* Acts of Ireland.

† Butlerage was levied, as in England, for the patent appointing Slegh and Sologhan as controllers of Cork and Kinsale empowered the grantees to collect the customs Cocket duties, and the custom of 2s. on every cask of wine imported by merchant strangers.

‡ The Patent Rolls of Richard II. furnish evidence that the king occasionally sent an agent into Ireland to pre-empt hawks and falcons. It appears also that there was a law against absentees, for in the patent appointing Richard's yeoman Lowyk gauger and general surveyor in Ireland the grantee was directed, after rendering an account to the Irish Exchequer, to bring his takings to England, the statute against absentees notwithstanding.

Poundage was levied by statute at 12d. on all goods exported or imported; wine and oil, which were subject to Prisage, excepted. (Bulk not to be broken at import till goods entered in the customer's books.) Most writers on Irish revenue seem to have thought that this was the first levy of poundage. The quotations furnished above may perhaps be held sufficient refutation. It is tolerably clear that poundage was introduced into Ireland soon after its appearance in England (and that Prisage and the Ancient Custom existed from the beginning of English occupation). Yet it is unlikely that it was collected regularly in the districts beyond the Pale.*

Henry VIII. prohibited the exportation of Irish wool. The Act was extensively infringed, and it appears to have been imperfect, as no provision was made towards granting the customs officers power of 'entry and search.' It was reaffirmed and amended by a later Act, which provided heavy penalties upon negligence on the part of the searchers. One Edward Abecke, a Manchester merchant, was allowed partial exemption. He was empowered to ship £40 worth of Irish wool per year to England.

The three ports mentioned were farmed by four merchants, who paid £307 a year, made up as below:

For Dublin	..	..	..	..	£146	13	4
For Drogheda	..	..	..	..	138	6	8
For Dundalk	..	..	..	..	22	0	0

During Elizabeth's reign it was found that the prohibition of wool had been frequently evaded, both by 'stealing' (smuggling) and by the obtaining of licences

---

* During Henry IV.'s reign William Mirson and John Mirson, Englishmen who acted as collectors of Irish customs, were allowed to employ deputies, the country being in so mutinous a condition that the Mirsons found it dangerous to visit remote ports unless formidably guarded. (It is possible that the unfortunate deputies went without escort, and took more chances than duties.) Ireland seems to have suffered in trading with England. The Rolls show that much 'old' (corrupt) wine was shipped to Ireland. In one of the licences it was stipulated that the wine should be of a kind not drinkable in England.

from the higher resident officials. Therefore a prohibitive duty was levied, applying not only to wool, but
to several other agricultural products. Below are the
rates (outward) :

Wool, 5s. per stone (8 pounds).
Flax and yarn, 1s. a pound.
Fells, 4d. each.
Deer-skins, 2s. 6d. each.
Beef (salted), 1d. a pound ; 5s. a firkin ; 10s. a half-
barrel ; £1 a barrel ; £2 a hogshead ; £4 a pipe.
Tallow, 2s. a stone.
Wax, 1s. a pound.
Butter, 6d. a pound.

Heavy port duties were levied on the goods, in addition
to the customs.

Another statute restricted the importation of wine to
certain ports, and prescribed the following imposts :

Spanish and Levant wines in denizens' ships : 40s. a tun (coin
of Ireland).
French and German wines in denizens' ships: 26s. 8d. a tun
(coin of Ireland).
Spanish and Levant wines in aliens' ships: 53s. 4d. a tun (coin
of Ireland).
French and German wines in aliens' ships : 40s. per tun (coin
of Ireland).

The Lord Deputy was allowed 20 tuns a year duty-free
for the use of his household, and empowered to prescribe
the quantities to be granted duty-free to peers and to
members of the Council.

It was enacted that woollen cloth and woollen stuff
might only be exported by merchants of the Irish staple
towns, or by such English merchants as bought from
them.

The next Act rendered smuggling of wool felony, the
heavy duty having failed to keep the wool in the country.

On account of depredations committed by French
pirates, Messrs. Walsh and Wise, Waterford merchants,
were allowed to take certain duties upon the ships and
goods of French traders in Irish ports, till they recovered
the amount lost by piracy (£1,300). They levied 18d. a

ton as tonnage dues, 3s. a tun on wine, 2s. a ton on iron, and 18d. a ton on salt.

The wine impost was reaffirmed.

In 1610 Robert Cogan was made surveyor-general of Irish Customs, his appointment being ' a reward for good and painful services taken in setting of the Customs of Ireland.' He had a salary of £100 a year, and was allowed to nominate officers.

In 1627 Charles increased the duties upon certain Irish goods exported otherwise than to England. The principal commodities surtaxed were fish, butter, salted flesh, hides, candles, iron, wool, cattle, horses, and corn. Wool and hides might only be exported under royal licence. The reason furnished was that Ireland, ' by reason of peace and plenty,' had been enabled to export goods not only to England, but to countries not friendly. Falkland was Chancellor of Ireland, and it is evident that Butlerage was still levied, or that Elizabeth's wine impost survived, for Lord Hay held a lease of the Irish wine duties, granted in 1613, and paid £1,400 a year for his farm. Charles I. issued a close writ, directing Falkland to pay one Cave, a customs officer, a special fee of £107 10s. a year, Cave having been diligent ' in reforming the " Book of Rates " and advancing the Irish Customs.' Later Cave petitioned, stating that his wages were in arrear.

Meanwhile Lord Hay repeatedly complained that the Irish wine importers were destitute of money,* and that he had frequently taken bonds from them for subsequent payment, released their goods, and failed to recover. Charles directed Falkland to exert himself on Hay's behalf. It seems that Falkland was unable to render much assistance, for Charles communicated with him again, stating that it had been stipulated in the patent of grant that the rent should be abated if trade declined ; that trade had declined, and Hay had not complained, yet

---

* Yet the king's Declaration (see above) had stated that Ireland had become a land ' of peace and plenty ' !

he should not suffer. Therefore the Irish Exchequer officials were instructed to allow the expenses of Hay's agents ' in a large, ample, and beneficent manner.'

In 1631 Charles laid a heavy impost upon Irish exports and imports.

Irish Commissioners of Revenue were appointed soon after the Restoration. The first was Sir George Blundell. In 1662 five others were appointed—Gorges, Smith, Dodson, Bligh, and Muschamp. They managed the tunnage on wine and oil, and the poundage on imported and exported merchandise, as granted by an Act dating from December 31, 1661. Later they received another commission, empowering them to manage ' the Excise or New Impost,' and the inland excise on beer, ale, etc. Later ' additional duties ' were placed upon certain imported goods. The ' New Impost ' was paid by the first buyer of foreign merchandise and wine.

An official was appointed, described as ' Taster of Wines and other Liquors, and Surveyor of the Outs and Defects of the same.' By ' outs ' were meant such casks of imported wine or spirits as were found almost empty when landed. The servants of this patentee (the work was performed by deputies) surveyed all ' outs,' and if satisfied allowed them to pass duty-free. They had also power to taste all imported wine and spirits, and decide as to quality. It is conceivable that there were many persons in Ireland, and in England too, who would have desired no better occupation than to act as deputies gratis. The patentee took fees, and his office was tolerably lucrative. Sometimes the patent was divided between two.* The fees incidental were as follows : ' For every butt, pipe, puncheon, or large cask tasted or surveyed, 6d. ; for every hogshead, tierce, barrel, rundlet, or smaller vessel, 3d.'

The ' king's ports ' were Dublin, Wexford, Waterford, Kinsale, Cork, Dingle, Limerick, Galway, Carrickfergus,

* In 1772 it was held by the Hon. John Beresford and Marcus Beresford.

Strangford, and Drogheda.   Drogheda included Dundalk and Carlingford, Carrickfergus included Belfast, Dublin included Wicklow and Arklow.

According to Sir William Petty, England exported goods to Ireland to the value of £60,000 a year, and the Irish exports to England reached a yearly value of £150,000, the excess being principally in Irish cattle and sheep.   Irish agriculture had prospered since the settlement of the Cromwellians.   (It will be remembered that the exportation of Irish live stock to England was forbidden in 1664.)   Sir William estimated the average weight of an Irish fleece at two pounds.   He commented upon the extensive use of tobacco, and stated that the smoking of that weed in short pipes, together with ' sneezing ' (snuff-taking), formed the chief pleasure of the Irishmen's lives.*

The newly appointed Commissioners at once started a survey, there being many arrears.   It is stated that up to 1658 the amount overdue had been £6,300 ; thence to 1660, £35,000 ; thence to 1662, £29,000.   £25,800 was owing in the port of Dublin alone.

The Commissioners had to manage the Crown-rents, composition-rents, and quit-rents.   Crown-rents were

* Undoubtedly he regarded the native Irish with unmeasured contempt.   His treatise teemed with bitter reflections upon their habits.   The spectacle of a well-ordered, well-meaning Englishman, busily applying cold figures to the inner life of a quaint and vagarious race, is by no means rare, yet not one whit the less amusing.   Indeed, Sir William's book is well worth reading on this account alone.   What can be better than his lugubrious reference to the condition of affairs at an earlier date, when an Englishman was held guiltless for killing an Irishman ?   His summary of matters relative to Irish shipbuilding is equally quaint.   It appears that even in his day the Irish attributed Ireland's deficiency in shipping solely to ' the policy of the English.'   He treated the argument in ruthless fashion.   Said he : ' I have never perceived any impediment of building or having ships in Ireland but men's own indisposition thereto.'   He went on to state that the Irish preferred buying ships from the Dutch to building them, and that most Irishmen were naturally averse to a seafaring life, and would rather ' eat potatoes and milk on dry land than contest with the winds and waves with better food.'

proceeds of patents granted to favourites, enabling them to hold Church lands vacated at the Reformation, and lands forfeited by rebels. Composition-rents were acknowledgments from the holders of certain lands in Clare and Connaught, made in lieu of ' Cess and Press,' and dating from the time of Elizabeth. Quit-rents were dues from lands which had been forfeited in the rebellion of 1641, and then granted to adventurers (mostly Cromwellians). The Commissioners also accounted for ' Hearth-money '— in short, they supervised the entire Irish Revenue. They had not all equal powers ; the usual number of their body was seven, of whom only five were competent to deal with the inland duties. The arrangement of the Irish Board down to 1772 furnishes a confusing branch of study ; therefore it may be best to give only a rough indication of the history of the staff, ending with as concise a description as possible of the course of revenue practice, and a few pages of narrative.

In 1663 one of the Privy Councillors was appointed to sit with the Commissioners. The king leased the tunnage, poundage, and import excise, the farmers paying £55,000 a year, and being allowed to act as extra Commissioners. Then he leased the inland excise to the Earl of Orrery and Lord Kingston for £36,600 a year. Only three of the original Commissioners remained in office, to audit the farmers' account.

In 1664 the inland excise was let to farm at £39,000 a year. The odious tax of Hearth-money was instituted, and farmed for £30,000 a year.

In 1669 the king let the entire Revenue to eleven persons, mostly citizens of London.

In 1671 the farm was granted to Lord Ranelagh and others. The Lord Lieutenant, the Archbishop of Dublin, the Lord Treasurer, and six others, were made temporary Commissioners, to supervise the farmers' proceedings.

In 1675 the king leased the Revenue to twelve farmers, and appointed the Irish Chancellor of the Exchequer, with ten others, as supervising Commissioners. In the following year he leased it afresh to a number of financiers, mostly London citizens, for £240,000 a year, and appointed Commissioners to supervise and audit.

In 1677 the brothers Bridges, London citizens, advanced the king £36,000 odd for the Irish military establishment, and were put on the Revenue to recoup. They were empowered to recover the money advanced, and other sums which would amount to a surplus of about £11,000. To secure this they levied 1s. in the £1 on the farmers' payments.

Some of the officers' legal perquisites, as stated in the regulation 'Table of Fees,' were taken in the form of petty prisage. The following have a quaint suggestiveness :

'Out of every barque or boat for bringing in apples : To the Searcher, one hundred of the same.

'Out of every barque or boat for bringing in oysters : To the Searcher, one hundred of the same.

'For Gaging every Tun of wine : To the Gager, fourpence : Besides out of every ship bringing in wines, one small bottle of wine for a Gaging bottle.'

Farming ceased in 1682, and thenceforward the Revenue was under sole management of the Commissioners. A Receiver-General was appointed in 1683, to act instead of the Vice-Treasurer. The new official was one Price, a London merchant, who had lent the king £16,000. He received a salary of £1,000 a year, besides fees. In 1688, two persons named Bond and Doe were allowed to pay him out, and divide the appointment between them.

When William III. reconquered Ireland, new Commissioners and a new Receiver-General were appointed. The Commissioners were called upon to manage additional quit-rents upon lands forfeited because their owners had supported James II. (In 1715 the renowned duke of Ormond was expatriated. The Ormond family had furnished a couple of Lord Treasurers, and held the Prisage of Ireland for many years.)

In 1704 the Board were entrusted with the collection

of the tonnage dues on vessels, which dues were appropriated to the upkeep of lighthouses on the Irish coast. The tonnage duties had been imposed soon after the Restoration, and their proceeds granted to Sir Robert Reading and his heirs, on condition that the grantees kept the lighthouses in good working order. This they had failed to do, so the Irish Parliament dispossessed them.

The Prisage was taken from its holder, the Earl of Arran, who had succeeded to the forfeited estates of the Ormonds, but he and his family were granted £3,500 a year as compensation. Later the grant was made £4,000.

Some rather interesting correspondence took place between the Irish Commissioners and the Treasury in 1724 on the subject of 'Wood's halfpence.' On August 29 the Commissioners wrote, acknowledging receipt from the Treasury of a copy of the bond entered into by Wood. Their letter continued :

'We humbly beg leave to assure your Lordships that we never gave any orders or Intimations to prevent or obstruct ye circulation of ye said Halfpence.

'As to your Lordships' commands to order all our officers not to receive in any one Paiment above fivepence-halfpenny in ye said copper coin, we think it our indispensable Duty—from ye Disorder this nation is in at present about these Halfpence, & ye Declarations that have been sign'd by all sorts of People & publish'd that they will not receive or utter them. We are under ye utmost difficulty to execute the same. . . .

'Y^e Acts of Customs & Excise having upon this occasion been inculcated into ye minds of ye People, by repeated Pamphlets and Papers dispers'd over ye Kingdom, informing them that all ye King's Dutys are to be paid in Sterling Money, or current money of England, as ye said Acts express :—And tho' we apprehend that Mr. Wood's Halfpence are not intended by your Lordships to be paid otherwise than by way of change, yet ye Prejudice conceiv'd against them is such that this Argument will have but little force.'

They proceeded at some length, stating their belief that the introduction of the halfpence would disturb and complicate the collection of revenue, and that there were not sufficient safeguards against Mr. Wood issuing and circulating more than the £40,000 worth stipulated in the patents.

The issue of port-books to the collectors was continued up to the middle of the eighteenth century, though the books were obsolete. It appears that this was done for no other purpose than to enrich the Remembrancer and the Pursuivant. These Exchequer officials charged heavy fees, the Remembrancer extorting 10s. for issuing each book, and the Pursuivant 3s. 4d. for delivering the same. The collectors refused to pay the fees, and the issue of the unwelcome documents ceased.

Separate Boards were appointed in 1772, one set of Commissioners managing the tunnage and poundage, the other the remaining branches of revenue.

In 1783, that year of disastrous inquisition into revenue methods both in Great Britain and Ireland, elaborate instructions were sent from Dublin as to the transmission of outport accounts and balances, the Board stating that many collectors had deceived the Accountant-General by means of false returns, and shown considerable sums as 'arrears of duty' which had been collected. About a dozen collectors were dismissed, the total defalcations amounting to a huge sum.

In 1779 the Irish Parliament passed resolutions in favour of free trade. In 1793 an Act was passed empowering Ireland to share in the East India trade.

The business of the port of Dublin had increased so much during the eighties that the 'Old Custom House' was found unsuitable, and a new one was erected. In 1796 docks were opened at Dublin.

A general review of the Irish revenue, from 1662 to the end of the eighteenth century, reveals little of interest, compared with the varied aspects of English revenue during the same period. The customs duties were much lighter than those obtaining in England. The allowances for leakage and damage on wines imported were much the same as the English allowances. The poundage was preferential with regard to British and Plantation goods, which paid about six-sevenths of the amount charged upon foreign merchandise.

The 'import-excise' levies were payable by retailers. Merchant-importers were exempt, provided they entered into bond for securing payment of the duties by the retailers who bought the goods from them. Retailers were not allowed drawback if they exported goods after paying the import-excise, but a merchant-importer might discharge his bond for the excise duties by exporting his goods. Thus there were two distinct classes of importers. The most favoured were the 'merchants,' but they might only sell their goods to be sold again ; they might not offer them to the actual consumers. The other class included the retailers, and those who imported for private use. These last were called 'consumptioners.' In practice, the merchants usually found it profitable to pay the import-excise themselves, as they secured an abatement by doing so, and then charged full prices to the retailers, who were not entitled to abatement in any case.

Most of the 'additional duties' were appropriated to various branches of expenditure—'the Loan,' 'the Tillage,' 'Lagan navigation,' etc. One of the later inland duties, the hawkers' and pedlars' licence branch, went to the maintenance of 'Protestant Schools.'

There is not much worth quoting as regards the interior economy of the Irish revenue department. The salaries paid were merely nominal, but the officers reaped an abundant harvest of fees. The duties were loosely collected ; even the imposition of fees appears to have been conducted in vagarious fashion, for when in 1762 one of the landing-waiters complained that the merchants refused to give him the usual 'gratuities,' the Board merely directed him to furnish a return upon oath of the total amount withheld, and they would make it good. It seems that some of the officers' relatives had queer notions upon such matters, for in 1781 the Board found it necessary to proclaim that the right of taking fees ceased at death. It must not be inferred from this that the shades of the departed continued to plague merchants ; the fact was that certain officers' widows had appealed to be allowed to continue their husbands' depredations.

Some of the instructions to officers were comical. Goods ' infected with the plague ' were directed to be sunk ' in 20 fathoms water at 14 leagues from land,' and we presume that the collector who tried to carry out this order literally had some trouble in finding the regulation depth at the regulation distance. Coast-waiters were ordered to go at sunrise and sunset to ' the highest spot in the neighbourhood,' and take a good long look around, to ascertain if any suspicious vessels were in sight. The customs gaugers seem to have been on capital terms with the wine-merchants, for in 1725 these latter were forbidden to continue a practice of giving the officers, *before the casks were gauged*, ' some gallons thereof under the name of the gauger's bottle.'*

Certain prohibitions and restrictions may be quoted :

1. East India goods might only be imported via England.

2. Asiatic, African, and American goods were subject to the Navigation Act.

3. Russian goods might only be imported in British, Irish, or Russian ships.

4. Plantation goods might only be imported via Great Britain.

5. Hops might only be imported via Great Britain.

6. Glass might only be imported when British.

A few articles of merchandise were duty-free inwards, the most important being dyeing drugs, linen cloth *made in Great Britain*, looms, and wool. Irish fustians, Irish

* See p. 431. It appears that the 'small bottle ' had grown into a demijohn.

flax seed, Irish flour, Irish linen cloth, and Irish rape oil were duty-free outwards. A premium was granted on Irish corn and flax seed exported in British or Irish shipping, when the price in Ireland did not exceed a certain specified sum. Irish fish and Irish sail-cloth were also bountied.

It must be admitted that the revenue regulations applicable to Irish commerce favoured Great Britain and harassed Ireland. The restriction most baneful was that upon wool and woollen products, which might only be exported to British ports. Thus the Irish woollen manufacture was slowly strangled. Irish agriculture also suffered, both by this and restrictions upon the exportation of Irish cattle to Great Britain. The products of the Plantations and the East Indies might only reach the western island through the ports of her more powerful rival. An utter and appalling selfishness was manifest in all English commercial dealings with Ireland. On certain occasions relaxations were made, noticeably towards the end of the American war, but they were relaxations dictated by selfishness. In the struggle for commercial supremacy, neither nations nor individuals have ever shown tenderness to each other. The strong have always oppressed and defrauded the weak, and, so long as men or nations subsist and prosper by buying and selling, this will be the case.

A remarkable instance of this grim practice with commercial men of thrusting burdens upon the feeble, and setting the able free, is discovered in the continuance in Ireland of that dreadful tax, Hearth-money, a duty of 2s. per annum on every hearth, firing-place, or stove. If a house had no chimney, and there were many such ' houses ' in the Ireland of that day, it was charged for two hearths. This practice actually found support amongst certain writers, who urged that it was likely to bring about the building of one-chimneyed houses. But Hearth-money was levied on *the tenant ;* therefore the landlord continued to build and let chimneyless hovels. Paupers were exempt under the Act, but in practice none was let off unless '*unable* to labour by reason of age, sickness, or bodily infirmity.' A man might be unemployed half a year at a time, but Hearth-money was still demandable from him. The following quotations give different but interesting views on the Hearth-tax.

The first is from a book published by Nicholas Eaton, Equalizer of Duties at Dublin in 1767. Said Eaton : ' There are Numbers of idle lazy Beggars in this Kingdom who live entirely upon the mistaken Charity of the Publick. . . . Such indolent vagrants were never designed to be favoured by this Act, which ought strictly and literally to be put in Force against them.'

The next is an utterance by Mr. Howard, Attorney to the Exchequer, a gentleman who in 1772 produced a luminous treatise on Irish revenue. He expressed himself thus with regard to Hearth-money : ' I could wish that the Hearth-tax were arranged as the House-tax is in England, under which cottages are exempt, and that the occupiers of the many wretched hovels here had been exempted even as the cottagers there, and the deficiency supplied by enlarging the tax upon those of sufficient ability to pay.'

The returns of Irish revenue are vague, and appear to be full of confusing contradictions. It is rather strange that in 1664 the Revenue should have been *farmed* for £124,000, and in 1676 for £240,000, and that the net return in 1688, when no farmers' profits preyed upon the balance, should have been only £150,000. The land was convulsed by rebellion at the latter date ; still, the statements are curious. The Revenue swelled gradually from £150,000 in 1688 to £1,560,000 in 1801—say an average rise of £12,500. Yet the return in 1799 shows an increase of £200,000. Perhaps a deal of revenue had been left uncollected during 1798, and the arrears were made good in 1799.*

* It is evident that trade was suspended for a time at Wicklow in 1798 (*vide* p. 439).

The Wicklow records furnish rather interesting details of the Irish practice towards the end of the century.

In 1795 the Irish Board apprised the Wicklow collector that they had received the Lord Mayor of Dublin's quarterly statement of the prices of corn ; that the said prices were on the high scale, except as regarded beans ; and that consequently all corn except beans must be prohibited from exportation ; also that vessels carrying butter from Ireland to Portugal (about the only export trade to that country) were to bring back salt. Bond was to be insisted on for fulfilment of this condition, the amount of such bond to be £1,000 for a vessel under 200 tons, £2,000 for a larger vessel.

An importer applied to Dublin for leave to land ' a general cargo ' at Ballymoney, consisting of salt, tobacco, pipes, scythe-stones, and shot. The Board directed the collector to ascertain the use to which said shot was to be put. The collector replied that it was for the use of sportsmen. ' This,' he stated, ' I have no doubt of.'

There were mines at Arklow, worked by the ' Hibernian Mine Company.' The Company were constantly complaining that their importations of coal, etc., were obstructed by the customs officers. The Board wrote the collector, directing him not to delay the Company's business. Later Sackville Hamilton, Secretary to the Lord Lieutenant, apprised the Board that a gold mine had been discovered near Arklow, and that thousands of people were resorting thither, and gathering the ore.

Evidently great things were expected, for the Secretary complained that whisky booths were becoming plentiful in the vicinity of the mine. The Board told the Wicklow collector to proceed to the locality and protect the ore, ' as the property of His Majesty's Government.'

But the collector was not going to trust himself amongst the mustering peasantry, especially as whisky booths were plentiful thereabout. He sent word back that sufficient force could not be gathered in the neighbourhood to overawe the amateur miners. Besides, he was suffering from rheumatism. Further instructions desired. Directly afterwards he wrote again, asking if his letter had miscarried, as 'he had heard nothing of the soldiers.' Evidently the collector knew how to take care of himself. Soldiers were sent in plenty, and he then carried out his instructions.

In 1796 the Board received a memorial from the Hibernian Mine Company and the inhabitants of Arklow, stating that though they imported annually 5,000 tons of coal, besides large quantities of iron plates and fire-bricks, there was no adequate provision for reporting vessels and paying duty ; that each shipmaster had to go to the Custom-house at Wicklow to report, clear, etc., and thus had to travel in all seventy-two miles on customs business. They suggested that the officer stationed at Arklow should be allowed to 'invoice and clear vessels,' and to take duties. This the collector stoutly opposed, no doubt with an eye to his fees. He stated that Arklow was only twelve miles away, and that the masters made but two journeys, thus travelling only forty-eight miles. It seems that the petitioners had exaggerated ; still, the Board thought fit to comply, deeming the mines 'of great public utility.' So the collector was ordered to entrust the customs business of Arklow to a 'proper person,' who might take duty on bricks, coal, iron plates, rock-salt, and slate inward, and on copper, ore of copper, and iron outward.

In 1798 the collector reported thus : 'The very wretched and disturbed state of this part of the kingdom has put a total stop to all business, consequently neither duties can be ascertained or obtained, nor vouchers returned.' The Board asked for fuller particulars. The collector then sent word that there was no part of the county of Wicklow but was in a state of disturbance, that the troops had been 'watching the rebels day and night,' and that during the night previous there had been an engagement,* in which

* There is an account of this battle in Sir Jonah Barrington's 'Rise and Fall of the Irish Nation.'

General Needham, at the head of a force of yeomanry and militia, had defeated a body of insurgents 20,000 strong. ' The rebels,' said he, ' burn and destroy the houses of all the protestants they come to, and massacre such as they can find.'

Later the collectors on the east coast of Ireland were told to supply the collectors of the western English ports with specimens of their handwriting, and of the form of passport issued to persons leaving Ireland for England. All collier brigs arriving from England were to be searched for arms and ammunition. During the whole of the year the Irish collectors sent the officers commanding the militia supplies of money, usually in halved bank-notes. Towards the end of 1798 the Board called on the collectors for reports as to how persons licensed to deal in gunpowder had demeaned themselves during the disturbances.

An application being made for a sufferance to land salt at Arklow, the collector advised that permission should be withheld, stating that if the salt were landed and stored at Ballymoney parties friendly to the rebels would make it their business to supply them, and that this would defeat the intentions of the generals commanding the loyalists in the district, they having up to that time been successful in preventing the rebels from obtaining salt to use with their provisions, ' thereby causing the death of numbers of them.' The Board considered this benevolent missive, and directed the collector to see that the salt was landed at Gorey, and placed under customs lock.

In 1799 a large vessel, with a valuable cargo, and bearing letters of marque, went ashore near Arklow, and had to be lightened by delivering part of her goods. The Board ordered the collector to see that the cargo delivered was lightered safely to Dublin, and to obtain soldiers to guard the ship during the transaction.

There was a deal of trouble with the Wicklow light-house-keepers, whose wages, together with the upkeep of the lighthouses, were paid out of the customs receipts. It was common for shipmasters to lodge complaints at

Dublin that the lights could not be seen, yet the light-house-keepers' affidavits that the lamps had been kept regularly burning came in every quarter as usual.   In the end the Wicklow gauger, a Mr. Dudgeon, was ordered to ride the coast at night, to keep an eye upon the lights, and to make occasional surprise visits, to see that the attendants were awake and alive to their duty.

The collector complained that a number of soldiers were billeted in the Custom-house, that they were usually in a condition of drunkenness, and that he was afraid they might set fire to or rob the building.   He stated that the soldiers kept the doors open night and day, and came and went as they pleased, and that he was constantly in great apprehension, 'from the character of such people.' The Board told him they were unable to interfere, but that he might apply to the magistrates.   (It is probable that the magistrates were equally indisposed.)

In 1800 the Board called for a return of bounty-money paid to Irish fishing vessels.   The Wicklow collector reported that nothing of the kind had been paid in his district since 1789.   Thus it would seem that the Irish fisheries were in a poor condition—even bounties failed to keep them going ; and that the Board did not interest themselves much in the matter, or they would have called for the return earlier.

Indeed, the customs business seems to have been con-ducted in happy-go-lucky fashion.   Letters on important matters sometimes remained unanswered for months, and returns asked for at the beginning of one year were sometimes supplied at the end of the next, and then only after repeated inquiries.   For instance, in 1800 the Wicklow collector was drummed up for a return of the values of revenue offices in his district, a return which should have been supplied long before.   He sent an account of the values of the excise offices, but not of the customs. Later he supplied the values of all the customs posts except his own, so the Board fined him 10 guineas for the omission.   Then he sent an account of his own complete receipts, placing them at £400 per annum—a considerable sum for that period, in a poverty-ridden land too. The Board were appeased, and remitted the fine.

Mr. Dudgeon, the gauger appointed to watch the lights, sent in a statement, vouched by several fishermen, to the effect that since his appointment as watcher the lights at Wicklow Head had been kept going better than at any time within memory. Soon afterwards there were several complaints from shipmasters, and the Board called upon Dudgeon for an explanation. Dudgeon thereupon furnished affidavits from the lighthouse-keepers, corroborating his statement. He was told that his allowance of 30 guineas per year for watching would be continued 'experimentally,' on condition that he did his duty. This put him upon his mettle, and later he furnished a report that, detecting a dulness, he visited, and found that the dulness was due to want of snuffing.

The coasting trade was almost at a standstill. During six months of 1800 only five coasters discharged in Wicklow Bay, the total deliveries being 10 barrels herrings, 26 tons potatoes, 510 barrels oats, 3 tons meal, 50 barrels wheat, and 5 barrels tar.

The Board asked for an account of some wine and fruit seized at Arklow in 1798. The landing-waiter there reported thus : ' The oranges melted away in the cases, and the wine was taken by the soldiers during the rebellion.'

The coast-waiter at Bray applied for permission to take entries and duties at that place. He had succeeded his father in the employment, and the father had been allowed to deal with moneys. But the Wicklow collector reported against the application, stating that the father had rarely returned any duties, and had been altogether an unsatisfactory official. Indeed, 'the late Mr. Brown' had for years succeeded in baffling all attempts at investigation of his very peculiar revenue transactions. Quoth the collector : ' When vessels were found by the Dublin officers to have discharged there, Mr. Brown said the duties had been paid at Wicklow, and when found by the Wicklow officers, Mr. Brown said the duties had been paid at Dublin. At last we made a clean detection,' etc. But what was done to Brown, senior, does not appear, nor any explanation as to why Brown, junior, was allowed to succeed him.

It will be seen from these brief memoranda of practical matters that the Irish Customs, compared with the English, was a quiet and unpicturesque department. There was occasional smuggling, but the contrabandists, with the exception of ' Jack the Bachelor's Gang,' made a poor figure beside the smugglers of Dorset, Hampshire, Sussex, and Kent. The extreme poverty of the land, and the Irish deficiency in maritime enterprise, may have been responsible for this. It needs a numerous class of skilled watermen and a tolerably free circulation of money, as well as a tremendous tariff, to bring smuggling to the perfection it reached in southern England during the eighteenth century. The contingencies must be favourable, and the actors fitted for their parts, ere the drama of lawlessness can be properly played.

It has been thought judicious to end the volume here, in order to begin the next with an account of the amalgamation of British and Irish Customs under the Act of Union. It would be idle to pretend that full justice can have been done, in one book, to the huge possibilities of the older Customs history. We have tried to present a simple and coherent narrative, and, in dealing with the history of smuggling, to display, not the most picturesque incidents, but those which appear to illustrate the spirit of the time, and the practice of a venerable Revenue department. It is impossible that the Customs history of the nineteenth century will be so deeply impregnated with the glamour of contraband, yet it may be found to possess even more potent elements of interest. The records will be more comprehensive, easier of access, perhaps more reliable.

LIST OF AUTHORITIES.

Act of Consolidation : 27 Geo. III., c. 13.

Imposts subsequent to consolidation : 27 Geo. III., c. 28 ; 31 Geo. III., c. 15 ; 34 Geo. III., c. 4 and 15 ; 34 Geo. III., c. 20 ; 34 Geo. III., c. 27 ; 35 Geo. III., c. 20 ; 36 Geo. III., c. 123 ; 37 Geo. III., c. 15 ; 37 Geo. III., c. 110 ; 38 Geo. III., c. 43 ; 39 Geo. III., c. 63.

Excise duties : 27 Geo. III., c. 31 ; 31 Geo. III., c. 1 ; 32 Geo. III., c. 7 ; 35 Geo. III., c. 10 ; 35 Geo. III., c. 12, 13 ; 36 Geo. III., c. 13 ; 38 Geo. III., c. 89 ; 40 Geo. III., c. 23 ; 34 Geo. III., c. 3.

Preventive measures : 27 Geo. III., c. 32 ; 33 Geo. III., c. 70 ; 34 Geo. III., c. 50 ; 36 Geo. III., c. 82 ; 38 Geo. III., c. 33.

Departmental incidents : Sir William Musgrave's 'Customs Memoranda'; Montrose Letter Books.

Repeal of Ancient Duties : 28 Geo. III., c. 16.

Protective measures and prohibitions : 28 Geo. III., c. 38 ; 30 Geo. III., c. 4 ; 30 Geo. III., c. 27 ; 31 Geo. III., c. 30 ; 32 Geo. III., c. 43 ; 33 Geo. III., c. 2 ; 33 Geo. III., c. 3 ; 33 Geo. III., c. 27 ; 33 Geo. III., c. 63 ; 34 Geo. III., c. 68 ; 36 Geo. III., c. 79 ; 36 Geo. III., c. 86 ; 37 Geo. III., c. 97 ; 38 Geo. III., c. 79 ; 39 Geo. III., c. 65 ; 39 Geo. III., c. 95.

Slave trade : 28 Geo. III., c. 54.

Establishment : 29 Geo. III., c. 64 ; 38 Geo. III., c. 86 ; Fourth Report of Select Committee on Finance.

Tobacco : 29 Geo. III., c. 68 ; 30 Geo. III., c. 40.

Coasting trade : 32 Geo. III., c. 50.

Aliens : 33 Geo. III., c. 4 ; 38 Geo. III., c. 50.

Drawbacks : 33 Geo. III., c. 48.

Privateers : 37 Geo. III., c. 109.

Isle of Man : 38 Geo. III., c. 63.

Convoy duties : 38 Geo. III., c. 76.

East India Company : 37 Geo. III., c. 117 ; 39 Geo. III., c. 59.

Exemptions (special) : 39 Geo. III., c. 96.

Quarantine : 39 Geo. III., c. 99.

London Dock Charters : 39 Geo. III., c. 69 (Local Act).

Irish Customs : Irish Acts, 12 Edw. IV., c. 1, 2 ; 20 Edw. IV., s. 2, c. 1 ; 14 Hen. VII., c. 1 ; 15 Hen. VII., c. 1 ; 13 Hen. VIII., c. 2 ; 28 Hen. VIII., c. 17 ; 11 Eliz., s. 3, c. 10, and s. 4, c. 1 ; 13 Eliz., c. 1, 2 ; 28 Eliz., c. 4 ; Lodge's 'Patentee Officers'; Patent Rolls, 19 Rich. II., p. 1, m. 19 ; Patent Rolls, 1 Hen. IV., p. 6, m. 8 ; Irish Calendars, 1532 ; Acts of Privy Council, 1579 ; Irish Calendars, 1625, 1626, 1627 ; Fœdera (' De Declaratione pro incremento Subsidiorum in Regno Hiberniæ '—' Declaration for the Imposition of divers Subsidies '); Petty's 'Political Anatomy'; Irish Table of Fees ; Treasury Papers, vol. 248 ; Dublin Order Books ; Eaton's ' Book of Rates ' ; Wicklow Letter Books.

CUSTOMS LITERATI

| GEOFFREY CHAUCER | JOHN DENNIS |
| WILLIAM CONGREVE | ADAM SMITH |

CHAUCER.

THE Chaucers were originally a family of cordwainers. Geoffrey's grandfather, Robert le Chaucer, became attorney or clerk to the king's Butler during Edward II.'s reign, and was afterwards made collector of the ' Petty Custom on Wine ' (Butlerage). It seems that the family abjured connexion with their ancient calling, for they left the Ward of the Cordwainers, and settled in the Vintry. Robert's son John, Geoffrey's father, became deputy to the king's Butler at Southampton, and for a time was collector of customs at that port.

Geoffrey appears first as a servant in the household of the countess of Ulster, and afterwards as an esquire in the French wars. His military experience was brief and disastrous. He returned to England, and stepped into the good graces of John of Gaunt. Another upward step brought him upon the threshold of the king's favour, and he was employed in various confidential foreign missions. There is every reason to believe that he displayed great tact and intelligence while thus occupied, and that the allusions to ' good service done,' which appeared in one or two of the patents subsequently endowing him with office, were no idle formulæ.

In 1374 he was granted a pitcher of wine daily from the London Prisage, and later in the year he was made controller of the Custom and Subsidy of wool, fells, and leather in the port of London, the patent to continue 'during the king's pleasure.' The appointment was reaffirmed in 1377.

At this time Chaucer lived in Aldgate, and must have been in affluent circumstances. Both he and his wife Philippa were in receipt of annuities. Occasionally he was employed oversea, and the advances then made him to cover expenses were extremely liberal. His regular income may be stated thus :

By his wife's pension ..	..	..	25 marks a year.
By his own (paid by the king) ..		..	20 ,, ,,
By his own (paid by John of Gaunt)		..	15 ,, ,,
By his salary as controller	..	..	15 ,, ,,
By value of his wine allowance..		..	12 ,, ,,
			87 ,, ,,

He must also have saved money out of his allowance when employed abroad on the king's business. None can doubt that as controller of the London wool duties he received many secret gifts from merchants, and there were other perquisites ; for instance, in 1376 he gained over 100 marks in one sum, as reward for a seizure of uncustomed wool. His total income may be stated as about 150 marks—say £1,500 in modern money.

In 1382 he was made controller of Petty Custom in London, and permitted to employ a deputy. In 1385 he was allowed a permanent deputy, and that period may be deemed the high-water hour of his prosperity. It is likely that he did little customs work, for he gave up his Aldgate house. Soon after this he was made a justice of the peace in Kent. Few poets have done as well, but be it borne in mind few have so well deserved.

In 1386 misfortune overtook him. He lost both his customs appointments—Adam Yerdley succeeding him as controller of the wool duties, Henry Gisors as controller of Petty Custom. In 1388 he lost his annuity ; but in 1389 he was taken into partial favour, and made Clerk of Works, receiving 2s. a day. As he was empowered to pre-empt building materials, it may be assumed there were perquisites appertaining.   Perhaps 60 marks a year (£600 in modern money) may represent his annual income. The duties of the new office must have been onerous.   At various periods he had to supervise the repair of the Royal Chapel at Windsor, and of the historic Wool Quay. He was employed for a time as Commissioner of Sewers and Drainage on the upper marshes of the Thames, and while thus occupied lived at Greenwich.

In 1390 Chaucer, while employed on his official duties, fell into the clutches of one of the gangs of brigands that infested the highways during Richard's reign, and was robbed of horse, equipment, and a considerable sum of money.   The robbery took place 'near the Fowle Oak, Hatcham.'   Thus much is certain, but in some of the records two subsequent robberies are mysteriously inter-woven with the Hatcham affair.   That Chaucer should have allowed himself to be robbed three times within a few months, and on two, if not three, occasions by mem-bers of the same gang, is almost incredible, yet the records appear to avouch it.   It is possible that the mystery attaching to the thefts may have discredited him, for he ceased to be employed officially.

Later he was granted 30 marks a year, an annuity but imperfectly paid ; and later still a cask of wine yearly (in some records quoted as a tun, in others as a butt).   He fell into pecuniary difficulties, and at one period was compelled to shun the attentions of the sheriff's officer. In 1399, with the proverbial inconstancy of a poet, he burst into song in welcome of the man by whom his late benefactor had been dethroned and imprisoned.   Henry granted him an annuity of 40 marks.   Upon this allow-ance—for his previous grant had lapsed—he subsisted for a brief space, residing in a house that stood in the garden of St. Mary's Chapel, Westminster.   His remains ennoble the historic ' Poet's Corner.'

He died poor, and, as ' The Retractation ' shows, sin-cerely penitent.   Other poets have died as poor as he.

Few, it is to be feared, have died as penitent, yet many have had more to repent of. The man who regretted having written the ' Canterbury Tales ' must have been a vassal of Contrition.

CONGREVE.

William Congreve was born at Bardsey, in Yorkshire. The date of his birth lies somewhere between 1669 and 1672. Shortly after the event his father, who was a younger son of an ancient Staffordshire family, obtained a military appointment in Ireland. Thus it came about that Congreve's boyhood was spent in the Irish Midlands, and that his earliest studies were performed in the famous town of Kilkenny. The elder Congreve obtained a situation as manager of an estate owned by the Burlington family, and vacated his military employment.

Congreve went from Kilkenny to Trinity College. From Dublin he proceeded to London, and studied at the Temple ; but he had no liking for the law, and the effects of distaste were soon manifest in the form of fictional literature. He wrote a novel entitled ' Incognita, or Love and Duty Reconciled.' (Dr. Johnson declared that he would rather praise the work than read it, and Leigh Hunt stated that he had read it, and was unable to praise it.)

Congreve's first play, ' The Old Bachelor,' came out in 1693. It gained the enthusiastic approval of John Dryden, and was tolerably successful. Soon after this he produced the ' Double Dealer,' which gained little favour. In 1695 appeared ' Love for Love,' which must have been more fortunate, for the celebrated Betterton, then manager of the New Theatre, made an arrangement with the author, under which Congreve was to supply him with a play a year.

Congreve failed to observe the letter of this agreement, and his next piece, ' The Mourning Bride,' did not appear till 1697. It was eminently successful ; why is difficult for plain thinkers to divine. Congreve's previous productions had been brisk, sparkling comedies, and the ' Mourning Bride ' was an extremely turgid tragedy.

In 1700 Congreve made his final effort in comedy, and it was unsuccessful with the public. ' The Way of the World ' fell flat, and its talented author retired, disgusted and incurably resentful. Its collapse has been attributed to the assaults of the celebrated Jeremy Collier, who had initiated a crusade against the obscenities of the stage. Congreve produced afterwards many pieces of verse, but these were not even of ordinary merit. Some of them, indeed, are utterly ridiculous. It is marvellous that so witty a man could have written them.

It seems that Congreve gained little money by his plays, but he was a keen man of the world, and well able to profit by the impression they had made in certain quarters. He stood high in the esteem of Lord Halifax, and repaid with a deal of bad verse the valuable assistance of his aristocratic patron. Halifax procured him a Commissionership of Hackney Coaches, and other valuable offices. In 1700 he was made patent* customer of Poole, in 1714 one of the five under-searchers in the port of London, and later he was endowed with a colonial secretaryship. The appointments were practically sinecures, and must have brought in considerably over £1,000 per annum. Congreve's remarkable personal gifts, placable manners, and aristocratic bearing, endeared him to many women of quality, and several of the leading ladies of the stage. Thus he was enabled to live in a style suitable to his extremely elegant inclinations. To the end of his life he was a true specimen of the ' fashionable gentleman ' of his day. He died in 1729, leaving a considerable sum of money, and was buried in Westminster Abbey.

* The London grant does not appear on the Roll, but there can be no doubt as to the appointment, for there is a transcript of the patent in ' Customs Book, 15,' and another of the Treasury order directing that Congreve should be ' sworn in,' and appointing Joshua White as his deputy.

DENNIS.

John Dennis was born in 1657. He was educated at Harrow, and later went to Cambridge. It has been stated that he was expelled from the latter seat of learning for drawing sword upon a fellow-collegian.

His first attempt upon the public favour was made in 1697, when he produced a play called 'A Plot and no Plot,' which failed utterly. In 1700 he brought out 'Iphigenia,' and this also failed. It was followed by an adaptation of 'The Merry Wives of Windsor,' also unsuccessful.

In 1704 he made another attempt, bringing out 'Liberty Asserted.' This was his only success. In 1705 he produced 'Gibraltar,' another fiasco, and followed with a rather grotesque adaptation of Shakespeare's 'Coriolanus.' During the same year he was appointed queen's waiter in the port of London.* Still he could not refrain from flirting with the Tragic Muse. In 1709 out came 'Appius and Virginia.' He also wrote various pieces of verse, mostly addressed to great men of the day, and as fulsome as such pieces usually are.

The best of Dennis is in his criticisms, which are powerfully written, and impregnated with humour of a peculiarly pungent kind. His analysis of Addison's 'Cato' is masterly, and in all English literature there is nothing more amusing than the paper war between Dennis and Steele. Both antagonists are at their best, but Dennis

---

* Dennis's appointment appears on the Roll (m. 13) dated June 14, 1705. He succeeded one 'Tutchin Martin, defunct.' On the accession of George I. the appointment was reaffirmed, Dennis, of course, becoming a 'king's waiter.' The Treasury notice was signed by Godolphin, the notice of reaffirmation by 'Halifax,' R. Onslow, William St. Quintin, and Edward Wortley. See Swift's amusing lines :

> 'Why has my Lord Godolphin's special grace
> Invested me with a queens-waiter's place,
> If I, debarred of festival delights,
> Am not allowed to spend the perquisites ?'
> *John Dennis the Sheltering Poet's Invitation.*

wins easily.   His ' Sir John Edgar ' is one of the most
telling and ferocious satires ever penned.

In 1715 Dennis sold his post in the Customs, and thenceforward his experience was one of disaster.   He lived to
the age of seventy-seven, and it is distressing to learn that
he died blind and poverty-stricken.   His latter days are
stated to have been intensely wretched, but this is unlikely, for he was a man of indomitable spirit, and his
keen and vigorous wit seems to have been unimpaired
to the last.   It may reasonably be asserted that the
English estimation of Dennis's literary powers is by no
means as high as it should be.   His plays were undoubtedly bad, but there have been few critics as able
and fearless, and as skilled in wielding English, as old
' John Dennis of the Custom House.'

SMITH.

Adam Smith came into the world on June 5, 1723, as
the posthumous child of the customs controller of Kirkcaldy.   During his infancy he was kidnapped by gipsies,
and only recovered after a strenuous search.   The dark
people have been credited with a deep purpose in stealing
the children of house-dwellers.   Strong and healthy
infants, likely to effect profitable ' crossing ' in the
Romany blood, were the usual objects of depredation.
As little Adam was an extremely delicate child, it is likely
they anticipated need of a ' patrico.'

Adam received his early education at the Kirkcaldy
Grammar School.   His mental gifts were even then conspicuous, for he was a greedy and discerning reader, and
his powers of memory were remarkable.   As is usual in
such cases, he was physically feeble, and unfitted to take
part in the tumultuous recreations of boyhood.

At the age of fourteen he went to Glasgow University,
and three years later to Balliol College, Oxford, where he
remained till he was twenty-four.   His immense application to study was not encouraged by the English pro-

fessors. Oxford furnished him with books and leisure, and little else. He had been intended for the Church, but his extensive studies and philosophical turn of mind frustrated the scheme. So he returned to Kirkcaldy, and till the end of 1748 resided with his mother.

Later he gained the patronage of Lord Kames. He removed to Edinburgh, and became distinguished as a lecturer upon polite literature. In 1751 he was made Professor of Logic and Moral Philosophy at Glasgow University. In 1759 he published his ' Theory of Moral Sentiments,' a work which at once secured popularity. Then he accompanied the young duke of Buccleuch in a tour upon the Continent.

On his return to Scotland, he threw himself with great ardour into the prosecution of a long-cherished literary project. After a severe course of study, he produced his ' Wealth of Nations,' a treatise at once acclaimed, and destined to found an entirely new scheme of economics. His lordly patrons appear to have resolved that the author of a work so creditable to the Lowland Scottish mind should not depend for pecuniary reward solely upon the shillings of a responsive public. In 1778 Adam was made a Scottish Commissioner of Customs. It is our opinion that the stately pronouncement upon the erratic practice of the ports of Montrose and Ferryden was furnished by him. His salary would certainly not be less than £500, and as he appears to have enjoyed an annuity of £300 as well, he was undoubtedly ' in a tolerable position.' He seems to have been fond of a bottle of wine, a game of whist, and the society of well-informed people, and it is likely that auld Edinburgh provided him with many an opportunity towards such eminently rational enjoyments.

One of his biographers has expressed disapprobation of the Customs appointment, asserting that it arrested Smith's literary labours. ' The performance of petty routine duties,' says the uncompromising commentator, ' engrossed the greater part of his time.' No doubt Adam

Smith was an earnest and painstaking Commissioner, but it should be borne in mind that he had several assistants, and the task of supervising the collection of the trifling revenue then furnished by Scotland could scarcely have wearied the mind that had constructed the 'Wealth of Nations.' And though the duties were light, they were not mechanical. They involved *practical* contact with matters of trade and revenue—a form of discipline which a scholarly recluse like Adam Smith stood in urgent need of. The great defects of the 'Theory of Moral Sentiments' and 'Wealth of Nations'—the great and apparent defects—were lack of knowledge of the world and the innumerable complexities of human nature. It is possible that Adam Smith, being an eminently receptive person, learned much while he was a Commissioner of Customs. And perhaps this may explain why he ceased to write books.

Undoubtedly he had given the world his best, and was conscious that a sedate and restful autumn should follow the abundant yield. So he did as Johnson had done. It should be remembered that he had acquired a position much more lucrative than that enjoyed by the Sage of Fleet Street. Yet Johnson had outdone him in literary achievement, though compelled to fight a way through obstacles which Adam Smith would never have been able to overcome.

Smith's society was almost as ardently courted in Edinburgh as Johnson's had been in London, yet modern students of 'the original' in mind and character would have deemed five minutes of Johnson worth a year of the Scottish philosopher. The milder social virtues may have been preferred in Edinburgh, and in these Smith certainly excelled. His benignity and sweetness of character are manifest in all his writings.

In 1787 Smith was made Lord Rector of Glasgow University. His extreme sincerity and loyalty were fully exemplified in his acknowledgment of the distinction. He attributed all his success to the managers of the institution. ' They educated me ; they sent me to Oxford.' He might with justice have added : ' And at Oxford I educated myself.'

He died in 1790, of a most painful disorder, the pangs and distresses of which he endured with characteristic firmness and dignity. Many men have possessed more striking gifts, few have been more deserving of the title of ' Scholar.' His works bear every evidence of sustained and laborious though occasionally imperfect thought. And he wrote ' the English ' beautifully.

APPENDIX

ILLUSTRATIVE DOCUMENTS

Preamble of C. 4, 3 Edw. IV., prohibiting foreign manufactured goods.

' COME en le dit p'lement, p' lartificers des mestiers mainuelx, homes & femes, en la Cite de Loundres & autres Citeez, Villez, Burghs, & Villages, deins cest roialme & Gales inhabitaunz & reseauntz, piteousment ad estre monstre & compleigne coment toutz ceux en gen'all & chun deux sont gᵃundement empov'ez & grevousment endamagez & p'judicez de leur encrece du mond & vivre cotidian, p' la gᵃund multitude des div's chaffares & wares, a leur mestiers & occupacions app'teign'tez, esteantz pleinement ov'ez & p'st faitz al vende, si bien p' les mains destraungez esteantz enemiez du Roy, come autres en cest roialme & Gales de la le mere amesnez, si bien p' m'chants estranges come deinszeins & autre p'sones,' etc.

The above may be freely rendered thus : ' Whereas piteous complaint has been made in the said parliament, by the artificers of mysteries of handicraft, men and women, inhabiting and resident in the City of London and other cities, towns, boroughs, and villages in this realm and Wales, how that they all, each and in general, are greatly impoverished and grievously injured and prejudiced in their worldly increase and daily living, by the great multitude of various commodities and wares appertaining to their mysteries and occupations, being fully wrought and made ready for sale, as well by the hands of strangers being enemies of the king, as by others of this realm and Wales brought oversea, as well by merchant strangers as by denizens and other persons,' etc.

(The context prohibits a variety of manufactured articles.)

455

Extract from ' A Remembrance to my Lord Protectours Grace'
(Duke of Somerset), 1547. *Probably supplied from the*
Exchequer Memoranda. Embodying suggestions of a new
tax upon cloth, and a tax of 1d. *on each sheep, etc.*

' The p'fetts of Custome and subsidie of wolls, wollfells &
clothes* and the Aulnage therof, in the 28th yere of the reigne
of Kyng Edward the thirde,

	£	s.	d.
' Shipped over the same yere in wolle, 34,760 sacks, whiche rated at 40s. the sacke for Custome and subsidie amountithe to	69,558	0	0
' Shipped over the same yere in fells, 348,451, whiche was rated at 2d. the fell, amountithe to	2,900	0	0
' Shipped over the same yere in Clothes, 2,483, wch rated after 14d. the cloth amountithe to	144	0	0
' The p'fetts of the Alnage the same yere	344	3	7
	£72,946	3	7'

(Noted on document) ' Memorand.†—that here is no difference made betwene the Custome of the Straungers and
Englysshmen, but all rated after one soorte, that y^s, after
40s. the sacke, where the Straunger paieth for ev^y sacke
£3 16s. 8d.'

(Noted in other handwriting) ' *And so it maye be gathered*
that the p'fett of the Custome and subsidies was greater.'

(Original handwriting) ' Sacke of wolle conteyneth 13 todde.
A todd conteyneth 28 li.‡

' Allowed to ev^y todd 20 sheere shepe, because it is thought that ther was not so many pasture sheepe in the tyme of Kyng Edward the thirde as be nowe, but moste Men kept on the Comons. And after that rate for ev^y sacke there must be accompted 260 sheepe. Accompted after that rate for 34,760 sacks..	9,037,600 sheepe.
' Allowed for every clothe 3 todde and to ev^y todd 20 sheepe, and so for ev^y clothe 60 sheepe. To make 2,483 clothes ther must be accompted	148,980 sheepe.
' It appeareth also by the Wolfells that were shipped, whereof the bodies were eaten or perisshed in the Realme, that ther were that yere also	348,451 sheepe.
' So that after this rate it may be justly and truly saied that ther were in the Realme in the 28th yere of the reigne of Kyng Edward the thirde	9,535,031 sheepe.'

* Cloths.
† Evidently denizens were not allowed to export wool during that
year. ‡ Lbs.

' The p'fetts of Custome and Subsidie of Wolle, Wollfells, and clothes, and the Aulnage thereof, the 38th yere of the reigne of Kinge Henry the eight.

	£	s.	d.
' Shipped over the same year in wolle by Englysshmen 1,136 sackes, and whiche rated at 40s. the sacke Custome and Subsidie amountithe to	2,272	0	0
' Shipped over the same yere by Straungers in Wolle 419 Sacks, which rated at £3 16s. 8d. the sacke amountithe to	1,625	3	4
' Shipped over the same yere in wollfells 363,829, whiche rated at 2d. the fell amountithe to ..	3,031	4	10
' Shipped over the same yere in Clothes 172,017, rated after 14d. the clothe, amountithe to ..	10,056	13	2
' The p'fetts of the alnage of the same yere	758	14	0
	£17,743	15	4

' And so it appereth that Kyng Edward the third had more yerely by his Custome then Kyng Henry the eight had by*..	£55,202	8	3

' And before the said Kyng Edwarde had for two yeres a Subsidie of the 9th sheepe, the 9th fleese,† the 9th Lambe, and the 9th parte of all the goodes of Marchaunts and Denyzyns.

' At the rate of 20 sheepe to the todd, 260 to the sacke and 60 to a clothe it appereth by the woll, wollfells and clothes carried out of the Realme in the 38th yere of the reigne of Kyng Henry the eight that ther were in the realme the same yere .. .. 11,089,149 sheepe.

' In all this accompte no mention is made of the sheepe whose wolle was made into Clothe and cappes spent that yere in the Realme, nor of skynnes tanned, lether, or parchement. And therefore it maye be trulye saied that ther wer more sheepe than is before reherste.'

(This curious document may not be altogether reliable. It will be observed that the amounts of duty, except in one instance, do not agree exactly with the quantities and rates, but there may have been ' remnants.' It is by no means certain that the 40s. rate quoted for wool and fells in Edward III.'s reign includes the Ancient Custom, or that 2d. a fell represents the fell duty even at the 40s. rate, for the duty was then charged on 300 fells, instead of 240 as computed. But the calculations as to sheep are worked out correctly, and the totals are rather surprising. If an estimate

---

* Henry had tunnage, poundage, and the wine impost.   † Fleece.

be made to account for the wool used in the kingdom the results will be almost incredible. It is likely that the estimate of sheep for Henry VIII.'s time is approximately correct as regards its connexion with the wool, fells, and cloth produced for shipment. If we increase it by one-half to account for the wool used in England, the result may be stated as 15,000,000 sheep. If the same proportion per head of population obtained at the present day, what a noble shearing-time! It appears that the old writers were correct when they maintained that English wealth was founded on English wool, and that the true emblems of England's strength were the long bow and the shepherd's crook.)

Order in Council, supporting the Merchant Adventurers in their dispute with one Thomas Clecher. Date, 1570.

' Trustie and welbeloved, we grete you well, and beinge enformed that divers p'sonnes not free of that your Company, nor brought upp in trade of m'chaundize, do not only empeche your trade, as well by unskilfull and disorderly occupyinge, as also by violatinge suche yor pryveleges by great traveile and charge of o^r progenito^{rs} graunt apteyned and graunted : And amongst other, that one Thom^s Clecher dothe without order or Authoritie entermeddell wth trade of m'chaundize in the lowe Countreis of Holland, Zeeland, Brabant, and Flaunders, and non'thelesse dothe stubbornely and obstinatly refuse to abide suche orders as other of yor compeny doo, and also dothe attempte to caull s^d previleges in question by the Lawe there : Wee, myndinge the p'servacon of good orders and the may'tennance of that your compeny, do will and comaund ye that by vertue of theis s^d Letters ye do in o^r name comaund the said Thomas to s^rcease* his sewte† there and stande to abide and obey suche yor orders as is amongst ye provyded for suche offenders : And o^r further will and pleasure is that if at anny tyme hereafter anny p'son not free of that compeny do attempte to trafficke into the said lowe Countreis, or to break or violate your privileges and good orders, that ye doe likewise by vertue of these our L^{res} comaund in o^r name all and any suche p'son and p'sonnes to appere before ye, and to stande to abide and obey all suche good orders and ordinaunces as by ye have bynne made and ordeyned. And if either ye said Clecher or anny other disordered p'sonne do refuse to accomplish the contente of theise our L^{res} that then ye do comaund hym or them in o^r name to appere before o^r Pryvie Councell, and that ye do

---

* Surcease. † Suit.

adv'tise o^r said Councell thereof with the p'ticulars of his or their offence or mysdemeano^r, to th'entent we may take suche order wth hym as may be to the example of anny attempting the like, and the p'servacon of yor previleges and good orders wch we mynde by all meanes to mayneteyne.'

Précis of a Warrant to pay certain customs moneys to Raleigh and Hawkins. Date, 1591.

' Whereas there is paieable unto Sr Walter Raleigh, Knight, at the Ann'ciation of O^r Lady next, the some of £1,000, and at Michael^s then next following £1,000, to be taken out of such Customes as shall growe due for the Custome of ov^r-lengthes* and remnaunts of clothes† to be transported, this to give order unto the Customers of the port of London to paie unto the said Sr Walter Raleigh such somes of money as shall appeare to be in theire hands, arising out of the Customes aforesaid since Michal‡—last past : And in case the same shall not suffice to make up the some of £2,000, then to paie unto him of her M^s treasure in the Receipt such further somes as shall want of the said some of £2,000, and to recale the same againe into the Receipt of th' Exchequer at the hands of the said Customers as it shall growe due upon the said Customes of ov^r-lengthes and remnaunts of clothes : And further to paie unto Sr John Hawkins, knight, Treas^r of her Ma^{tys} navie, the some of £500 of her M^s treasure in th' Exchequer, for the furnishing and setting in order of her Ma^{tys} Shipp called the *Crane*, appointed to serve at sea under the charge of the saide Sr Walter Raleigh.'§

A Scheme for remodelling James I.'s ' Book of Rates.' (The document appears to have been submitted to Cranfield, the surveyor-general of Customs, and is a fair specimen of the incoherent propositions occasionally tendered by interested fiscal ' reformers.')

' Comodities not to be altered in Custome or Impost, but to remayne in the book of rates as they nowe are :

' *Outwards.*—Baies.‖ (This may well be put into the rate, and the Imposicon removed). Lead. Tynn.

' *Inwards.* — Sugars (In Farme to the Queenes Matie), Beaver hatts, starche (both forraine manufactures), Whale-fynns, cloves, mace, nutmegge, Synnamon,¶ gynger.

---

* Over-lengths.   † Cloths.   ‡ Michaelmas.
§ Against the Spanish plate-fleet.   ‖ Bays.   ¶ Cinnamon.

'Comodities wch are to be Improved* in the rates and Impost :

'Silk of all kynds, wrought and unwrought, one-third in both, except Rawe Silke long and short, wch shalbe improved ⅓ in the rates onlie, w^{thout} anie imposicon at all. Pepper ⅓ in both. Lawnes and cambricks to be improved ⅛ both in custome and Impost. Incle,† wrought, to be improved ⅓ in both. Fustians of all kyndes to be improved ⅓ in the rates onlie, and the imposicon to be whollie taken away. Currants, the imposicon of them to be setled at 5s. 6d. p-hundred, as the late Queene left them. Tobacco to be improved to 20s. in the rates onlie, as the king's ma^{tie} wth his privie counsell latelie ordered it. French wynes to be improved in the rates onlie to 16£ a tonn. Sweet wynes to be improved in the rates onlie to 8£ p-butt. Rhenish wynes to be improved in the rates onlie to 3£ p-aum. Wyne vinagar to be improved in the rates onlie to 8£ a tonn.

'Comodities uppon wch are Impost, wch shalbe whollie taken off and put into the rates, w^{thout} streyning‡ uppon the subject, and must be done out of necessitie, for the tyeng§ strang^{rs} to make imployement.

'Holland cloth, callicoes, dyap^{er},|| damask, and all other kyndes of forraine lynnin cloth, excepting 8 or tenn sorts. Playing cardes, Estridge fethers, hopps, pynnes, oyle, tap'strie, indico,¶ qucheneile,** druggs, cloth of gold or silver.'

(Here follows a recapitulation. Then the proposer continues his rambling statement.)

'As alsoe all the other 1,200 Comodities conteyned in the book of rates, and here not menconed, to remayne as nowe they are, w^{thout} improvement or alteracon, ether in Custome or Impost.

'Memoranda.

'The ports are whollie eased in this alteracon, who, being manye in parliament, make all the claime. The comon wealth in gen'all eased, there being nothing nowe chardged but Dellicacyes and sup'fluityes, wch beggers the state. The kynge looseth as much on the necessarie things by under-valuing as he gaynes by these fewe sup'fluityes, they being manye in number, and these but fewe. So that the chardging the one and undervaluing the other is done by his Matie wth the advise of his Counsell, for the publique good, and not for gayne as is surmysed. This maie be done, and all the farmes manteyned, w^{thout} anie alteracon or difficultie. For the

---

* Raised.   † Inkle (linen tape).   ‡ Oppressing.
§ Compelling. ||Diaper.   ¶ Indigo.
** Cochineal.

kynges Offic^{rs} may receave to his Maties use the difference
betweene the Customes and Imposicons, wch are nowe fell,
and wch were before. And they maye lykewyse forbeare to
demaund these wch his Matie hath remytted. And there is
no alloweance to be made to anie farme^{rs}, by cause all the
Imposicons wch his Matie hath dischardged are in his owne
hands.'

Part of C. 24, 16 Chas. I. (Long Parliament), 1640.

'Whereas many thousands of your Majestie's good and
loving subjects, with their ships and goods, have of late time
beene surprised and taken at Sea * * * by Turkish, Moorish,
and other Pirats. * * * And whereas as well your Majestie's
subjects as Strangers * * * have ever sithence your Majestie's
accesse unto this Crowne been charged with the payment of
great Sums of money under the name of Custom, and that
without consent of Parliament ; which, had they been legally
taken, ought to have been cheifly imployed to the safeguard
of the Seas * * * but have been exhausted by evil Ministers,
and not applied to their proper uses :'
(The Act stipulates that an additional levy of 1 per cent.
on all duties—presumably 1 per cent. extra on all goods
liable to poundage—shall be made, to provide immediate
protection against the aforesaid pirates. The moneys to be
received by the Mayor and Chamberlain of London. The
Act concludes as below.)
'That your Majesty would in time to come be pleased
to intrust such Ministers as may faithfully imploy the moneys
raised by Tunnage and Poundage unto the right and proper
uses,' etc.

Order to the Remembrancer of the Exchequer to proceed for arrears against the lessees of the Customs farm of 1662-1667. Date, August 25, 1671.

'After our hearty commendacones :
'Whereas the late Farmers of his Ma^{ts} Customes for
five yeares ending at Michael — 1667, are indebted to his
Matie in a greate sume of money upon their Accompt, wch they
have long delayed to pay. & doe still detaine in their hands to
his Mat^{es} greate p'judice. & whereby the same is in danger to
be lost, these are therefore to desire and direct you forthwith
to cause pro^{sses}* of immediate payment to issue out against

* Processes.

the bodies, goods, and lands of ye said farmers & their heires, Execut^{rs}, & Adm^{rs}, in order to ye satisfaccon of his Ma^{ty's} debt due from them : And soe now bid you heartily farewell, and remaine, &c.'

Petition of Joshua Wright, referred favourably by the king to the Treasury, in order that the Commissioners of Customs might provide employment as requested. Date of transmission to Treasury, December 6, 1679.

' Humbly setting forth to his Ma^{ty} that his father, Erasmus Wright of ye Citty of Bristoll, Merch^t, in ye yeare 1643—his Highness Prince Rupert then besieging ye s^d Citty—was by a great shott slayne, whiles he was giveing his Highness an acco^t of the Rebells strength in ye sayd Citty, whereby his famely suffered much : Ye Petit^r also beeing taken in ye yeare 77 by two Algerine men of warr in sight of Silly,* lost all his goods to his utter ruine : That in July, 1678, upon ye humble Peticon of ye s^d Wright for a Landwaiter's place in ye Port of London, his Ma^{ty} granted a Refference thereon to ye then L^d high Treas^r, but ye Petit^r not obteyning ye effects thereof prays that in memory & compassion of his father's death as aforesaid, & his own great losses, a speciall order to enter into ye s^d place or imploy, wth ye first vacancy that shall fall.'

Treasury Warrant to the Commissioners of Customs to unite two revenue offices in the American Plantations, and grant the combined salaries to the person remaining in office. Date, April 7, 1679.

' After our hearty Comendacions :
    ' You haveing presented unto us Nicholas Spencer, Esqr, as a fitt person to be Collector of his Mat^s Customes at Potomack River in Virginia, for the whole collection, Mr. John Washington† who was formerly joyned with him being deceased : These are to pray and require you to issue forth your deputacon to the said Nicholas Spencer to be the sole Collector at the said place accordingly, with the allowance of Sallary which both received, and under such instructions to be given him as you shall thinke fitt for his Ma^{ts} service : And for soe doeing this shall be your warrant.'

* Scilly.   † George Washington's great-grandfather : died 1677.

Précis of a Return furnished to Admiralty by Customs, January 29, 1702. (Illustrative of the effect of the Navigation Act.)

		1695. Total Tonnage of Ships that cleared from London.	1701. Total Tonnage of Ships that cleared from London.
English	.. ..	65,786	132,634
Foreign	.. ..	52,138	34,773
		117,924	167,407

Comparative Trade of Ports in 1701. (English tonnage.)

London, 132,634 ; Bristol, 17,338 ; Ipswich, 11,170 ; Newcastle, 11,000 ; Yarmouth, 9,914 ; Liverpool, 8,619. (Bideford furnished almost as large a return as Liverpool ; so did Exeter. Scarborough's tonnage almost equalled that of Hull.)

From 1695 to 1701 inclusive, over 1,000 ships in ballast entered the port of London. Thus it would seem that the export trade preponderated.

Extract from a statement of the Public Revenue of Scotland for five years subsequent to the Union (May 1, 1707, to May 1, 1712).

			£	s.	d.
' The Excise from 1st May, 1707, to 1st May, 1712..			259,175	10	6¼
' The Customs in that time	£171,811 16s. 7¼d. £55,435 7s. 3d. £18,205 7s. 6¾d.	In Money Outstanding Bonds Seizures actually paid	245,452	11	5
			£504,628	1	11¼

' These two Revenues of Excise & Customes for these five years do make annually the sum of £100,000, and a surplus £4,628 1s. 11¼d. to compensate the drawbacks which may happen to be taken out of the Bonds stated above as a part of the Customes, and is given here by gross, because the Commissioners of ye Customes have not thought fitt that the amount of those drawbacks should appear by the account sent to the Commissioners of Equivalent.'

(By the same return it appears that the Crown rents produced annually about £5,500, the Compositions in Exchequer £1,943, the Land Tax £48,000, and the ' poste office ' *about £3,000 !* The Coinage duty brought in about £1,500. Thus the total annual Scottish revenue barely reached £160,000.)

English Export Trade in Corn, Malt, and Oatmeal.

'An Account of Corn exported out of England from Christmas, 1720, to Christmas, 1727, with the value thereof by the medium prices that the several sorts of Corn bore at Bear Key* at Midsummer Day in the several respective years.

Years.	Barley.			Malt.				Oatmeal.			Rye.				Wheat.			
	Qrs.	s.	d.	Qrs.	£	s.	d.	Qrs.	s.	d.	Qrs.	£	s.	d.	Qrs.	£	s.	d.
1721	11,608	15	6	338,942	1	3	0	3,538	10	6	69,697	0	14	0	81,632	1	5	0
1722	37,730	12	0	366,526	0	16	6	1,000	11	0	42,579	0	12	6	178,880	1	3	6
1723	45,789	19	6	305,063	1	2	0	541	13	6	12,737	0	16	6	157,719	1	10	6
1724	10,289	15	6	241,895	0	19	0	516	12	0	23,441	0	18	6	245,864	1	5	6
1725	13,782	18	6	294,025	1	2	6	1,447	12	0	20,539	1	4	0	204,413	2	7	6
1726	20,017	13	0	325,925	1	3	6	1,412	11	6	18,835	0	16	0	142,183	1	12	0
1727	8,688	18	0	241,428	1	3	0	2,204	11	0	9,169	1	1	0	30,315	1	10	0

'Inspector-General's Office,
'Custom House,
'15th August, 1728.'

'John Oxenford, A.S.I.G.

* Bear Quay stood near the Custom-house, London. It should be observed that the figures are Midsummer prices (just prior to harvest-time, when corn would be at its highest value).

Extract from the collector of Colchester's letter to the Board of Customs, April 16, 1748.

'This morning about two o'clock two persons went to John Bloys (he being then at a granary upon the Town Key) and inquired where the Custom-house was, pretending that a Seizure of Tea had been made, and must be immediately lodged there, or it would be rescued by the Smuglers who were in pursuit of it : Upon which Bloys went to the Custom-house with the said men, and called upon Thomas Coker the collector's servant : Upon which Coker came downstairs and opened the door of the collector's house : Immediately upon the door being opened the two men took hold of Bloys and Coker by the collar, and, presenting pistols to their breasts, swore they'd kill them that moment if they made any noise or resistance : Near Thirty Smuglers armed with Blunderbusses and Pistols came into the courtyard, threat'ning with dreadful Imprecations,' etc.

(The letter proceeded to state that the smugglers broke into the King's Warehouse, and carried off a quantity of tea, previously seized near Woodbridge Haven by Robert Martin, captain of a revenue cruiser. It ended as below.)

'The King's Warehouse is a very secure place, but the greatest security imaginable would not have prevented these desperate villains from effecting their design, they having told Bloys and Coker that had they met with resistance they were resolved to have murdered every person that obstructed them, and came fully determined to have the goods or die in the attempt. Mr. William Lisle, supervisor of the riding-officers, and several other persons, went after the Smuglers, and heard they were got to Hadleigh in Suffolk by 6 o'clock in the morning, and what became of them afterwards they could not hear.'

Specimen of Information laid in the Irish Court of Exchequer relative to East India goods, imported into Ireland without previous unshipment in Great Britain.

'Be it Remembered, that Thomas Foorder, who as well on behalf of our sovereign lord the King as of himself prosecutes in this behalf, came before the barons of his Majesty's Court of Exchequer on the 2nd day of June in this term, in his proper person, and as well on behalf of our sovereign lord the

King as himself gave the said Court to understand that on the 2nd day of July, in the year of our Lord one thousand seven hundred and fifty nine, at Shiphaven in the county of Londonderry, he did seize and arrest to the use of our said lord the King and himself the said Thomas Foorder a certain ship or vessel called the *Swift* sloop, with all her guns, tackle, furniture, ammunition, and apparel, and the following goods and commodities then and there on board the said ship, that is to say, 21 casks of green tea, 102 casks of bohea tea, and one cask of rhubarb, for that the said goods and commodities, being of the growth, produce, and manufacture of the East Indies,' etc.

Extract from a Letter furnished by Mr. Heron, collector of Potomac River in Maryland, January 3, 1765, giving particulars of an assault committed on him whilst he was trying to sell a ship and certain goods, condemned under the Plantation Acts.

' The numberless abuses and continual threatnings to shoot me, &c. makes me sensible of the melancholy situation of this office * * * this office is seated, as I can almost say, amongst nothing but a gang of smuglers. * * * No one would bid, most of them being concerned in the illicit trade. * * * On the day appointed for sale of the brig I gave attendance for that purpose, accompany^d by Mr. Gibbs, Comptroller of the Customs at Annapolis,' etc.

(The letter goes on to state that none would bid for the condemned ship, and that her captain, with a number of supporters, ' all Scotch,' attended. The captain, after making himself furious with drink, attacked Heron with a club, the other Scots holding Heron's arms meanwhile. ' He certainly would have murdered me, had not the man of the house, who is a very strong bold fellow, released [rescued] me.' The letter ends as below.)

' I humbly hope your Honours will contrive ways and means for our better protection from the Insults of such a Villanious set of People. I never go out but am doubly armed with a hanger, a pair of pistols in my Pockets, and another before me.'

Patent appointing Resident Commissioners of Customs in the American Plantations (September 8, 1767).

' George the Third by the Grace of God, &c. : To our Trusty and Wellbeloved Henry Hulton, John Temple, William Burch, Charles Paxton, and John Robinson, Esquires, Greeting : Whereas by an Act of Parliament lately passed to Enable us to put the Customs and other Duties in the British Dominions in America, and the Execution of the Laws relating to Trade there, under the management of Comissioners to be appointed for that purpose and to be Resident in the said Dominions, It is Enacted that the Customs and other Duties Imposed by any Act or Acts of Parliament upon any Goods or Merchandises brought or Imported into or Exported or carried from any British Colony or Plantation in America may from time to time be put under the management and direction of such Comissioners, to reside in the said Plantations, as Wee, our heirs and Successors, by our or their commission or commissions under the Great Seal of Great Britain, shall Judge to be most for the advantage of Trade and Security of the Revenue of the said British Colonies,' etc.

(The new Commissioners were given powers similar to those exercised in England by the Commissioners at London. They might appoint, remove, or displace inferior officers, or take security for their good behaviour. They might issue warrants for payment of rewards and ' incidents,' and compound for petty seizures. They might administer oaths, and empower the Cashier to pay salaries out of the customs takings. They might search ships by day or night, and—bearing a writ of assistance—warehouses, etc., by day. Admiralty officers, justices, etc., were enjoined to assist them. They were to obey orders received from the Treasury, and to see that the duties were properly collected and paid in to the Cashier. After salaries, etc., had been paid, the surplus was to be remitted to the Receiver-General of Customs in England, who was to apportion the moneys to the respective Customs branches, and pay them into the Exchequer. An advice of moneys thus remitted was to be sent to the English Commissioners of Customs.

The salary of a resident Commissioner was £500. The Commissioners' powers extended over the whole coast of the American Colonies, from Davis's Straits to the Capes of Florida, as well as Bermuda and the Bahamas.)

*Extract from a Petition sent by the collector of Boston, Massa-
chusetts, to the Commissioners of the Treasury, December 16, 1775.*

' Humbly Sheweth : That your petitioner was appointed
collector in August, 1773.

' That soon after, that spirit of Resistance to the Revenue
Laws, which had shewn itself on many occasions, began then
to breake out into open Acts of Violence, particularly in the
Destruction of the Tea belonging to the East India Company,
during which Transaction your Petitioner executed at hazzard
of his life the Duties of his office, and although left without
any other support than the Comptroller he never quitted
his station during all that scene of anarchy and Confusion
which then prevailed in the Town of Boston, and when all
the other officers of the Crown were obliged to leave the
Place, and take Refuge in the Castle and elsewhere.'

(He went on to state that when the port was closed by the
Act of 1774 he and the comptroller were removed to Plymouth,
Massachusetts, that the ships usually discharging at Boston
entered and cleared at Salem, and that he thus received nothing
but his salary—£100 a year—and lost the fees he had been
accustomed to take from the merchants and shippers of
Boston.)

' Your petitioner is the more encouraged to hope as he has
been informed that your Lordships had ordered a Minute
to be made that the Officers of the Customs should be compensated,' etc.

(He stated he had his account made up accordingly.)

' But your petitioner has received for answer that the
People of the Country had stopped all communication between
Boston and Plymouth,' etc.

(The books and accounts had been removed to Plymouth.)

' And in all probability would be destroyed by the Populace, as they had seized the Boat belonging to the Custom-
house and dragged her up into the middle of the town,' etc.

(He asked for compensation, and furnished an account of
the perquisites he gained from August 16, 1773, to June 1,
1774. It appears that the collector's fees in the port of

Boston for ten and a half months amounted to £1,259 9s. 6½d.
'lawful money,' which represented in 'sterling value'—lawful
tender of the Colonies = ¾ths sterling—£944 12s. 1¾d.)

'The above is a true account of the money I received for
my Fees of Office during the Time therein specified.

'RICHARD ACKLOM HARRISON.'

*Specimen of a customs document, securing to the bearer immunity
from impress (vide p. 421).*

'These are to certify whom it may concern : That the
bearer *Edward Reed* aged *36* years, *5 feet 8 inches high, brown
complexion, wears his hair, the middle finger of his right hand
crooked*, is a
'*Harpooner*, belonging to the ship *Marianne* in the Greenland Trade, and hath given security to the Commissioners
of His Majesty's Customs to proceed in the said Ship to
Greenland the next season, and is not to be imprest from or
out of the said Service ; By virtue of an Act of Parliament
passed in the eleventh year of his present Majesty's Reign,
intituled, *An Act for the better support and Establishment of the
Greenland and Whale Fishery :* Witness our hands and Seals
of Office, Custom House, *London ;* Dated the *3rd* day of
August, One thousand Seven Hundred and Eighty *Two*.

'WM. BATES, Dy. Coll^r.
W. FLETCHER, Dy. Comp^{tr}.
I. FATHWELL.'

*Statement made before the collector of Penzance, by an inhabitant
of Newlyn, Cornwall.*

'Deposeth : That on the 17th day of July, 1783, he, with
Anthony Hallah, Francis Hocking, John Tregurtha, John
Maddein, Richard Kelynack, Paul Tonkin, Richard Tonkin,
William Maddein, Thomas Rowe, John Thomas, James
Goodlines, Jacob Thomas, Richard Yeoman, Francis Ruff-
neck, a man nicknamed " Jolly," and six others, boarded a
foreign brigantine, about six leagues from the Lizard, and
feloniously and piratically took and carried away about
60 loaves white sugar, a quantity of spices, about 1,000
pounds coffee, &c. &c. * * * And out of another foreign
brigantine three casks and one chest silk handkerchiefs, and
about three gallons brandy, &c. &c.'

(The collector in his report on this deposition stated as below, for the information of the Board of Customs and the Admiralty.)

' We are now surrounded with a set of the most abandoned fellows in this Nation, and it is almost impossible for any of the officers of this Revenue to make their appearance out of doors without being insulted and ill-used.'

Letter from the Secretary of Customs to the Secretary to the Admiralty, December 17, 1788.

' The Commissioners finding it necessary to apply to Captain Horatio Nelson, Commander of one of His Majesty's Ships of War on the West India Station, in respect to the Seizure of two vessels carried into Nevis in the year 1785 : I am commanded to request you will favour me with his address, in order that a Letter may be written to him on that Subject.' (Minute, endorsed by Admiralty : ' Let him know it. Burnham, Norfolk.')

Treasury Warrant empowering the Commissioners of Customs to pay an additional sum to Nelson, on account of the seizure of a vessel in the West Indies.

' Having considered your Secretary's letters of the 20th Decr. 1797, and 9th and 11th January, 1798, with their several enclosures, upon the subject of a Decree made by the High Court of Admiralty, reversing a Decree of the Court of Admiralty at Nevis against a ship called the *Jane and Elizabeth*, which was seized by Sir Horatio Nelson in the year 1786 at Barbadoes, and we being of opinion that Sir H. Nelson should be indemnified at the expense of the Crown : These are, under the particular instances of the case, to authorise and require you to direct payment to be made, out of the King's share of seizures, of the sum of £1,131 6s. 6d. which, with the sum of £175 8s. 7d. received by Sir H. Nelson, will make up the sum awarded to be paid by the Decree of the Court of Admiralty, for which this shall be your warrant.'

*Extract from the journal of Pendock Neal, captain of the Lord
Hawke, a vessel cruising under letters of marque. Journal
forwarded to Admiralty by the collector of Plymouth, 1798,
(vide p. 402.)*

' Aug. 12th, 1798. Took the brig *Argo* with Brandy and
dry goods (Chartered by French merchants).
' Aug. 16th, 1798. Retook the *Mary and Elizabeth* of
Dartmouth.*
' Aug. 23rd, 1798. Captured the *Nostra Senora del Car-
mena* (with four others, names unknown) loaded with wheat,
and a lugger with coffee and sugar.
' Sept. 6th, 1798. Destroyed a French privateer with
40 men, which had taken our boat.
' Sept. 7th, 1798. Took the Spanish packet *La Edad del
Oro*, loaded with cocoa, from Vera Cruz. She threw the mail
overboard, which was recovered after it had sunk by John
Watson, a seaman of the *Lord Hawke*, who cut the ballast
from it after it was a considerable way under the water.'

*Extract from declaration made before the collector of Greenock,
September 3, 1798, by John Jamieson, master of the
' Margaret' of Greenock, who shortly after leaving Sligo with
a cargo of kelp had been captured by the French squadron
that conveyed the troops used in Humbert's invasion.*

Jamieson deposes that his ship was seized by ' Three
French vessels full of troops. That he thinks the total number
of Troops landed did not exceed Eighteen Hundred men.
That his vessel was filled with Military stores, and discharged
the same at Killala on the morning of the 23rd August. That
the declarant was permitted to remain on board his vessel
all the time that the French were at Killala, and was allowed
to go on shore to the bishop's house with a guard. That he
was in the town of Killala on Wednesday last the 29th ult.
about two o'clock in the afternoon, by which time the Enemy
were joined by a great number of the country people, who
were immediately clothed in uniform, and furnished with
arms and ammunition. That he heard that upwards of
3,000 of the country people had joined the enemy at Killala.
That he was informed by the Frenchmen that they had landed
60,000 stand of arms. That the French frigates left the
Bay early on the morning of the 24th with a contrary wind.
That in the afternoon of the 28th a 64-gun ship, three

---

* This vessel had been captured by the enemy.

frigates, and a King's Cutter* came into the Bay, and burnt the brig and some other vessels lying there, and remained there. Declared that when at Killala on Monday the 27th† he heard that on the day before the enemy had defeated General Lake at Castlebar, and that he saw some of the King's troops brought in as prisoners to Killala.

'JOHN JAMIESON, *Deponent.*
CHAS. OGILVIE, *Collector.*'

* Revenue cruiser. These vessels often performed most valuable work in addition to their ordinary spells of duty, being used as advice boats, transport boats, etc.

† 27th altered to 28th.

INDEX